BOSTON'S
Copp's Hill
Burying Ground
Guide

D0905508

By Charles Chauncey Wells

CHAUNCEY PARK PRESS
Oak Park, Illinois, USA

Boston's Copp's Hill
Burying Ground Guide© 1998 by
Charles Chauncey Wells and Chauncey Park Press.

For information, write to

CHAUNCEY PARK PRESS
735 N. Grove Avenue
Oak Park, Illinois 60302-1551 USA

email: chauncey@wells1.com
Our Trademark was taken from a Mt. Lebanon Lodge
Commemorative book, published in Boston in 1885.

Cover and inside design by Leigh Dezelan of Dezelan Dezign,
Oak Park, Illinois. Digital photos taken on a Kodak 210 Digital camera
by Suzanne A. Wells. Printed on #60 recycled Husky acid free offset
text on a Heidelberg 19 x 25 MOZP press. Text and headlines
were set in Janson Text with decorative headlines in Masterpiece.

Library of Congress Catalog Card Number 98-74412

ISBN: 0-9667808-0-9

Table of Contents

Section B The 1878 edition, *Graveyards of Boston:* 1st Volume, *Copp's Hill Epitaphs*, by William Whitmore and Thomas B. Wyman, noted historian of Boston. This complete rare volume is published here.

Section C The 1986 Inventory of Graves, conducted by the Historic Burying Ground Initiative, Boston Parks & Recreation Department, City of Boston, 14 Sept. 1986. Listing of the then existing tombstones in Copp's Hill. . . . . Listed Alphabetically by Name

Section D Complete 1986 Burying Ground Initiative mapping contained in three maps in the back flap envelope. These illustrated maps have never been released in book form to the public before.

How to use this guide

This book is both a guide for Boston visitors and for historians or genealogists needing information on families living on Boston's North End. It is divided into four sections.

Section A tells about Copp's Hill Burying Ground itself both today and historically.

Section B is a reprint of the 120-year-old book, *The Graveyards of Boston*, First Volume, *Copp's Hill Epitaphs*, published in 1887.

Section C is a 1986 alphabetical inventory of Copp's Hill tombstones. See the Key Page C-2 for important information.

Section D locates the tombstones inventoried in Section C on three maps. In Section A, for example, you may find the designation "Loc. W-22." This means that tombstone is located in area W (Hull Street Fence) at Location 22.

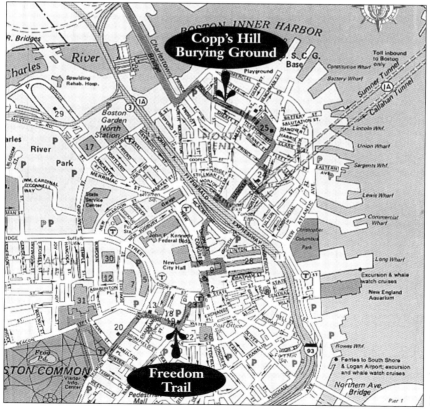

Massachusetts Highway Department

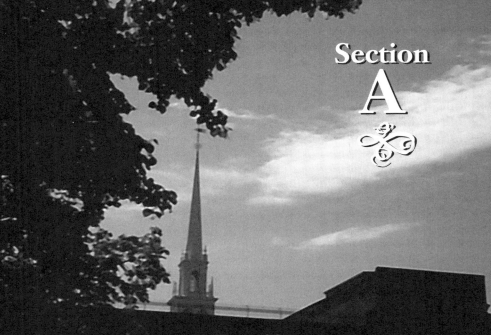

Section
A

Let us now sing the praises of famous men, our ancestors in their generations. The Lord apportioned to them great glory, his majesty from the beginning; there were those who ruled in their kingdoms, and made a name for themselves by their valor; those who gave counsel because they were intelligent; those who spoke in prophetic oracles; those who led the people by their counsels and by their knowledge of the people's lore, they were wise in their words of instruction; those who composed musical tunes, or put verses in writing; rich men endowed with resources, living peacefully in their homes.

All these were honored in their generations, and were the pride of their times. Some of them have left behind a name, so that others declare their praise.

But of others there is no memory; they have perished as though they had never existed; they have become as though they had never been born, they and their children after them. But these also were godly men, whose righteous deeds have not been forgotten; Their offspring will continue forever, and their glory will never be blotted out. Their bodies are buried in peace, but their name lives on generation after generation.

Ecclesiasticus 44: 1-10, 13-14

Copp's Hill Burying Ground, dating back 340 years, is Boston's second oldest and largest Burying Ground with 10,000 - 11,000 graves, about 1,000 African American. Beginning in the mid-1600s, the North End had many upper class residents: merchants mixed in with middle class artisans and mechanics, and laborers, especially in the maritime trades. African Americans lived here, too, in an area called "New Guinea" near the bottom of the hill. Right after the Revolution, the North End began to decline and later poorer Irish, Jewish, and Italian immigrants settled here. It remained primarily Italian after being cut off from the rest of the city by the expressway in the 1950s. Today it is being gentrified as buildings are purchased and rehabilitated and the expressway put underground. ❦

Robert Newman

Robert Newman (1752 - 1804) is for some people today the most famous person buried in Copp's Hill. He hung two lanterns in the Old North Church steeple for the Patriots in Charlestown to see. "One if by land, two if by sea," as the Longfellow poem goes. The British went across the Charles River and marched to Lexington and Concord on that night of 18 April 1775.

Robert Newman was sexton of Christ Church, the formal name of "Old North." He had the keys and knew his way up a "steep and trembling ladder" to the upper windows where he hung the lanterns. Later, he lived at Salem and Sheafe Streets and was made poor by the Revolution. He was a Freemason.

Because Revere knew Newman well, he could trust him to send the signal about the British. Although Revere lived on the North End, he is buried in the Granary Burying Ground downtown.

The Newman marker is next to Tomb 27. To find it, walk along the Hull Street side to the end, turn right along Snowhill Street, and it is about 30 feet along the fence. Loc. W-22.

Prince Hall

Prince Hall (1735 - 1807) is perhaps Copp's Hill's next best-known personage today. Believed born in Barbados, he was a slave of Wm. Hall, leather dresser, who freed him in 1770 after Prince Hall had been a Hall family slave for 21 years. He is believed to have fought at Lexington and Concord and Bunker Hill and tradition says he influenced George Washington to allow Black soldiers to serve in the Army. More than 5,000 did serve.

Continuing as a leather dresser and laborer, he educated himself and led the abolitionist cause to end slavery in Massachusetts in the 1780s. Petitioning the Massachusetts Assembly, he pointed out that Blacks were taxed just as whites and paid their share, and therefore "means [must] be provided for the education of colored people." Not getting this, he started a school in own home, moving to African Society House on Belnap Street, where his son Primus continued it.

He is best remembered for the Prince Hall Lodge of Free and Accepted Masons. That started as African Lodge No. 459, under a charter from the Grand Lodge of England, with Prince Hall as master. Today many prominent African Americans are among 500,000 claiming membership in 44 grand lodges across America. Prince Hall and other primarily white Grand Lodges are now increasingly recognizing each other's validity.

The Prince Hall grave is near the Robert Newman tomb, about 30 feet farther on the Snowhill side, a tall black monument in the grave section. The old tombstone reads "Here lies the body of Prince Hall, First Grand Master of the colored Grand Lodge of Masons in Mass., Died Dec. 7, 1787." Loc. D-16.

8

The Mathers

Increase, Samuel & Cotton Mather

Increase Mather

The Mathers are not well known today, but were the powerhouse family of American Puritanism from the founding of New England until about 1785 and their influence lasted long after.

The Mather Tomb holds the remains of Increase (died 1723, ae 84), Cotton (died 1727, ae 65), and Samuel (died 1785, ae 79).

Increase is hailed as "the greatest American Puritan," the voice of Puritan orthodoxy. His father Richard started the beginnings of American Puritanism and Increase's time marks the end of the middle era. He followed his father into the pastorate of 2nd or Old North Church on North Square in 1664 and stayed 50 years. In 1685, he also became president of Harvard College, reorganizing and revitalizing it. He insisted students know Latin, Greek, and Hebrew. ➥

Cotton, his son, was named for his grandfather Rev. John Cotton. He was a great evangelist at Old North, and canvassed Boston house by house, teaching his parishioners and evangelizing the unchurched.

Cotton Mather   Unfortunately, he believed in witches and wrote in defense of witch trials in general, but condemned those at Salem because of the way they were conducted. His and other Boston clergy opposition was crucial to stopping the trials. His early work set the stage for America's first great religious awakening 10 years later.

Samuel, Cotton's son, was elected to the pastorate of 2nd Church in 1732. Charged with "loose doctrines" and so called "improper conduct," he was dismissed. Some 93 out of 356 remained with him and they formed "Samuel Mather's Church," a thriving Congregational Church built at the corner of Bennett and Hanover Streets nearby on the North End. There he remained for 44 years, until he died in 1785 and its members rejoined the then 2nd or New Brick Church. His conduct remained exemplary, so the earlier charges had more to do with belief rather than what we would term bad conduct today.

Their remains are not in the brick superstructure; that is for inscriptions. The coffins were interred below ground in a brick tomb. That is true of the other table top tombstones in Copp's Hill also. Loc. I-23. ☙

Edmund Hartt

Tomb 55 along the Snowhill Side toward Charter Street without a marker is the tomb of Edmund Hartt who built the famous frigates *Constitution* and *Boston*. Hartt lies buried in full view of his famous ship, moored across at the Charlestown Navy Yard. He died in about 1806. The Hartt family were the first widely-known shipwrights in America. At one time, seven members of the family were naval contractors at various shipyards along the East Coast. Hartt's shipyard is now Constitution Wharf on Atlantic Avenue.

The *Constitution* is uniquely Boston: Paul Revere made the copper sheathing and bolts and the masts, sails, anchors, and gun carriages were all made in Boston or nearby. It was launched Oct. 21, 1797, the pride of the U. S. Navy. At first it was considered an ill-fated ship because it took three attempts to launch her: the first time it only slid about 8 feet down the ways, disappointing hundreds who had gathered. The second also failed. Then, on the third attempt, the launch was successful. Commodore Samuel Nicholson, her skipper and first commandant of the Charlestown Navy Yard, is buried in a crypt just down Hull Street at Old North Church. ✹

Worthylake Tombstone

One of the saddest is the three-in-one Worthylake tombstone. George Worthylake was one of the first keepers of the Boston lighthouse. He and his family drowned while sailing in Boston Harbor. He was 45, his wife Ann was 40, and his daughter Ruth 13. Benjamin Franklin wrote a poem about it. Loc. F-257.

Another sad life is that of Betsy, wife of David Darling, died 23 March 1809, ae 43. She had 17 children and "around her lie 12 of them and two were lost at sea." Loc. A-5. &

Malcolm Bullet-Ridden Stone

Cpt. Daniel Malcolm was an ardent patriot, especially disliked by the British. He was a smuggler and organized opposition to British duties on imported goods. His inscription reads: "Capt. Daniel Malcolm, Merchant, who departed this life Oct. 23d, 1769, aged 44 years.

"A true Son of Liberty, a friend to the Publick. An enemy to Oppression and One of the foremost in opposing the Revenue Acts on America." Is it any wonder why they used it for target practice? The bullet markings are visible even today. Loc. D-86. &

Dupee Monument

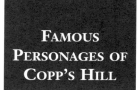
This, the most elaborate monument in the burying ground, demands a level of religious understanding few of us have today. It was erected by Isaac Dupee in 1846 and tells little about him or about the Dupee Family. Some were involved with early Boston education and later generations owned mills at Lowell and started copper mines in Upper Michigan. Loc. G-297

It says "God is Love," and then lists four Biblical verses, one on each side:

1 Corinthians xv. 49: *"As we have worn the likeness of the man made of dust, so shall we wear the likeness of the heavenly man."*

1 John iv. 8: *"Everyone who loves is a child of God and knows God, but the unloving know nothing of God."*

Matthew v. 9: *"How blest are the pacemakers; God shall call them his sons."*

Ephesians 1:9: *"He had made known to us his hidden purpose: that the universe might be brought into unity in Christ"*

Those verses were then used to form the following verse:

> *"My name from the palms of his hands*
> *Eternity will not erase;*
> *Impressed on his heart, it remains*
> *In marks of indelible grace.*
> *Yes, I to the end shall endure,*
> *As sure as the earnest is given*
> *More happy, but not more secure,*
> *The Glorified spirits in heaven."*

From our viewpoint today, it is difficult to see how the couplets could be made from the verses cited. ☙

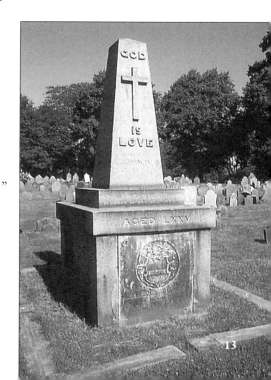

Judge Samuel Sewell

Judge Samuel Sewell (1652 -1730) sold a large portion of the land to allow enlarging Copp's Hill. He had a life of public service, blemished only by his relentless pursuit of "witches," to many of whom he gave death sentences. He realized his error and begged public forgiveness, asking "That God might not visit his sin upon him, his family, or upon the land." A leading figure of Boston of his time, Judge Sewell is today remembered for his diary, which gives a vivid picture of the time he lived. ☙

A Notorious Sinner Repents

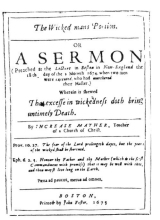

Increase Mather in this 50-year pastorate at 2nd or Old North Church (Puritan) had to censure only two members: one was a sister and one was John Farnum. In 1665-66, John Farnum did much telling of untruths, he condemned the whole church at Charlestown, broke his covenant, and was guilty of schism. He talked with excommunicated persons, lied, disagreed with the pastor's sermons in the middle of the service, and there continued a whole list of his other offenses against the church and its doctrines. He was denied communion and so he refused to attend services. Church officials went to reason with him, but he refused to change. "His heart is so strangely besotted and hardened with guilt and sin, and the wrath of God against his soul, that he even laugheth at the calamity which is coming upon him," Increase wrote. After several more attempts at changing him, he was voted out. "Now out of the hands of Satan, whose at present he is, the Lord, if it be possible deliver him." Then, 17 years later, John Farnum, after being an Anabaptist, returned to 2nd Church and begged pardon of the Lord and community. He died 20 Jan 1701/2, ae 69) forgiven by God and man. Loc. C-432. ☙

Hutchinson Family Tomb

Built in 1711, this tomb holds remains of some of the famous Hutchinson Family. However, history's two most famous Hutchinsons are not buried here. Ann, who fled with her husband Gov. Wm. to Rhode Island because of religious persecution, is not buried here. Neither is her descendant, Gov. Thomas Hutchinson, who was British governor of Massachusetts and had to flee to London in 1774.

Here's who is buried here: Ann's grandson, Elisha, prominent North End merchant and selectman from 1678 - 87 who began a salt manufactory at Boston neck. He died in an attack made by Indians at Quaboag in Brookfield. His son Col. Thomas, prominent in real estate and who paid for the first schoolhouse on the North End is also buried here. Col. Thomas's children included Sarah, who married Samuel Mather and is buried in the Mather Tomb; and the Gov. Thomas (1711-1780) mentioned above and who is buried in London.

Son Gov. Thomas produced *History of Massachusetts Bay*, the first written history of Boston. In 1765, when he was lieutenant governor, a mob sacked his house in reaction to his actions in enforcing the Stamp Act. He was colonial governor from 1771-74 during the tea crisis and the hated Port Bill, which resulted in closing the Port of Boston before the Revolution.

"Had he fallen upon more peaceful times, he would easily have attained the fame to which his varied accomplishments and his blameless character entitled him; but his over estimate of power, his want of sympathy with popular rights, and his great ambition led him to the losing side of the controversy," the *Memorial History of Boston* said of Gov. Thomas. The Hutchinson tomb interests many, not for what it contains, but for the historical memories it inspires. Thomas Lewis purchased this tomb and "Lewis" is engraved upon it. Loc. G-295 is just two tombs toward Hull Street from the Dupee Monument. ☙

The Reveres

PAUL REVERE'S SISTER

Mary Revere was Paul's younger sister, born 10 July 1743, a twin of John and about 10 years younger than Paul, is buried in Copp's Hill. She married first, Edward Rose in 1765, a mariner, and they had three children. He died on a trip from Guinea to Barbados in 1771. In March of 1791, she married Alexander Baker, caulker on Hull St., but he died in May, ae 72 and was buried in Copp's Hill. Mary died 27 Dec. 1801, ae 58. Loc. F-70.

PAUL REVERE'S DAUGHTERS

Lincoln Tomb No. 7 – Amos Lincoln (1753 - 1829) participated in the Boston Tea Party. He was a Lt. Colonel in Craft's Regiment, served against Shay's Rebellion and was in charge of building the State House. He married successively two daughters of Paul Revere: Deborah, Revere's daughter by his first marriage who was born in 1758 and they had 9 children. After she died in January, 1797, he married Elizabeth, Revere's daughter by his second marriage. Amos Lincoln married her in May of 1797 and they had 5 children before she died in 1805, ae 35. All are likely buried here. Amos' brother Jedediah Lincoln, housewright, married Mary Revere, Elizabeth's sister. The two brothers married two sisters, not uncommon in those times. This is located at W-7, about 20 feet to the right as you enter the burying ground.

Rachel Walker Revere

Paul Revere

PAUL REVERE'S NIECE

Revere's nephew through his brother John was Edward Revere, goldsmith, who worked with Paul. His wife was Eliza Maria Revere, who died 5 Nov. 1804, ae 28. Her marker is hard to read but easy to find at Loc. F-212. ☙

Eliza Maria Revere's Tmbstone

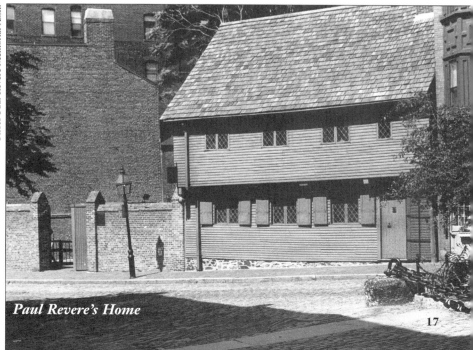

Paul Revere's Home

Opens China Trade

Major Samuel Shaw's tall white marker, erected in 1848 but nearly unreadable, tells of his exploits in the Revolution. He opened the China trade Feb. 22, 1784, sailing from New York to Canton on his ship, the *Empress of China*. "It was the first vessel that sailed from the United States to that place," the inscription reads. George Washington named him consul to China and he died in 1794. Between the circles is a crossing of paved walks and this marker is located there. ✎

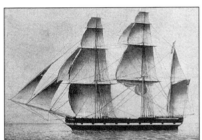

William Clark/ Winslow Tomb

As you enter the main gate and turn right, you will see one of the finest carved markers in Copp's Hill. It marks Tomb 15 of Wm. Clark, the wealthiest of Boston's ship owners. During the French & Indian War (1744 - 1749), he lost 40 ships and that hastened his death shortly afterward. Adjoining it is the tomb of his brother, Dr. John Clark, physician and its inscription is in Latin. Seven succeeding generations all produced doctors with the same name. This tomb is called "the Winslow Tomb," because Samuel Winslow, sexton of 1st Baptist Church, took it over and carved his name as rightful owner. See chapter on Scandal at Copp's Hill. Loc. W-10. ✎

Mayor
Charles Wells

In 1814, Charles Wells (1786 - 1866) purchased land and built 55 tombs in the New North Burying Ground section. Then in 1819, he built 34 more tombs in the area fronting on Charter Street near the school. He served on the Common Council and the Board of Aldermen and was elected mayor in 1832/33 as a reaction of the common people against Mayors Quincy and Otis and what was called the high-handed and extravagant way they had run Boston. "A master builder, by training he was little fitted for public office, his two terms were uneventful," a biography reads. A son of Thomas Wells, Boston Tea Party participant, he went on to become the 6th president of Mass. Charitable Mechanic Assn., and, for many years, was president of Mass. Mutual Fire Insurance Co., a predecessor of Mass. Mutual Life Insurance Co. In 1854, he laid the cornerstone on the Franklin Monument to Franklin's parents in the Granary Burying Ground. He is not buried at Copp's Hill even though Tomb 18 bears his name along with his brother John B. Wells. By the time they died, the area had become rundown and Charles chose a crypt in fashionable Mt. Auburn in Cambridge. Loc. J-9. ✆

THE COPP FAMILY

WILLIAM COPP – No stone, died about 1670, gave his name to the Hill, was cordwainer or shoe-maker. Goodeth his wife (their way of pronouncing Judith) died 25 March 1670. Loc. C-280. Most notable Copp is David who died 20 Nov 1713, ae. 78. He was an elder in 2nd Church, prominent on the North End, and lived on Hull near Christ Church. Loc. C-218; his second wife Amy died in 1718, Loc. C-353. Obedience, his first wife, died in 1678. Loc. C-358.

HOPESTILL CAPEN (1731 - 1807) – He owned the building now housing the Union Oyster House. From 1769 - 1826, when it became a restaurant, the building housed Hopestill Capen's fancy dress goods, importers of fancy clothing and the ships could unload right into the upper windows. Also in the upper part, the *Boston Gazette* was published by Benjamin Edes and Isaiah Thomas from 1771 to 1775. AHAC, 1763. Loc. A-291.

This 1909 photo shows a clear line of sight view of the Bunker Hill Monument. From here, General Gage could view how his artillery was hitting the Patriots. This artillery also started the raging fire that destroyed Charlestown.

*AHAC denotes member of Ancient & Honorable Artillery Co., whose headquarters is located in Faneuil Hall. Its four- volume history is one of the best sources on Boston and North End residents.

CARNES: JOHN, EDWARD AND THOMAS – Lt. Col. John was commander of AHAC, 1733); son Major Edward, born 1730, served in the Continental Army, was a ropemaker, and lived on Hull St. across from Copp's Hill. Tomb loc. W-6. Brother Cpt. Thomas (1731 - 1793) was a shopkeeper and trader who encountered trying economic times and went bankrupt. He died at Governor's Island, NY on a journey from Philadelphia of yellow fever, Loc. A-61.

SARAH CHAMPNEY – died 13 Oct. 1800, ae 60. Member of prominent Champney family of North End. "The joys of faith triumphant rise/ and wing the soul above the skies." Loc. G-122.

JOHN COOKSON, who along with his Negro slave Tobey swept chimneys of the North End from 1711 to 1733 and also reported to selectmen about unsafe chimneys. He was also a gunsmith. AHAC, 1701. Loc. Near Tomb 16, J-7.

ROBERT CUMBY – 1654/5 - 1717, Deacon of New North Church, 1717, AHAC member in 1691. Loc. H-2.

DEACON SHEMM DROWNE – Boston carver who carved the grasshopper on the Faneuil Hall weather vane. Died. 1774, ae. 90. Loc. A-164.

EDES TOMB – THOMAS EDES (1715 - 1794), baker, was part of the mob that attacked and destroyed Gov. Thomas Hutchinson's mansion during the Stamp Act riots of 1765. He was buried from the home of his son Edward near the North Grammar School. Tomb Loc. W-28. Benjamin Edes (1732 - 1803), printer and publisher of *Massachusetts Gazette*, was one of the early leaders of Revolutionary activity. AHAC, 1760. It is probable he is buried in the Edes Tomb at Copp's Hill. Loc.W-28.

REV. ANDREW ELIOT (1719 - 1778) – Beloved pastor from 1742 - 1778 of New North (5th) Church at Hanover & Clark Streets, now St. Stephen's Roman Catholic Church. He was devoted to the Patriot cause and remained in Boston during the siege, and cared for that portion of his congregation which remained in the city. He was called to the presidency of Harvard College in 1769, but declined, and elected in 1773, but declined. His son John succeeded him from 1779-1813. Loc. W-25.

JOSHUA GEE, wealthy shipbuilder, whose son was pastor of 2nd Church 1742 - 48, once had the only privately owned family plot in the burying ground. His wife "wanted to be laid away from the multitude," instead of the helter-skelter way the other graves were arranged. The plot was taken over by Deacon Moses Grant of the Tea Party and Revolutionary War fame who also was a noted temperance lecturer. (C-58 between two paved circles)

CHRISTOPHER GORE TOMB (1758 -1827) MA governor in 1810. Some sources say he is buried at the Granary Burying Ground. Loc. W-46

REV. FRANCIS W. P. GREENWOOD, D.D., rector of Kings Chapel in the early 1800s. Tomb 57, Loc. G-294.

CAPT. RALPH HARTT (1699 -1776) Patriarch of famous shipbuilding family and uncle of Edmund and Zephaniah, builders of the U.S. Constitution. AHAC. Loc. A-195.

Hunt Family

Ephraim Hunt, born 1681,blacksmith, son of Cpt. Thomas and Judith Hunt, he was a deacon of New North Church in 1726. He became special justice of the Court of Common Pleas, moving upward from justice of the peace in 1702. AHAC, 1717. No marker.

Thomas Hunt – Lynn Street anchor smith, died 1721, ae 73, AHAC, 1685. Loc. C-80

Charles Jarvis Tomb – Noted local politician who died in 1807, ae 59. He was "a physician, statesman, a patriot, an honest man, whose dignified deportment, sublime eloquence, unbounded philanthropy, and other virtues endeared him to his fellow citizens." Loc. A-385.

Cpt. Thomas Lake – Very wealthy man who owned large tracts in Maine and New Hampshire; killed by Indians at Kennibeck 14 Aug. 1678. Body not found for 7 months. Legend says the lead from bullets which killed him was poured into a deep slit in the tombstone. AHAC commander in 1662 and 1674. Loc. C-143.

Caleb Lyman (1678 - 1737) Indian fighter in 1704 in Connecticut River area near Northhampton. Later shopkeeper, founder in 1712 and deacon of New North Church, and constable, justice of the peace and selectman. Tomb loc. Unknown.

Mariner's Tomb – Dedicated to the Seamen of All Nations, by Phineas Stowe, pastor of 1st Baptist Bethel Church, Boston 1851. Built by seamen's contributions, it contains the remains of Stowe's wife Emily, who died the day the marker was completed, and four seamen. Most prominent marker at Hull and Snowhill streets, near Malcolm tomb.

Edward Martyn (1665 - 1717/8). Tomb 10 is the first one to the right as you enter Copp's Hill and bears a coat of arms. He was a merchant, living on Hanover near Richmond, and served on many selectmen's committees. He left 10 pounds to 2nd Church for a "piece of plate and 20 pounds to be distributed to the poor of the flock." He owned most of the land from Hanover St. to the water. AHAC, 1702.

John Milk: Milk St. downtown is named for him. Loc. F-289. →

OTHER
PERSONAGES OF
COPP'S HILL

MOUNTFORT FAMILY

TOMBS 17, built in 1711 on Hull Street for John Mountfort (Loc. W-13) and Tomb 59 for Jonathan (J-3a), built in 1724, reprsent the Mountforts, long a prominent North End family. They were sons of Edward Mountfort who fled political troubles in London in 1656. John (1670 - 1711), a cooper or barrel maker, later owned Mountfort's Wharf and lived on Prince St. AHAC, 1696. Jonathan was a wealthy but eccentric doctor, owned a pharmacy, and was a founder and treasurer of the New Brick Church. It is highly probable that Joseph Mountfort of the Boston Tea Party and latter a cooper is buried in another Mountfort tomb located at J3a.

PARKER TOMB – Tomb of Chief Judge Parker. Loc. C-400

EDWARD PROCTOR (1691 - 1751) Tailor and prominent in North End affairs, lived on Wood Lane, now called Proctor Lane. AHAC, 1699. Grandson, also Edward (1733 -1811), participated in the Tea Party and was a prominent citizen of Boston. He had a West India goods store on North Street in the North End and had the Schooner Tavern on Fish St. A friend of Paul Revere, he was an ardent Patriot, rising to the rank of colonel during the Revolution. He joined St. Andrew's Lodge of Freemasons and rose to high office in the Grand Lodge of Massachusetts. The funeral was from his mansion house on North Bennett St. to Tomb 16 in Copp's Hill. AHAC, 1756.

SARAH RULE – died 5 July 1690, ae. 9, moved Cotton Mather to great wrath when she drew pictures in ink on his sermons.

ANDREW SIGOURNEY (1766 - 1820) – Boston treasurer from 1814 until he died. He was active in Boston Freemasonry and in AHAC, 1806. Members of this family were French Huguenots as were the Reveres, Mountforts, and Johonnots, all of the North End. They left France for America to escape Catholic persecution for their being Protestant. Loc. J-33.

THOMAS STODDARD (1699-1763) He with Newman and John Greenough (also buried in Copp's Hill) built the landing for the ferry coming from Chelsea to the town slip located at the lower end of North Street. He owned extensive real estate and slaves, and was an Indian fighter on the Connecticut River. Loc. A-300.

THOMAS THORNTON – Born in England, 1647, died Boston 1726. Merchant, ship owner, and selectman in charge of docks and wharves on the North End. Representative to General Court, 1693-95, and served the town of Boston on a committee to regulate the price of corn for bakers and the committee to purchase additional land for Copp's Hill Burying Ground. AHAC. Loc. G-244.

NICHOLAS UPSHALL – Friend to Quakers who were persecuted and hanged. For bribing the jailer to take food to two imprisoned Quaker women, he was fined 20 pounds and banished to Rhode Island for the rest of the six years of Gov. Endicott's rule. When he returned, he allowed the Quakers free use of a room in his house. In 1637, he owned about a fourth of the North End. AHAC 23rd founding member. Loc. A-409.

JAMES VARNEY, bricklayer, built house on Sheafe Street, served as constable of North End. AHAC, 1711. Loc. D-147.

RECOMPENSE WADSWORTH – First headmaster of Grammar Free School, died 9 June 1713, ae 25, after teaching for only six months in the new school house on Bennett St. His marker was lost, having been used to close a tomb, and found by Copp's Hill Supt. MacDonald in 1878. Loc. now unknown again. ❧

Participants in the
Boston Tea Party
of 1773

History often produces an inexact record and the Boston Tea Party is an excellent example. Unlike the Declaration of Independence, which had signers, the Boston Tea Party was veiled in secrecy. In fact it was not called the "Tea Party," until many years later. It was called "Destruction of the Tea in Boston Harbor."[1]

Participants swore themselves to secrecy and some did not acknowledge each other even when boarding the ships, breaking open the chests and dumping the tea. Some never talked about it except among close family members. Lists were produced, but were incomplete. So today, 225 years later, we have those incomplete lists, family oral tradition, and almost no artifacts to trace participation. Even years later, some retained secrecy for fear of lawsuits possibly being brought by the British East India Company. Also, some of the participants' families had become well to do and were not proud of identifying with "civil disobedience," even though it was the most significant act leading to our nation's break with Great Britain.

We believe 29 Tea Party participants are probably buried in Copp's Hill. Some we are positive about. Others we believe are buried from the evidence available.

[1] Discussions 2 October, 1998, with [1]Alfred F. Young, *The Shoemaker and the Tea Party: Memory and the American Revolution,* (Beacon Press, forthcoming), which Young shared with the author in manuscript form.

Where Patriots met before Destruction of the Tea.

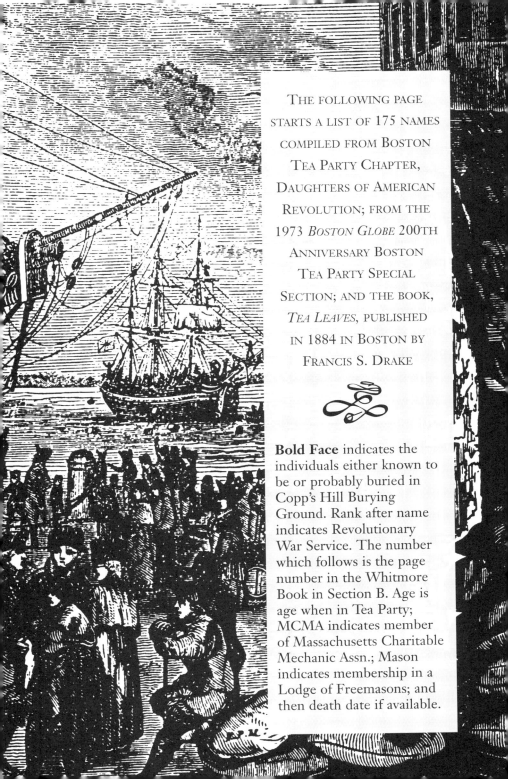

THE FOLLOWING PAGE
STARTS A LIST OF 175 NAMES
COMPILED FROM BOSTON
TEA PARTY CHAPTER,
DAUGHTERS OF AMERICAN
REVOLUTION; FROM THE
1973 *BOSTON GLOBE* 200TH
ANNIVERSARY BOSTON
TEA PARTY SPECIAL
SECTION; AND THE BOOK,
TEA LEAVES, PUBLISHED
IN 1884 IN BOSTON BY
FRANCIS S. DRAKE

Bold Face indicates the individuals either known to be or probably buried in Copp's Hill Burying Ground. Rank after name indicates Revolutionary War Service. The number which follows is the page number in the Whitmore Book in Section B. Age is age when in Tea Party; MCMA indicates member of Massachusetts Charitable Mechanic Assn.; Mason indicates membership in a Lodge of Freemasons; and then death date if available.

THE TEA PARTY LIST

Francis Akeley (Eckley), only one imprisoned for Tea Party.

Nathaniel Barber (Major) Tomb 28 Old Burial Ground (xiv), early revolutionary and soldier, Mason, died 1787.

Samuel Barnard (Maj.), died 1782.

Henry Bass, early revolutionary, died 1813.

Joseph Bassett (Cpt.), Tomb 65 (xv).

Edward Bates.

Adam Beals Jr.

Thomas Bolter (Cpt.), 38, died 1811.

David Bradlee (Cpt.), 31, died 1811.

Josiah Bradlee, 19, died 1798.

Nathaniel Bradlee, 27, MCMA, died 1813.

Thomas Bradlee, 29, MCMA, Mason, died 1805.

James Brewer (Cpt.), possibly Tomb 22 Old Ground, MCMA, Mason, died 1805.

John Brown (Cpt.), entry 1718, 27, died 1782.

Seth Ingersoll Browne, 23, Bunker Hill, died 1809

Stephen Bruce, 356, Mason, died 1801.

Benjamin Burton (Maj.), 24, died 1835.

Nicholas Campbell, 41, died 1929.

George Carleton

Thomas Chase, early revolutionary, Mason.

Nathaniel Child

Benjamin Clarke, Tomb 104, xvi, MCMA, died 1840, three sons may have been in Tea Party also.

Jonathan Clark (Sgt.), possibly Tomb 77 (Dana & Clark) xv.

John Cochran, 24, died 1839.

Gilbert Colesworthy, 29, died 1818.

Gersham Collier, Mason, died 1825.

Adam Collson, 35, early revolutionary, Mason, died 1798.

James Foster Condy, died 1809.

Daniel Coolidge

Joseph Coolidge

Samuel Coolidge

Samuel Cooper (LT), 18, died 1840.
William Cox
Thomas Crafts (Col.), 33, early revolutionary, died 1799.
John Crane (Brig. Gen.), 29, early revolutionary, Mason, died 1805.
_______ Crockett
Obadiah Curtis
Thomas Dana, Jr. possibly Tomb 77 (Dana & Clark).
Robert Davis (Maj.), 26, early revolutionary, Mason, died 1798.
John DeCarteret
David Decker
John Dickman
Edward Dolbeare, died 1796.
Samuel Dolbeare
John Dyar, Jr.
Joseph Eaton (Cpt.)
Joseph Eayres
Eckley (see Francis Akeley)
Benjamin Edes, possibly 482, 41, early revolutionary, died 1803.
William Etheridge
Samuel Fenno, died 1806.
Samuel Foster (Capt.), died 1778.
Thomas Fracker, Entry 884 (Charter St tombs), died 1806.
Nathaniel Frothingham, Jr. (LT.), Entry 1738, Tomb 27 (Thomas Frothingham and others) Also possibly 1837, Tomb 56; 27, died 1825.
John Fulton, 40.
John Gammell, revolutionary war soldier, died 1827.
Eleazer Gay, possibly 1733 (Ebenezer Gay Tomb 21, 1819)
Thomas Gerrish
Samuel Gore, probably Tomb 112 (1810) with brother Gov. Christopher Gore; 22, MCMA, Mason, died 1831.
Moses Grant, entry 1030, 30, MCMA, died 1817. →

Moses Grant

Nathaniel Greene, early revolutionary, MCMA.

Timothy Guy

Samuel Hammond, 24, died 1842.

Peter Harrington

William Haskins

William Hendley, 25, Mason, died 1830.

George Robert Twelves Hewes, 31, shoemaker,
    left memoir of Tea Party, died 1840.

John Hicks, 48, killed at Arlington by British retreating from
    Lexington-Concord, died April 19, 1775.

Samuel Hobbs, 23, died 1823.

John Hooton (Sgt.), possibly Tomb 15--Hooten & Watts
    Family Tomb (13).

Elisha Horton

Elijah Houghton

Samuel Howard (born Hayward), Tomb 120 Old Ground, 21, died 1797.

Edward Compton Howe, 31, died 1821.

Jonathan Hunnewell, possibly Copp's Hill , 14,
    6th president MCMA, died 1842.

Richard Hunnewell, probably Copp's Hill Tomb 36,
    Mason, MCMA, died 1805.

Richard Hunnewell, Jr., possibly Copp's Hill, 16.

Thomas Hunstable, 20, Mason.

Abraham Hunt (Col.), 25, Valley Forge, died 1793.

Daniel Ingersoll, 23, Mason, died 1829.

Daniel Ingoldson

Charles Jameson

Robert Jameson (Cpt.)

Jared Joy

David Kinnison (doubtful he was in Tea Party), died 1852.

Robert Lash, probably because wife Johanna buried here (1114).

Amariah Learned

Joseph Lee (Cpt.), 28, Mason, died 1831.

Nathaniel Lee (Cpt.)

Amos Lincoln (Lt. Col.), Tomb 7 (1805) Old Burial Ground (697), 20, Bunker Hill, married 2 daughters of Paul Revere, MCMA, Mason, died 1829.

John Locke (Sgt.)

Matthew Loring, possibly Tomb 88; Loring Family Tomb, 1806; 23, died 1829.

Joseph Lovering, 15, MCMA, died 1848.

Joseph Ludden (Sgt.)

David Lyon

Thomas Machin (Cpt.), 29, Bunker Hill, Mason, died 1816.

Ebenezer MacIntosh, 36, early revolutionary, died 1812.

Peter McIntosh

Archibald MacNeil, 23, died 1840.

John Marston (Bombadier), J. B. Marston Tomb, 1810,131)

Martin, probably Wm. P., MCMA.

Thompson Maxwell (LT.), 31, Concord, Bunker Hill, died 1835.

John Marston

John May (Col.), 25, died 1812.

Mead, probably John, probably Copp's Hill Tomb 22 New Ground, MCMA. ➥

Henry Mellius

Thomas Melville (Maj.), 22, early revolutionary, Mason, MCMA, died 1832.

Aaron John Miller (Dr.)

James Mills

William Molineaux, 57, early revolutionary, died 1774.

Francis Moore

Thomas Moore, 20, died 1813.

Anthony Morse (LT.)

Joseph Mountfort (LT.), 23, MCMA, died 1838.

Eliphalet Newell, 38, artillery officer, Mason.

Joseph Nicholls (Cpt.)

Samuel Nowell

Joseph Pearse Palmer (Major), Mason, died 1788.

Jonathan Parker

Joseph Payson, 30.

Samuel Peck, early revolutionary, Mason.

John Peters, 41, Lexington, Bunker Hill, died 1832.

William Pierce, 29, barber, MCMA, died 1840.

Isaac Pitman (Cpt.)

Lendall Pitts, 26, early revolutionary, MCMA, died 1787.

Samuel Pitts, 28, also early revolutionary.

Thomas Porter, died 1800.

Henry Prentiss (Cpt.), 24, MCMA, Mason, died 1821.

Nathaniel Prentiss, probably 1626 (N. S. Prentiss).

Rev. John Prince, 22, Mason, died 1836, later said he was a witness and not a Tea Party participant.

Edward Procter (Col.), 40, early revolutionary, Mason, died 1811.

Henry Purkitt (Col.), 18, MCMA, Mason, died 1846.

Seth Putnam

John Randall

Joseph Reed (Cpt.)

Paul Revere (Col.), 38, early revolutionary, MCMA founder, Mason, died 1818.

Benjamin Rice (Cpt.)

Jonathan Dorby Robins

Joseph Roby

John Russell, MCMA, Mason, died 1778.

William Russell (Sgt.-Maj.), 25, Mason, died 1784.

John Sawtelle

George Sayward
Edmund Sears (Cpt.)
Robert Sessions (LT.), 21, died 1836.
Joseph Shed, 41, died 1812.
Benjamin Simpson, soldier, died 1849.
Peter Slater, Jr. (Cpt.), 14, died 1831.
Samuel Sloper
Ephriam Smith
Josiah Snelling, Tomb 31 (1803)(xiv,1681), MCMA, died 1873.
Thomas Spear, died 1789.
Samuel Sprague (Sgt.),19, MCMA, died 1844.
John Spurr (Maj.), 25, died 1822.
James Starr, 32, died 1831.
Phineas Stearns (Cpt.) 32, Lexington, Dorchester Hts., died 1798.
Ebeneezer Stevens (Gen.), 22, Revolution + War of 1812, died 1823.
James Stoddard
Elisha Story (Dr.), 30, Lexington, Bunker Hill, died 1805.
James Swan (Col.), 19, Bunker Hill, Mason, died 1831.
Abraham Tower (Sgt.)
Bartholomew Trow (Cpt.)
John Truman, xvi, Tomb 118 Old Ground.
Benjamin Tucker Jr.
Thomas Urann (Cpt.), Mason, died 1791.
James Watson (Cpt.)
Henry Wells (Cpt.), Mason.
Thomas Wells, probably Tomb 18, 26, Tea Party evidence at
    Old South Meeting House, died 1810.
Josiah Wheeler (Cpt.), 30, Dorchester Hts., died 1817.
John Whitehead (LT.)
David Williams
Isaac Williams
Jeremiah Williams
Thomas Williams (Sgt.), 19, Lexington, died 1817.
Nathaniel Willis, 18, MCMA, died 1831.
Joshua Wyeth, 16, Revolutionary soldier, died after 1827.
Thomas Young (Dr.), 41, early revolutionary, Army svc., died 1777. ❀

Copp's Hill

Soldiers of the Revolutionary War and War of 1812

The following list of Revolutionary War and War of 1812 veterans is taken from "Who Fought? Boston Soldiers in the Revolutionary War," an honors thesis in American History at Tufts University, 1981, by Dr. Philip C. Swain, now an attorney of Manhattan Beach, CA.

Additional information was taken from a *Boston Globe* Tea Party special section and *Old Copp's Hill, 1900*, by Edward McDonald, the cemetery's superintendent. These names should be checked with other sources such as the Adjutant General's multi-volume set on Massachusetts Men in the Revolution for further authentication.

REVOLUTIONARY WAR LIST

Alexander, Wm., service began 1780.

Barber, Nathaniel, began 1777, 16 mos, Maj. Muster master for Suffolk Co., later Naval officer in Boston 1784., died 1787, ae. 59.

Bassett, Joseph, Cpt.

Brewer, James, began 1775, 3 mos, Matross, Cpt, also privateer and prisoner of war in 1781, blockmaker, lived Summer St., died 1805.

Brown, John, Cpt, died 1782.

Brown, Deacon Jonathan, began 1775, 59 mos, Pvt., died 1785.

Burbeck, Henry, began 1775, 72 mos, Cpt., died 1820.

Burbeck, Joseph, began 1775, 3 mos, Matross, married 1784., died 1820.

Carnes, Edward, began 1776, 32 mos, Maj., died after 1790, ae 53.

Champney, Caleb Distal, died 1802.

Clark, Jonathan, began 1775, Sgt, age 29.

Clark, John, began 1777, 41 mos, Pvt. Also Matross, 5 mos. svc.

Dolbeare, John, Cpt., died 1794.

Doubleday, Benjamin, began 1777, 43 mos, Pvt, died 1784, ae 49.

Dupee, Anthony, began 1779, 28 mos, Matross.

Green, John, began 1777, 6 mos, ae 44, tinsmith living on Market St.; also could be John Green Jr., began 1780, 6 mos, Matross, ae 17, tailor on Federal St., died 1800.

Hall, John, began 1778, 36 mos.

Hartt, Ralph, Cpt, died 1776.

Hart, Wm., began 1776, 9 mos.,
Sgt, died , 1741

Hichborn, Samuel Jr., died 1812.

Hooten, John, Sgt., oarmaker, later
wood warfinger in North End.

Hopkins, Thomas, began 1777,
11 mos, Pvt., died 1804.

Hudson, Thomas, began 1780,
12 mos, Fifer, ae. 17, died 1816.

Hutchinson, James, began 1775,
3 mos, Matross.

Ingraham, Joseph, began 1777,
36 mos, drummer., died 1811.

Jackson, Eleazer, began 1775,
8 mos, Pvt., died 1809.

Johnson, John, began 1777/1778,
may be Jr. or Sr. and may be Pvt
or Matross or both, died 1804.

Jones, Benjamin B., began 1777,
13 mos, Sgt, died 1813.

Marston, James, began 1775,
23 mos. Bombardier, married
1757, died 1810.

Miller, John W., began 1778, 9 mos.,
ae 25, housewright on Hanover St., died 1813.

Mills, Wm., began 1777, 77 mos, Cpt., died 1792.

Mountfort, Joseph, Lt, cooper, died 1838.

Rose, Phillip, began 1776, 46 mos, Sgt, died 1800.

Rumney, Edwd., began 1775, 3 mos, Cpt., married 1771,
shopkeeper, lived Middle St., died 1808.

Seward, Thomas, Maj, died 1800, ae 60.

Shaw, Samuel, Maj, China trader and consul to China, died 1794.

Sigourney, Andrew, began 1777, 43 mos, Pvt.

Smith, Benj., began 1780, 10 mos, Pvt, ae 33., died 1805.

Smith, John, began 1775, 2 mos, Matross, ae 21
or another John Smith, began 1780, ae 29.

Snelling, Joseph, began 1779, Cpt, married 1763,
baker, Salem St., died 1799.

Sullivan, James G., began 1776, 6 mos, Matross, prob. Lawyer,
Cambridge St, died 1807.

Webber, Seth, began 1777, 36 mos, Sgt, Middle St., died 1806.

Wilson, John, began 1777, 12 mos. Matross, died 1828. ✤

**Hartt, Edmund, builder of
frigate Constitution
(Old Ironsides) and Boston.**

**Lang, John, Coxwain,
Navy service, died 1838.**

NOTE: It may say Cpt. on tombstone, but Captain is not necessarily
the rank attained. Cpt. was often
applied to any aged man believed to
have fought in a war. Likewise the
term "deacon" indicates a religious
lay position, but not necessarily the
official position of deacon.

Members of Charitable Mechanic Association Buried in Copp's Hill Burying Ground

The Massachusetts Charitable Mechanic Assn. was organized in 1794 and Paul Revere became its first president from 1795-99. Its purpose was to advance the cause of tradesmen and artisans, especially in training apprentices and in advancing and promoting American-made and invented products and services. Up into the 1950s, it had a large exhibition hall for trade shows and apprentice education located where the Christian Science Plaza now is. It continues today as the "Quiet Philanthropy," headquartered in Quincy, dispensing up to $300,000 yearly to various Boston area charities.

We know the members listed are definitely buried in Copp's Hill or, in the case of family tombs, it is highly probable they are buried here.

Alexander, William, O.M., cabinetmaker
Bassett, Joseph, cooper, died 1852
Bassett, Samuel, sailmaker
Clark, Benjamin, cooper, died 1840
Clark, John, tobacconist, died 1853
Cushing, Benjamin, cooper, died 1820
Dalton, Michael, type founder, died 1879
Darracott, George, tinplate worker, died 1865
Davis, Samuel, jeweler
Dodd, John, tobacconist
Dupee, Isaac, blockmaker, died 1850
Folsom, John W. O.M., printer
Gilman, Peter, tailor
Grant, Moses, upholsterer, died 1861
Gore, Samuel, O.M., painter, died 1831

Greenough, John G., carpenter
Greenough, Joseph, stonecutter
Hall, John, dyer
Harris, Leach, shipwright
Hartt, Samuel, ship carpenter
Hitchborn, Samuel, Jr., sailmaker, died 1854
Hill, Samuel, engraver
Hunt, Joab, shipjoiner, died 1828
Hunnewell, Jonathon, O.M., bricklayer, died 1842
Hunnewell, Richard, O.M., bricklayer, died 1805
James, Francis, mason
Jones, Joseph, sailmaker, died 1851
Leman, John, shipsmith, died 1841
Lewis, Joseph, baker, died 1858
Lewis, Thomas, cooper
Libbey, J.G. L., jeweler, died 1847
Loring, John, baker, died 1821
Loring, Josiah, bookbinder, 1841
Low, John, bricklayer

Marston, John, pump &
block maker
McClennen, Wm., rigger,
died 1833
McClennen, Wm. 2nd, rigger
Mead, John, bookbinder,
died 1836
Miller, Charles, gilder
Mountfort, Charles, sailmaker
Mountfort, Joseph, cooper,
died 1838
Nichols, Samuel, bricklayer,
died 1810
Nichols, Smith W., bricklayer,
died 1881
Parsons, Ebenezer, carpenter
Parsons, Edmund, cabinetmaker,
died 1837
Phillips, James, O.M.,
ropemaker, 1853
Pond, Moses, Jr., tinplate worker,
died 1870
Sargent, Edward, cooper,
died 1848
Singleton, George, cooper

OTHERS:
Callendar, Joseph, engraver,
did not sign constitution so
not a member, but listed.
Wells, Mayor Charles, bricklayer,
died 1866 is named on marker,
but buried in Mt. Auburn.
Wells, John B., cooper,
also Mt. Auburn. ☙

Singleton, Samuel, pump &
block maker
Skillin, Simeon, carver
Snelling, Josiah, baker
Starr, Joseph, shipwright
Tuttle, Samuel, tailor, died 1832
Vannevar, Alexander, cooper,
died 1863
Vannevar, George, carpenter,
died 1863
Varney, Benj., pump & block
maker, died 1809
Wade, Joseph, carpenter
Wells, Benj. T., coppersmith,
died 1822
Wells, John, O.M. coppersmith,
died 1832
Wells, Thomas, bookbinder,
died 1830
Willard, Josiah, chairmaker
Willcutt, Joseph, housewright,
died 1843
Willett, Joseph, carpenter,
died 1824
Wilson, John, tailor, died 1856
Wyler, John, O.M., rigger
Yendell, Samuel, boatbuilder,
died 1861

O.M. means Original Member.

All you ever wanted to about Copp's Hill

What was Copp's Hill like? Picture in your mind an ancient graveyard on a hill with a view of the shore in almost every direction. There were no planned walkways between the scattered gravestones, no entrance gates or walls surrounding it.

How has it changed? The burying ground has been changed several times so that stones do not necessarily mark the exact burial place of the person named on the gravestone. In 1807, the highest point was lowered several feet. Some tombs were rearranged in 1838 and the pathways laid out. Additional changes were made in 1878.

Why aren't families always buried together as in other places? The term cemetery (from the Greek; sleeping place) was not in common use until after the spread of the Rural Cemetery Movement in the mid-1800s. A cemetery is thought of as a planned and regulated landscape where families may have title to their own family plot. In early burial grounds, people did not own defined plots and, although family members were usually buried nearby, they were not always able to be buried next to each other. The large vault tombs of the more well to do (Mather tomb, for example) could accommodate multiple burials in one location. However, as it filled in, burials were made wherever space was available. Graves are close together, newer graves were sometimes placed on top of older ones.

If there were 10,000 - 11,000 burials here, where are all the tombstones? There are 2,230 tombstones remaining, down from 3,000 of 120 years ago. Many graves are unmarked (See Chapter on Tomb 18, which has 10 burials in one tomb). Some markers were stolen for foundations in nearby buildings; some were used as closures to entrances to below-ground tombs; many are probably sunken or buried, and some were removed for other uses. A baker, for example, used a tombstone for his hearth and the bread he produced had the markings of the stone on it. Over the years, there have been losses from normal aging and damage from natural disasters such as the gale of 1888 or the hurricane in the 1950s that took the steeple off Old North Church.

What are the tombstones like? The earliest markers were small, thick, and undecorated with upper case lettering for the carved inscription. Stones with winged skulls were very popular until the late 1700s. The stones with faces and wings began to dominate in the middle to late 1700s. The classical urn and willow motif appeared toward the end of the 1700s and remained popular well into the 1800s.

What are their condition? Remarkably good considering the 325 years some of them have been here. Don't be afraid to get down on your hands and knees to inspect the stones. The artwork and inscriptions don't always show up well as you look down on them. There are al least 50 really outstanding examples.

What are they made of? Most of the stones are of slate, produced locally.

Who carved them? We know at least 18 carvers who placed stones at Copp's Hill. Two are buried here: Wm. Mumford (died 1718, Ae 77; his son died 1707, Ae 27 – Loc. C-283; Loc. C-356) and Wm. Codner, Loc. H-52. ➥

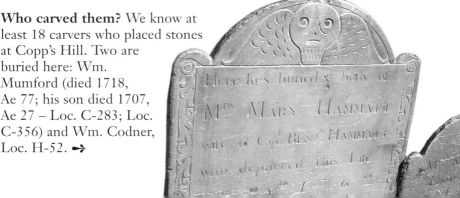

Why the Roman Numerals? Roman numerals were not widely used on tombstones, but you do see some here. Some elaborate stones and a few where the person wanted to lend a certain ambiance of class did use them. They are the exception, not the rule; fads that went in and out of style. Roman numbers were often used on most clocks and building cornerstones. Up until about 75 years ago, most people could read them easily. M = 1,000, D = 500, C = 100, L = 50; X = 10, V = 5, and I = 1. For example, VIII = 8, but IX = 9; and MDCCCCXIII = 1908. Numbers before the main numeral subtract and those after add. It'll soon get easier: the year 2000 will be MM.

Child's Grave

Why are the demographics of Copp's Hill? The burying ground reflects all classes: wealthy appointees of the Royal Government, old established families with their coats of arms, shipbuilders, sea captains, teachers, tradesmen (and sometime tradeswomen), artisans, laborers, sailors, slaves and indentured servants, and free Blacks. It was very much a community burying ground. An estimated 1,000 African Americans are buried the unmarked area near Snowhill and Charter Streets.

What do the tombstones reflect? There are wealthy North End resident buried here and their markers reflect that wealth. Trades people (mechanics) and artisans have more modest tombstones. As families moved out to the developed Back Bay and outlying areas of Boston in the 19th Century, the North End neighborhood slowly became a less desirable place to live. Many Bostonians chose inter-ment in nearby Mt. Auburn or other garden style rural cemeteries. Monument styles changed; slate and skulls were no longer appropri-ate reflections of the new ideas.

What was their religion? Almost entirely Protestant. At first, all were Puritans because that was the only recognized religion. Then later, other denominations were represented here. Few if any Roman Catholics or Jews are buried here.

How did most of these people view death? The earliest Puritans were anxious about death; anxious about whether they were one of the chosen few to enter heaven. The last judgement was definitely important in their theology. Later theology held out hope that heaven could be achieved if one lived righteously. St. Paul says it well, "The trumpet shall sound, and the dead shall be raised." This is reflected in some of the tombstones motifs.

What was their attitude regarding death? Death was very much with them and they lived in the shadow of it. Infant mortality was much higher than today. Children died more frequently than today. Infection, childbirth, communicable diseases (small pox , diphtheria, and measles), drowning and other accidents were responsible for many deaths. Puritans focused on the soul of the deceased, not the body left behind by death. Early burials were considered to be a civil, rather than a religious function.

Why is it called Copp's Hill? In 1653, the elevation was originally known as Milfield or Windmill Hill because of a windmill used here to grind grain. Later it was called Snow Hill and finally Copp's Hill after Wm. Copp who lived at the southeast corner near Prince Street. Some jokingly called it "corpse hill."

Terms for Death Causes

PAST TERM	MODERN TERM
Apoplexy	Stroke
Bad Blood	Syphilis
Blood Poisoning	Septicemia
Bright's disease	Glomerulonephritis
Consumption	Tuberculosis
Cretinism	Congenital Hypothyroidism
Dropsy	Congenital Heart Failure
Fatty Liver	Cirrhosis
Glandular Fever	Mononucleosis
Grippe	Influenza
Jail Fever	Typhus
Lock Jaw	Tetanus
Lung Fever	Pneumonia
Lung Sickness	Tuberculosis
Plague/Black Death	Bubonic Plague
Podagra	Gout
Pott's Disease	TB of the Spine
Quinsy	Streptococcal Tonsillitis
Scrofula	TB of the Neck Lymph Nodes, Hodgkin's disease
Toxemia of Pregnancy	Eclampsia (high blood pressure and seizures)

What have been its other uses? The site has been a pasture, a parade ground for the Ancient & Honorable Artillery Company, and a community meeting place. Sometimes, on Pope's Day for example, or when news of Quebec's surrender reached the city, or when the Stamp Act was repealed, there were bonfires and parties to celebrate the special day. The French Revolution was commemorated by an ox roast in 1793. It was a British cannon site during the Battle of Bunker Hill. In 1828, a gas works became the most prominent North End landmark, but was removed in recent times. At the bottom of Hull Street, a giant tank used to store molasses for the United Liquor Company burst on Jan. 15, 1919, flooding the area with a 15-foot wave of molasses which killed 21 people. The parking garage just beyond the Seaman's tomb once housed Brinks Armored Car Co. It was robbed of $1.2 million, Jan. 19, 1950, an event that made headlines across America. ➨

43

When did the land become a burial ground? The area was laid out in 1659 to become the North Burying Ground. The city of Boston officially purchased it on Nov. 5, 1660, and it became the city's largest, with 88,800 square feet. It is the second oldest burial ground (only King's Chapel, 1630, is older) in the city proper. By 1760, about one-fourth of the city's burials were contained at Copp's Hill. Portions have also been called Hull Street, Charter Street, and New North Burying Ground. When Snowhill Street was widened, remains there were transferred to Mt. Hope Cemetery in 1861.

What are the oldest and newest burials in Copp's Hill? Exact date of the first is unknown, but first inscriptions date from 1661. "David, son to David Copp and Obedience his wife, aged 2 weeks Dyed Dec. 22 1661." New below ground burials were outlawed in 1833, but tomb burials continued until 1968, Marian L. Bray (CH/I-1a).

Where are the tombs located? There are 230 tombs in Copp's Hill. A below ground tomb is made with brick walls and a brick crown roof covered over with earth and grass. An opening was built into the roof to allow for burials. To use it, the grass and earth were removed, exposing a slab cover, which had to be removed to expose the opening. Then the coffins in the tomb could be moved over and the new one deposited. The box tombs and table stones one sees in early New England burial grounds are simply grave markers. The vault tombs are in the ground beneath the elevated stones.

What was a tomb like? Copp's Hill Supt. Edward MacDonald describes the one tomb as dry as the cellar in a well-drained house. "The interior is by no means cheerful, but they are not as repulsive as might be expected. A body deposited in one of them soon loses all offensive odor, and, until the inevitable crumbling of the coffin occurs, there is nothing to offend either sight or smell." Bodies went back to dust quickly because there was no embalming until about the Civil War.

Why isn't Copp's Hill used for burials anymore? It simply filled up. The Boston Council officially closed the main part of the burying ground in 1833. "It being the order of the Mayor and Aldermen that the old part of the North Burying Ground be closed and" no new graves be opened or dug nor tombs built therein." New tombs were permitted in the depressed section to the right of the entrance. This also applied to Kings Chapel and Granary Burying Ground downtown. At Copp's Hill, most burials ceased by about 1850. See chapter on "Scandals at Copp's Hill."

Is anything being done to preserve it? Boston Parks & Recreation Department of the City of Boston is responsible for the 16 burying grounds within the city. Beginning in 1986, it inventoried the tombstones and more than 300 slate gravestones and other monuments were restored in 1988, 1990, and 1995. This is ongoing as funds permit. There is a separate office within the department called the Historic Burying Ground Initiative created to oversee these hallowed landmarks.

What about the future for Copp's Hill? Plans in 1998 called for the adjacent unused Michaelangelo Junior High School to be converted to senior citizen's housing. The Hull Street entrance of the school's 1930 annex would provide restrooms for those walking the Freedom Trail plus an information desk staffed by the residents. Those markers in or near the walls would be reset and restored. Within Copp's Hill, $400,000 is needed for a full restoration.

What can I do to help preserve Copp's Hill? Individual and family financial support along with civic and corporate assistance is welcomed. Bequests earmarked for burying ground restoration also would be welcome. Historic Burying Ground Initiative is located at 1010 Massachusetts Ave., Boston, MA 02118; Tel. 617-635-4505.

Are there other ways to learn about Burying Grounds and Tombstones? The Association for Gravestone Studies is a national non-profit association whose members are interested in cemeteries and gravestones. Their address is: 278 Main Street, Suite 207, Greenfield, MA 01301, or phone 413-772-0836, email: ags@javanet.com Also see section at back of book for more information on the association. ☙

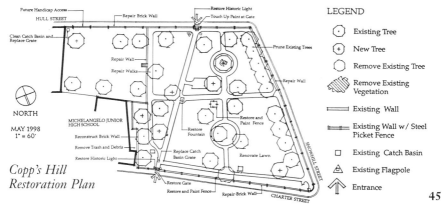

Copp's Hill Restoration Plan

LEGEND

⊙ Existing Tree
⊕ New Tree
◯ Remove Existing Tree
▨ Remove Existing Vegetation
▭▭ Existing Wall
▬▬ Existing Wall w/ Steel Picket Fence
▢ Existing Catch Basin
△ Existing Flagpole
⇧ Entrance

SCANDAL AT
Copp's Hill

THIS 1851 ACCOUNT TELLS SOME OF THE EARLY PRACTICES THAT DISCOURAGED NORTH END FAMILIES FROM BURYING THEIR LOVED ONES AT COPP'S HILL. THE AREA ALSO HAD BEGAN TO DECLINE, RESIDENTS MOVED TO MORE DESIRABLE LOCATIONS, AND TO MORE ATTRACTIVE CEMETERIES LIKE MT. AUBURN IN CAMBRIDGE.

"An infamous custom has prevailed among some of the sextons in this city of speculating in tombs. Finding a poor widow or dilapidated heir, having a share or fractional interest in some old tomb under his care, the grave-digger, aware of the absence or death of the principal owner, and that a 'living dog is better than a dead lion,' purchases it for a trifle, seizes the whole by prescription, or threats of the law, calls it his own, erases the family name, clears out the sacred relics which lie there, and then makes a trade of his mortmain right, by selling a berth for dead strangers in the city, at $8, or $10 or $12 apiece, as the case may be. This has been repeatedly done on Copp's Hill, King's Chapel, and other burial grounds in the city.

"Nor is this all. After the tombs have been filled up by the remains of strangers, their corpses have been carted out of town in the night season, or buried in a hole dug at the bottom of the tomb, pounded down in one horrid, hideous mass, and covered over, to make way for more death money. An aged gentleman of respectability, residing near Copp's Hill, told me he has seen loads of broken-up coffins removed from the tombs thus desecrated; and a lady in this city recently remarked that within 15 years she was in that cemetery, and there saw a collection of coffins heaped up for removal; on the fragments of one of which skin and hair adhered – the hair black and glossy – the long, fine hair of a female; and she shuddered and turned away from the spectacle!

"The grave is no resting-place for the dead; the sacred ashes of a husband or father will one day be scattered by the hand of the sexton, and a greedy, unprincipled grave-digger will claim your ancestral tomb for a mere pittance, and turn it into a mercenary charnel-house to suit his purposes," he concluded.*

Reacting to the scandal, The Boston City Council passed The Cemetery Ordinance of 1833, which provided that "no person shall remove any bodies, or the remains of bodies, from any of the graves or tombs in the city, or shall disturb, break up, or remove any body in any tomb or grave without special permission of the Superintendent of burials."

It is evident that this was specially aimed at the scandal Thomas Bridgman wrote about. The ordinance also said that no grave or tomb could be opened from June 1 to Oct. 1 without special permission.

Tombstones were also regulated: Length 4.5 feet, breadth of 1 foot 10 inches, thickness 3.5 inches, having the person's name and age, the number of the grave, the number of the range cut thereon, and placed perpendicularly six inches from the head of the grave, settled in the earth 18 inches from a level surface.

"Such grave shall be reserved for the use of the same family: Provided, the top of any coffin placed therein, be not within three feet of the surface of the ground. Further, that no new range of graves shall be commenced, until the preceding range shall be taken up by deposit of one or more bodies therein." ❧

"The grave is no resting-place for the dead; the sacred ashes of a husband or father will one day be scattered by the hand of the sexton, and a greedy, unprincipled grave-digger will claim your ancestral tomb for a mere pittance, and turn it into a mercenary charnel-house to suit his purposes."

Bridgman, Thomas, Epitaphs from *Copp's Hill Burial Ground*, Boston, 1851, pages 20-21.

TOMB 18
Tells a Typical Story

Of the 11,000 estimated Copp's Hill burials, only about 3,500 had tombstones or inscriptions. Survivors simply did not purchase a marker either because of cost or because they thought it unimportant. Others buried in the tombs did not always have an epitaph either. These deaths may be recorded in newspapers, municipal death records, church records, or are not recorded at all. Most, especially those before 1800 are unrecorded.

From the author's research, his ancestral Tomb 18 illustrates this problem well. The tomb inscription says "Nathaniel, John and Charles Wells," leading one to think there are three burials there. Yet, there are 10 and perhaps 11. In researching the Boston Death Index for 1800 -1848, we found other family member's deaths, which are found nowhere else. Others may have the same experience in tracking their ancestors having tomb interments in Copp's Hill. The only way to know for certain who is interred in a tomb is to research the family name in the Boston Death Index.

And, Mayor Charles and John B. Wells weren't even buried here. They decided to be buried in Mt. Auburn Cemetery in Cambridge. They had become more prosperous and could afford better.

Here are the other Wells burials in Tomb 18, which gives an idea of how many undocumented burials a tomb can actually contain:

Hannah Clarke Wells (daughter of Nathaniel Wells), died 21 Sept. 1813, ae. 3 of a canker. Buried 23 Sept, 1813, Comfort Claflin, undertaker.

Francis Wells (son of Mary Wells), died 15 Feb 1814, ae. 10 mos. of typhus, buried 17 Feb. 1814, by Monroe, undertaker.

Albert Wells (son of Nathaniel), died 18 Oct 1814, ae. 10 mos. of consumption (TB), buried 20 Oct. 1814, Comfort Claflin, undertaker.

Infant w No Name (Son of Nathaniel) died 26 April 1815, ae. 21 days of infantile death, buried 27 April 1815, Comfort Claflin, undertaker.

Nathaniel Wells (baker), died 16 June 1815, ae. 33 of consumption (TB), buried 19 June 1815, Comfort Claflin, undertaker. He is named on the marker.

Hannah Clarke Wells (widow of Nathaniel), died 21 Jan 1821, ae. 42 of consumption, buried 23 Jan 1821, Comfort Claflin, undertaker.

Sarah Wells (daughter of Thomas Wells) died 22 Sept. 1821, ae. 21 of brain fever, buried 24 Sept 1821, Sam'l Winslow, undertaker.

Joseph S. Wells (son of Charles Wells), died 5 July 1822, ae. 13, drowned, buried 6 July 1822, Sam'l Winslow, undertaker. Another son, Charles, is buried in Tomb 100. He died 25 Sept 1817, ae. 1 year, 7 mos. of dysentery.

Elizabeth White Wells (widow of Thomas), died 20 Jan 1825, ae. 78, buried 22 Jan 1825, Sam'l Winslow undertaker.

Mary Frances Wells, died 29 June 1837, ae. 2 years, 6 mos. of "abscess of brain."

The patriarch of the family, **Thomas Wells** (blacksmith), who died 13 March 1810, ae. 64, is probably buried here also. His death is listed in Boston Records, but with no record of burial place. It is quite possible he is buried in Tomb 18 because his death in 1810 and the year 1811 on the tomb are so close together and no other burials were made until 1813. 🕯

Death Index 1801- 1848, City of Boston Archives, Room 13, City Hall, Boston. ✓

How the Modern Funeral CAME TO BE

"IN THE OLDEN TIME, BURIALS WERE CONDUCTED IN A VERY DIFFERENT MANNER FROM WHAT THEY NOW ARE.*

"When a death occurred in a family, it was generally made known very widely; and on the day of the funeral, the relatives and friends, far and near, assembled at the house of the deceased, and carried the body to the burial ground, unless, as in many of the towns in the Plymouth Colony, there were places for burial upon the farms, which was not the case, of course, in Boston. As our fathers eschewed everything that resembled the church customs of their fatherland (Puritan Boston vs. Anglican England), no prayers or particular services were had at the house or even at the grave; but after the funeral, the mourners and their friends returned to the house and there, if we can believe the charges in the old administration accounts, there sometimes must have been pretty high times. Instead of the prayers and addresses which are now part of the funeral ceremonies at houses, the prayers, and now and then a funeral sermon, were reserved for the ensuing Sunday forenoon religious services at the meeting-house.

"The first prayer made at a funeral in Boston is said, on good authority, to have been offered by the Rev. Dr. Charles Chauncey, at the interment of Rev. Dr. Jonathan Mayhew, pastor of the West Church, who died on the 9th of July, 1766, and was buried from the West Church on account of the great concourse who desired to pay respect to his memory by being present on the occasion. The assembly being in a meeting-house, it was deemed proper and expedient that a devotional exercise should be had; and this incident led to a custom which is now universal.

* Shurtleff, Nathaniel B., *A Topographical & Historical Description of Boston*, Boston, 1872, 2nd Edition, Page 263.

"The sermon which introduced the present custom of funeral sermons over the body was preached by the Rev. Dr. John Clarke in Brattle Street Meeting House, at the interment of Rev. Dr. Samuel Cooper, who died on the 29th of December, 1783, and was buried on the following Friday; which being the day the usual sacramental lecture was delivered in Brattle Street Church, and the body having been taken into the meeting-house on account of the great number of persons who desired to attend the funeral, Rev. Dr. Clarke, the junior pastor of the First Church, who was to have preached the lecture, changed it into a funeral service, and thus set an example which has been much followed since. The sermons which are usually designed as funeral sermons were generally in the early times preached, as before said, upon the Sunday after the funeral; although occasionally, by accident, the funeral sermon was preached at the time of inter- ment, as exception to the general rule.

"There were no hearses in the early days of the town. The coffin, which was generally of pine, hemlock, or cedar, and sometimes of harder and more costly wood, was usually stained black or red, and some- times covered with black cloth; and this was ornamented with capacious hinges and a plate, all stuck up into form from sheets of tinned iron, the plate being marked with black letters, neatly painted upon a plan- ished surface. This was carried by hand upon a bier to the grave, or tomb, as the case happened to be, by bearers, who were from time to time relieved by others who walked by their side; and these were followed by the mourners and friends, who walked two by two, man and woman, arm and arm, and boy and girl hand and hand together. After the funeral, ➥

Hearses were not introduced into Boston until about the year 1796, when, on account of the great distance of the burial grounds from some parts of the town, their use became necessary.

the bier was left standing over the grave ready for use when occasion should require. This custom prevailed till within a period which can be well remembered by our oldest people. The bearers were generally rewarded with a present of gloves, and sometimes scarves, and the mourners had funeral rings of black enamel, edged with gold, bearing as inscriptions the name, age, and date of death of the deceased. Hearses were not introduced into Boston until about the year 1796, when, on account of the great distance of the burial grounds from some parts of the town, their use became necessary. Carriages, for the women to ride in, were introduced into use not long afterwards, although the men continued to walk until the establishment of suburban cemeteries.

"Until the purchase of "Sweet Auburn," on the confines of Cambridge and Watertown, for a rural burial place, very little had been done towards ornamenting and beautifying the graveyards in Boston and the neighboring  towns; but since the establishment of Mt. Auburn Cemetery, much has been done to expel from the old graveyards their forbidding appearances. In later years, since the abolishment of burials in graves within the limits of the peninsula (Boston proper), the greatest number of interments have been made in the rural cemeteries, that at Mt. Auburn being the oldest of those most generally used."

Mt. Auburn in Cambridge was the first of America's modern garden cemeteries. The earliest ones of this type had begun near Paris. The Massachusetts Horticultural Society established the cemetery June 23, 1831, for the erection of tombs, cenotaphs, or other monuments for or in memory of the dead. Features included family plots, shrubbery, flowers, trees, walks, and other rural ornaments. Located near the borders of Cambridge and Watertown, it rises 125 feet above the Charles River on its southern border. Many of Boston's late and great are buried here and it is truly a cemetery in a garden. It proved so successful that Forest Hills was established in 1848 near Roxbury and Mount Hope in 1868, near West Roxbury.

By 1878, the manufacture of coffins had grown to become a major Boston business. In a section entitled, "New Businesses Introduced into Boston since 1800, Alfred Mudge & Son's *Historical Sketch of Boston* tells of the development of the coffin and casket industry:

"The funeral business has had many changes within the present century. Formerly, the business was divided: the funeral being ➝

1833 Schedule of Fees for Undertakers

For each person buried, 75 cents.

For each mile for the distance out of the city for any distance that a funeral be sent out of the city, $1 per mile.

To the City of Boston as a tax:
For each person buried, 75 cents
For each mile traveled outside of the city for burial, $1.

To the Undertakers:
For digging a grave 8 feet deep and covering the same, $2.50.
~ 6 feet, 6 inches deep, $1.50.
~ 5 feet deep, $1.25.
~ 4 feet deep, $1.00
~ Children under 10, 3 and a half feet deep, 75 cents.

Open and closing a tomb, 75 cents.

For attendance and service in the home of a person deceased, in collecting and returning chairs and other service, $1.

For every family notified by request, 5 cents.

For tolling a bell by special permission, 50 cents.

For placing a corpse in a coffin, when requested, and removing the same downstairs, $1.

For use of one horse with the car and leader, $1.50; for each additional horse, 75 cents.

For carrying a corpse from the house to the car, and from the car to the grave, tomb, or vault, and placing the same therein and closing the same, including the assistance of the funeral porters, $3.

For carrying a corpse into a church for a funeral service, $2.

attended by the sexton of some church; and the coffin, provided by some carpenter or cabinet maker, made of plain wood, without ornamentation, and of cheap quality. The hurry of getting those articles ready after the death of a person was not in keeping, oftentimes, with the position of the person in life.

"But within the last 20 years, the business has entirely changed. Caskets of beautiful wood and finish are kept ready made, with such ornaments as may be selected by the means and taste of the relatives needing such articles for the burial of deceased friends.

"Within the city of Boston, there are a number of warerooms devoted to this purpose, one of which is at No. 2302 Washington St., Boston, kept by Mr. Joseph S. Waterman."

The section goes on to list other so called new products like the carpet sweeper, introduced in Boston in 1859; photographs, introduced in 1852 with a photo of the Harvard graduating class; life insurance in 1851; bed springs in 1853; city and state directories and fine lithograph printing; and cemetery monuments in marble, freestone and granite.

" ...the monument business has grown to be one of the most extensive among us. In this city, the business has reached to a most remarkable degree of beauty and perfection; and among the expert beautifiers of the art, none excel in the point of artistic skill and expression as Mr. F. Dolan, whose place of business is at No. 500 Tremont St. His work is highly commended by all who have availed themselves of his experience."

These markers were not used in Copp's Hill because by 1850 burials had ended there, and the garden cemeteries like Mt. Auburn and Forest Hills were more popular. &

Hot Spots...

BOSTON'S HISTORICAL

The best way to learn Boston history is to walk the Freedom Trail either on your own or with a National Park Service guide. The Boston National Historical Park Visitor Center has information, tours, and an excellent bookstore at 15 State St., near the Old State House downtown. Tel: 617-242-5642; Website: www.nps.gov/bost

If you haven't the time or energy for all of the Freedom Trail, at least do part of it. The Freedom Trail Foundation website is: www.thefreedomtrail.org

So, whether you have a day or a week, here are places and activities that will greatly increase your historical fun in visiting the wonderful place that is Boston:

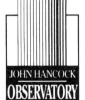

JOHN HANCOCK OBSERVATORY

This gives an over-all perspective you will get nowhere else. Its relief map of Old Boston + the view of Boston today takes you back to the days when Boston was smaller and more connected to the sea. Today it's hard to imagine what it was like because of the filling in of Boston Harbor to make more city. Located at Copley Square in Boston's Back Bay, it's easily reached by car or public transit. Hours: 9 a.m. to 10 p.m. daily except until 5 p.m. on Sundays Nov - March. Tel: 617-572-6429; website: www.jhancock.com then "Search the Site," then "Observatory."

BOSTON BY FOOT

Wonderful tours, wonderful information, wonderful prices. Here are just a few tours that pertain to Boston and Copp's Hill: The North End Tour, Saturdays at 2 p.m.; The Heart of the Freedom Trail, Tue. - Sat. at 10 a.m.; The Waterfront, Friday at 5:30 p.m. and Sunday at 10 a.m.; Victorian Back Bay, Fri., Sat., 10 a.m.; Beacon Hill, Mon. - Fri., 5:30 p.m., Sat. at 10 a.m., and Sun at 2 p.m. There are many more tours given by knowledgeable, educated, helpful guides. Tel: 617-367-2345 for bookings and information or 617-367-3766 for recording. Website: www.bostonbyfoot.com

Hot BOSTON'S HISTORICAL
Spots...

PAUL REVERE HOUSE
Paul Revere is the North End's most famous citizen. Visit his house if you want to understand life in the 1700s. It was built in the 1680s and he lived here 1770-1800. Located at North Square (North & Prince). Open year around 9:30 a.m. to 5:15 p.m., April 15 - Oct. 31 and until 4:15 from Nov. 1 - April 14. Tel: 617-523-2338. Website: www.paulreverehouse.org

OLD NORTH (CHRIST) CHURCH, EPISCOPAL
Everyone visits this church at one time or another. Attending church here as the colonials did is unique, though. Visitors welcomed Sundays at 9 a.m., 11 a.m. (choir) and 5 p.m. Communicants used to have to pay pew rent, but they don't charge that today. Located at 193 Salem St. Free or reduced parking for those attending Sunday service. Usher will validate. Parcel 7 Garage (Congress & Sudbury) and Kinney Garage, Commercial & Hull. Outstanding gift shop. Church: 617-523-6676; Gift Shop 617-523-4848. Website: www.oldnorth.com

SUNSET CRUISE
The 90-minute Sunset Cruise offers not just a historic view of Boston Harbor, but you also see the impressive "Retiring of the Colors" at *Old Ironsides* including firing the cannon.

Boston Harbor Cruises

Departs Long Wharf at 7 p.m. Boston Harbor Cruises at 617-227-4321; website: www.bostonboats.com Many other cruises available.

UNION OYSTER HOUSE
UNION OYSTER HOUSE est. 1826 Originally Hopestill Capen's store, this is Boston's oldest restaurant and oldest restaurant in continuous service in the U.S. Specializing in seafood, its ambiance takes you back into history and the food is excellent. Located at 41 Union near Boston City Hall and Quincy Market. Make reservations in the evening. Open 11 a.m. - 9:30 p.m. daily, Fri., Sat. until 10 with the bar open until midnight. If you're on a tight budget, try the luncheon. And to think that our ancestors fed lobsters to the pigs. Tel: 617-227-2750. Website: www.unionoysterhouse.com

OLD SOUTH MEETING HOUSE

At 310 Washington Street just up from the Old Statehouse, visit Old South Meeting House, where the debates raged over what to do with the tea. The presentation takes you back to 1773 for the debate. Baptismal place of Benjamin Franklin. Other special events and noonday lectures. Outstanding gift shop and accessible facilities. Tel: 617-482-6439. Website: through Freedom Trail.

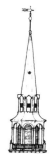

BOSTON TEA PARTY SHIP & MUSEUM

Once you've heard the debate, now you should be enraged enough to go down to dump the tea. Located down Congress Street on the Freedom Trail at the Congress Street bridge, the 110-foot long

brig *Beaver II*, a working replica of one of the three Tea Party ships. Open March - November 9 to 5 Spring & Fall and 9 to 5:45 Summers. Tel: 617-338-1773. Website: www.historictours.com

MT. AUBURN CEMETERY

If you have the time, Mt. Auburn is well worth the trip over to Cambridge. Visit the Washington Memorial Tower. It has unique vistas of Boston, the Charles River, and Cambridge. Many well-known national personages are buried here. Audio tape tour. Located 1.5 miles west of Harvard Square on #72 or #73 bus line. Open every day from 8 a.m. to 5 p.m. Tel: 617-547-7105. Website under development.

MUSEUM OF FINE ARTS

Outstanding collection of early American paintings including Paul Revere, Geo. Washington, Mercy Otis Warren, and others. Also furniture and many other items of early America. Located one mile west of Copley Square at 465 Huntington Avenue in the Fenway neighborhood. Public transportation and parking. Accessible. Open 7 Days a week, Call 617-267-9300 for hours. Some reduced admission days and hours. Website: www.mfa.org ☙

Where else
to look...

Boston's North End can be an elusive place to find people in history. For example, Copp's Hill Burying Ground has an estimated 11,000 burials, but we can only document about 3,000 from present tombstones in Section C of this book, the Whitman book in Section B, and other sources. So how to find the "lost"?

NEW ENGLAND HISTORIC GENEALOGICAL SOCIETY
This is the first place to look for anything about Boston families. It is one of the top genealogical research libraries in America. There may already be a genealogy for your family. Everyone shows up sometime in Boston city records; check this 20+ volume source. For hard to find situations, check their manuscript listings. Churches, for example, may show baptisms, membership, etc. Numerous other sources are available. Daily fee applicable to membership. NEHGS, 101 Newbury St., Boston, MA 02116-3009. Toll Free 888-906-3447. Website: www.nehgs.org

NEHGS sales department has many publications on Boston and New England. Two especially helpful ones are: *Boston Deaths: 1700 - 1799* and *Boston Cemeteries* (Kings Chapel, Granary, Central Burying Ground, and Copp's Hill), both by Robert J. Dunkle and Ann S. Lainhart. Toll Free: 888-296-3447.

BOSTON CITY ARCHIVES
Boston's Death Index from 1800 to 1848 documents most of the deaths within the city of Boston, next of kin, cause, and where the person is buried. Researchers can use this facility personally one day per month, usually 10 a.m. - 2 p.m. on the last Tuesday of each month. There are many duplicates of church records here also. Call 617-635-359, City Hall Archives, Rm. 13, in advance for appointment. Charge is $10.

By mail, write: Registry Division, City of Boston, Rm. 13 City Hall, Boston, MA 02201 Cost is $10 for a search and $9 per record, $6 additional after the first. Send a check for all your searches. They will refund the amount, not needed.

ANOTHER NORTH END BURIAL PLACE

"Old North" or Christ Church (Episcopal). The church, opened in 1723, is, and always has been, Anglican: part of the Church of England before the Revolution; part of the Episcopal Church of the United States since. It has an estimated 1,000 - 1,100 burials in the 38 crypts in its undercroft. Not all members were buried here; many were buried in Copp's Hill.

It will help the Archivist, who has limited time for research, if you send as much information as possible about the person whose history you seek and an approximate five-year period for burial if the exact date is unknown.

Enclose a donation and self-addressed stamped envelope to: Archivist, Old North Church, 193 Salem St., Boston, MA 02113. Tel: 617-523-6676; Website: www.oldnorth.com

BOSTON PUBLIC LIBRARY

Besides being an excellent resource, the library building itself is worth the trip. Check the card catalogs first for easy-to-access materials. Then the Rare Book & Manuscript Dept., which has originals of many Boston church records if originals need to be viewed. However, much of this information is already available from other sources, either from books within the library itself or other places. Save this specialized area of the library for those rare searches you can find nowhere else. Hours: 9 a.m. - 9 p.m. Mon. -Fri., 9- 5 p.m. Fri. - Sat., and 1 - 5 on Sun. Located at Copley Square, 666 Boylston St., Boston, MA 02116-2813. Tel: 617-536-5400. Website: www.bpl.org

MASSACHUSETTS HISTORICAL SOCIETY

The Thwing Index is a huge collection of notes on Boston families before 1800 from various sources written by Boston author, Annie Haven Thwing. Located at 1154 Boylston St., Boston 02215-3631. Hours: 9 a.m. - 4:45 p.m. Mon. - Fri. Tel: 617-536-1608 Website: www.masshist.org ➡

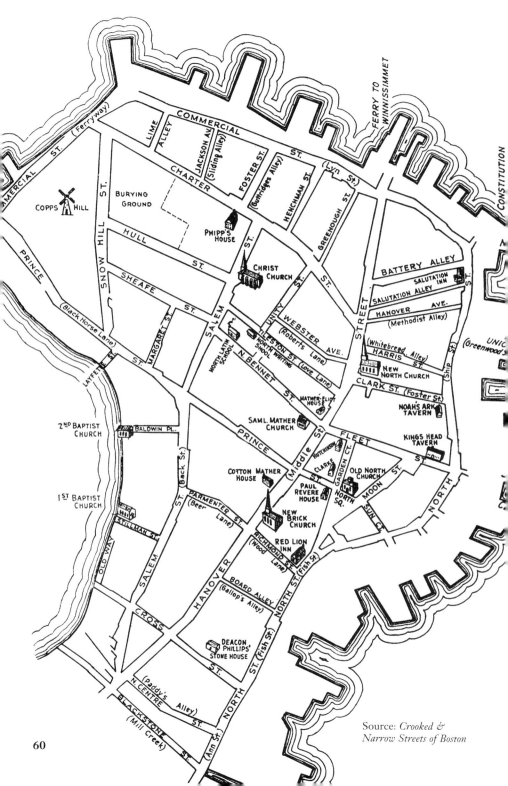

Source: *Crooked &
Narrow Streets of Boston*

60

Where else to look...

CHURCHES

Up until the 1840s and the coming of the Irish, most North End residents were Protestants. They tended to go to the church nearest their home. To miss church was to be fined in earliest times and the tradition of churchgoing continued. If the person you are looking for attended one of the following North End churches, it is probable burial was in Copp's Hill even though no exact record may exist. This becomes less true the later the person died up to 1850 when most burials ceased in Copp's Hill.

OLD NORTH CHURCH (Puritan), gathered June 5, 1650, this later became 2nd Church and was torn down by the British for firewood. It was located at North Square, Prince & Garden Court, across from the Paul Revere House and after the Revolutionary War merged with the New Brick.

NEW NORTH 5TH CHURCH (Puritan/later Unitarian). Organized at Hanover & Clark Streets in 1714, the building built in 1804 became St. Stephen's Roman Catholic Church in 1862.

NEW BRICK CHURCH, also called "Cockerel Church," it was located Hanover & Richmond Streets and began in 1719. For a time, the Revere family attended here.

SAMUEL MATHER'S CHURCH, located near Hanover & Bennett Streets from 1740 -1790. This became First Universalist from 1793 - 1863, with a new building erected in 1838. In 1864, it became 1st Baptist Mariner's Church.

1ST BAPTIST CHURCH, located on the Mill Pond, it began in 1679 and existed at Stillman and Salem Streets until about 1829, when their new home was at Hanover and Union.

2ND BAPTIST (Baldwin Place Baptist) Also called Samuel Stillman's Church, it separated from 1st Baptist and located just to the north in 1743. Located in an alley off Salem, its new building was built in 1810 and this was a congregation until 1865 when the building was sold for secular use. Then from 1889 - 1920, it was Temple Bethel to serve the Jews who had move to the North End.

1ST METHODIST CHURCH began in 1792 on the North End and was located on North Bennett Street in 1828.

SEAMAN'S BETHEL on North Square formed late and was sold in 1888 to become Sacred Heart Roman Catholic Church. ➨

Where else to look...

HIGHLY SPECIALIZED AREAS

ANCIENT & HONORABLE ARTILLERY COMPANY
Museum and references located 4th Floor, Faneuil Hall, Boston, MA 02109. Open 9 a.m. - 5 p.m. Mon. - Fri., AHAC has an excellent 4-volume history with many Boston biographies dating from its founding in 1638. Tel: 617-227-1638.

MASSACHUSETTS CHARITABLE MECHANIC ASSN.
History of Boston tradesmen, merchants, and craftsmen from its founding in 1795. Limited research available on members and development of Boston commerce and artisans. Mail: MCMA, 353 Southern Artery, Quincy, MA 02169. Tel: 617-479-1795.

GRAND LODGE OF MASSACHUSETTS
Information on Freemasonry in Massachusetts and lodge rolls of the craft, some very early lodges. This symbol on tombstone indicates Masonic membership. Samuel Crocker Lawrence Library and Museum of the Grand Lodge of Massachusetts. Located at 186 Tremont St., Boston, MA 02111. Tel: 617-426-6040. Fax 617-426-6115, email www.glmasonsma@aol.com

GENEALOGICAL ETIQUETTE
If you are asking for information, it is only proper manners to enclose a self-addressed stamped envelope with your query. If it is going to take time to research your question, enclosed a check for $5 or $10 for the effort and copying expense. That will greatly improve your return rate on queries. And, it's the nice thing to do. ❧

Historic Burying Grounds Initiative
✺ SAVING BOSTON'S ✺
CHERISHED CEMETERIES

Organized in the early 1980's, Boston's Historic Burying Grounds Initiative (HBGI) has saved its ancient cemeteries from extinction. It is a public/private cooperative venture administered by the City of Boston Parks & Recreation Dept.

So far it has accomplished indexing the condition of more than 16,000 gravestones and physical properties of the burying grounds in the city. HBGI developed a master plan to conserve and improve the sites and spent $3.5 million implementing the plan.

Some of this has included restoration of walls, walkways and ornamental fencing, conserving thousands of markers, installation of signage, lighting, and a bicycle pilgrimage called "Tour de Graves." It has developed a broad base of "friends" groups and community support. It publishes "Common Ground," a newsletter on its activities. Occassional tours are offered on a reservation basis.

To contact HBGI, call 617-635-4505 or write to HBGI Project Manager, Boston Parks & Recreation Dept., 1010 Massachusetts Ave., Boston, MA 02118. Donations and bequests are greatly appreciated.

BOSTON BURYING GROUNDS INCLUDE:
- Bennington Street Cemetery (1838) - East Boston
- Bunker Hill Burying Ground (1807) - Charlestown
- Central Burying Ground (1756) - Boston Common, a National Historic Landmark
- Copp's Hill Burying Ground (1659) - North End, listed on the National Register of Historic Places and located on the Freedom Trail
- Dorchester North Burying Ground (1633/34) - Dorchester, listed on the National Register of Historic Places
- Dorchester South Burying Ground (1814) - Dorchester
- Eliot Burying Ground (1630) - Roxbury, listed on the National Register of Historic Places and located in the Eustis Street Architectural Conservation District ➥

- Hawes/Union Burying Grounds (1816/1841) - South Boston
- Granary Burying Ground (1660) - Downtown, located in Beacon Hill Architectural District and on the Freedom Trail
- King's Chapel Burying Ground (1630) - Downtown, located on the Freedom Trail
- Market Street Burying Ground (1764) - Brighton Center
- Phipps Street Burying Ground (1630) - Charlestown, listed on the National Register of Historic Places
- South End South Burying Ground (1810) - South End, located in the South End National Landmark District
- Walter Street Burying Ground (1711) - Roslindale, located in the Arnold Arboretum, a National Historic Landmark
- Westerly Burying Ground (1683) - West Roxbury, listed on the National Register of Historic Places ❧

Join the Association for Gravestone Studies

CONTINUE YOUR INTEREST BY JOINING US:

- AGS Quarterly: Bulletin of the Assn. for Gravestone Studies, published four times yearly.
- Conferences, events, and workshops across America.
- Publications including *Markers*, the annual journal, plus other papers, newsletters, etc., and items. Also, a growing archive at headquarters in Greenfield, MA, a lending library, and a research clearing house.

For further information, call 413-772-0836 or write
THE ASSOCIATION FOR GRAVESTONE STUDIES
278 Main St., Suite 207, Greenfield, MA 01301
Website: www.berkshire.net/ags

THE GRAVEYARDS

OF

BOSTON.

———

FIRST VOLUME, COPP'S HILL EPITAPHS.

———

PREPARED FOR PUBLICATION

BY

WILLIAM H. WHITMORE.

———

ALBANY:

JOEL MUNSELL.

1878.

Section

B

PREFACE.

It is always an ungrateful task, to criticise the work of one's predecessors in any branch of inquiry. When, however, that work is one which does not call for any mental labor, when it admits neither of reasoning, fancy or invention, when, as in the present case, it calls simply for accuracy, criticism becomes justifiable and unavoidable.

In 1852, the late Thomas Bridgman published a book entitled "Memorials of the Dead in Boston; containing an exact transcript from Inscriptions, Epitaphs and Records on the Monuments and Tombstones in Copp's-Hill Burying Ground," etc., etc.

The justification for the present volume lies in the fact that Mr. Bridgman's transcript was not exact, and was very far from exhaustive. The errors in transcribing, though very numerous, were mostly trivial; but the omissions were inexcusably numerous. Out of the 2000 inscriptions here copied, about 800 are not to be found in Mr. Bridgman's book.

It may therefore be claimed for this volume, that as supplementing his work, it has added nearly as many facts to the knowledge of the antiquary as the original afforded him. It is not a re-casting of old material, but a large contribution of material not before accessible.

As to the accuracy of the present transcript, it should be stated that the editor employed the late Thomas B. Wyman, Jr., to prepare it from the original stones, carefully comparing all of Mr. Bridgman's text, and noting all errors and omissions. The work was done deliberately, and no one who has had the pleasure of knowing Mr. Wyman, will doubt that it was done with conscientious care.

The printed text has been carefully compared with Mr. Wyman's copy, the original of which, containing a full annotation in regard to the position of each stone, is deposited in the office of the City Registrar of Boston.

In order that the truth of history may be preserved, the reader is warned that Mr. Bridgman admitted some inscriptions into his book which never existed in the Copp's Hill yard. Especially was this the case in regard to coats-of-arms. Thus, on page 2 of his book, he gives the Lake arms, which are not on the stone. On page 162 he gives the Thornton arms and an inscription in form of an epitaph; but no such stone ever existed. On page 221 the Loring arms figured without any authority, though as this appears among the notes, the cautious reader might not be misled. On page 186, there is a list of persons deposited in the Shute tomb, but whose names are not inscribed on it. So also, all the names on pages 198, 199 and 200 are those of persons buried elsewhere.

The true record of all the coats-of-arms inscribed on stones in this yard will be found in the Introduction.

The most economical form of printing has been adopted for this volume, from necessity. The object sought has been to give a faithful transcript of the reading of each inscription, with such an approximation to the spelling and lettering as ordinary type would yield. No attempt has been made to add punctuation, except in the few cases where the sense might be obscured by a too literal transcription.

Lastly, the editor has ventured to place his name upon the title page, as the inciter of the enterprise, cheerfully acknowledging, as he already has, the merits of the transcriber. But he cannot leave unrecorded his sense of the public spirit which has impelled the publisher to undertake the enterprise.

The patronage afforded to such works is too scanty to make them attractive to publishers, and the citizens of Boston may well return thanks to one who has thus put a portion of their records beyond the reach of ordinary dangers.

Equally faithful copies of the inscriptions in the other grave-yards in old Boston, were made by Mr. Wyman for the editor. Should the present volume meet with moderate success, an attempt will be made hereafter to print those transcripts also.

W. H. WHITMORE.

Boston, July 1st, 1878.

INTRODUCTION.

The grave-yards in Boston proper, have been the King's Chapel yard, the Copp's Hill yard, the Granary, the Quaker's yard in Congress street, the yard on the Common, the one on Boston Neck, and five collections of tombs under as many of our churches.

Of these the King's Chapel yard was the first in use, and in 1642 an order was passed by the town for the constables to fence it.

The second in date, was the Copp's Hill yard, concerning which the following order was passed by the town, Nov. 5th, 1660 : "It is ordered that the old burying place shall be wholly deserted for some convenient season, and the new place appointed for burying only made use of."

The town had already bought a piece of land as appears by the following deed, dated 20th Feb., 1659–60, and recorded in Suff. Deeds, lib. 53, fol. 153. 'John Baker and Daniel Turell, sell to the selectmen of Boston, a lot of land, 294 feet on the northerly side, 252 feet on the southerly side ; in breadth on the easterly end 120 feet. Butting on the way that leadeth from the new meeting house in Boston towards Charleston ferry, on the north ; on the lands of William Phillips southerly ; on the land of John Baker and Daniel Turell easterly ; and on the way that leadeth from Senter-haven towards Charleston ferry westerly.'

The first yard then was a parallelogram with its longer sides facing north-east and south-west, so that the left hand upper corner, at the junction of Charter and Snow-hill streets, pointed almost due north.

After some forty years, an enlargement was desirable, and the corresponding lot on the south-west was purchased by the town of Judge Samuel Sewall and his wife.[1] (Suff. Deeds, lib. 26, fol. 97.)

---

[1] Already, January 7, 1708, Sewall and his wife Hannah had sold to Joshua Gee, the following named lot (Suff. Deeds, lib. 25, fol. 174). One rod square in their pasture "adjoining the north burying place, in which parcel of ground Mrs. Mary Thacher now lyeth buried," bounded north by the said burying place and on all other sides by Sewall's land, with no way to said land except what he has through the burying place.

Deed dated 17 Dec., 1707 ; in consideration of £50 paid and the re-
lease from the payment of an annual quit-rent of 40 shillings for a
certain cedar swamp in Brookline, Samuel Sewall and wife Hannah, sold the town of Boston land for enlarging the north burying
place.   It adjoined said place northerly, measuring 250 feet ;
southerly it bounded on Hull street, measuring across in a straight
line to the burying place, 140 feet.   On Hull street it measured
180 feet ; westerly on Snow hill 170 feet.

The yard thus increased was nearly a square, bounded on three
sides by streets.

In 1809 another enlargement was made, by the purchase of the
adjoining lot, on Hull street, east of the Sewall portion of the old
yard.   The deed was dated 18 Dec., 1809, and was recorded in lib.
231, fol. 199.   It states as follows.   For $10,000, Benjamin Weld
and wife Nabby sold the town of Boston a parcel of land, bounded
south-west on Hull street 148 feet, north-west on the burial ground
138 feet 6 inches ; north-east on land of Goodwin and other 153
feet south.east on land of Jonathan Merry 123 feet : being land
conveyed to Weld by Merry, 21 Oct., 1809, recorded lib. 230, fol.
191.

This lot is nearly square and is rather less than one-half the size
of the old yard.   Like the first, it is surrounded with a row of tombs.

(Suff. Deeds, lib. 262. fol. 296,) 3 June 1819, John Bishop of
Medford, sold to Charles Wells, for $1.051.30, land in Charter street
bounded north-east on said street 20 feet north-westerly, 70 feet on
the burying ground 20 feet wide, then continuing 50 feet more,
28 feet wide ; southwest 28 feet on land formerly of Dr. Wm. Clark,
but now a burying ground ; then south-east 50 feet, 28 feet wide,
then continuing 70 feet more 20 feet wide, on land formerly owned
by Wm. Fowle.   It was the land which Stephen Gorham as admin-
istrator of Nathaniel Holmes, sold to said Bishop, 14 Dec., 1791,
recorded lib. 184, fol. 59.

This lot of land, now bounded on the north-east by Marshall place,
seems to be entirely covered by tombs, thirty-four in number, erected
by Mr. Charles Wells with the consent of the town.

The following extracts from the town records throw some light
upon the history of particular tombs.   These tombs in the old yard
are numbered consecutively as follows.   Beginning on Hull street,
at the south-east corner, next to the new yard, and running westerly
numbers 1 to 21 inclusive.   On Snow hill street, numbers 22 (at
the corner of Hull street), to No. 55 at the corner of Charter street.

Then returning to the south-east corner on Hull street, and running north-east along the line of the yard to Charter street, numbers 56 to 83 inclusive. Then westerly on Charter street, numbers 84 to 115 inclusive.

In the open yard are situated tombs numbered 116 to 125 inclusive.

The list of tombs and the owners thereof, now preserved in the office of the Board of Health, is quite modern and very unsatisfactory as regards the earlier ownership. We can discover, however, that in 1717 the first row of tombs was in process of erection.

These grants, as nearly as can be ascertained from the modern list, were as follows, and bear date in 1717–1718 :

1
2   John Charnock.
3   Joshua Gee.
4   John Frizell.
5   James Pecker and Benjamin Edwards.
6   Thomas Lee.
7   ? James Grant.
8   John Baker.
9   John Ruck.
10   Edward Martyn.
11   ? James Pitts.
12   John Clark.
13   William Clark.
14   Robert Orange.
15   ? Mrs. Mary Hough,   ? Samuel Burnell.
16   Edward Proctor.
17   John Mountfort.
18   John Langdon.

A careful search on the town records, fails to give any more information in regard to the grants of tombs from 19 to 32. The official list contains only the names of modern families.

In 1722 it seems that a new range of tombs was commenced at the south-east corner on Hull street, running north. Here we identify

56   John Greenough.
57   Samuel Greenwood.
58   Thomas Hutchinson.
59   Jonathan Mountfort.
60   Walter Goodrich.

61 Edward Pell.

62 John Roberts.

63 John Cookson.

In 1743, grants are recorded, on the Snow hill street side, to

33 Cap't Parker.

34 John Larrabee.

35 Samuel Hunt.

36 ? Richard Hunnewell.

37 ? Daniel Bell.

38 ?   do.

In 1801, Thomas Godfrey and others were allowed to build No. 39, hence we may conclude that the range for a long time, ended with 38.

Undoubtedly our examination of the county records would reveal many facts in regard to the transfer of tombs, and thus throw light on their history. But this is hardly the occasion for such an investigation, and it may well be postponed until such time as the Board of Health of the city of Boston shall decide to exercise its new power as custodian of the several graveyards.

We proceed therefore to give all the passages in the Selectmen's Records which relate to this yard.

SELECTMEN'S MINUTES.

Vol. 3, P. 38.   1717, June 18.   " Liberty is granted to Mr. John Frizzel to erect a Toomb in the North burying place, next unto Mr. Joshua Gee's spot there, in the skirt or side of the s^d burying place, which of them he shall think best."

P. 40   1717 June 27.   " Liberty is granted to Mr. James Grant to erect a Toomb in the Line or range of Toombs now begun at the southerly side of the North burying place, provided that he carry up the Brick wall thereof next the H. way so as to be a sufficient fence.

The like is granted to Mr. James Pecker and his Bro. Mr. Benj. Edwards.

The like is granted to Capt. John Charnock.

The like is granted to Mr. John Baker."

P. 45.   1717, July 25.   " Liberty is granted to Thomas Lee to digg and erect a Toomb in the North Burying place, provided he carry up the brick wall thereof next the H. way so as to be a sufficient fence."

P. 48. 1717, Aug. 13. " Liberty is granted to Capt. Edward
Martyn, Mr. Joshua Gee and Mr. Robert Orange, for each of
them to make a Toomb in the new Range of Toombs in the North
Burying place. Provided they carry up the Brick wall thereof
next the H. way so as to be a sufficient fence."

P. 48. 1717, Aug. 20. "Liberty is granted to Mr. William
Clark to made a Toomb in the New Range of Toombs on the
southerly side of the North burying place, provided he carry
up the brick wall," etc., etc.

P. 48. 1717, Aug. 28. " Liberty is granted to John Clark, Esq.,
Capt. James Pitts and Mr. John Ruck, each of them the liberty
of making a Toomb in the new range of Toombs on the north
side of the North burying place next to Hull street, provided
each of them carry up their Brick wall next the H. way, so as
to be a sufficient fence."

P. 49. 1717, Aug. 26. Drain laid from " the new range of
Toombs in the North burying place into the common shore in
Salem street, which runs into the Mill Pond."

P. 54. 1717, Oct. 28. " Liberty is granted to Mr. Elias Callendar, to make a vault in the old burying place in the spot of
ground where his relations are buried, provided no monument
above ground, over the same, be there raised."

P. 64, 1717-8. March 18. " Liberty is granted to Widdo Mary
Hough to erect a Toomb in the New Range of Toombs in the
North Burying place next Hull street, provided she carry up
the brick work, next the H. way, so as to be a sufficient
fence."

Pp. 82-3. 1718, Sept. 9. " Liberty is granted to Mr. Edward
Proctor, to make a Toomb in the New Range of Toombs on the
southerly side of the North Burying place, next to Mrs. Hough's
Toomb, provided he carry up the Brick wall thereof, next Hull
street, so as to be a sufficient fence. The Like Liberty of a
Toomb is granted to be placed next to Mr. Proctor's Toomb.
The Like Liberty of a Toomb is granted to Deacon John Bar-
nerd, to be placed next to Mr. Mountfort's Toomb.
Liberty is granted to Edward Durant to erect a Toomb at the
north end of range of new Toombs in the Old burying place,
provided he carry up the wall thereof, next the adjoining Land
in conformity to the other Toombs in that range."

P. 84. 1718, Sept. 23. " Liberty is granted to Mr. John
Langdon, to make a Toomb in the new range of Toombs on the

southerly side of the north burying place, provided he carry up the brick wall thereof next to Hull street, so as to be a sufficient fence."

P. 203. 1722, July 30. "Liberty is granted to Thomas Hutchinson, Esq., Mr. Samuel Greenwood and Capt. John Greenough, to build each of them a Toomb in the North burying place on the south-east side, provided they take the direction of Mr. William Clark and Mr. Ebenezer Clough therein."

P. 205. 1722, Aug. 27. "Liberty is granted to Mr. Jonathan Mountfort, Mr. Walter Goodrich and Edward Pell to build each of them a Toomb in the North burying place on the eastwardly side as others had done."

P. 207. 1722, Sept. 24. "Liberty is granted to John Roberts to build a Toomb in the North burying place on the easterly line next to Mr. Edward Pell's."

P. 257. 1724, April 27. "Liberty granted to Samuel Burnell to build a Toomb in the North burying place, next Hull street and next to the widow Mary Hough's Toomb; he carrying up the brick wall for a sufficient fence."

P. 262. 1724, June 29. "Liberty granted to Mr. John Cookson to build a Toomb (probably No. 63) in the North Burying place, on the easterly line next to Mr. John Robert's Toomb (probably No. 62) on the same conditions with the former."

Vol. 4, P. 249. 1735, June 25. "Liberty is granted Benjn Swain to build a new Toomb at the North burying place, next to " . —— [blank]

P. 257. 1735, Sept. 3. "Mr. Benj. Swain informs that Mr. Peter Thomas desires Liberty to build a Toomb in the North Burying place; which was accordingly granted; and the Town Clerk directed to view the place and take the number of it, that it may be entered in the Records as usual."

P. 292. 1736, April 14. "According to order Mr. Swain attended and enformed. That he has built three Tombs in the North Burying place and disposed of them as follows, viz : One to Capt. Caleb Lyman, one to Mr. Peter Thomas, and the other to himself. He was thereupon ordered to acquaint those gentlemen with the orders of the Town respecting tombs, that so they might make proper application for a confirmation of the said Tombs to them as usual. And further he was ordered immediately to put up and secure the Fence which at present lyes waste, until he can have opportunity to build the Brick wall."

P. 298.   April 21.   Tombs granted to Capt. Lyman and Mr. Thomas as above " upon condition that they each of them respectively erect a Brick wall at their own charge, of the full breadth of their said Tomb, and that they at all times hereafter maintain and keep the same in good Repair, to the satisfaction of the Selectmen for the time being."

Vol. 8 or H., p. 2.   1743, Aug. 3.   " Liberty is granted to Mr. Daniel Bell, to build Two Tombs on the westerly side in the North Burying place, he performing the conditions of former grants."

H. p. 10. 1743, Aug. 29.   " Voted that Capt. John Larrabee have Liberty to build a Tomb in the North Burying place on the north-west side next to that granted to Mr. Parker, he performing the conditions of former grants."   (Probably No. 34.)

I., p. 145.   1749, Aug. 31.   " Mr. Samuel Hunt desires Liberty to Build a Tomb in the North Burying place, adjoining to Mr. Richard Hunnewell's lately dec^d, at the End of the Line of Toombs on the Top of the Hill running towards Charlestoun. Voted that Liberty be granted him accordingly, he Building a sufficient Brick Wall the width of the same and keep the same in repair'forever."   (Probably No. 35.)

1801, Aug. 5.   " Deacon Benjn. Henderson has liberty to build a Tomb in the North Burying Ground on the spot formerly assigned to Josiah Copeland, and which he has neglected to improve."   (Probably No. 70.)

P. 76.   1801, Aug. 12.   " Mr. Turel Tuttle has liberty to build a Tomb in the North Burying Ground, next to the one the last granted, conditioned as usual."   (Probably No. 72.)

P. 77.   1801, Aug. 30.   " On application of William Emerson, Jon^a. Merry, and Thomas Godfrey, liberty is granted to each of them to build a Tomb in the North Burying Ground.'

P. 78.   1801, Sept. 16.   " Mr. Nathaniel Valentine, Robert Crocker, and William Andrew have liberty to build a Tomb in No. Buryal Ground."

P. 103.   1802, March 31.   " Mr. Samuel Brintnel has liberty to build a Tomb in the North Burying Ground on the west side (Probably No. 42.) Mr. John Sullivan has liberty to build another Tomb on the east side of said Burying Ground." (Probably No. 73.)

P. 107. 1802, May 5. " Mr. John Wait has liberty to build a Tomb in the North Burying Ground on the south side, on the usual conditions."

P. 291. 1806, March 5. " Messrs. Adam French, and James Farrar have liberty to build a Tomb in the North Burying Ground. (Probably No. 81.) Mr. Joshua Ellis has the like liberty both to be on the East side of the Burying Ground." (Probably No. 82.)

The lists now preserved in the office of the Board of Health are as follows : The words and figures in brackets have been added on the authority of the stones themselves, or on information presumed to be of equal value.

OLD BURIAL GROUND, COPP'S HILL.

1 Broudens Heirs — Mrs Curtis
2 Charnoks. Eben Shute — John Turner
3 Joshua Gee — Susan Hunt — Joshua G. Davis
4 Elizabeth Conant
5 B. Edwards — Alex^r Edwards — Jedediah Lincoln
6 Thomas Lee — Nathaniel G. Snelling
7 Bants. A & J. Lincoln – F. & I. Lincoln
8 Baker — John Carnes — William Baker. [Edward Carnes.]
9 John Ruck — Edward Cruft.
10 Martyn — Timothy Martyn Minot — J. U. Hinkley
11 Ezekiel Goldthwait — John Williams
12 Dr Johannes Clark — Peter Wainwright
13 William Clark — Samuel Winslow
14 R. Orange & Silas Atkins
15 Watts & Hooton — Mary Hooton — Sarah Waldron — John Waldron
16 Col. Edward Proctor —— Tuckerman
17 John Mountfort heirs
18 Dea. Langdon — Wid° Smith formerly Langdon
19 John Skillings — Margaret S. Palfrey ¼ — A. Butrick
20 Jenkins — Jacob Hall
21 Dagget — Wm J. Hammett — Erastus Thompson — sold to Seamen — Rev. Phineas Stowe, pastor
22 Pierpont — Brewer   Darracott — Cook
23 Halsey — Richard Wellen — James Pierce

24 Ann Brown [Joseph Callendar, 1823]; W^m B Callendar —
   Elizabeth Hudson
25 Sigourney — Daniel A. Sigourney
26 Barnard — Brown — S. Edes — Dea. Kendall
27 P. [eter] Thomas — Thos K. Thomas
28 Nathl Barber. W^o Barber [Mrs Elizabeth Barber]
29 Swain & Pidgeon. James Sherman [1801]. W^o Sherman
30 Harris   Andrew Eliot. John Eliot
31 Harrods. Josiah Snelling [1803]
32 Jonⁿ Snelling
33 Caleb Parker. Isaac Harris
34 Capt Larrabee — Rev Henry Edes. James Carter
35 Sarah Hunt. Dr. Dixwell
36 Vernon. Stephen Brown
37 John Osborn. J. W Folsom. Jos. Bennett. Isaac Gardner
   Wm Bennett
38 Enoch Rust. Ruth Ridgway [L. Ridgway]
39 Thos Godfrey. William Dodd.
40 Loring & Smith — Benj^a Smith
41 Andrews. Crocker. Valentine
42 Samuel Brintnal [1802] — Charles Brintnall
42½ Hannah Barker ½ no. side; Mary F. Bartlett ½ south side
43 William McKean. Henry Swift [1804]
44 Norcross. [Zephaniah] Sampson. Benford. [John] Snelling [1805]
45 Asa & Cyrus Holbrook. Jon^a Wild
46 Francis & Enoch James [1805]
47 James Davis. Warren Jacobs   Seth Lothrop
48 I. L. Dimmock. John H. Whitman [? Pitman 1828]
49 Jacob Hyler [1805]
50 James Washburn — Daniel Ballard
51 Widow Susan Bass
52 E. Rogers. Benjⁿ Varney
53 Holmes & Foster. John Shelton. Nathl Blake
54 Charles Holmes. Henry Lane. D. Johnson [1807]
55 Edmund Hunt [Hart]
56 John Greenough. Joseph Greenough
57 Samuel Greenwood
58 [Thomas] Hutchinson — Thos Lewis — John Lewis
59 Jon^a Mountfort. [1724] Elizabeth Seaver. W^m J Seaver
60 [Walter] Goodrich — Isaac Dupee

61 E[dward] Pells   Joseph & Nath[l] Hall
62 [John] Roberts. Daniel Ingersoll
63 John Cookson. Widow Dashwood
64 Sam[l] Clark. James Clark
65 Alex[r] Forsyth — Joseph Bassett
66 Thomas Goodwill. W[m] Fowle
67 Kennedy. Dr Prentiss of Roxbury
68 Hayward. Tho[s] Oliver. Mass. Gen. Hospital
69 William Sherburn. Benj[n] White. Holmes
70 Benjamin Henderson — Francis Green
71 Turrel Tuttle
72 Joshua A & John Binney
73 Sullivan & Barber
74 Frink Stratton — Thomas Gould — [Ezra] Hawks [1812]
75 Elijah Nickerson — Thomas Hopkins, Elijah Nickerson's heir
76 Davis Whitman
77 Dana & Clark. Benj[n] West. Sam[l] H. Hewes. Henry Davis
   Elijah L. Green — Rowe
78 City Tomb for Infants
79 Mather — Samuel Parker
80 none
81 French & Farrar — Charles French
82 Joshua & Rowland Ellis
83 Ephraim & Ebenezer Tufts
84 Thomas Tracker. Cotton Thayer. George Domett
85 Samuel Clark. John Neat. Nancy Clark
86 Seth Webber. Joseph Grammer of Malden
87 Thomas Page. Kilby Page
88 John Loring — John Howard
89 Benjamin Cowey [1807] — Leach Harris
90 Joseph Adams — Philip Adams
91 William Learned — Norton Newcomb [1807].
92 John Rice — Jacob H. Kent
93 Elijah Loring
94 William & Isaac Harris [1808]
95 Edward Chamberlain — B Tilden — Frederick Gould
96 John Wells. Samuel Tuttle
97 Henry Atkins — Salome Rich [ards ?] [1807]
98 Thomas Haskell
99 Ann Freeland
100 Edward Winchester. Cha[s] Wells. Moses Pond — John
   Spence

101 Ephraim & Larkin Snow. C. T. Benson.   John S. Somes
102 William Boynton — John F. Low [1809]
103 Henry Hutchinson — James Penniman.   William Mills
104 Benj[n] & John Clark
105 George Southerland [1809]
106 Tyler & Russell.   Moses Bass [1819]
107 Mitchell Lincoln
108 Elijah Adams
109 Isaac Durell — James Bird — Isaac Berry
110 Thomas Laton — Joseph Barnes — Samuel Winslow
111 Joseph Cullender.   Elisha Learned
112 James Marston.   Christopher Gore.   [1810]
113 John Russell — Samuel Brown [1811]
114 J. Cooms.   H. Pearson.   J. Wilson
115 James W. Burditt [1869]
116 Dr Jarvis; monument.
117 Franklin Smith
118 Middlecot — John Trueman
119 Brondson — William Abrahams
120 Howard's heirs — Judge Parker. — Jarvis
121 Marston   David Marston
122 Buckley's grave
123 Lemick's grave
124 John Ruddock's grave
125 Grant's grave

NEW BURIAL GROUND, COPP'S HILL.

1 Benjamin Sweetser.   Enoch H. Snelling
2 John P. Sholes.   John J. Ulmer
3 Elizabeth Williams
4 David E. Powers [1811]
5 Othniel French.   John Leman [1811]
6 John Suter.   Francis Walker [1811]
7 Nath[l] Alley, jr.   Geo. Rodden.   John Eames [1811]. Samuel
    Eames
8 Ann Curtiss. [Joseph Willcutt jr 1811]
9 Jacob Rhoades [1811]
10 Thomas Coburn. Henry Goodrich. Elizabeth Wakefield [1811]
11 Robert Barber.   Thomas Holt.   Asher Davenport
12 Samuel Nichols.   Lewis Leland.   Jesse Kingsbury.   [1825]
13 Jacob Sanderson.   Josiah Gilmore.   Sam[l] & W[m] Hart [1841]

14 Robert Thompson. John Wade [1811]
15 Joab Hunt
16 Joseph Austin
'17 William Ward
18 Joseph Starr. Nathaniel, John B. & Charles Wells
19 I. Percival. N. Parker. Ezra Dyer
20 Thomas Capen
21 John Aiken. Ezra Dyer. Benjamin French
22 Daniel Stanwood. Joseph Willcutt [1831]. James W. Fenno
23 William Fenno
24 Thomas Green. John Lewis [1812]. Jabez Allen
25 James Bartlett. John Thayer. Joseph Urann [1813]
26 John B. Bannister. Simeon Boyden [1828]. Sam¹ Noyes
27 Wᵐ McClennen. Joseph Jones [1812]
28 Noah Lincoln. Jonathan Thaxter [1812]
29 Samuel Hichbon. Gedney King [1812]
30 Josiah Marshall. [John Marshall 1812]. Thomas Badger
31 Giles Richards. Amos Lawrence. Henry Davis. George
      Low [Abiah P. Low 1836]
32 Daniel & Samuel Adams [1813]
33 John Smith
34 Nathaniel Faxon [1814]
35 Rainsford & Farrington [1814]
36 Ross Family tomb. Thoˢ Ross.
37 James Weld, [sold to Phineas Capen, May 23, 1851]
38 Simon Wilkinson. Thomas Hudson. Sam. Yendell [1816]
39 Amasa Winchester
40 Andrew J. Allen. Thomas Mickel
41 R. E. Newman. James W. Carter. John B. Bolton. O. J.
      & O. S. Davis [1819] — F. B. Woods
42 Isaac F. Rowe
ᵢ43 Merrill & Tarbell
44 Parker Emerson, Warren Claflin [1815]
45 John F. Newton. Joshua Loring [1819]
46 Ephraim B. Bouvé. Lewis Kupfer
47 Edward Bell [1825]
48 Nathaniel Nottage. Jonᵃ Loring, Jr. [1828]
49 Robert Baron. Frances E. Alden. Danˡ Dickinson [Lorenzo
      Alden]
50 Susan Richardson. Lydia Baker [Joel Richardson 1828]
51 Benjᵃ Lamson. Joseph Lewis [1828]
                    1ʙ

52 Libeus Stetson [1828] John Peak
53 Abiel Buttrick. Abijah Patch. Artemas Tirrill. Tho⁴ French [1828]
54 Abigail Furber. John D. Furber
55 Andrews. Parsons. Penniman
56 Ebenezer Frothingham [1814]
57 Peter Brigham Andrew Harrington [1814]
58 Aaron Bancroft. Galen Holmes
59 Sam¹ & Edward Chessman
60 Tho⁴ Kendall, Ezra Hawkes, Jonⁿ Carlton

SECOND RANGE

1 Charles Henderson. John Peak
2 John H. Pray. J. G. Libby
3 Ephraim Milton. John Tremere. Henry Gurney [1828]
4 Daniel Dickerson
5 John Winslow
6 Elizabeth Sigourney [Andrew Sigourney]
7 David Marden [1828]

CHARTER STREET CEMETERY.

1 Asahel Stockwell — Daniel Wise
2 William Thompson. Tho⁴ Richardson — William Badger
3 William & John Howe
4 Utley. Heath. Rayner. Reuben Read — Baker [1819]
5 John Gale— Francis Masse. Levi Haskell —Leonard Spalding.
6 E & J. Sargent. Ann Burchsted [1820]
7 John Wyer. [1820]
8 Joseph Wheeler. [1820] Geo. W. Clarke
9 Ichabod Macomber, Ezekiel Sawin [Charles Howard].
10 Thomas Haskell
11 Lemuel Crackbone. Samuel H. Hewes. Samuel Winslow, John Venivar [George Vannevar, 1845]
12 Abraham Millett [1821]
13 J. Jenkins, L. Felton, S. Jenkins, Solon Jenkins, Earl Goddard [1821]
14 Rufus Baxter [Eliza Stephens, 1821]
15 Josiah Ayres
16 A[dams] Bailey, jr, S[amuel] Noyes. M[ary] Blanchard [1821]
17 Robert Ripley [1843]
18 Thomas Haskell
19 B. Lewis. J. Bailey. E. Thomas. S. Winslow
20 Elliot. Kimball. Pratt [1819.]

21 Eben' Gay — Eli Veazie [1819]
22 Jabez & Nath¹ Fisher. Washington Monroe. Jos. Mead.
23 Alexander Vanever. J. Barstow [1819]
24 Francis Holmes. Benj³ Cushing [1819]
25 Edmund Parsons. Sam¹ Hills [1820]. Job Turner
26 Edmund Winchester [1819]
27 Thomas Frothingham [1819]
28 James Davis .
29 Bradley N. Cummings   S. W. Robinson
30 Pliny Clapp. [Henry Clapp & Jonathan Forbes, 1819.]
31 Josiah Brown. Isaac S. Tompkins
32 John Fenno. Capt John Howes [1819]
33 Ward Jackson — Heman Lincoln
34 William Hall.   Cornelius B. Simmons [1819]

Finally we have to point out and give engravings of such stones bearing coats-of-arms, as do exist in the yard.

I.

Goodrich arms. The inscription is our number 581.

II.

Clark Arms. These arms are on the stone bearing inscription No. 992, and are repeated on the stone inscribed with epitaph No. 997. The reader may learn that inscription No 991 " the tomb of Samuel Winslow " is also on the first of these Clark tombs, and indicates that Mr. Winslow, a former sexton of the neighborhood, obtained possession of the tomb in some manner.

III.

Watts. On the reverse of the stone bearing the inscription No. 1199, to the Rev. Andrew Eliot, will be found the following arms.

This however was an honest transaction, as is pointed out in the Heraldic Journal, ii, 119, as the Eliots bought the tomb and paid for altering the stone. The presumption is that the Watts family represented the original owner, and that perhaps the stone came from tomb No. 15. The arms are not inscribed to any family of the name of Watts.[1]

IV.

Gee arms. Epitaph No. 1333.

V.

Hutchinson arms. This stone bears the well-known arms of the Hutchinsons. Upon it has been placed the names of T. & J. Lewis (our epitaph No 1641), but we know not by what authority they took possession of the tomb.

VI.

Mountfort arms.   Inscription No. 793.

VII.

Hutchinson.   The following cut represents a stone bearing the Hutchinson arms but no inscription.   It is now separated from its proper place and we cannot determine its original location.

VIII.

Martyn arms.   Epitaph 1202.

IX.

Greenwood arms.   Epitaph 1387*a*.

COPP'S HILL EPITAPHS.

1. Mather Tomb. The revere . . Doctors Increase, Cotton & Samuel Mather were interred in this vault.
℣ is the Tomb of our Fathers. Mather. Croer's.
I. died Aug: 27th, 1723 æ. 84.
C ' died Feb. 13th 1727 æ. 65
S died June 27th 1785 æ. 79.

2. Here lyes yᵉ Body of Mrs SARAH MATHER, Wife to Mrs Joseph Mather, who Died Febʳʸ 21st, 1737, in yᵉ 41st Year of her Age.

3. Adam French & James Farrar's Family Tomb. 1806.

4. City Infant Tomb.

5. Joanna yᵉ daughter of William & Anne Copp aged 6 monthes, died March yᵉ 20, 1695-6.

6. Ebenezer & Ephraim Tufts Family Tomb. 1806.

7. Here lyes bur ... the Body of ... Mrs. Lydia Amee... aged 81 yea... died July yᵉ ... 1749.

8. Martha Amee. Dauʳ to John & Desire Amee Aged 21 Years, Died Sept. yᵉ 22, 1704.

9. Benjamin, Son of Benj. & Sarah Abrahams died Sept 5, 1817 a. 15 months. [Two lines.]

10. ..... Andrews. ... Augˢᵗ 19ᵗʰ 1806 æ. 54. A kind husband and tender parent. Also his grandson Ezekiel, son of Thomas & Eliza Andrews æ. 3 mo.

11. Capt. Thomas Lake, aged 61 yeeres. an eminently faithfull servant of God. and one of a pvblic spirit: was perfidiously slain by yᵉ Indians at Kennibeck, Avgvst yᵉ 14, 1676, and here interred the 13 of March following.

12. Here lyeth yᵉ body of John Lake, Son to Capt Thomas Lake, Aged abovt 24 years. Deceased yᵉ 27 of June 1690.

13. Hooton & Watts Family Tomb. No 15.

14. 1680 Hezekiah Hares aged 1 year 11 mo. dec'd yᵉ 31 of January. John Hares aged 9 months dec'd yᵉ 23 of August 1674. The 2 children of Wm. & Hannah Hares.

15. Here lyeth buried yᵉ body of Hannah Harris Aged 11 years & 5 mo. deceased December yᵉ 13, 1686.

16. Here lyeth buried yᵉ body of William Harris Aged 16 years & 10 mo, deceased January yᵉ 31, 1688-9.

17. Here lyes yᵉ Body of Capt. William Hares Aged 37 Years. Decᵈ June yᵉ 14th 1729.

18. William Harris, son of William & Abigail Harris Decᵈ June 28th, 1730. Aged about 10 monᵗˢ.

19. Here lies buried the Body of Capt Ralph Hartt who departed this Life the 14th of March 1776. Aged 77 years.

20. Here lyes yᵉ body of Mary Nevill aged 81 years & 4 months decᵈ Decʳ the 31ˢᵗ 1723.

21. John yᵉ Son of John & Annabel Salisbury, Died December yᵉ 15, 1704, in yᵉ 14 year of his age.

22. Elizabeth, wife to Niclas Salsbvry aged 53 years departed this life yᵉ 17 of February 1687–8.

23. Elizabeth, late wife to George Robinson, aged about 40 Years deceased yᵉ 7 of July 1697.

24. Here lyeth yᵉ Body of Thomas Luscombe aged about 35 Years, decᵈ October yᵉ 15, 1694.

25. Here lyeth buried yᵉ Body of Grace Berry, yᵉ Wife of Thomas Berry. Age about 58 years, who died May yᵉ 17, 1695.

26. Here lyes buried the body of Mr. Daniel Berry aged 66 years decᵈ June yᵉ 18th, 1738.

27. Memento Mori Fugit Hora. Here Lyes the Body of Nathaniel Adams. Aged 60 years. Deceased the 29ᵗʰ of March 1689–90.

28. Here lyes Buried The Body of Mr. Nathaniel Adams aged 37 years & 3 months who Departed this Life May yᵉ 26th, 1745.

29. Here lyes the Body of Mr. Joseph Adams dyed August yᵉ 13th 1745, in yᵉ 26th year of his age.

30. Joseph Adams, son of Mr. Nathˡ & Mrs Mary Adams Aged 3 years & 6 mo. Decᵈ Augˢᵗ 6th, 1737.

31. .. re lyeth buried ... . ody of Elizabeth . .eare Relict of . illiam Weare, aged 90 years, decᵈ yᵉ 27 of September, 1681.

32. Deacon John Phillipes Aged 77 yeares Deceased the 16 day of December 1682.

33. Johana Phillipes the Wife of John Phillipes Aged 80 Yeares deceased yᵉ 22 of October, 1675.

34. Here lies buried the body of Thomas Aubins aged 20 Years died Sept. yᵉ 14, 1750.

35. Here lyeth buried the Body of John Saxton, Aged 38 Years, departed this Life the 31 day of July 1686.

36. Here lyes ... .. of Phil... wife of Rowler Aged 28 years, Died June yᵉ 12th 1749. Also Cæsar, a child.

37. 1677. Abigail Ayres aged 27 years, dyed yᵉ 2 of Janwary

38. Elizabeth Shute, late wife to Richard Shute, Aged 63 years & ½, decᵈ September yᵉ 8ᵗʰ 1691

39. Elizabeth Shute, aged 1 Week. Dyed ye 12 Febuar. 1665.

40. Here lyes buried ye body of Richard Shut, aged 72 years, died October ye 2^d 1703.

41. Elizabeth Chapin ye Daughter of Ebenezer & Elizabeth Chapin, aged about 16m^o. Died August ye 23, 1694.

42. Michael Powell aged 67 Yeares, desesed the 28 of December 1672.

43. Lydia Broun, Wife to William Broun aged about 46 Years, dec^d July ye 30, 1680.

44. Isaac Griffen aged about 55 Years died July ye 29, 1693.

45. Samuel, ye son of Samuel & Anna Engs, aged 1 day died October 21, 1701.

46 Sarah Rule aged 9 Years died July ye 5, 1690.

47. Elizabeth, Daughter of John & Elizabeth Pickerin Aged 16 m^o Died August ye 27, 1690.

48. In memory of Mr. John Barnicoat; dec^d Feb. ye 23, 1809 aged 70 Years.

49. Ales Howard, Relict of Left^e William Howard Aged 72 years dec^d November ye 18, 1681.

50. Here lyeth buried ye Body of Edward Grant Aged about 50 Years, dec^d ye 19 day of June 1682.

51. Mr. Joseph Grant. (Foot stone.)

52. Here lies the Body of Experience Miles, Aged 49 years, died January the 26, 1690-1.

53. William Tyer Aged 26 Years died January 14, 1666.

54 Martha Hasey, Aged 12 Yeares dyed the 4th of May 1676.

55. Sacred to the memory of Mr. Christon Albry who died Sept. 1st 1802 aged 57 years. [7 lines.]

56. Rebekah Hooper, the Daughter of Georg Hooper Aged 2 Yeares, and 10 Weekes, Dyed the 15 of October 1675.

57. Nathaniel Saxton Aged 19 Yeares dyed ye 15 of September 1677.

58. Here lyeth Buried ye Body of Samuel Saxton Aged about 39 years, died iuly ye 21, 1693.

59. Here lyeth buried ye Body of Alexander Adams Aged 62 years, dyed ye 15 day of January 1677. [On reverse " Marston's Tomb."]

60. Here lyeth buried ye Body of Mary Bill Wife to James Bill, Aged about 75 yeares, died ye 29 of Aug^{ust} 1688.

61. Here lyeth buried ye Body of James Bill, aged 73 years, departed this life ye first of February 1687-8.

62. Here lies the Body of Mrs Mary Bill who died August 7th 1766 aged 77 years.

63. Lydia Hough, Wife to William Hough, aged 38 years, dec^d ye 26th day of February 1682-3.

64. Here lyeth buried ye Body of William Kent Aged 57 years dec^d June ye 9, 1691.

65. Charles Farnum Aged 3 years & 6 m. Dec^d January ye 21 1677-8.

66. Elizabeth ye daughter of Jonathan & Martha Farnam aged 2 years & ½ died April ye 26, 1694.

67. In memory of Martha S. Farnham, who died March 23, 1819, aged 7 months & 10 days (4 lines).

68. In memorial of Dorathy Upshall, Aged 73 Yeares deceased the 18 of September 1675.

69. Annah Reade, Wife to Obadiah Reade, aged 33 years Dyed ye 13 day of September 1680.

70. Here lyes ye body of Elizabeth wife to Obadiah Reade aged 67 years, died Feb^{ry} ye 26, 1712-13.

71. Here lyeth buried ye body of Esdras Reade, aged 85 years dec^d July ye 27, 1680.

72. Sarah .... to Esdras ..... aged ... dec^d Ma.. 16..

73. Here lyeth buried ye Body of Mary Winslow, Daughter to Mr. Samuel Winslow, aged 3 years, Departed this life June ye 2d, 1681.

74. Here lyes the Body of Francis Ward, wife to Samuel Ward, Aged 83 Years, dyed the 10 of June 1690.

75. Here lyes the Body of John Pittom, Aged about 54 years died Feb^r. ye 30 (?) 1699.

76. The 3 children of Obadiah & Elizabeth Gill. Obadiah Gill aged 7 months & 1 half, dyed ye 9 day of August 1682. Obadiah Gill aged 6 months dyed ye 3 of July 1678. Samuel Gill aged 3 years & 7 months dyed ye 6 day of June 1679.

77. Elizabeth, daughter of Obadiah & Elizabeth Gill Aged 12 months & 5 D^s Died October ye 1, 1687.

78. Sarah Gill ye daughter of Obadiah & Elizabeth Gill, Aged 3 months & 17 d. died April ye 20 1691.

79. Here lyeth buried ye Body of Richard Collacott, Aged 83 years. Dyed July ye 7, 1686.

80. Here lyes ye body of Jonathan Frost, son to Samuel & Elizabeth Frost, aged 21 years, died June ye 23, 1706.

81. Mary Hunting, ye daughter of Samuel & Mary Hunting Aged 13 months & 25 days, Died July y^r 29, 1699.

82. In memory of Capt. Joseph Hunting who departed this Life July 26, 1755, Aged 55 years.

83. Here lyes buried the body of Mrs Mary Hunting wife to Mr Samuel Hunting, aged 47 years, died June ye 7th, 1745.

84. Here lyes yᵉ Body of John Maverick, Son of John & Mrs Elizabeth Mavericke who died July 17th 1734, aged 10 years & 6 mᵒ.

85. Here lyes yᵉ Body of Mrs Mehitable Mavericke wife of Mr Jotham Mavericke Aged 24 years dyed June 30ᵗʰ 1747.

86. Here lyes buried the Body of Mrs Mary Gilburt Relict of Capᵗ Thomas Gilburt aged 63 years. Decᵈ Decemʳ yᵉ 30ᵗʰ 1733.

87. Mrs Sarah Shaw 1799.

88. Here lyes yᵉ body of Henry Dickerson, Aged 54 years died March yᵉ 21ˢᵗ 1719–20.

89. Jacob Hall's Tomb. No. 20.

90. Custin, son of John & Mary Bushnell Aged 9 weeks, died July yᵉ 13th, 1718.

91. Here lies intered the mortal part of Mr John Adams who departed this life March yᵉ 1ˢᵗ 1783 Æ 67 years.

92. Here lieth buryed yᵉ Bodi of Obodiah Gill, Deacon of yᵉ North Church in Boston. Aged 50 years decesed January yᵉ 6, 1700.

93. Here lies the bodies of Custin & Michael Bushnell Aged 20 months died August 12ᵗʰ, 1758.

94. Here lyes yᵉ Body of Mrs Mehitable Mavericke Wife of Jotham Mavericke Aged 24 years, dyed June 30ᵗʰ 1747.

95. Here lyes yᵉ body of Elizabeth wife to Edward Bickford Aged 40 years & 5 months, died the 4ᵗʰ of June 1740.

96. Here lyeth buried yᵉ Body of Joseph Shaw Senier Aged 56 years, died May yᵉ 7, 1701.

97. Sacred to the Memory of Mr. Jacob Hawkins, who professed faith in Jesus Christ about 14 years & about 1 year a Preacher of the Gospel. He was one of a sound Judgment, meek & happy spirit. He ended his days in peace July 19ᵗʰ 1797, Aged 31 years.

98. Edward Carnes Tomb. No. 8.

99. In memory of Thomas, son of Edward & Martha Carnes was accidentally killed Dec 22, 1818, aged 5 years & 5 mo.

100. In memory of Mr Joshua Bowles who died Augˢᵗ 31, 1794 æt. 72.

101. In memory of Mrs. Mary Bowles, Wife of Mr Joshua Bowles, who died Janʳy 16 1780. Æt. 52.

102. Here lyes yᵉ Body of Joshua Bowels, Jun. son of Mr Joshua and Mrs Mary Bowels; who departed this Life June yᵉ 3d 1772, in yᵉ 18ᵗʰ year of his age.

103. Here lyes yᵉ Body of Mrs Hannah Stoddard, Wife to Mr After Stoddard, who died December yᵉ 29ᵗʰ 1755, Aged 42 Years.

104. Here lyes the body of Mrs Tabitha Stoddard, wife to Mr

Thomas Stoddard, and daugʳ. to Mr. Nathˡ & Mrs Susanna Hodgdon, aged 31 years & 5 mo. decᵈ June yᵉ 3d, 1734.

105. Here lyes Buried the Body of Mr. Josiah Clark who decᵈ. August the, 27,ᵗʰ 1726. Aged 45 Years.

106. Here lyes yᵉ body of Mrs Hannah Bodge, wife to Mr Benjamin Bodge, died Novʳ yᵉ 10ᵗʰ 1745 in yᵉ 38 ʰ year of her age.

107. Reader !!! Beneath this Stone is deposited the Remains of Major Thomas Seward. Who gallantly fought in our late Revolutionary War, and through its various Scenes behaved with Patriotic Fortitude & Died in the Calms of domestic Felicity as becomes a universal Christian Nov. 27ᵗʰ 1800 ætat 60.

> The lonely turf where silence lays her head
> The mound where pity sighs for honᵈ dead,
> Such is the grief where sorrow now doth sigh,
> To learn to live is but to learn to die.

108. Also, Sarah Seward his Wife Obiit March 14ᵗʰ 1800 Ætat. 63.

109. Here lyes yᵉ body of Marcy Buckman Aged 27 years died April yᵉ 4ᵗʰ 1719.

110. Here lyeth Bur... yᵉ body of Agnis Booden, yᵉ wife of John Booden Aged 59 years. Dyed yᵉ 8 of March 1684.

111. Sacred to the memory of Mrs Nancy Burr, wife of Mr Peter Burr, who died Octʳ 3d, 1804. Æt. 25
[6 lines of verse.]

112. In memory of Mrs Susanna Gray, wife of Capt Daniel Gray, who died July 9ᵗʰ 1798, in the 42ᵈ year of her age
[4 lines of verse.]

113. Here lies buried in a Stone Grave 10 feet deep Capᵗ Daniel Malcom, Merchᵗ who departed this Life October 23ᵈ 1769 Aged 44 Years. A true Son of Liberty, a Friend to the Publick, An Enemy to Oppression and One of the foremost in opposing the Revenue Acts on America.

114. Harris son of John & Elizabeth Dutch, Born yᵉ 23ᵈ of August & died Sept. yᵉ 10, 1712.

115. Sarah King. (footstone.)

116. Here lyes yᵉ Body of Mrs Mary Hartt, Wife to Mr. Ralph Hartt, Aged 34 years and 2 mo. decᵈ August yᵉ 2ᵈ 1733.

117. Here lyes Buried yᵉ Body of Mrs Lois Hartt. The Wife Capt. Ralph Hartt Aged 46 years. Deceased Novʳ yᵉ 5ᵗʰ 1751.

118. In memory of Mr Eleazer Jackson, who died June 6ᵗʰ 1809 aged 26, also 3 children of Eleazer and Mary Jackson. Walter died June 21ˢᵗ 1809, aged 4 months & 14 days. Mary Ann died July 24ᵗʰ 1809 aged 10 days. Eleazer died Octʳ 22ᵈ 1809 aged 9 years, 9 months, & 18 days.

119. Here lyes Buried yᵉ Body of Mrs Mary Thatcher Widdow late Wife of Judah Thatcher of Yarmouth, departed this life Novʳ yᵉ 30, 1708 in yᵉ 68ᵗʰ year of her age.

120. Here lyes yᵉ Body of Mr Frances Hudson, aged 55 years, decᵈ June yᵉ 13th 1732.

121. Here lies buried yᵉ Body of Mrs Sarah Hudson, Wife to Capt. Joseph Hudson who Departed this Life, December 17ᵗʰ 1778, Aged 39 years & 5 mo.

122. Here lies buried the Body of Mrs Ann Hudson, Widow of Mr. Joseph Hudson, who departed this Life Novʳ 18ᵗʰ 1793 Aged 85 years.

123. Nathˡ Greenwood, son of Nath & Elizbᵗʰ Greenwood Aged 1 year & 6 days Died July yᵉ 7ᵗʰ 1730.

124. Here lyes buried yᵉ Body of David Copp, Elder of yᵉ Old Church in Boston, Aged 78 years decᵈ November the 20, 1713.

125. [O]bedience, wife to David Copp aged neer 37 years dyed 30ᵗʰ May 1678.

126. Goodeth Copp, Aged 65 years dyed yᵉ 25ᵗʰ of March 1670.

127. Here lyes yᵉ body of Dau... the son of David & Patience Copp, aged 14 years, died yᵉ 24 of Febʳʸ 1712.

128. Here lyes buried the body of Mrs Patience Copp, wife to Mr. David Copp, decᵈ April yᵉ 4ᵗʰ 1736, in yᵉ 60ᵗʰ year of age.

129. Here lyes Interred yᵉ Body of Capᵗ Richard Thomas Aged 57 years, Decᵈ August yᵉ 16ᵗʰ 1728.

130. Here lyes the Body of Mr. Harvey Thomas Aged 39 years, who departed this life Sept. yᵉ 12ᵗʰ 1750.

131. J. B. Marston & Chris Gore's Tomb. 1810.

132. Here lyes the Body of Mrs Mary Coney, who died Janʳʸ yᵉ 30ᵗʰ 1749–50 aged 80 years.

133. Joseph Chandler & Elisha Learned's Tomb.

134. Here lyes yᵉ Body of Mr. Nathaniel Ayers, aged 67 years & 6 mo. decᵈ December yᵉ 4ᵗʰ 1731.

135. John Russell & Samuel Brown's Family tomb. 1811.

136. Here lyes yᵉ Body of Mrs Sarah Wales, Wife to Mr. Timothy Wales, decᵈ May yᵉ 3ᵈ 1726, in yᵉ 57ᵗʰ year of her age.

137. Here lyes yᵉ Body of Hannah Green, wife to John Green, Cenʳ. Aged 63 years & about 4 mo. Died January yᵉ 3, 1717–18.

138. In memory of Elizabeth Green, Dau ʳ of Mr. William & Mrs Elizabeth Green who died April 27th, 1766. Aged 12 years.

139. Here lyes buried . . . Body of Mrs S . . . . Barington wife . . Richard Baring . . . aged 32 year & . . . yᵉ 22ᵈ . . . .

140. Here lies yᵉ Body of Mrs Abigail Furbur, the Wife of Mr Richard Furbur, who died July yᵉ 11ᵗʰ 1750. Aged 33 years.

141. Here lyes buried the Body of Capt. William Dowrick aged 38 years & 3 mo. died March y⁰ 10ᵗʰ 1748–9.

142. Here lies yᵉ body of Mrs Martha Dowrick, widdow of Capt. William Dowrick, Aged 54 years, Died October 16ᵗʰ 1757.

143. Here lyes yᵉ Body of Hannah Shutt, Daughter of Capt Michael and Mrs Mary Shutt, Aged 16 years and 8 months, who Deceased April the 29ᵗʰ 1709.

144. Here lyes yᵉ Body of Mrs Mary Shutt, the Wife of Capt Michael Shutt, agett 45 years and eight months. Who Deceased September the 16ᵗʰ 1709.

145. Here lyes the body of Mrs Lydia Shute, Aged 42 years Decᵈ Octʳ yᵉ 3ᵈ 1721.

146. Here lyeth Buried yᵉ Body of John Green, Senior, aged 59 years, Died February yᵉ 25, 1701–2.

147. Here lyes yᵉ Body of Anne Green, Daugᵗʳ of Mr. Samuel and Mrs Anne Green, who Died June yᵉ 9ᵗʰ 1730, Aged 17 years.

148. Here lies the Body of Mrs Elizabeth Austill, Wife of Capt. Joseph Austill, who dyed June yᵉ 18ᵗʰ 1767, in the 80ᵗʰ year of her age.

149. Abigail Furber & John Furber Tomb. 1828.

150. Here lies buried the Body of Mrs Rebecca Clarke Widow of Mr John Clarke, Aged 82 years died Janʳʸ 2ᵈ 1763.

151. Here lyes buried the body of Mr Humphrey Scarlet Aged 46 years Decᵈ Janʳʸ yᵉ 4ᵗʰ 1739.

152 Here lyes buried the Body of Mehetebel Scarlet, Wife to Mr Humphrey Scarlet, Decᵈ June yᵉ 26ᵗʰ 1733 In yᵉ 43ᵈ year of her age.

153. Here lyeth buried yᵉ Body of Mr Joseph Buckley Aged 42 years & 6 mounthes. Died Jan. yᵉ 1, 1701.

154. Here lyes buried the body of Mr James Watson decᵈ July yᵉ 22ᵈ 1738, in yᵉ 58ᵗʰ year of his age.

155. Here lies the Body of Mrs Mary Watson, wife of Capt James Watson aged 59 years. Died Octʳ 1ˢᵗ 1743.

156. Here lyeth buried yᵉ Body of Joseph Glidden aged about 32 years. Died Novᵉʳ yᵉ 24, 1700.

157. Here lyes buried yᵉ Body of Mʳˢ Mary Glidden, yᵉ Wife of Mr Joseph Glidden Aged 41 years. Died August yᵉ 23ᵈ 1746.

158. Sarah, dauʳ of Mr Joseph & Mrs Mary Glidden Aged 18 months, Decᵈ Novʳ 1ˢᵗ 1737.

159. Sarah Glidden, Dauʳ of Mr Joseph & Mrs Mary Glidden, Aged 1 year & 10 mᵒ decᵈ Octʳ 16ᵗʰ 1739.

160. Judith Glidden Dauʳ of Mr Joseph & Mrs Mary Glidden Aged 12 years & 4 mᵒ Died Augˢᵗ yᵉ 5ᵗʰ 1744.

161. Here lyes buried the Body of John Goodwin, aged 65 years departed this life June ye 21st 1712.

162. Here lyes buried ye Body of Mrs Mary Goodwin aged 85 Years, died July ye 16th 1759.

163. Here lyes buried ye Body of Mrs Martha Pearson (formerly ye wife of Mr John Goodwin), Aged 76 years, who departed this life Sep^t ye 26th 1728.

164. George ye son of Mr Joseph & Mrs Samuel Person, aged 2 years, Died Sept ye 17, 1727.

165. John ye Son of Mr Thomas & Mrs Eunice Pearson, Aged 1 year & 7 m^o Dec^d Octr ye 7, 1729.

166. Here lyes ye Body of Dorcas Ballard, Wife to Daniel Ballard, aged about 57 years, died June ye 22^d 1719.

167. Dorcas Ballard, Dau^r to Mr Daniel & Mrs Mary Ballard, aged 13 mouths, Dec^d Jan^{ry} ye 25^h 1737.

168. Here lyes ye Body of Benjamin Ballard, aged about 30 years Dec^l Novem^{br} the 15ta 1718.

169. Here lies Buried the Body of Mrs Margaret Ballard wife to Mr. John Ballard Died May 3, 1767 Aged 47 years.

170. Here lyes buried the Body of Mrs Anna Ballard wife to Mr John Ballard, Aged 32 years, Died Feb y 15, 1750–51.

171. In memory of Betsey Ballard (Eldest daug^r of Daniel & Betsey Ballard who died Augst 30th 1801, Aged 2 years & 8 M^{os}.

172. Here lyes ye Body of Abigail Cooper, Wife of Edward Cooper, died March ye 11th 1718, in ye 31st year of her age.

173. Here lyes Buried ye Body of Mrs Hannah Woodbury Wife to Mr. Andrew Woodbury, Who departed this Life, July 28th 1733, .. ye 37th year of her age.

174. Andrew, son to Andrew & Hannah Woodbury Aged 5 years & 5 M^o Dec^d Oct^o ye 21st 1725.

175. James Washburn & Samuel Ballard. Tomb. No. 50.

176. Here lyeth ye Body of Susannah Wadsworth, ye Wife of Timothy Wadsworth, Dec^d April ye 3^d 1704, in ye 37th year of her age.

177. .... lyes the ..dy of Mr ..mothy Wadsworth, ...d June ye 20th [174]4, in the .. ..

178. Here lyes buried ye Body of Capt. Richard Harris aged about 63 years who dec^d March ye 10th 1713–14.

179. Amos, son to Mr. Amos & Mrs Mary Carterit, Aged 3 months, Dec^l Septr ye 26th 1731.

180. Here lieth ye Body of Michael Nowel, aged 33 years & ½. Died Aug^{ust} ye 27th 1696.

181. Here 1... ye Body of Mr George Nowell, aged 74 years died June ye 8, 1742.

182. Here lyes buried the Body of Mr Dean Grover, aged 46 years, dec^d Aug. ye 15th. 1734.

183. Here lies ye Body of Rebecca Wife to Obdiah Wakefield, Aged 38 years, died May the 28, 1715.

184. Here lyes buried the body of Mr Samuel Cockran, died May 9th 1763, in ye 48th year of his age.

185. Here lyes Buried ye Body of Mr Robert Seares, who Departed this Life Decem^{br} 29th 1732, in ye 76th year of His Age.

186. Sacred to the Memory of Mr Paul Farmer, who died December 26th 1791 aged 77 years.

187. Here lyes buried the body of Mrs Abigail Freeman, dec^d Feb^{ry} ye 21st 1734, in ye 61st year of her age.

188. Here lyes ye Body of Abigail Thomas, Wife to William Thomas, dec^d May ye 4th 1717, in the 33^d year of her age.

189. Here lyes ye Body of Mrs Abigail Ingham, late Wife of Mr North Ingham, who dec^d April ye 10th 1728 in ye 36th year of his age.

190. Here lyes ye Body of William Mumford, aged 77 years, died Novr ye 21st 1718.

191. Here lyes buried ye body of William Mumford son to William & Ruth Mumford Aged 27 years & 5 months, died Decr ye 18, 1704.

192. Mary Munford, aged 3 years Died January ye 24, 1687–8.

193. Here lyeth enterred ye Body of Michael Martyn aged 60 years dec^d March ye 26, 1682.

194. Here lyeth ye body of Capt. Michael Martyn, ye son of Richard Martyn, who died October ye 27, in ye 35 year of his age.

195. Here lyes ye Body of Mr Joseph Hood, aged 55 years, dec^d December ye 14th 1729.

196. Here lyes ye body of Joseph, son to Joseph & Judith Hood, aged 6 mo. dec^d Sept ye 4th 1713.

197. Elizabeth Greenough, the dafter of John & Elizabeth Greenough, Aged 7 years & 6 mon ... Died y^e ......

198. In memory of Mrs. Margaret Clark the Virtuous Consort of Capt. Joseph Clark. She died Jany 11th 1761 Ætat 69.

199. Here lies the Body of Capt. Joseph Clark, who Departed this life March ye 17th, 1760, in the 81st year of his age.

200. In Memory of Mr Joseph Clark, died Oct. 16th 1783, aged 67 years.

201. In memory of Mrs Prudence Clark, Widow of Mr Joseph Clark, deceased 13 December 1789, aged 68 years.

202. Here lyeth ye Body of Elizabeth, wife of William Greenough, Aged 38 years, Dec^d May ye 23^d 1688.

203. Buckland Clark, aged 3 years & 4 months, died Novr 6th 1748. Also Elizabeth Clark aged 1 year & 2 months, died Oct. 20th, 1751. The children of Mr James & Mrs Ruth Clark.

204. Here lyes ye Body of Mrs Sarah Clark, Wife of Mr. Samuel Clark, died August 9, 1799, aged 56 years.

205. Here lyes the Body of Mrs Hannah Clark, the wife of Mr Samuel Clark, who died Feb^{ry} 13, 1764, Aged 35 years.

206. Here lyes y^e Body of Sarah y^e daughter of William & Sarah Clark, aged 18 months, died August y^e 15th 1704.

207. Here lyes y^e Body of John Russell aged 64 years, who departed this life September y^e 28$^{t 1}$ 1709.

208. Here lyes enterred the Body of Mr William Hough, aged 67 years, died November y^r 8 ^{h} 1714.

209. Here lyes buried y^e body of Mr William Hough Junr Aged 20 years & 4 mo. Dec^i June y^e 18th 1716.

210. Mary Hough, daughter to William & Mary Hough, aged 3 years & 9 Mo. dec^d Sept y^e 29, 1692.

211. Here lyes ye Body of Mrs Hannah Russell, wife of Mr Samuel Russell. Died March 21st 1737–8.

212. Here lyes ye body of Susannah Russel, dec^d Octr y^o 17th 1721, in ye 17th year of her age.

213. Here lyes ye Body of Mrs Mary Attwood, wife to Deacon John Attwood, aged 63 years, dec^i March ye 18th 1728–9.

214. Here lies buried the Body of Mr Thadeus Sargent, to Son Mr Thomas Sargent, died ye 26th of January 1773, in the 37th year of his age.

215. Here lyes buried the Body of Mrs Mary Hicks, the wife of Mr Zachariah Hicks, aged 49 years, who died December ye 30th 1747.

216. Here lyes buried the Body of Mrs Elizth Fifield Widow of Capt Giles Fifield aged 84 years, who died June ye 16th 1743.

217. Here lies the Body of Capt. Thomas Stoddard, who departed this Life April the 12^{tn} 1763, in the 64th year of his Age.

218. Thomas Stoddard, son of Mr Thomas & Mrs Abigail Stoddard Aged 1 year & 2 Mo. Died Sept ye 3^d 1743.

219. Here lyes ye Body of Mrs Abigail Stoddard, Wife to Capt. Thomas Stoddard, & daughter of Mr Benjamin Barker of Andover, who died July 23^d 1761, in ye 60th year of her age.

220. Elizabeth Peirse, Dau^r to Moses & Elizabeth Peirse, aged 7 years, died Nov. ye 1st 1721.

221. Here lies enterred yᵉ body of Elizabeth Pearse, yᵉ Daughter of John and Elizabeth Pearse Aged .... who departed this life September yᵉ 20, 1708.

222. Samuel Winslow's Tomb. No. 117.

223. Here lyes the Body of Capt. William Troutt, Died March 31ˢᵗ 1742, in yᵉ 53ᵈ year of his age.

224. Sarah Trout, Dauʳ to Mr Joseph and Mrs Sarah Trout aged 3 weeks, died Augˢ 35ᵗʰ 1753.

225. Here lyes yᵉ Body of Edward Ransford, aged 48 years, died December the 27ᵗʰ 1717.

226. Here lyes the Body of Mrs Elizᵗʰ Stoddard, wife to Mr Daniel Stoddard, dauʳ to Mr. John & Mrs Elizᵗʰ Ballard aged 70, years, decᵈ Febʳʸ yᵉ 20ᵗʰ 1732.

227. Here lyes yᵉ Body of Mary, wife to John Pittom, aged 69 years, died March yᵉ 17 1712–13.

228. Here lyes yᵉ Body of Samuel Greenwood, aged about 65 years, died yᵉ 19 of August, 1711.

229. Here lyes the Body of Samuel son of Samuel & Mary Greenwood, aged near 34 years, died Dec. yᵉ 10, 1711.

230. Here lies yᵉ Body of Thomas Stoddard Capen, son to Mr Hopestill & Mrs Patience Capen, who Died Decemᵉʳ the 21ˢᵗ 1761 Aged 3 months.

231. Erected to the Memory of Mrs. Patience Capen, the Consort of Mr Hopestill Capen who died Jan. 19ᵗʰ 1791 Aged 57 years.

232. Erected to the memory of Mr Hopestill Capen, who died March 2, 1807 aged 76 years.

233. Here lies the Body of Mrs Martha Capen wife to Mr William Capen who departed this Life April the 23ᵈ 1780, Aged 35 years.

234. Here lies the Body of Miss Hannah Langford, Dauʳ of Mr Nicholas & Mrs Joanna Langford, who died Nov. 19ᵗʰ 1796 Aged 15 years & 6 months.
[6 lines of poetry]

235. Here lyes the Body of Mr. Richard Jones, aged 28 years decᵈ Dec. yᵉ 8ᵗʰ 1731.

236. Here lyes yᵉ Body of Nathaniel Gill, aged 30 years & 7 mo. deceased Octʳ yᵉ 3ᵈ 1720.

237. Here lyes buried the body of Mrs Elizabeth Kenney, died May 6ᵗʰ 1753, aged 65 years.

238. Here lyes yᵉ Body of Mrs Mary Scott, Widdow of Capt. John Scott, aged 87 years, died Novʳ 23ᵈ 1754.

239. Here lies Buried the Body of Mrs Mary Farrinton, wife to Mr Joseph Farrington, died July yᵉ 12ᵗʰ 1752 (in) the 65ᵗʰ year of her age.

240. Joseph Farington son to Joseph & Mary Farington, aged 4 m⁰ dyed Nov yᵉ 5 ʰ 1721.

241. Joseph Farington, son to Joseph & Mary Farington Aged 16 Mo. decᵈ Sept yᵉ 2, 1724.

242. Here lyes buried the Body of Mrs Hannah White Widdow of Capt Samuel White, aged 73 years, Decᵈ Decʳ yᵉ 9ᵗʰ 1736.

243. Mary White, dauʳ to Mr Joseph & Mrs Mary White Aged 14 dayes, Decᵈ October yᵉ .. 1727.

244. Mary White, daughter of Samuel & Ann White, aged 4 years & 7 mo. who deceased October yᵉ 10ᵗʰ 1702.

245. ..... lies buried .. body of Mary White wife of Mr Isaac White, died April yᵉ 16ᵗʰ 1763.

246. Here lyes yᵉ Body of Mr Benjamin Pullinton aged 51 years decᵈ June the 11ᵗʰ 1735.

247. In memory of Mr Gershom Whittemore, son of Mr Thomas & Mrs Anna Whittemore, who died Nov. 1ˢᵗ 1795, Aged 20 years.

248. Here lies yᵉ Body of Mr Leonard Barons, son to Mr John and Mrs Mary Barrons of Salcomb-regis in Devon, died Octʳ 25ᵗʰ 1765, aged 33 years.

249. Here lyes buried the Body of Mr John Waterhouse, aged 37 years, died Janʳʸ yᵉ 1ˢᵗ 1746-7.

250. Here lyes yᵉ body of Rachel Waterhouse, wife to Mr Samuel Waterhouse, decᵈ Janʸ yᵉ 23ᵈ 1726-7 in yᵉ 22 year of her age.

251. Here lyes Buried the Body of Capt Joseph Buckley who Departed this Life January the 2ᵈ 1764, aged 32 years.

252. Here lies Buried the Body of Mr Richard Buckley, who departed this Life May yᵉ 21ˢᵗ 1767 Aged 72 years.

253. Here lyes buried yᵉ body of Mrs Joanna Buckley, widdow to Mr Joseph Buckley, aged 54 years & 9 Mo. decᵈ March yᵉ 4ᵗʰ 1716-17.

254. Sacred to the memory of Miss Joanna Buckley who died Janʳʸ 3ᵈ 1803 Æ 64.

"Blessed are the dead who die in the Lord"

255. Rachel, dauʳ to Mr Samuel & Mrs Rachel Waterhouse aged 2 Dˢ died Janʳʸ 3ᵈ 1726-7.

256. Here lies Buried the Body of Mr Thomas Coverly, Died Janʳʸ 29ᵗʰ 1778 Aged 69 years and 8 months.

257. Here lies buried the Body of Mr John Clough died July yᵉ 6ᵗʰ 1756 aged 46 years.

258. Here lies Buried the Body of Mr Edward Edes, aged 55 years, Died Janʳʸ 19ᵗʰ, 1761.

259. Edward Edes, son of Mr Edward & Mrs Sarah Edes, aged 5 years, dec^d Nov. ye 5th, 1736.

260. Here lyes the Body of Mr Edward Edes, aged 49 years, dec^d Sepr ye 28th 1730.

261. Elias Parkman, son of Elias & Martha Parkman aged about 3 weeks Dec^d Sept ye 2^d 1721.

262. Here lyes buried the Body of Mr Elias Parkman, aged 52 years, 5 mo & 15 days, dec^d May the 24th 1741.

263. Here lyes buried the body of Mrs Elizabeth Parkman, wife to Mr Elias Parkman, who died Nov. ye 1st 1746, in the 58th year of Her age.

264. Here lyes buried the body of Mrs Elizabeth Parkman the virtuous & pious consort of Mr William Parkman, aged 85 years & 7 months, April ye 13th 1746.

265. This stone perpetuates the Memory of Doc^{tr} Elias Parkman, who departed this Life March ye 6th 1750–1, aged 33.

266. Here lyes buried the Body of Mr Samuel Goffe, dec^d Sep. the 11th 1740, in the 58th year of his age.

267. Here lyes ye Body of Hannah White, daughter to Samuel & Hannah White aged 20 years, dec^{end} April ye 8th 1718.

268. In Memory of Mrs Mary Stevens wife of Mr Thomas Stevens, who Departed this Life May 9th 1785 in the 75th year of her age.

"Blessed are the dead that die in the Lord, for they rest from their Labours, and their Works do follow them."

269. Here lyes buried ye body of Mr John Stevens, dec^d April ye 2^d 1721, in ye 50th year of his age.

270. Here lyes the Body of Sarah Stevens, wife to Thomas Stevens, aged about 52 years, dec^d Novr ye 30, 1723.

271. Joanna, Dau^r to Thomas & Sarah Stevens, aged 1 year & 2 Da^s Dec^d Novr ye 2^d 1718.

272. Edward, son of Thomas & Sarah Stevens, aged 3 months died Augst ye 31st, 1712.

273. Here lies Buried the Body of Mr. Thomas Stevens, Died May 6th 1751, aged 56 years.

274. Here lyes Buried the Body of Mr. John Stevens, son of Capt John & Mrs Abigail Stevens of Charlestown who died Sept. 26th, 1748 aged 23 years & 27 Days.

275. Here lyes buried the Body of Capt Thomas Porter, dec^d April ye 11th 1738, in the 63^d year of his age.

276. ...e dau^r to [T]homas & [E]lizabeth Porter, aged 3 monthes Died Sept ye 8, 1712.

277. Here lyes buried the Body of Capt. Alexander Seares who departed this life March ye 17th 1758, aged 60 years.

278. Here lies buried the Body of Mrs Hannah Sears, Widow of Capt Alexander Seares, who Departed this Life, June 25.ʰ 1769, In the 73ᵈ year of her Age.

279. Mr John Cooper (footstone).

280. In memory of Mr Edward Grant, who departed this life, June 28ᵗʰ 1797, aged 78.

281. Thomas, son of John & Ann May, Aged 3 years & 9 months, Died November yᵉ 10ᵗʰ 1710.

282. Here lyes yᵉ Body of William Rouse, died January yᵉ 20ᵗʰ 1704-5, in yᵉ 65ᵗʰ year of his age.

283. Here lyes buried yᵉ Body of Capt. Samuel Harris, aged 53 years, who died March yᵉ 20ᵗʰ 1741.

284. Here lyes yᵉ Body of Mrs Mary Richards wife to Mr Edward Richards, who departed this life Janʳʸ yᵉ 20ᵗʰ 1760, in yᵉ 84ᵗʰ year of her age.

285. Mrs Mary Richards (footstone).

286. Here lies the Body of Mrs Mary Richards wife to Mr John Richards, Aged 27 years, Decᵈ Octʳ the 22ᵈ 1713.

287. In memory of Mr Jonas Clark, who died Novʳ 28 ʰ 1790 Aged 64 years, 2 months & 17 Days.

288. Mrs Sarah Clark, 1779.

289. Here lies the Body of Mrs Martha Clark, wife of Mr Jonas Clark, who parted this life, March the 20ᵗʰ 1769, aged 36 years.

290. Here lyes entirred yᵉ Body of Arthur Smith, aged about 63 years, died May yᵉ 17ᵗʰ 1708.

291. In memory of Capt. John Pulling, who departed this life January 25ᵗʰ 1787, in the 51ˢᵗ year of his age.

292. Here lies yᵉ Body of Mr John Diamond, died March 8ᵗʰ 1763 aged 62 years. Also the body of Mrs Margaret Diamond Dauʳ of Mr John & Mrs Hannah Diamond, died May 9ᵗʰ 1769 aged 48 years.

293. Here lyes yᵉ body of Mrs Hannah Diamond, wife to Mr John Diamond, who died May 4ᵗʰ 1743 in yᵉ 32ᵈ year of her age.

294. Here lies interred the Body of Mrs Elizabeth Sheaffe, wife to Mr Willᵐ Sheaffe, who departed this life March yᵉ 17ᵗʰ 1731-2. In the 37ᵗʰ year of her age.

295. Here lyes yᵉ Body of Mrs Hannah Copp wife to Mr. Samuel Copp, decᵈ Feb. yᵉ 2ᵈ 1722.

296. Here lyes yᵉ Body of Mrs Amy Copp, Wife to elder David Copp, aged 82 years decᵈ Novʳ yᵉ 28ᵗʰ 1718.

297. ...... Copp .... about 32 years, decᵈ Octʳ yᵉ 3ᵈ 1732.

298. Here lyes yᵉ Body of Marcy Marshall, yᵉ Wife of Joseph Marshall, aged 36 years, dyed yᵉ 18 of yᵉ 2ᵈ mo. 1712.

299. Margrett Ruck, daughter to Samuell & Ann Ruck, aged 18 months, died July the 8, 1687.

300. Here lyes buried the Body of Mr Joseph Bill, aged 55 years, died Febʳʸ yᵉ 3ᵈ 1747–8.

301. In Memory of Mrs. Rebecca Littlefield, Consort of Capt James Littlefield, who departed this Life Sept 17ᵗʰ 1773, aged 23 years.

302. In memory of Elizabeth Ann, dau. to Elijah & Mary Bruce, who died March 12, 1815, aged 19 months.

[4 lines.]

303. Here lyes yᵉ Body of Deacon John Attwood, aged about 67 years, died August 26, 1714.

304. Here lies buried yᵉ Body of Mr Joshua Atwood, died August 31ˢᵗ 1770, aged 70 years.

305. Here lies yᵉ Body of Mrs Elizabeth Atwood, Wife to Mr. Joshua Atwood, died Janʳʸ 15, 1768, aged 63 years.

306. Here lies Buried the Body of Mrs Alice Attwood, wife of Mr Joseph Attwood, died the 10ᵗʰ of Octʳ 1770, aged 50 years.

307. Sacred to the memory of Martha Atwood, Relict of Capt. Joseph Atwood, died Novʳ 9 ⁿ 1809 Ae 62.

308. In memory of Mrs Ann Clough, wife of Mr Samuel Clough, died April yᵉ 2ᵈ 1772 aged 52 years.

[6 lines of verse.]

309. Mehetabel Clough, Daughter of John & Mehetabel Clough, aged 17 months & 18 days, Died October yᵉ 5ᵗʰ 1717.

310. Here lyes the body of Mrs Elizabeth Clough, wife of Mr. John Clough, aged 46 years, Dyed Novʳ yᵉ 6ᵗʰ 1745.

311. Here lies the Body of Mary Greenwood, Wife of Samˡ Greenwood, Departed this Life Sept. 21ˢᵗ 1774, aged 31 years.

312. In Memory of Miss Nancy Greenwood, daughter of Nathˡ & Priscilla Greenwood who departed this Life, May 5ᵗʰ 1802, aged 34 years.

313. In Memory of Mr Ebenezer Hancock; who died July 4ᵗʰ 1799, in the 50ᵗʰ Year of his Age.

314. Here lyes yᵉ Body of Mrs Abigail Beal, wife of Mr Othniel Beal, decᵈ Novʳ yᵉ 16ᵗᵃ 1719 in yᵉ 25 ⁿ year of her age.

315. Here lyes Buried the body of Mr Simeon Drowne, Aged 48 years, 3 Mo & 24 ...., Decᵈ Augˢᵗ yᵉ 2ᵈ 1734.

316. Here lies Buried the Body of Mrs. Katherine Drowne, Wife to Deacon Shem Drowne, Daughter of the late Timothy Clarke Esq. & Sarah his wife, who Departed this Life April 21ˢᵗ 1754, Aged 67 years & 4 Days.

317. The Remains of Deacon Shem Drowne who departed this Life January 13ᵗʰ 1774, Aged 90 years, 1 month & 9 days.

"For if we believe that Jesus died & Rose again, even so them also who sleep in Jesus, will God bring with him."

318. In Memory of Mr Shem Drowne Junʳ Anno Ætatis 39 ᵑᵒ Birth August 10ᵗʰ 1741, O.S. Death May 6ᵗʰ 1770 N.S.

319. John Drowne, son to Shem & Katherine Drowne, aged 16 days, died Sept. yᵉ 1ˢᵗ 1713.

320. Here lies yᵉ Body of Joseph Drowne, son to Shem & Katherine Drowne, Aged 3 years 10 Mᵒ 21 Daˢ Decᵈ Octʳ yᵉ 31ˢᵗ 1721.

321. Here lyes yᵉ Body of Capt. Thomas Barnard, aged 59 years, 5 mo. & 15 dˢ decesᵈ March yᵉ 14ᵗʰ 1715–16.

322. Here lyes yᵉ Body of Mr Thomas Barnard, aged 46 years decᵈ May the 16th 1730.

323. ⎧ Webster. No. 4.
⎪
⎨ Grant Webster died 1797 Æ 80.
⎪ John White died 1803 Æ 87.
⎩ Sarah White Conant died 1807, Æ. 77.

324. Here lyes yᵉ Body of Mrs Maria Elliot, Wife to Capt John Elliot, aged 27 years, 11 mo. & 8 dayes, decᵈ Sept. yᵉ 21ˢᵗ 1721.

325. Mrs Hannah Nichols 1760.

326. This Tomb No. 1. belongs to the heirs of Miss Elizabeth Bronsdson, who departed this life, March 20ᵗʰ 1810, Æ. 82 George Brondson Curtis died Augᵗ 20ᵗʰ 1800

327. In Memory of Ebenezer, son of Ebenʳ & Mary Sessions, who died Octʳ 18ᵗʰ 1813, Aged 15 months & 1 day.

[4 lines of verse]

328. Here lies yᵉ Body of Mr John Milk, decᵈ May 19th 1756, aged 47 years, 10 mᵒ & 27 dˢ.

329. Memento Mori, Fugit Hora. Here lyes yᵉ Body of Mr John Breck, aged 32 years. 1 Mᵒ & 3 Weekes, who deceased February yᵉ 16, 1712–13.

329. Here lies buried the Body of Mr William Beer, who died December yᵉ 11ᵗʰ 1759, aged 57 years.

330. Here lies Mr Thomas Lee, the Founder of this Tomb, who after a long and usefull Life, died on the 16th of July 1766, Anno Ætatis 93.

Give up his Body to death
his Soul to Immortality.

Also the Body of his Wife Deborah Lee, daughter of Edward Flint of Salem, who departed this life the 3ᵈ of April AD 1763, Anno Ætatis 91.

3

331. John Williams Departed this life Sept 9, 1845, aged 72 years.
[4 lines of verse.]

332. Here lies the body of Mrs Love Williams, wife to Mr. Nathaniel Williams, who died Octr the 19th 1755 ....

333. In Memory of 2 children, Twin sons of Peter & Huldah Gayetty. William died July 15th 1802, aged 1 year & 1 month. Joseph died Feb^ry 13th 1808 aged 6 years & 8 months.
[4 lines of verse.]

334. Here lyes buried ye Body of Mrs Dorcas Doublede, wife to Mr Elijah Doublede, who died March 3^d 1739–40, in ye 39th year of her age.

335. Here lies buried ye Body of Mrs Sibella Breck, wife to Mr Robert Breck, who departed this Life, April the 28th 1764, Aged 52 years.

336. Erected in Memory of Capt. Samuel Breck, who died suddenly March 20, 1809 ....

337. Margaret, ye wife of Willia. Snelling, aged 46 yeares deceased the 18 day of June 1667.

338. Here lyes ye Body of James Adams, died June 17th 1718 in ye 32 year of his age.

339. Here lies intered the Body of Thomas Drowne, who departed this Life 26th Feb^ry 1795 aged 79.
[2 lines.]

340. Here lies intered the Body of Sarah Drowne, Wife of Thomas Drowne, who departed this Life 26th Sept. 1795 aged 79.

341. Here lyes buried the Body of Mr Nathanael Newell, Junr aged 26 years, 10 m° & 15 days, dec^d April ye 24, 1717.

342. Mary Drowne, an Infant of 8 hours old, Dec^d February 11th 1726.   Elizabeth Drowne, aged 2 months, Dec^d March ye 15th 1728–9, children of Mr Shem & Mrs Katherine Drowne.

343. Sacred to the Memory of Mrs Henretta Harper, Wife of the Revd John Harper, late of the Island of St Christophers ; who having early in life obtained the faith which works by love ; endured as seeing him who is invisible ; and rested in peace from all her labours, May 23^d 1795, in the 27th year of her age.

344. Here lyes ye Body of Mr Phillip Hughes, aged 62 years dec^d June ye 16th 1720.

345. Here lyes ye Body of Mrs Elizabeth Tyley, wife to Mr John Tyley, dec^d Sep^t ye 1st 1727, aged near 37 years.

346. Here lyes ye Body of Davied Webb, dec^d Octr ye 9th 1722, in ye 35th year of his age.

347. Here lyes Buried the Body of Mr Alexander Parkman died March ye 6th 1747–8, in the 49th year of His age.

348. Here lyes buried the Body of Mrs Esther Parkman, the virtuous consort of Mr Alexander Parkman, aged 42 years who died Jan^{ry} ye 12th 1745–6.

349. Here lyes Buried the Body of Mr Samuel Parkman who departed this life August the 10th 1767, aged 72 years.

350. Here lyes Buried the Body of Mrs Martha Emmes wife to Mr Joshua Emmes, aged 22 years & 9 mo & 6^{ds} died Jan^{ry} ye 27th 1746–7.

351. Ann Emmes, wife to Mr Henry Emmes Dec^d Decr y^u 7th 1742, in the 31st year of her age.

352. Margaret Emmes, Wife of Mr Joshua Emmes, Dec^d who died August 31, 1778 aged 55 years.

353. Here lyes buried the body of Elizabeth Emmes, wife to Henry Emmes, aged about 65 years, dec^d Octo^r ye 15, 1715.

354. Here lyes buried ye body of Mr Henry Emmes dec^d February ye 12, 1724–5, in the 76th year of his age.

355. In Memory of Mr Joshua Emmes who Departed this Life the 6th of Augst. 1772, aged 53 years.

356. Here lyes ye Body of Sarah Swaen, wife to Benjamin Swaen & daughter to William & Elizabeth Parkman, aged near 97 years, died Feb^{ry} ye 10th 1710–11.

357. Here lyes buried ye Body of Mrs Martha Dixwell Wife to Mr. John Dixwell aged 48 years who dec^d Oct ye 3^d 1722.

358. Here lyes buried ye Body of Mrs Mary Dixwell, wife to Mr John Dixwell, aged 35 years, dec^d Sept ye 28th 1721.

359. Mary Dixwell, dau^r of Mr John & Mrs Mary Dixwell aged 12 days, died Sept ye 19th 1745.

360. Here lyes Intered the Body of Mrs Love Rawlins, Widow of Capt John Rawlins late of Boston, dec^d who Departed this life December 10th Anno Domi 1743, in the 66th Year of her Age.

361. Elizabeth Rawlings aged 1 year & 5 months dyed ye 12 of August 1685. Caleb Rawlings aged 8 weeks dyed January ye 12, 1682. Caleb Rawlings aged 2 years & 6 months dyed ye 16 of August 1678. The children of Caleb & Elizabeth Rawlings.

362. Ruth, daugh^{tr} to James & Alice Townsend aged 10 months dec^d Octr ye 23, 1713.

363. Here lyes ye body of Anna Townsend, aged 45 years & 9 Mo. dec^d Novr ye 11th 1717.

364. Here lyes buried the Body of Mr James Townsend dec^d April 18th 1767, in ye 70th year of his age.

365. Here lyes Buried the Body of Mr William Parkman aged 72 years, dec^d November 28, 1730.

366. William Parkman, Son to Mr William & Hannah Parkman, Aged 15 years 3 mo & 2 Dayes, Dec^d May ye 4th 1730.

367. Susanna Parkman, Dau' to William & Mrs Hannah Parkman, aged 15 years & 11 M° Died Nov' y° 16ᵗʰ 1743.

368. ....s Buried ..e Body of Dorothy Parkman, dau' to Mr Elias & Mrs Elizabeth Parkman, aged 15 years & 2 Mo. dec⁴ April y° 9ᵗʰ 1741.

369. Here lies the body of Wilᵐ Bowes Parkman, Son to Mr William & Mrs Dorcas Parkman, died Nov' 2ᵈ 1758, in the 24ᵗʰ Year of His Age.

370. Here lies y° body of Mrs Mary Revely, Wife of Mr Edward Revely, Died Janʳʸ 18ᵗʰ 1731, aged 44 years.

371. Here lyes y° Body of Mrs Elizabeth Belcher, Widow to Mr Joseph Belcher, who departed this life Aug 23ᵈ 1762, Aged 61 years.

372. Charles Jarvis, Died Nov. 15, 1807, Aged 59 Years. A Physician, a Statesman, a Patriot and an honest Man, whose dignified Deportment, sublime eloquence, unbounded Philanthrophy and other virtues, endeared his Memory to his Fellow Citizens.

373. S...., ... of Leonard & Mrs Sarah Jarvis, Died Dec' 17ᵗʰ 1753, Aged 2 years & 6 mo.

374. Here lies buried the Body of Lieuᵗ William Merchant, who departed this life, August y° 12th 1751 aged 61 years.

375. Thomas, son to John & Elizabeth Gand, aged 3 weeks & 5 dˢ Died Nov' y° 15ᵗʰ 1708.

376. William, son to Bartholemew & Mary Gedney, aged 6 weeks, Died Dec' y° 7ᵗʰ 1725.

377. William, son to Bartholomew & Mary Gedney, Aged 14 days, Died Dec' y° 14ᵗʰ 1726.

378. In Memory of Capᵗ Robert Newman, Who died March 23, 1806, Æ 51.
[12 lines of verse.]

379. Also, In Memory of Capᵗ Robert Newman Junʳ who died at sea, Dec 14, 1816 Æt. 31.

380. In memory af William Newman, who died at Martinico, Aug 28, 1817 : Æt. 26.

381. Here lyes buried the Body of Mrs Martha Sartly, aged 64 years, who died Febʳʸ y° 3ᵈ 1747-8.

382. Miss Mary Ann Newell Carlisle Died January the 22, 1807, in the Eleventh yʳ of Her Age.

383. Here lyes ye Body of Mrs Sarah Sharp, wife of Mr. Gibbins Sharp, died June 9ᵗʰ 1756, in the 78ᵗʰ year of her age.

384. In Memory of Mr Gibbins Sharp, who departed this Life Octʳ 24ᵗʰ 1740 Aged 22 years.

385. Joshua Ellis, born in Sandwich May 4, 1769, died July 29, 1829.

386. Sarah L. Ellis, born in Lynn, March 3, 1798, died April 2, 1823.

387. Lydia L. Ellis, born in Boston Aug. 13, 1798, died April 2, 1799.

388. Joshua Ellis Jun. born in Boston Nov 4, 1796, died June 7, 1820.

389. Emeline C. D. Joselyn, born in Boston Sept 2, 1732, died Oct 28, 1833.

390. J. Cullen Ayer, M.D. Died Jan. 22, 1846, aged 34 years and 4 mos Christus Resurrectio et 'Vita est.

391. Antoinette D. Ayer, Aug. 28, 1839, aged 3 years & 7 mos.

392. Emeline A. Ayer, Died Jan. 21, 1842, aged 2 months.

393. Henry D. Emerson, born in Boston April 19, 1836, died Aug. 16, 1846.
Like a bright flower he was cut down.

394. Sally Emerson, born in Boston July 19, 1793, Died at Lynn, Jan. 27, 1863, aged 69 years.

395. Scammell Penniman, James Parsons & Joseph E. Andrews' Tomb, 1821. No. 55.

396. Sacred to the Memory of Mrs Esther. wife of Janerson Baldwin, Daughter of Mr Parker Emerson, Died Decr 27th 1809, aged 37 years.

397. Here lies buried the Body of Colo. Leonard Jarvis, who departed this Life, the 30th day of September 1770, aged 56 years.

398. Here lies buried the Body of Mrs Elizabeth Jarvis, Widow of Capt Nathaniel Jarvis, died Feb^ry 13th 1760, Aged 82 years.

399. Sarah Jarvis, Dau^r of Mr Thomas & Mrs Sarah Jarvis, Died Decr 15th 1747, Aged 6 months.

400. Here lies Buried the Body of Mrs Elizabeth Jarvis, daughter of Leonard Jarvis Esqr and Mrs Sarah his wife, died May 9th 1760, Aged 17 years.

401. Here lyes buried the Body of Mrs Mary Jones, the wife of Mr Josiah Jones, aged 62 years, died May ye 7th 1746.

402. Here lyes buried the Body of .apt Josiah Jones, deo^d Jan^ry ye 17th 1744 in the 51st year of his age.

403. In memory of Mrs Betsey Jones, wife ef Mr Elisha Jones, who died April 22^d 1800, Æ. 20.

404. Here lyes ye Body of Thomas Jonson, dec^d Decr ye 31st 1722, in ye 28th year of his age.

405. Here lies ye Body of Mrs Sarah Melendy, Wife to Mr. William Melendy, Aged 70 years, Died Feb^ry ye 12th 1743–4.

406. Elizabeth, Dau. to Freeborn & Susannah Balch, aged 14 months Dec^d June ye 27th 1728.

407. Here lies yᵉ Body of Mrs Marcy White, Wife of Mr. James White, Died April 13ᵗʰ 1778, Aged 32 years.

[2 lines of verse.]

408. In Memory of Robert L. Tilden, son of Charles & Isabella, Tilden, who died Novʳ 6th 1801, Aged   years & 4 months.

(2 lines of verse.)

409. Here lyes buried yᵉ body of Archibald MacQuedy aged about 50 years, Died Octʳ yᵉ 11ᵗʰ 1717.

410. Here lies intered the Body of Capt. Patrick Connel, who was born in the countey of Kelcancy in Ireland, who Departed this Life June the 11ᵗʰ 1763, aged 50 years.   Also is buried here four of his children.

411. Mrs Mary Hedman (footstone).

412. Here lyes yᵉ Body of Thomas Kellon, aged 52 years died Decʳ yᵉ 25ᵗʰ 1708.

413. Here lyes yᵉ body of Mrs Elizabeth Kellen, wife to Mr Thomas Kellen, aged 76 years, decᵈ Janʳʸ yᵉ 22ᵈ 1728–9.

414. Erected to the Memory of Benjamin Eustis, who departed this Life May 4 ʰ 1804, aged 84.

415. Here lyes the body of Mary Forist, wife to Charles Forist, Decᵈ Sept 2ᵈ 1728, Aged 33 years.

416. In Memory of Mr Aaron McClintock, who died May 5ᵗʰ 1800, Ætat, 38.

417. In memory of Mrs Martha McClintock, who died Oct. 13ᵗʰ 1798 Ætat 67.

418. Here lyes yᵉ Body of Jane, wife to Onesimus, dyed April yᵉ 24, 1727, in yᵉ 32ᵈ year of her age.

419. Willᵐ son to Onesimus & Jane, aged 10dˢ dyed April yᵉ 28, 1727.

420. Here lyes yᵉ Body of Martha Knox, dauʳ of Mr Adam & Mrs Martha Knox, Aged 2 years & 7 mᵒ died May 15ᵗʰ 1748.

421. Here lies Buried yᵉ Body of Mrs Ann Knox, wife of Capt. Andrew Knox, who departed this life Janʳʸ yᵉ 25ᵗʰ 1760, aged 61 years.

422. In Memory of Mrs Eleanor Read; departed this life Sept 17ᵗʰ 1798 Aged 58 years.

423. Mrs Eleanor Gere ; departed this Life Sept 19ᵗʰ 1798, aged 30 years.

424. Miss Elizabeth Berry ; departed this Life, Sept 21ˢᵗ 1798 Aged 25 years.

(2 lines of verse.)

425. Margarett, yᵉ daughter of Thomas & Margarett Berry Aged 1 Mᵒ & 2 Dˢ Died July yᵉ 27, 1692.

426. Erasmus, son to Erasmus & Persis Stevens, aged 2 years dec⁴ Novʳ yᵉ 1ˢᵗ 1721.

427. Here lyes Buried the Body of Mʳ Erasmus Stevens, who died yᵉ 22ᵈ June 1750, aged 64 years.

428. Here lies buried the Body of Mr John Pulling, Obᵗ 18ᵗʰ Janʳʸ 1771 aged 71 years.

429. Here lyes the Body of Mrs Mary Pullen, Wife to Mr. John Pullen, Aged 66 years, dec⁴ Janʳʸ 15ᵗʰ 1735–6.

430. Here lies the body of Mrs Martha Pulling the wife of Mr John Pulling, aged 43 years, Died Janʳy 31ˢᵗ 1753.

431. Here lies buried the Body of Mrs Ann Malcom, Widow of Capt. Daniel Malcom, died April 4ᵗʰ 1770, aged 40 years.

432. Here lyes yᵉ body of Mr John Viall, aged 76 years, died November yᵉ 13ᵗʰ 1720.

433. Elizabeth Viall, daughter of John & Mary Viall, aged 9 weeks died January yᵉ 17, 1682.

434. Lydia Wair, yᵉ wife of Daniel Wair, died January yᵉ 2ᵈ 1704–5, in yᵉ 43ᵈ year of her age.

435. Here lyes yᵉ body of Ezekiel Cleasby aged 57 years, died April yᵉ 27, 1720.

436. Abigail Dauʳ to Ezekiel & Abigail Cleasby aged about 11 mo. dec⁴ Augᵗ yᵉ 20ᵗʰ 1718.

437. Here lyes yᵉ Body of Sarah Cleasby wife to Ezekiel Cleasby, Aged about 53 years, Dec⁴ Novʳ ye 21ˢᵗ 1716.

438. Here lyes yᵉ Body of Sarah Cleasby, Dauᶠ to Ezekiel & Sarah Cleasby, Aged about 25 years, Dec⁴ Novʳ yᵉ 25, 1716.

439. In Memory of Mrs Elizabeth Coleman : who died Sept. 5ᵗʰ 1798 Æ. 58.

440. Also, Miss Temperance Coleman, who died Sept. 13ᵗʰ 1798, Æ. 32.

441. Here lyes yᵉ Body of John Manley, son of Capt. John & Mrs Hannah Manley Died Sept yᵉ 7ᵗʰ 1767, aged 8 Months & 7 Days.

442. In memory of Deacon Josiah Willard ; died Augˢᵗ 20ᵗʰ 1807, Aged 57 years, 9 mᵒ.

443. To the Memory of William Francis, son of Mr Asa Francis of Hartford Connect. who died June 26 AD 1804, aged 20 years.
[4 lines of verse.]

444. Capt Moses Chadwell (footstone).

445. Here lyes Buried the Body of Mrs Elizabeth Fullerton, the wife of Mr Edward Fullerton, Aged 51 years, who Departed this Life, April yᵉ 19ᵗʰ 1747.

446. ... in yᵉ Shir... Aged 35 ... Dec⁴ Febʳ .... 1736–7.

447. Here lyes ye Body of Mr James Shirley, son of Mr John & Mrs Jenet Shirley, who died August ye 2^d 1749, in ye 31st year of his age.

448. Here lyes ye Body of James Humphres, died October ye 30th 1721, in ye 36th year of his age.

449. Here lyes the Body of Deacon Edward Allin, died Sept ye 29^{:h} 1739, in ye 30th year of his age.

450. Ebenezer son to Ebenezer & Elizabeth Allin, still-born August ye 31st 1719.

451. Here lyes the Body of Mrs Theodocia Hay, aged 65 years, died May ye 31st 1751.

452. Here lyes ye Body of Mrs Abigail Goffe, wife of Mr William Goffe, died Augst 21st 1744, in ye 49th year of her age.

453. Abigail Goffe, dau^r to Samuel & Sarah Goffe, aged 15 months dec^d August ye 23^d 1727.

454. Here lyes buried the Body of Mrs Mary Holmes, wife to Mr Nathaniel Holmes, aged 34 years, died July ye 16th 1742.

455. ..aph Dell aged .o years, died the .. of September in the year 1681.

456. Here lyes ye Body of Mr George Ingersull, aged 78 years and 3 months, died August 19^{:h} 1721.

457. Here lies ye Body of Nehemiah Ingersoll, son of Capt Nehemiah & Mrs Elizth Ingersoll, died Augst 25th 1782, aged 21 months & 22 days.

458. Here lyes buried the Body of Thomas Goodwell, aged 62 years, who died Decr 21st 1749.

459. Here lyes ye Body of Mrs Elizabeth Lidston wife to Mr Thomas Lidston; who departed this life Feb^{ry} 6th AD 1752, aged 52 years.

460. Here lyes ye Body of Ann Crighton, widdow of James Crighton, aged 27 years, 1 mo & 17 days, Dec^d April ye 25th 1717.

461. Here lyes ye Body of Mrs Elizabeth Lamson, wife to Mr Nathaniel Lamson, who died August the 10th 1766, aged 33 years.

462. Here lyes ye Body of Mrs Abigail Low, wife to Mr John Low, aged 32 years & 11 m^o dec^d Augt ye 21st 1738.

463. Sacred to the Memory of Mrs Lucy Parry, wife of Mr Richard Parry, who departed this life Sept. 23rd A.D. 1800, in the 40th year of her age.

464. Also, her son, Cornelius Cook; died Nov. 2^d 1791.

Remember the great teacher — Death.

465. In Memory of Mr John Williston who departed this life 7th April 1776, aged 56 years.

466. Also, Mrs Ann Willeston, who departed this life, 28 Sept 1775, aged 52 years.

467. Sacred to the memory of Mr John Williston, died Octr 8, 1807, Æt. 32.

468. Here lyes buried ye Body of Mr Joseph Grouard Junr, aged 22 years & 1 m^o, died Nov. ye 19th 1746.

469. Here lyes ye Body of Mrs Elizabeth Grouard, wife of Mr Joseph Grouard, Aged 52 years, & 3 Mo Died July ye 5th 1747.

470. Elizabeth, Dau^r to Joseph & Eliz^th Grouard, aged 4 years & 2 m^o Dec^d May ye 21, 1730.

471. Here lies buried the Body of Mr Alexander Campbell, who departed this life August 4th 1770, aged 55 years.

472. Here lyes Buried the Body of Mr William Campbell, who was born April 23^d 1733, and departed this Life Jan^ry 17th 1773 Aged 40 years.

(5 prose lines.)

473. Sacred to the memory of Mrs Lucy Pomroy, Wife of Mr Daniel Pomroy, who died Jan^ry 1st 1805, aged 24 years.

474. In memory of Miss Mary Pomroy, Died May 8th 1790, aged 67.

475. Vernon & Brown's Tomb. No. 36. Here lies the body of Fortesque Vernon who departed this life Dec 21, 1778, Æt. 63.

476. Also; Tho. C. Vernon, who departed this life Nov 3, 1809, Æt. 60.

477. Here lyes ye body of Mrs Mary Demeret, aged 43 years, Dec^d March ye 20th 1735-6.

478. Here lyes the Body of Mrs Mary Hunt, Wife of Mr Daniel Hunt; who departed this Life Octr 25th 1801, aged 66 years.

(2 lines of verse.)

479. Henry Atkins, son to Mr Silas & Mrs Mary Atkins, aged 3 months 6 days, Died Dec. 31st 1750.

480. Nathaniel Atkins, son to Mr Silas & Mrs Mary Atkins, died Aug^st ye 14th 1753, aged 13 days.

481. Here lies buried the Body of Mr Joseph Gillander, of Aberdeen in Scotland, died the 31st May 1774.

482. Edes.

483. L. Ridgway's Tomb, 1819. No. 38.

484. Silas Atkins' Tomb. No. 14.

485. .... lies ye Body .. John Atkins, son of Mr Silas & Mrs Mary Atkins, aged 5 months, Died May 7th 1765.

486. Here lies the body of Isaiah Atkins, son of Mr Silas & Mrs Mary Atkins, who died May the 13th 1763, aged 8 months.

487. In memory of George, son of Thomas and Sarah Robbins, Died Sept 19ᵗʰ 1792, aged 14 months, 13 days.

488. In memory of Mr Thomas Robbins, who died March 11ᵗʰ 1803, in the 49ᵗʰ year of his Age.

(4 lines of verse.)

489. Here lies the Body of Mrs Patience Higgins, widow of Mr John Higgins, aged 59 years, Died Febʳʸ yᵉ 4ᵗʰ 1760.

490. Sacred to the Memory of Mrs Betsey Pitman ; wife to Mr Joshua Pitman, who departed this life March 8ᵗʰ 1784, aged 27 years.

(7 lines of blank verse.)

491. ... . wife of .... who departed .... April 2ᵈ, 1801, age 42 years.

492. John Maverick.

493. John, son to John & Elizabeth Maverick aged about 8 years, decᵈ Janʳʸ yᵉ 24ᵗʰ 1719–20.

494. Here lyes buried the Body of Mr Richard Henchman aged 70 years, decᵈ February yᵉ 15ᵗʰ 1724–5.

495. In memory of Mr John Lucking, a native of England who died Apr. 14ᵗʰ 1804, Æt. 36.

(3 lines of verse.)

496. Here lyes Buried the Body of Mr Jonathan Tarbox, who Departed this Life May the 3ᵈ 1769, aged 72 years.

497. Here lies the Body of Mr Jonathan Tarbox, eldest son of Mr Jonaⁿ & Mrs Mary Tarbox, who departed this Life, July 7ᵗʰ AD. 1760, In yᵉ 34ᵗʰ year of his age.

498. Here lies the Body of Mrs Mary Tarbox, wife of Mr. Jonathan Tarbox, who departed this life Janʳʸ the 19ᵗʰ 1763, in the 60ᵗʰ year of her age.

499. In memory of Capt Benjⁿ Hammatt, who died Apr 7ᵗʰ 1805, Æt. 93.

500. Here lyes yᵉ Body of Mrs Elizabeth Barnard, wife to Capt. Thomas Barnard, aged about 58 years, deceased September yᵉ 14ᵗʰ 1716.

501. Richard Hazly (footstone).

502. Here lyes buried the body of Mr John Briggs, aged 34 years, Died Novʳ yᵉ .. 1721, aged 34 years.

503. John yᵉ son of John & Deborah Briggs, deceasᵈ September yᵉ 4ᵗʰ 1717, aged 18 dayes.

504. Sacred to the memory of Mr Nicholas Brown, who died May 14ᵗʰ 1801, aged 49 years.

505. Here lyes buried the body of Mrs Lettuce Hood, wife to Mr Cumbey Hood, aged 25 years, died July yᵉ 10ᵗʰ 1747.

506. ... Brown, who died July ye 14th 1761, aged 6 months.

507. Sacred to the memory of Mrs Elizabeth Brown, wife of Mr Nicholas Brown, who died Decr 11th 1803, aged 35 years.

(14 lines of verse.)

508. Sacred to the Memory of Mr John Bankamp, who died March 21st 1805, aged 34 years. He was a native of Prussia, on his return from the West Indies to his native country. It may with truth be said of this worthy stranger, in his life he was an example of goodness & greatness of mind rarely to be met with, and died the Death of the Righteous Man.

509. Here lyes the Body of Mrs Mary Neck, widdow, Dec^d March ye 27th 1729, in ye 80th year of her age.

510. Mr William Clough, 1798 (footstone).

511. Here lyes buried the Body of Mrs Hannah Tuttle, wife to Mr Elisha Tuttle, dec^d May ye 15th 1736, in ye 67 year of her age.

512. Here lyes ye Body of Joses Tuttle, son of Mr. Elisha & Mrs Hannah Tuttle, aged 17 years 10 m^o Died July 17, 1712.

513. Here lyes buried the Body of Capt Thomas Templer, who was born in the city of Exeter, & died August ye 3^d 1745, aged 47 years.

514. Here lies the body of Mrs Anna Blair, wife of Mr Brice Blair, died Sept 13th 1756, aged 80 years. As also the Body of Mrs Rosanna Creighton, daughter to said Mrs Blair, died Octr 12th 1756, aged 42 years.

515. Here lyes ye Body of Mr David Crawford, born in Greenock in Scotland, who dec^d Novr 20th 1738, aged 54 years.

516. Sacred to the memory of Ebenezer Woodward, who died Novr 9th 1805, in the 54th year of his age.

517. In memory of Mrs Margaret, wife of Mr John Boies of Waltham & daughter of Mr Robt Duncan, died Oct. 21st 1779 Æt. 60.

518. Sacred to the memory of Mrs Elizabeth Cutter, wife of Mr Ammi Cutter, Junr, who departed this life June 13th 1801, aged 28 years.

Blessed are the dead, that die in the Lord.

519. Here lies buried the Body of Mrs Mary Blackador, widow of Capt. Christopher Blackador, aged 43 years, died Oct 23^d 1751.

520. Here lyes ye Body of Mrs Sarah Brown, Relict of Mr James Brown late of Ipswich dec^d, departed this Life May 16th 1772, aged 76.

521. Here lyes ye Body of Mr Thomas Lasinby Who Died June 24th A.D 1747, aged 60 years.

522. Here lyes ye Body of Capt John Sunderland, aged 64 years, deceased September ye 11th 1724.

523. Nathaniel y·· son of John & Mary Sunderland, aged 6 days, died June yᵉ 22, 1699.

524. Here lies deposited the Remains of Hezekiah Wyman. son of Wᵐ & Elizabeth Wyman, who died Oct. 24, 1808, Æ. 6 years & 5 mo.

(6 lines of verse.)

525. Sacred to the Memory of Mr Peter Gilman, who departed this life, April 12ᵗʰ 1807, aged 42 years.

(4 lines of verse.)

526. Here lyes yᵉ Body of Mrs Mary Brown, Wife to Mr Benjamin Brown, Decᵈ Nouʳ yᵉ 25ᵗ 1728, in yᵉ 45 year of her age.

527. Samuel. yᵉ son of James & Mary Traworthy, aged 2 Mᵒ died April yᵉ 19, 1697.

528. Here lies buried the Body of Capt John Troth, who died Sept. 19ᵗʰ 1781. aged 79 years.

529. In memory of Mrs Judith Troth, Wife of Capt. John Troth, Died May 17ᵗʰ 1786, aged 75 years.

530. This Monument, erected June 4. 1848, by Robert G. Shaw, Son of Francis Shaw, Jr. & Hannah Nickels, as a tribute of respect to his deceased Relations.

531. Major Samuel Shaw, third son of Francis & Sarah, served as an Officer in the Revolutionary War, from its commencement to its close. On the 22d of Feb. 1784, he sailed from New York in the Ship Empress of China, for Canton, as Supercargo & part ownerₜ: this being the first vessel that sailed from the U. States for that place. He was appointed by Washington, Consul to China, which office he held until his death, in 1794.

532. In Memory of Francis Shaw, born in Boston 1721, died Oct. 18, 1784 aged 64. Sarah Burt, his wife, born in Boston 1726, died Sept. 1799, aged 74. Their children were Francis, jr. died at Gouldsboro, Me. 1785 aged 37. John died at Gouldsboro, Maine, 1780 aged 30. Sarah, wife of Samuel Parkman, Esq. Died at Boston, 1782, aged 30. Samuel, died on his passage from Canton 1794, aged 39. William died while on a journey at Charlemont 1803, aged 46. Abigail, wife of Jⁿᵒ Crocker, died at Washington D.C. Aug 12, 1797, aged 40. Benjamin, died at New York, 1807, aged 49. Nathaniel died on his passage from Canton 1791, aged 30.

533. In memory of John Burt died Jany 1745, aged 54. Wᵐ Burt, died Feb. 1752 aged 26. Susannah Burt, died Feb. 1752, aged 21. Samuel Burt died Sept 1754, aged 30. Abigail Burt. died Aug. 1778 aged 90. Benj. Burt, died 1803, aged 75. Nath. Howland, died July 1766, aged 62, and Abigail Burt his wife, died July 1766, aged 49.

534. John yᵉ son of John and Mary Robinson, aged 17 months died August yᵉ 2, 1690.

535. Here lyes Buried the Body of Mr. Harbottle Dorr, Died June ye 12th 1746, Ætatis suæ 50 years, one month and 8 D^s.

536. Here lies Buried the Body of Mrs. Dorothy Dorr, widow to Mr. Harbottle Dorr, Died April 16th 1765. aged 65 years.

537. In memory of Stephen Kent Chadwick, son to Capt. Nathaniel and Mrs. Sibbil Chadwick. died April 27th 1790, aged 2 years and 8 months

[Verses.]

538. Mrs. Mary Hudson (footstone.)

539. Here lyes ye Body of Mr. Timothy Thornton, aged 79 years, dec^d Sep^t ye 19th 1726

540. Here lyes ye Body of Mrs Sarah Thornton, wife of Mr. Timothy Thornton, aged 86 years, dec^d Decr ye 3^d 1725.

541. Elizabeth Loring, Dau^r to Mr David & Mrs Eliz. Loring, died Sept 23^d. 1767. aged 17 months.

542. Here lyes Buried the Body of Mr John Butler, who departed this Life June the 14th 1748, aged 37 years 5 m^o & 16 D^s.

543. Susanna. Dau^r to Mr John & Mrs Thankfull Butler. Aged 14 M^o. Died Octr 5th 1738.

544. Thankfull Butler, Dau^r of Mr John & Thankfull Butler Aged 1 year, 7 m^o, & 23 D^s Died Octr 1st 1741

545. In memory of Mrs Ann Butler. Wife of Mr John Butler of Falmouth & Dau^r of Mrs Parnell Codman of Charlestown, Died May 18th 1783 Ae. 50 years & 6 m^o. A kind & tender wife.

546. Here lies Buried the body of Mrs Abigail Adams, Wife of Mr Benjamin Adams, who departed this Life, Jan^ry the 17th 1764, in the 35th year of her age & Eunice her babe seven weeks old.

547. Here lies buried the Body of Capt John Dobel, died the 8th of April 1773, aged 70 years.

548. Here lies buried the Body of Mrs Abigail Dobel, wife to Capt. John Dobel. who departed this life, November the 5th 1769, aged 59 years.

549. In Memory of Mrs Mary Dobel, who died Decr 3^d 1709, Æ. 55, also her husband, Capt. Joseph Dobel Senr died March 19, 1801, Æt. 71

[4 lines of verse.]

550. Here lies buried the Body of Mrs Sarah Butler, wife to Mr Joseph Butler, died Oct. 25, 1754, aged 38 years & 7 months.

551. Here lyes the Body of Mrs Hannah Butler, aged 59 years, who died May ye 20th 1749

552. Sarah Butler, Dau^r to Mr Joseph & Mrs Sarah Butler Died Octr 9th 1751, aged 1 year, 5 m^o & 19 D^s.

553. Sarah Butler, Dauʳ of Mr ... Sarah Butler, Died Sept yᵉ 11ᵗʰ 1747, aged 1 year & 4 mo.

554. Mathew, son of Mr John & Mrs Thankfull Butler aged 8 months, died July 30ᵗʰ 1743.

555. Here lyes yᵉ Body of Mr Thomas Hunt, aged 73 years & 7 months, who decᵈ Febʳʸ yᵉ 11ᵗʰ 1721–2

556. Here lyeth yᵉ Body of Nicholas Stone, aged 76 years, died December yᵉ 9ᵗʰ 1689.

557. Jacob Hewens, aged 36 years, decᵈ July yᵉ 6, 1690

558. Also Jacob Hewens, yᵉ son of Jacob & Martha Hewens, aged 4 days, died Oct yᵉ 7, 1673.

559. Here lies buried the body of Mr John Demery, who died March yᵉ 13ᵗʰ 1758, in yᵉ 77ᵗʰ year of his age.

560. Jean Treuis, late wife to Daniell Treuis, aged near 100 years, died June yᵉ 30ᵗʰ 1706.

561. ...... son ..... .ohn .... 9 years. 5 months .... yᵉ 11ᵗʰ ..31–2.

562. In Memory of Mr Benjamin Goodwin. died Nov. 30ᵗʰ 1792, aged 61 years. Mrs Hannah Goodwin. died Octʳ 25ᵗʰ 1775, aged 42 years; Wife of Mr Benjamin Goodwin. Nancy Weatherston Goodwin, died Oct. 21ˢᵗ 1775, aged 11 Days, daughter of Mr. Benjamin & Mrs Hannah Goodwin.

563. Sacred to the Memory of Mrs Sarah Bennett, Wife of Mr. Briggs Bennett, who departed this Life, April 9ᵗʰ 1803, aged 20 years. Allso Her Infant daughter.

564. Here lies the Body of Mrs Sarah Bennett, Widdow of Capᵗ Elles Bennett, who departed this Life July 31ˢᵗ 1765, in yᵉ 68ᵗʰ year of her age.

565. Ann Hobby, daugʳ of John & Ann Hobby, aged 7 days, died yᵉ 3ᵈ of April 1711. Richard Hobby, son of John & Anna Hobby, aged 13 years, Died Apr yᵉ 13ᵗʰ 1711.

566. In memory of Mr Elijah Swift, who died May 9ᵗʰ 1803; aged 73 years.

567. Here lies yᵉ Body of William Swift, son of Mr Elijah & Mrs Eddee Swift, aged 6 months. Died April yᵉ 1ˢᵗ 1765.

568. In Memory of Mrs Edee Swift, Wife of Mr Elijah Swift, who died Octʳ 12ᵗʰ 1795, Aged 64 years.

569. Here lies yᵉ Body of Mary Swift, Dauʳ to Mr James & Mrs Mary Swift, died April the 9ᵗʰ 1764, aged 10 years.

570. Here lyeth buried yᵉ Body of Lydia Garish yᵉ wife of John Garish, aged about 27 years ; decᵈ January yᵉ 8ᵗʰ 1697–8

571. John B. Sholes, John J. Ulmer's Tomb. No. 2.

572. Here lyeth buried yᵉ Body of Lydia Watts. aged 55 years, decᵈ September yᵉ 29, 1700

573. Benj^a Tout, aged 4 years, 5 m^o & 5 D^s, Dec^d July ye 20, 1729, Martha Tout aged 4 months, Dec^d Novr ye 19th 1727; ye children of Benjⁿ & Jane Tout.

574. Elizabth Tout, aged 42 years, dec^d Oct ye 24 1678.

575. Sarah Tout, aged 5 weeks, died 1678.

576. Mary Tout aged 1 year, dyed October ye 19, 1678.

577. William Ellis, son to William & Susannah Ellis, aged 2 year & 7 m^o died Sep^t ye 8th 1694.

578. Ellis, son to Mr Ellis & Mrs Sarah Bennet, aged 5 months, deceased July ye 23^d 1733.

579. Here lyes ye Body of Mr Richard Hunnewell; who Died Nov^{br} ye 27th 1742, in ye 61st year of his age.

580. Here lyes ye Body of Mrs Sarah Hunywell, wife to Mr Richard Hunywell, aged 66 years, Dec^d July ye 30, 1723.

581. Isaac Dupee. Heir to Goodridge. Erected by Isaac Dupee, Grandson to G., aged LXXV August 31, 1846.

582. Here lyes Buried the Body of Elizabeth Dupee Freeland, died Sept 22^d 1766, aged 20 years and 2 months.

583. In Memory of Mr James Freeland, who departed this life July 20th 1802; aged 64 years. In all his connections, as a Husband, Parent and Friend, he was amiable, beneficent and true. (7 lines.)

584. Susanna Barr, wife to John Barr, aged 40 years died March ye 6, 1701–2. also Elizabeth ..... aged 17 years Died Nov. ... 1700.

585. Here lyes ye body of Charles Demery aged about 60 years. Died Nov^{br} y^d 22, 1717

586. Here lyeth buried ye Body of James Ingles, aged 70 years & 6 mo. deceased February ye 6, 1702–3.

587. Here lyeth intered the body of Joanna ingles, wife to James ingles, aged 37 years, departed this life the 11^t of September, 1678.

588. Here lyes ye Body of Mrs Martha Tucks, aged 65 years dec^d November ye 4th 1729

589. Here lies ye Body of Mrs Mary Perkins, ye wife of Capt. William Perkins. She died July 8th 1756, aged 38 years

590. David Watson's Tomb. 1811. No. 3.

591. Here lyes y^r Body of Mrs Sarah Sarvise the Wife of Mr Samuel Sarvise, dec^d Augst 4th 1739, in the 32^d year of her age.

592. Here lyes Buried the Body of Maria Servise, wife to Mr Samuel Servise, died Decr ye 17th 1742, in the 35th year of her age.

593. Here lies ye Body of Mr George Sharrow, aged 54 years, who Died Octr 6th 1743.

594. Allso, Hemmen Henderson, aged 18 years, Died April 19th 1738.

595. Here lyes y⁰ body of Mr Jeremiah Cushing, aged 55 years, died July y⁰ 18, 1722.

596. Here lies y⁰ Body of Mr Jeremiah Cushing. Died October y⁰ 24ᵗʰ 1755, aged 63 years.

597. Here lies y⁰ Body of Mrs Ann Cushing, wife of Mr Jeremiah Cushing, Died August y⁰ 15 ᵗ 1759, aged 55 years.

598. Sacred to the Memory of Capt Ralph Beatley, who departed this Life, Oct. 16ᵗʰ 1804, aged 42 years

[4 lines of verse.]

599. Mrs Sarah Hodge (footstone)

600. In Memory of Capt John Buckley, who died on Fryday, 9ᵗʰ August, 1799, aged 58 years.

601. Mr John Morrison. Mrs Nancy Domack.

602. In Memory of Mrs Nancy Holden, the wife of Mr. Thomas Holden, who died 25 May. 1802; aged 19 years, 2 months & 4 days, also an infant buried with her.

603. Here lies the remains of David Alexander. son of Mr. John & Mrs Ellen Morrison, who died May 1ˢᵗ, Æt. 14½ months.

604. In Memory of Mr. Enoch Hopkins, who departed this Life Decʳ 27ᵗʰ 1778, Æ 55 years

(4 lines of verse)

605. Here lyes ye body of Mr Thomas Nowel, aged .. years, decᵈ ... y⁰ 13, ...0.

606. Lidia Nowell, wife to George Nowell, aged 68 years, died Decemʳ y⁰ 18ᵗʰ 1704.

607. In Memory of Mrs Deborah Nowell, wife of Mr George Nowell, died May 6ᵗʰ 1794, aged 56 years.

608. Here lyes the Body of Mr Samuel Jones, decᵈ Augᵗ y⁰ 26, 1731, in y⁰ 42ᵈ year of his age.

609. Thomas Nowell son to Mr Thomas & Mrs Elizᵗʰ Nowell, decᵈ Decemʳ y⁰ 30, 1739, in y⁰ 9ᵗʰ year of her age.

610. Edmund Hartt's Tomb. 1806 No. 55.

611. In memory of Mr George Nowell obᵗ Augᵗ. 29 1802, Æt 64. Also a grand-child, William, son of John & Sarah Taylor, obᵗ Octʳ 3ᵈ 1808, Æt, 15 m.

612. Here lyeth buried y⁰ Body of John Ireland, aged 18 years, 7 months & 10 days, died February y⁰ 15, 1701-2.

613. Here lyes y⁰ Body of Mary Hill, Wife to Edward Hill, aged about 42 years, died Janʳʸ y⁰ 20ᵗʰ 1721-2

614. Here lyes y⁰ Body of Mrs Mary Nowel, Wife to Mr Thomas Nowel, aged 45 years, decᵈ May y⁰ 29ᵗʰ 1739.

615. Here lies yᵉ Body of Mrs Lydia Cullam, Wife to Capt John Cullam, who Died Novʳ yᵉ 3ᵈ 1761, aged 42 years.

616. Here lyes buried the body of Mr Richard. True, aged 38 years, who died ye 29th of Aug. 1744.

617. In memory of Mrs Hannah Giles, Wife of Mr John Giles, who died August 12th 1805, aged 26 years.   A native of Plymouth, England.   Also her Infant Son.

(4 lines of verse.)

618. Benjamin Chub. the son of Mr Benjamin & Mrs Lydia Chub, aged 3 months died Decr ye 4th 1722.

619. Here lies Buried the Body of Mrs Hannah Bill, Wife of Mr Hezekiah Bill, Died Nov 20th 1760, in the 40th year of her age.

620. Here lyeth buried ye Body of Abigail Bill, wife to Thomas Bill, aged 63 years, died Novem. ye 7th 1696.

621. Here lies Buried the Body of Miss Polly Bill, who Departed this Life August 30th 1782, in the 21st year of her age

(2 lines.)

622. Here lies buried the Body of Capt John Dorrington Obit 14th March 1772, Ætatis 44

623. Here lyes ye body of Eliphal Graves, wife of Ebenezer Graves, & Dau^r of William & Elizabeth Stretton, aged 27 years, 11 m^o & 20 days, Dec^d April ye 15th 1717.

624. Here lyes ye Body of Mrs Ann Waldo, Wife to Mr John Waldo, aged about 31 years, died Feb^{ry} ye 2^d 1723.   Also a child still-borne.

625. Sarah Rous, Wife to William Rous, Aged 61 years, died August 29. 1705

626. Here lyes ye body of Mrs Rebecca Rouse, wife of Mr. William Rouse, Aged 28 years & 7 M^o. died Augst 15th 1742

627. Underneath this monumental Stone, lies deposited the Body of Mr Joseph Hemmenway, who departed this Life Jany 15th 1806, aged 59 years.   He was a respectable man & worthy citizen to his country

(4 lines of verse.)

628. Here lies ye Body of Samuel Hopkins, son to Mr Enoch & Mrs Mary Hopkins, who died Sep^t 23^d 1767, aged 1 year & 8 months.

629. Mary. Dau^r to Joseph & Rebecca Snelling, aged 9 mo. & 21 days, Dec^d Augt ye 29, 1719

630. Nath^{el} Snelling, Son to Mr Joseph & Mrs Priscilla Snelling Died May 26th 1745, aged 8 months & 12 D^s.

631. Here lyes ye Body of Mary Snelling, wife to Mr Joseph Snelling, aged 26 years, 9 m^o & 19 days, Died Jany ye 28th 1724.

632. In Memory of Mrs Priscilla Snelling, widow of Joseph Snelling who departed this life Augst 2^d 1791, aged 79 years

633. In Memory of Mrs Eliza Fuller, wife of Mr John Fuller, who died Sept. 16th 1806, aged 22 years.

(2 lines of verse)

634. Here lyes Buried ye Body of Mrs Rebeckah Snelling, wife to Mr Joseph Snelling ; who Died Novmbr 7th 1730 aged 56 years, 7 mo & 20 Ds.

635. In Memory of Miss Rebecca Snelling, who departed this life May 26th 1802, in the 63d year of her age.

636. Here lies ye Body of Rebecca Snelling, Daur of Mr Josiah & Mrs Mary Snelling, Died April ye 20th 1777, Ae 5 years & 10 Ds.

637. John, son to Thomas and Silence Barnard, aged 16 mo & 28 days, died Sept ye 5th 1719.

638. In Memory of Mrs Hannah Brown, widow of the late Bartholomew Brown, obt. March 29th 1810, aged 50 years

(6 lines of verse.)

639. John Bowman, son of Mr Jonathan & Mrs Mary Bowman, Died July 4th 1730, aged 3 years.

640. Here resteth the Body of John Buckley, Junior ; son of John Buckley of Saddleworth near Manchester, old England, Merchant, who departed this Life the 23d day of August, 1798, in the 23d year of his age.

(8 lines of verse.)

641. In Memory of Mary Buckley, who departed this Life Octr 21st 1793, aged 64 years.

642. Here lyeth buried the Body of Artor Kaind, aged 75 years, Departed this Life, the 24 day of March, 1686–7.

643. Here lyes Interred ye body of Jane Kind, widdow of Arthur Kind, aged 86 years, died ye 3d of April 1710.

644. Mary Kind, age, dyed ye 15 of August, 1662. William Kind, aged about 1 year, dyed ye 14 of February 1666. The children of Arthur & Jane Kind.

645. Thomas Kaind, son to Arthur & .ane Kaind, aged .0 years, died August 25, 1678.

646. Here lyeth ye body of Rachel ye wife of John Kind, aged about 38 years, Decd July ye 6 1690.

647. Here lyes ye Body of Elizabeth King, Wife to John King aged about 38 years, died Novr ye 29th 1715.

648. This Stone is in Memory of Mrs Elizabeth McKean, Wife of Mr William McKean, who died 8 July, 1792, in the 44th Year of her Age.

649. Here lies ye Body of Mrs Rebekah Welch, Widow to Mr. William Welch, & Daur of Mr John & Mrs Mary King of this town, died Octr 23, 1767, in ye 38th year of her age.

650. ....er buried ..e Body of Mrs Hannah Nichols, wife to Mr William Nichols, dec^d March 22^d 1769, aged 56 years.

651. In Memory of Mary Creighton, dau^r of George & Mary Creighton died April 5th 1801, Æ 2 years & 7 months.

652. Sacred to the memory Mr. Sampson Mason, who departed this life Aug^st 28th 1807, Aged 36 years

653. Sacred to the Memory of Mr Elijah Corlew, who departed this life May 25th 1804, aged 31 years ; also his infant child

(2 lines of verse.)

654. Sacred to the memory of Lydia Mason, wife of Sampson Mason, who died Decr 30th 1803, aged 29 years

(4 lines of verse.)

655. Here lyes ye Body of Mrs Dorcas Peggy, wife to Mr. Edward Peggy, aged 65 years, died October the 24th 1720.

656. Capt. Henry Atkins & Mrs Salome Rich's Tomb. 1807 No. 97.

657. Here lies ye Body of Eliz^th Adams, daut. to Joseph & Eliz^th Adams, aged 30 years & 6 m^o dec^d Novr ye 2^d 1725

658. Joel Shipley & Hiram Smith's Tomb. 1818. No. 98.

659. Here lyes ye Body of Richard Furbur, son of Mr. Richard and Mrs Abigail Furbur, who died March 8th 1749, aged 6 years & 8 months.

660. Here lies buried the Body of Mr Richard Furber, died Feb^ry 15th 1753, aged 38 years,

661. In Memory of Miss Elizabeth Furbur, Dau^r of Mr Richard & Mrs Abigail Furbur, who Died May 10th 1790, aged 41 years.

(5 lines of verse.)

662. Tomb of Ann Freeland, Repaired 1845. No. 99.

663. Here lyes buried the Body of Mr Jonathan Marsters, aged 44 years, dec^d Feb^ry ye 12, 1732

664. Tomb of John Spence & Moses Pond. 1852. No. 100.

665. Here lyeth buried ye body of Matthew Armstrong, aged 37 years, departed this life, May ye 10 1671.

666. Here lyes burried ye body of Matthew Armstrong, aged 43 years, departed this life September the 21st 1709.

667. Here lyeth buried ye Body of Moses Draper, aged about 31 years, dec^d ye 14 of August 1693.

668. Here lyeth buried ye Body of Mathew Pittom, ye son of John & Mary Pittom, aged near 20 years, died January ye 26th 1693–4.

669. Here lyes the Body of Mr James Barter, aged 71 years died May 16, 1757

670. .ere lyes y⁰ Body of .annah Carthew, aged 66 years dec^d Jany 20th 1713–4.

671. Here lyes y⁰ body of Mr Isaac Adams aged 59 years, who died December y⁰ 30th 1732.

672. Here lyes interred the Body of Mr Leonard Drowne, who departed this life, October y⁰ 31st 1729, in y⁰ 83^d year of his age.

673. William Mason, son to Mr William and & Mrs Deborah Mason, aged 15 days, Dec^d Novr y⁰ 24, 172. .

674. William, son to Mr William & Mrs Deborah Mason, aged 10 weeks, & 1 day, Dec^d Septr y⁰ 23^d 1732.

675. Here lyes the Body of Mr Philip Merritt, dec^d March ye 29th 1741, in y⁰ 70th year of his age.

676. Here lyes the Body of Mrs Mary Merritt, wife to Mr. Philip Merritt, dec^d Sept y⁰ 20th 1735, in y⁰ 60th year of her age.

677. Here lyes y⁰ body of Joseph Lewis, aged 30 years, & 6 m⁰ dec^d Novr ye 23^d 1729.

678. Beneath this stone are deposited the Remains of Mrs Mary Lewis, Widow of Capt Winslow Lewis, who departed this life Dec. 31st 1806, aged 60 years.

The memory of the just is blessed.

679. William, son to William & Elydia Letherbee, aged 16 m⁰ died Sept ye 21st 1710.

680. This Monument is erected in Memory of Mrs Sarah Mulvana, who died July 4, 1805, aged 68 years.

(2 lines of verse.)

681. In Memory of Wm Albert Palmer, son of Ezra & Elizabeth Palmer, who died May 19th 1813.

682. Sacred to the memory of Mrs Bethia Gilman, wife of Peter Gilman, who departed this life Jany 22^d 1806, aged 40 years

683. Here lies the Body of Sally Goodwin, Wife to Capt. Nathaniel Goodwin of Charlestown, and Eldest Daughter of Mr John & Sarah Stone of Newbury Port, who departed this Life, Aug^st 23^d 1781, aged 25 years.

684. Here lyes the Body of Mrs Rebecca Parham, widow of Mr. Joseph Parham, died April 28th 1753, in ye 82^d year of her age Also the Body of Mrs Sarah Parham wife to Mr Joseph Parham died May ye 27th 1752, Aged 41 years & 5 m⁰.

685. Mrs Abigail Roberts (footstone.)

686. In Memory of Mrs Lydia Gilman, Wife of Mr Peter Gilman who died March 6th 1796, in the 28th year of her age.

2 lines of verse.

687. In Memory of Mrs Abigail Gilman, Wife of Mr Peter Gilman who died July 3^d 1802, aged 29 years.

688. Sacred to the Memory of Peter Gilman Juʳ Son of Peter and Lydia Gilman, who died July 11ᵗʰ 1804, aged 13 years.

689. Harris C. Proctor, son of John C. Proctor, died March 9ᵗʰ 1818, Æt. 17 hours.

690. In Memory of Eliza Lane Proctor, daughter of Mr Benjamin and Mrs Eliza Proctor, who died Octʳ 15ᵗʰ 1802, aged 1 year and 6 months

691. Sarah, daughter of John & Experience Roberts, aged 4 years & 11 mᵒ, decᵈ Decʳ yᵉ 9, 1690.

692. Here lies buried the Body of Mr John White Roberts, died Novʳ 20ᵗʰ 1771, aged 36 years.

693. Abigail Larrabee, Daughᵗʳ of Deacᵒⁿ William & Mrs Lydia Larrabee, Decᵈ July yᵉ 3ᵈ 1729, aged 15 months.

694. Benjamin Larrabee, son of Deacon William & Mrs Lydia Larrabee, decᵈ May 9ᵗʰ 1730. Aged 3 years and 10 months.

695. In Memory of Mrs Mercy Roberts, Relict of Mr John White Roberts, who died May 2ᵈ 1799, aged 61 years.

(2 lines of verse.)

696. Bethiah Way, the Wife of Richard Way, aged 40 years died August the .. 1678.

697. A & J Lincoln's Tomb. 1805. No. 7.

698. Here lyes Buried yᵉ Body of Mrs Jane Chamberlain, Relict of Mr John Chamberlain, who Died May 20ᵗʰ 1738, aged 68 years.

699. Here lyes yᵉ body of Mrs Martha, wife to Mr Ebenezer Chamberlin, aged 50 years, dec. April yᵉ 10ᵗʰ 1734.

700. Here lyes yᵉ body of Mr Ebenezer Chamberlin, aged 50 years, decᵈ Febʳʸ yᵉ 26ᵗʰ 1729–30.

701. William Dodd's Tomb. 1807 No. 39.

702. Benjamin Smith's Tomb. Built 1805. No. 40.

703. Capt Benj. Edwards' Tomb.

704. John & James Dodd 1821. Tomb No 10.

705. Here lyeth buried yᵉ Body of William Waters, yᵉ son of Samson & Rebecca Waters, aged 21 years, 3 mo & 12 days, Decᵈ June yᵉ 15, 1691

706. Here lies Buried the Body of Mr William Waters, He died Augᵗ yᵉ 10ᵗʰ 1757, aged 85.

707. Here lyes buried the body of Mrs Rebeckah Watters, widdow of Mr John Watters, aged 44 years, Dyed April yᵉ 9ᵗʰ 1745.

708. In Memory of John Waters, son of Capt Abraham & Mrs Sukey Waters, who died Octʳ 24ᵗʰ 1799, aged 1 year & 9 months

709. Here lyes the Body of Mr Bartholomew Stretton, aged 60 years, decᵈ Janʳʸ yᵉ 9, 1686–7.

710. Here lyes ye body of Mrs Eliphal, wife to Mr Bartholomew Stretton, dec^d Jan^ry y^c 19, 1724–5, in y^c 88th year of her age.

711. Here lyes ye Body of Eliz^th Stretton, dau^r of William & Eliz^th Stretton, aged 33 years, 9 mo & 26 days, dec^d Feb^ry ye 15, 1720–1.

712. Here lyes ye body of Mrs Elizabeth Stretton, wife to Mr William Stretton, dec^d May ye 14th 1727, in ye 64th year of her age.

713. Here lyes ye Body of Mary Adams, Wife to Nathanel Adams, aged 77 years, died June y^c 11th 1707.

714. Here lies Burried the Body of Mrs Elizabeth Sargent, Wife to Mr Thomas Sargent, who Departed this Life, May the 19th 1770, aged 60 years.

715. Here lyes ye Body of Mrs Dorcas Demount, Wife to Mr John Demount, Who Died May 19th 1738, aged 55 years

716. Here lyeth buried ye Body of Kathron Way, y^c wife of Richard Way, aged about 55 years, who deceased ye 28 day of April 1689

717. Lydia, wife to Robert Millar, aged 32 years, Dec^d December ye 11, 1678

718. Samuel Miller, aged 7 months and odd dayes, died ye 10 of June 1697, ye son of Alexander & Dorcas Miller,

719. Here lies the Body of Mrs Sarah Miller, Wife of Mr James Miller, aged 45 years, died Feb^ry 6th 1755

720. Jane, dau. of Joseph and Mary Burdsell, aged 1 year & 8 mo. died 1721

721. Here lyes ye body of Mrs Elizabeth Douglis, wife to Capt. Joseph Douglis, aged about 30 years, Deceased Jan^ry y^c 22^d 1725–6.

722. Underneath this Turf rest the Sacred remains of Mr Caleb Beal, who died Decr 10th 1801 ; Ætat. 55 years.

723. Sacred to the memory of Mrs Judith Adams; wife of Mr. Elijah Adams, who departed this Life Aug^st 22^d 1808, in the 55th year of her age. Also her former husband, Mr Nathan Townsend, who departed this Life Octr 12th 1786 in the 42^d year of his age.

724. Here lyes ye Body of Mrs Elizabeth Burrington, wife to Mr. Thomas Burrington, died June ye 2^d 1723, in 24th year of her age.

725. Here lyeth buried ye Body of Grace Gamman aged 74 years dec^d July ye 27, 1702

726. Jeremiah Tounzan, ye son of Samuel & Abigail Tounzan, aged about 26 years, died September ye 6, 1690.

727. Here lyes the body of Elizabeth Townsend, wife to Solomon Townsend, aged 47 years & 7 m^o Dec^d Sept. ye 21st 1713.

728. In Memory of Judith Townsend, died Oct^o 16th 1771 aged 3 days. Nathan Townsend died Oct^o. 17th 1772, aged 15 months.

Nathan Townsend died April 16th 1777, aged 10 months. John Townsend died June 27th 1783, aged 2 years & 7 mos. the children of Mr Nathan and Mrs Judith Townsend.

729. Here lyes ye Body of Rebecca Twing, wife to Benjamin Twing, aged 36 years, died Jany ye 5th 1717–18.

730. Here lyes ye body of Mrs Abigail Bickford wife to Mr Thomas Bickford, aged 26 years, Decd January ye 21st 1728.

731. Sarah Ellis aged 70 years deceased on ye 4th day of September, 1681.

732. Moses Bass's Tomb. No 106. 1819

733. Susan Bass. No 51. John Bass, died Jan 30, 1848, aged 47 years & 4 mos.

734. Sarah Thomas. Tomb 1805. No 51.

735. Here lys Bury'd the Body of Master Robert Patridge, son of Robert and Mary Patridge, who departed this Life, Nov. 10th 1802, Aged 14 years, 1 Month, and 27 days.
"Sleep on dear youth and take thy rest."

736. John Frost, 1776 (footstone.)

737. In memory of 3 children of Francis & Rebecca Hardy. Francis died Oct. 26th 1807, aged 2 months. John died Augst 28th 1808, aged 2 days. Margaret died Sept. 16th, 1809, aged 6 weeks.

738. Mary, daur to Mr. Abraham & Mrs Mary Gybuat, aged 1 year & 11 Mo Decd July ye 16, 1735

739. Here lyes ye body of Mrs Hannah Elphs, ye wife of Mr William Elphs, aged 27 years, decd June 3d 1737. Hannah Elphs Born & Died May 15, 1737

740. Memento Mori Fugit Hora. Here lyes ye Body of Furnell Smallpeace son of John & Olive Smallpeace, aged 6 years & 4 mo. died August 28th

741. Here lyes ye Body of Left. Mathew Barnard, aged 54 years, decd ye 9th day of May. 1679. Also his mother Alce Barnard dyed 1663 & Mary Barnard his last child dyed 1663.

742. Richard Barnard aged about 44 years died Decr ye 20, 1703

743. Here lyes burried the Body of Mr Richard Barnard, aged 47 years. Died May ye 31st 1745.

744. Here lyeth interred ye Body of Thomas Kemble aged 67 years & 14 days decd January ye 26, 1688.

745. Here lyeth interred ye Body of Maior Anthony Haywood aged about 50 years, departed this life ye 16 of October, 1689

746. Here lyes ye body of Mary Grater, ye Daur of Mr Robert & Mrs Abigail Grater, died June ye 21st 1741, in ye 20th year of her age.

747. Here lyes yᵉ Body of William Lowd, Son of John & Dabrah Lowd, aged 28 years, deceased yᵉ 17 of December 1690.

748. Elizabeth yᵉ wife of William Lowd aged 23 years Died November yᵉ 25, 1689.

749. Here lyes yᵉ Body of Mrs Margaret Thacher, Wife to Mr Thomas Thacher, aged 38 years, died Sept yᵉ 14, 1719.

750. Here lyes yᵉ Boddy of Mrs Jerusha Caddall, wife of Mr Roburt Caddall, died Novʳ 14ᵗʰ 1771, in yᵉ 30ᵗʰ year of her age.

(4 lines of verse.)

751. In Memory of Mr Clement Collins, who departed this life April the 24ᵗʰ 1787, Æ. 83 years.

752. Here lies burried yᵉ Body of Mrs. Sarah Collins the wife to Mr Clement Collins, departed this life March 29, 1771, aged 62 years.

(Text.)

753. Here lies buried the Body of Capt. Philip Breading who departed this life November 22ᵈ 1764, aged 63 years.

754. Abigail Gyles, Dauʳ of Mr Charles & Mrs Mary Gyles, aged 2 years & 7 mᵒ Decᵈ July 2, 1740.

755. Here lyes the Body of Mrs Mary Gyles, wife to Mr. Charles Gyles, died Octʳ 30ᵗʰ 1757, in the 59ᵗʰ year of her age.

756. Here lies Buried the Body of Mrs Mary Gyles, Dauʳ of Mr Edward & Mrs Elizabeth Gyles, Died Octʳ 22ᵈ 1777, aged 25 years & 4 mᵒ

757. In Memory of Mrs Mary Gyles, Relict of Mr John Gyles, who died April 13th 1795, aged 70 years. well beloved in life & much lamented in death.

758. Here lyes yᵉ Body of Mr Peletiah Kinsman, aged 47 years, decᵈ April yᵉ 2ᵈ 1727.

759. Mrs Ruth Adams 1781 (foot-stone.)

760. Here lies Buried the Body of Mrs Sarah Malcom, Wife to Mr Richard Malcom, Died Sept. 23ᵈ 1767.

761. Here lies Buried the Body of Mrs Abigail Taylor, departed this life Octʳ 26ᵗʰ 1774, aged 75 years & 9 months.

762. Here lyes buried yᵉ Body of Mr Robert Cumby aged 62 years & 5 mo. decᵈ July yᵉ 17ᵗʰ 1717

763. Here lyes burried the Body of Mrs Rebecca Cumby wife to Mr Robert Cumby, decᵈ April yᵉ 26, 1731 in the 76ᵗʰ year of her age.

764. Here lyes buried yᵉ Body of Jonathan Adams aged about 64 years, died April yᵉ 7ᵗʰ 1707.

765. Here lyes Buried yᵉ Body of Mrs Rebecca Adams wife to Mr Jonathan Adams, who Died Decᵇʳ 22ᵈ 1731, Aged about 76 years.

766. Here lyes yᵉ Body of Josiah Adams yᵉ son of Jonathan & Rebecca Adams aged 16 Mᵒ Decᵈ September the 6, 1699.

767. In Memory of Mary Waters, Wife of Capt Daniel Waters, formerly wife of Mr Peter Mortamore, Born in the City of Waterford in the Kingdom of Ireland. She died June 7ᵗʰ 1802, Æt. 78.

768. Here lyes yᵉ body of Joseph Watters aged about 17 years & 3 Mᵒ Died May yᵉ 24ᵗʰ 1709.

769. George Sutherland's Tomb. No. 105. 1809.

770. Here lyes yᵉ Body of Ann Ruby, dauʳ of John & Elizᵗʰ Ruby, aged 17 years, died Septʳ yⁿ 19ᵗʰ 1741.

771. In Memory of John Kent, son of Seth & Elizᵗʰ Kent, who died 30ᵗʰ Sept. 1794, aged 6 years.

772. Sacred to the Memory of Mrs Elizabeth Kent, Wife of Mr Seth Kent, who died July 22ᵈ 1809, aged 41 years.

773. Here lyes yᵉ Body of Mrs Patience Collins, wife of Deacon Joseph Collins. who Suddenly Departed this Life June the 25ᵗʰ 1760, aged 67 years.

774. Here lyes yᵉ Body of Mrs Mary Collins, Wife to Deacon Joseph Collins; Who Departed this Life Decemʳ yᵉ 4ᵗʰ 1761 in yᵉ 78ᵗʰ year of her age.

775. Here lies Buried the Body of Mrs Charity Collins wife of Deacon Joseph Collins, who departed this Life Octᵒʳ 25ᵗʰ 1771 in the 67ᵗʰ year of her age.

776. Here lyes yᵉ Body of Mrs Mary Gardner, wife of Mr John Gardner, aged 39 years decᵈ May yᵉ 22ᵈ 1743

777. In Memory of Ellsy Gardner, Dauʳ of James & Ruth Gardner; who departed this Life Novʳ 17, 1800, aged 5 years & 9 months

(2 lines.)

778. In Memory of Mr James Gardner; who died March 22ᵈ 1802, aged 38 years. " Be ye also ready."

779. Capt. Peter Mortmer.

780. Here lyes the Body of Capt. John Hobby, aged about 50 years, died Sept yᵉ 7, 1711.

781. John Hobby, son of John & Hannah Hobby, aged 3 months, dyed yᵉ 17 of October, 1685.

782. Here lyes buried the body of Mr John Hobby, Aged 49 years, Decᵈ May yᵉ 14ᵗʰ 1741

783. In Memory of Betsy, wife of David Darling, died March 23ᵈ, 1809. Æ. 43. She was the mother of 17 children; and around her lie 12 of them; and 2 were lost at sea. Brother Sextons, Please to leave a clear birth for me near by this stone.

784. Mrs Barbara Patten (foot-stone.)

785. Here lyes yᵉ Body of Mrs Sarah Bass, yᵉ widdow of Capt Phillip Bass, died April yᵉ 26, 1746, in yᵉ 86ᵗʰ year of her age.

786. Sarah, Daughter of Phillip & Sarah Bass, Aged 3 Weeks & 3 dˢ Died July yᵉ 7. 1692.

787. James, son to Mr William & Mrs Lydia Maxwell, aged 2 years decᵈ July yᵉ 3ᵈ 1729.

788.   (Monument without a name thus inscribed
       A Samuel returned to God jn Christ
       after a short abode on earth
       To shun earths harmes & crimes
       Was here well put to bed betimes
       The grave ~ as short as thou : prepare
       Lest thy deat. come at unaware

789. Here lies Buried the Body of Mr Jonathan Farnum Who Died Octʳ 13ᵗʰ 1768, Aged 61 years.

790. In Memory of Mr Jonathan Farnham, who died Decʳ 6ᵗʰ 1804. Æt. 64 ....

791. Sacred to the Memory of Mrs Ruth Farnham, Consort of Mr Jonathan Farnham, Who died May the 23ᵈ, 1799; Aged 52 years.

792. Mr John Mountfort. Ætatis LIV. obt. Janʳʸ VI. MDCC XXIV. Benjamin Mountfort, son of John and Mary Mountfort, ætatis XXV, Obt. March X, MDCC XXI. Tomb No. 7.

793. Jonathan Mountfort   Tomb No. 59.

1724.

794. Here lies interred the Body of Mr James Mortimer, who Departed this Life Aug'st 18th 1773, Aged 69 Years. He was Born in the City of Waterford in the Kingdom of Ireland.

795. Here lies interred the Body of Mrs Hannah Mortimer, wife of Mr James Mortimer, who Departed this Life Augst. 21ˢᵗ 1773, Aged 81 years. She was Born in the City of Waterford, in the Kingdom of Ireland.

796. Sacred to the Memory of Mr Ebenezer Parsons, Who died Aug. 31, 1805 : Aged 23 years.

797. Here lies Buried the Body of Capt. Edward Page, who died July 27th, 1785, aged 34 years.

798. Richard, son to Richard & Maria Wells, aged 2 years, 10 months & 4 days, Dyed yᵉ 8 of Septʳ 1682.

799. Sacred to the Memory of Mr Samuel Wells, who resigned this Life, Novʳ 13ᵗʰ 1804, in the 26 ᵗʰ year of his age.

[4 lines of verse.]

800. Sacred to the memory of William Wells who died Aug^st 8th, 1808, Aged 32 years.

801. Here lyeth buried ye body of John Farnum Senr aged 69 years & 11 monthes & 18 dayes, dec^d January ye 20, 1701–2.

802. Here lyes ... . of Mrs Dorothy Far... wife to Mr John Farnum dec^d Octr ye 17th 1721 in ye 55 year .. ..

803. Joseph Farnum, aged about 30 years, dec^d Novr ye 30, 1678

Ultima semper expe..anda dies
homine dicique beatus
Ante obitum nemo
supremaque funera debet.

804. .... Farnum senior. Aged 85 years, departed this life December ye 6, 1686.

805. Here lyeth ye body of Susannah Farnum, aged 12 years, died September the 23, 1700.

806. Here lyes buried ye body of Susanna Farnum, wife of John Farnham aged 87 years & 7 mo. deceased April ye 26th, 1717.

807. In Memory of Mrs Eliz^th Farnham, wife of Mr Robert Farnham, who died March 20th 1799, Aged 27 years.

808. Here lyes buried the Body of Mr Daniel Graves of the island of Barbados, aged 32 years, died July ye 10, 1739

809. Sacred to the Memory of Mr. George Tompkins, who died Octr 21st 1801, Ætat. 25.

[4 lines of verse.]

810. Here lyeth buried ye Body of John Gill, aged about 60 years dec^d ye 10 Day of December, 1671. Thomas, son of John & Elizabeth Gill aged about 3 M^o Dec^d in Decr 1660.

811. Here lyeth buried ye Body of Elizabeth wife to John Gill, aged about 35 years, dec^d ye 28 of Septr 1666.

812. Here lyes ye body of Samuel, son to Obadiah & Elizabeth Gill, aged 3 year & ½, departed this life ye 29 of May, 1683.

813. Here lies the Body of Mr John Dethick, aged 68 years Dec^d July ye 2^d 1738.

814. Here lyes ye body of Mr Thomas Nowel, aged .. years, dec^d the 13th ....

815. Here lyeth buried ye Body of Sarah Grant, relict of Edward Grant, aged about 61 years, dec^d ye 25 of March 1690.

816. Here lies ye Body of Robert Edmunds, aged 89 years dec^d Novr ye 22^d 1717.

817. Here lies the Body of Mrs Abigail Cades, Wife of Mr John Cades, Died Sept 3, 1777 Aged 37 Years.

818. In Memory of Joanah Cades 4th Daugh^r of John and Abigail Cades, She lived 22 years & died Octr 9th 1792.

819. In Memory of Mary Cades, daugh^r of John & Abigail Cades; who died Augst 18th 1783, aged 6 years.

820. Here lyes ye Body of Mrs. Ann Hobby, Wife of Mr. William Hobby aged 74 years. died June ye 22th 1709   Mr. William Hobby aged 79 years Died August the 24th 1713

821. Here lyes Buried the Body of Mrs Susannah Bentley Wife to Mr. Thomas Bentley.   Aged 42 Years, who died Septr ye 9th 1748.

822. Here lyes ye Body of Mrs Dorcas Phillips, wife to Mr Anderson Phillips, who died Jany 9th 1763, in ye 42^d year of her age.

823. Here lies Buried the Body of Capt. Nathaniel Breed, who Departed this life Augst the 29th 1761, Aged 76 years.

824. Here lyes buried the Body of Mrs Sarah Breed, the wife of Nathaniel Breed, aged 54 years & 10 months, deo^d March 5th 1739–40.

825. Here lyes ye body of Mr Nathaniel Breed who died Jan^{ry} ye 27th 1765, aged 23 years.

826. Here lyes ye Body of Mr Josiah Baker; who Dec^d June ye 19th 1729, in ye 74th Year of his age

827. Sarah Ballard ye wife of Daniel Ballard, aged 46 years died December ye 15th in ye year 1704.

828. Here lyes ye Body of Mr. David Edwards, son of Mr David & Mrs Mary Edwards, aged 43 years & 4 mo. deo^d December ye 4th 1727.

829. Here lyes the body of Samuel Edward aged 38 years died June ye 7th 1710.

830. In memory of Mary Ballard died Decr ye 18th 1769. Aged 3 years; also Elizabeth Ballard, died Decr ye 20th, 1769, aged 1 year and 6 Mo. chil^n of Mr. Bartholomew & Mrs. Mary Ballard.

831. Here lies the body of Mr John Battens Junr late of St Johns Newfoundland who departed this life April 1st 1762. In the 23^d year of his age

832. Here lyes ye Body of Mrs Mehetebel Pratt, Wife to Mr William Pratt who Departed this life August 8th 1750 in ye 57th year of her age

833. Here lies Buried the Body of Mrs Abigail Sherburne Wife to Dea^n Thomas Sherburne departed this life April 8th 1778 aged 61 years & 7 mo.

834. Sarah Winslow aged 26 years died ye 4 day of April 1667.

835. Here lyes buried ye Body of Mrs Lydia Whitemore Wife to Mr John Whitemore Jr died 15th Jan 1750 aged 31 years.

836. Here lyes Buried the Body of Mrs Elizabeth Whittemore wife to Mr John Whittemore Aged 57 years Died Aug ye 13th 1746.

837. Hannah Whittemore Daughter of Benjamin & Elizabeth Whittemore aged about 21 years Died January ye 15 1693-4

838. Here lyes Buried the Body of Mr John Whittemore aged 63 years Died April ye 21st 1748

839. William son to Robert & Elizabeth Rand aged 13 months Died Sept y^e   1721

840. Elizabeth daughter of Thomas & Elizabeth Barnard aged 2 years dyed ye 5 of Sepr 1683.

841. Elizabeth daughter of Joseph & Lydia Williams aged 1 year & 8 mo died August ye 12 1690

842. Jeremiah son to Joseph & Sarah Williams aged 9 years dec^d Octr ye 30th 1721.

843. Rachel Williams Wife to Benjamin Williams aged about 56 years died ye 25 of March 1708

844. Ere lies ye body of Elizabeth Williams dau^r of Capt Henry & Mrs Mary Williams Died March 1st 1759 in the 16th year of her age

845. Mr Robert Fowler, footstone

846. Here lyes interred the Body of Hindreh Hirsst aged about 52 years deceased January y^r 30th 1717-8

847. Here lyes ye body of Mary Hirsst Wife to Hindreh Hirsst Dau^r of James Bill & Mehitable his wife died Novr ye 23 1717 in ye 37 year of her age.

848. In memory of Samuel Wakefied who died Nov 12. 1809
(six lines)

849. Here lyes ye Body of Mrs Ammey Hunt wife of Mr Benjamin Hunt who died Novr 20th 1769 aged 40 years
(4 lines)

850. Here lies buried the Body of Mrs Sarah Hunt who departed this life Decr 26th 1775 aged 90 years

851. John son to John & Rebeckah Hunt aged about 1 year dec^d April ye 11th 1714

852. Palsgrave son of Ephraim & Johannah Hunt aged 6 months & 17 days died Sept 19 1711

853.   No 102

| William Boynton |
| and |
| John F. Low's |
| Family Tomb 1809 |

854.   No 101

> Ephraim & Larkin
> Snow's Tomb
> 1808

855. Here lyes buried the Body of Mrs Mary Payson wife to Mr Jonathan Payson who died June 3ᵈ 1743 in the 36ᵗʰ year of her age

856. Here lyes buried yᵉ Body of Samuel Payson son to Mr Samuel & Mrs Mary Payson aged 17 years 6 mo & 2 days Died Octʳ yᵉ 11ᵗʰ 1741

857. Here lies buried the Body of Mr Joseph Beath who died July 28ᵗʰ 1780 aged 26 years.

858. Sacred to the memory of 4 children of Jabez & Lydia Sweet. Henry died Jan 13ᵗ 1800 aged 4 months. Ebenezer died April 14ᵗʰ 1802. aged 14 months. Jabez died Sept 6ᵗʰ 1805 aged 12 months. Jabez Henry died May 20ᵗʰ 1807 aged 10 months.

859. Here lyes buried yᵉ Body of Hannah Hobby yᵉ Wife of John Hobby aged about 27 years decᵈ June 26 1690.

860. Here lyes yᵉ Body of Mrs Mary Hughes dautʳ of Mr Richard & Mrs Sarah Hughes who died March ye 7, 1765 aged 47 years
(6 lines poetry.)

861. Here lies buried the body of Mr Richard Hughes died July 'yᵉ 8ᵗʰ 1757 aged 42 years

862. Here lyes yᵉ Body of Mrs Sarah Hughes widow of Mr Richard Hughes who died Nov 23ᵈ 1764 in yᵉ 77ᵗʰ year of Her age. (4 lines poetry.)

863. Here lies buried the Body of Mrs Elizabeth Hughes Daur of Capt Richard & Mrs Sarah Hughes aged 52 years Died May 29ᵗʰ 1771.

864. Here lyeth buried ye Body of Susanna Sweet ye wife of John Sweet aged 44 years deceased ye 16 of July 1666.

865. Here lyeth buried ye Body of John Sweet aged 82 years departed this life ye 25 of April 1685

866. Here lyeth buried ye Body of Daniel George aged 29 years deceased ye 18 day of July 1684

867. Here lies ye Body of Mr Abraham Gording aged about 76 years decd Sept ye 27ᵗʰ 1706

868. Here lies ye body of Mrs Hannah Gording decd March ye 3ᵈ 1724–5 in ye 80ᵗʰ year of her age

869. Here lyeth buried ye Body of Daniel Travis Senior aged 76 years departed this life ye 19 of January 1688–9

870. Here lyes ye body of Daniel Travis aged 55 years died May ye 9, 1720.

871. Here lyes ye body of Mrs Willmoth Hoar aged 78 years decd Feb'y ye 29th 1735-6

872. No 115

> James W. Burdett
> 1809

873. Here lyes ye Body of James Codner aged about 39 years deceased July ye 12th 1715.

874 Here lies Interred the Body of Mr James Codner Died Aug 5th 1784 aged 53 years

875. Here lies buried the Body of Mrs Mary Ela who decd March ye 6th 1737-8 in ye 55 year of her age

876. Here lyes ye Body of Mrs Mary Sumers Wife to Mr Edward Sumers aged 72 years decd Nov' ye 18th 1724

877. Charles Sumers son of Edward and Mary Sumers Aged 5 months Died ye 25 of January 168*

878. William Kingston Son of Elias & Martha Kingston Aged 5 weeks & 4 days Decd February 8th 1719-20

879. Sacred to the memory of Mrs Abiel Cogswell consort of Mr John Cogswell & Daughr of Edward & Rebekah Page who died suddenly Feb'r 12, 1804 in the 54 h year of her age. Mrs Abigail Cogswell Consort of Mr Jno Cogswell & Dau'r of Saml & Sarah Godiag who died Jan'y 19th 1782 in the 42d year of her age also five of their children died young.

880. Here lies buried the Body of Mr William Codner who departed this life Sept'r 12th 1769 aged 60 years

881. Here lies buried the Body of Capt Philip Bass who departed this life June 10th 1761 aged 76 years

882. Philip son of Capt Philip and Mrs Mary Bass aged 2 years Died August y 9 1720

883. Elizth Bass Dau'r to Capt Phillip Bass & Elizth his wife aged 5 months Died July 30 1758 also two more of their children

884. Thomas Fracker and Cotton Thayers, Tomb 1806.

885. Here lyes the Body of Mr Richard Trew died October 8th 1756 aged 26 years

886. Here lyes buried the Body of Mr John Goffe decd July ye 24th 1716 in the 67 h year of his age

887. In memory of Mr John Goff died Feby 26th 1807 in the 44th year of his age

888. Here lyes buried ye Body of Mrs Elizabeth Snelling wife to Mr Joseph Snelling who died April ye 1st A. D 1737 aged 32 years 11 mo & 14 ds.

889. Here lies ye Body of Mr Edward Lack died Feb⁷ 29 1760 Æt 86

890. (Also Randalls)

891. . (with Lack), Abagail & Sarah the children of Richard & Sarah Randolls.

892. Here lyes yᵉ Body of Richard Randalls who decᵈ Octobr yᵉ 10ᵗʰ 1730 aged 38 years

893. Here lies the Body of Mrs Mary Randall wife of William Randall Esq Died June 26ᵗʰ 1772 Aged 50 years.

894. Here lies the Body of Mrs Hannah Edmonds wife of Mr Joseph Edmonds who died suddenly Sept 19ᵗʰ 1778 aged 45 years.

895. Here lyes interred the Body of Mrs Ann Archer wife to Capt Thomas Archer who died Sept 20ᵗʰ 1738 in ye 69ᵗʰ year of her age

896. Here lyes ye Body of S.muel Knight aged 32 years died Oct yᵉ 25ᵗʰ 1721.

897. Here lyes buried the Body of Mr William Brown died Sept yᵉ 6ᵗʰ 1751 aged 54 years.

898. Here lies the Body of Mrs Mary Owen Wife of Mr William Owen who departed this life December yᵉ 14ᵗʰ 1767 aged 66 years

899. William son to William & Susannah Pike aged 15 mo & 8 Ds Decᵈ Sept yᵉ 25ᵗʰ 1721

900. Eliza Oakes 1681

901. Here lyes yᵉ body of Elizabeth Hannah dauʳ to William & Martha Hannah aged 5 years died January yᵉ 20 1703-4 Mary Hannah dauʳ to William & Martha Hannah aged 3 months Died July ye 31 1701

902. Here lyes ye Body of Mrs Mary Russell widdow who died Sept yᵉ 29ᵗʰ 1750 in yᵉ 71ˢᵗ ...

903. Here lyes buried the Body of Moses Paull, son to Mr Moses & Mrs Mary Paull aged 27 years 2 months & 25 d, decᵈ March yᵉ 25ᵗʰ 1730

904. Here lyes Buried the Body of Sarah Paull Dauʳ to Mr Moses & Mrs Mary Paull aged 18 years 8 months & 25 Dˢ Decᵈ March yᵉ 25ᵗʰ 1730

905. Here lyes buried the Body of Mrs Elizabeth Wiswall wife to Mr Peleg Wiswall aged 47 years who died December yᵉ 1ˢᵗ 1743

906. Here lies buried the Body of Mr Francis Marshall who departed this life the 24ᵗʰ of July 1767 aged 57 years

907. Francis Marshall son of Mr Francis & Mrs Abigail Marshall Died Augˢᵗ 23ᵈ 1740 aged 14 days.

908. Here lies buried ye Body of Mr John Brown who died suddenly March yᵉ 11ᵗʰ 1747-8 aged 45 years & 8 mo.

909. Thomas Gatte son to Capt Patrick Gatte & Rachel his wife aged 5 years & 2 mo died Dec[r] 7 1745.

910. Here lyes Buried the Body of Capt Patrick Gatte who Departed this life Nov[r] ye 19th 1746 Aged 33 years.

911. Here ly... Interred y[e] body of Mr Peter Oliver aged 30 years Deceas[d] April y 27th 1712

912. Here lyes y[e] Body of Mrs Charity Brown consort to Mr John Brown who departed this life April y[e] 13th A. D 1754 in ye 31st year of her age

913. Here lies buried the Body of Mrs Sarah Brown wife to Mr Samuel Brown who departed this life Febry 17th 1754 in the 41st year of her age.

914. Samuel Whitehead son of Samuel & Mary Whitehead aged 1 year 6 months and 22 days dec[d] August 26th 1719

915. Here lies buried the Body of Mr Samuel Brown who died Aug[st] 7th 1768 aged 57 years

916. Here lyes buried the Body of Nathaniel Newell aged 73 years dec[d] Nov[r] ye 29th 1731

917. Here lies interred the remains of Mr George Eustis, Son of Mr Benj[n] Eustis who departed this life Oct 19th 1779 in the 25th year of his age

918. Here lyes ye Body of Flora Eustis wife of Ceaser aged 33 years Died Sept 30 ....

919. Here lyes y[e] Body of Mrs Rebeca Blackman wife to y[e] Rev[d] Mr Benjam Blackman aged about 63 years dec[d] March y[e] 29th 1715.

920. Mrs Lydia Gendall

921. Edward Late y[e] son of Mr John & Mrs Mary Late aged 3 years & 3 mo Dec[d] May y[e] 13th 1734

922. Margret Nichols aged 7 weeks died Nov[r] 27 1753, Margret Nichols aged 8 days died Nov[r] 3[d] 1751. The two Daug[rs] of M Will[m] & Mrs Margaret Nichols.

923. In Memory of Capt Peleg L. Hillman who died March 25th 1798 Aged 41 years

924. Here lyeth ye Body of Capt David Edwards aged about 57 years died October ye first 1696

925. Here lyes ye Body of Mr Daniel Tucker dec[d] July 17th 1739 in ye 32[d] year of his age

926. Ebenezer son of Elisha & Elizabeth Tucker died Aug[t] 28 1816 aged 10 months

927. Here lyeth buried ye body of John Soames Sen[r] aged about 52 years departed this life November ye 16 1700

928. Elizabeth Somes aged 16 days dyed Sept⟨r⟩ ye 16 1685

929. In memory of Capt John Hyer who Died at Cape France-way, March 8ᵗʰ 1742–3 in ye 46ᵗʰ year of his age. Here lyes ye Bodys of two of the children of Capt John & Mrs Sarah Hyer, Sarah Died Nov⟨r⟩ 11ᵗʰ 1743 in ye 13 year of her age, Sage aged 7 months Died August 30 1734.

930. In Memory of Lucy Swier who died Oct 1 1795 ... Æt 63

931. Here lyeth buried ye body of Elizabeth Prout ye wife of Timothy Prout decd January ye 19ᵗʰ 1693–4 in 57ᵗʰ year of her age

932. Here lies the Body of Mr William Haly who died April ye 6ᵗʰ 1760 aged 86 years Also Mrs Sarah Haly wife of Mr William Haly who died May ye 15ᵗʰ 1752 Aged 77 years

933. .ere lies buried the Body of Mrs Hannah Collins wife to Mr Daniel Collins who died May 8ᵗʰ 1756 in the 42 year of her age

934. Here lyes ye body of Daniel Colins Aged 47 years & 17 months dec⟨d⟩ October ye 30ᵗʰ 1718

⁃935. In memory of Mrs Lydia Collins died June 10ᵗʰ 1789 Aged 64 years

936. Thomas son of Richard & Sarah Sheren aged 7 months Died July ye 4 1704

937. Here lyes ye Body of Sarah Sherrin wife to Richard Sherrin aged 46 years & 4 months decd Aug ye 26ᵗʰ 1715

938. Here lyes buried ye body of Richard Sharin aged 52 years departed this life October ye 22ᵈ 1710

939. Mary the daughter to Chor⟨r⟩ and Jane Marvin aged near 14 monthes died July ye 24ᵗʰ 1714

940. William son of Thomas & Ann Diamond aged 6 months died Sept ye 20 1711

941. In Memory of Mrs Anna Gladding who died June 18ᵗʰ 1801 Aged 66 years

942. Here lyeth buried the body of Samuel Winslow aged 39 years departed this life October ye 14 1680

943. Here lies buried the Body of Mrs Hannah Parkman wife to Mr William Parkman died May 14ᵗʰ 1756 Aged 62 years & 5 months

944. Sarah Iamson aged about 83 years died ye 25ᵗʰ daye of March 1696.

945. Here lies ye Body of David Norton aged 57 years Dec⟨d⟩ December 2ᵈ 1721

946. Here lyes buried ye body of George Norton who departed this life May ye 19ᵗʰ 1710 in the 39ᵗʰ year of his age

947. Here lyes ye body of Thomas Norton aged 21 years 1 mo & 20 Dˢ Decᵈ Sept ye 21ˢᵗ 1714

948. Here lyes ye Body of Mary Thomas dau^r to Mr John & Mrs Lydia Thomas of Brantry dec^d Sept ye 4th 1734 in ye 20th year of her age.

949. Here lyeth buried ye body of Judith Hunt ye wife of Thomas Hunt aged about 38 years departed this life ye 18 of October 1693 ye daughter of Capt William Torey of Waymouth

950. Josiah Clarke son of Josiah & Prissilah Clarke aged 9 months .. September ye ..

951. J. Adams 1804

952. Here lyes ye Body of Mr John Parker died Sept 27th 1744 in ye 80th year of his age

953. Here lyes ye Body of Mrs Sarah Parker wife of Mr John Parker died Sept 5th 1750 in ye 81st year of her age

954. Mrs Margaret Parker Aged 87 Died Oct 1815.

955. Sarah Greenough aged 5 m Dyed September 1676

956. Here lies Buried the Body of Mrs Hannah Harris Widow of Capt Leach Harris who died Dec 24th 1783 aged 67 Years
[poetry 2 lines.]

957. Here lies buried the Body of Mr John Harris died Decem^r 18th 1770 Aged 68 years

958. Here lies the body of Mrs Ann Harris Wife of Capt Samuel Harris who died 28th June 1748 Aged 42 years & 4 mo

959. Here lies buried the Body of Mrs Anna Harris Wife of Mr John Harris Died Sept 2^d 1778 aged 76 years

960. Here lies Buried the Body of Mrs Prudence Newell Wife of Mr John Newell Died Feb^{ry} 21st 1777 in the 36th Year of her age

961. Here lies ye Body of John Jenkins Parker son of Capt Robt Jenkins Parker Aged 3 years Dec^d May 17th 1758

962. In Memory of Mrs Sally Dumblide wife of John Steven Dumblide who departed this life Feb^{ry} 26th 1796 Aged 35 years

963. Here lies buried the Body of Nathaniel Harris son of Mr. John & Mrs Anna Harris aged 20 years died Feb^{ry} ye 12 1749.

964. In memory of Capt Nathaniel Langdon Harris, who departed this life Jan^{ry} 14th 1804 aged 29 years Also Catharine Butler Harris, Daughter of Capt Nathaniel & Susanna Harris Aged 10 months

965. Here lyes ye Body of Susannah Doubleday Dau^r of Capt John and Mrs Elizth Doubleday died Sept 5th 1773 aged 20 months

966. Sacred to the memory of Mrs Ann Singleton who died Sept 3^d 1805 aged 29 years
[poetry 4 lines]

967. John Lunne Aged 2 years 7 months Died Decr 10th 1747 Elizth Lunne Aged 9 Months Died Octr ye 20th 1748 the children of Mr John & Mrs Elizabeth Lunne

968. Here lies Buried the Body of Mr Phillip Howell Aged 39 years Died March 5th 1753

969. Here lyes ye Body of Mrs. Mary Howell Wife of Mr Phillip Howell Aged 30 years & 7 mo Died Augst 21st 1744

970. Elizth dau to Isaac and Rebecca Doubt aged 5 Mo Died Jan ^y ye 28th 1724–5

971. Here lies buried the Body of Mr John Carter who died Novr 26th 1765 Aged 65 Years. Also Mrs Jane Carter Wife to Mr John Carter who died July 28th 1772 Aged 57 Years
(poetry 4 lines.)

972. George Singleton departed this life Jan 24 1805 Æt 39. Samuel H. Singleton Aged 11 mos

973. In Memory of Mr James Carter Singleton who departed this Life Nov 26th 1800 Aged 34 years
(poetry 2 lines)

974. Here lies ye Body of Mrs Mary Hill aged about 35 years died the 20th of October 1714

975. Here lyes buried ye Body of Capt William King died June 20th 1768 Aged 43 Years Also William King son to Capt William and Mrs Mary King died April 7th 1767 Aged 14 years

976. Here lyes ye Body of Mary King Dau^r to Peter & Mary King Dec^d Octr ye 1st 1721 in ye 13th year of her age

977. Here lies buried the Body of Mrs Abigail King the Wife of Mr Peter King .. ied Novr 13th 1770 Aged 31 years

978. Here lyes ye body of William Leighton son to Joseph & Abigail Leighton aged 2 years died May ye 25th 1710

979. Nancy Barber Dau^r of Mr Samuel & Mrs Polly Barber died July 4 1799 aged 9 months

980. Here lyes ye Body of Mr. John Barber Senr aged 84 years dec^d December ye 4th 1726

981. Here lyes ye body of Mary Barber wife to John Barber aged 64 years dec^d March ye 5th 1717

982. Here lyes ye Body of John Tilestone dec^d Octr ye 7th 1721 in ye 16th year of his age

983. Here lyes the body of Mr James Tilston Aged 62 years Decd Feby 20th 1739–40

984. Here dies the Body of Mrs Joanna Tilestone the wife of Mr James Tilestone Aged 31 years died May 1st ...

985. Here lyes the body of Mrs Mary Tilestone Aged 34 years Died June ye 11th 17 . 2

986. Here lies the Body of Mr. Josiah King who departed this Life March 24th 1786 Aged 58 years

987. Here lies Interred the Body of Col William Burbeck died July 22d 1785 Aged 69 years.

988. Here lies Buried the Body of Mrs Jerusha Burbeck wife of Col William'Burbeck Died July 27th 1777 aged 54 years & 7 mo

989. Here lyes ye Body of Capt David Robertson aged 63 years died July ye 3d 1726

990. Here lyes ye Body of Martha Shute wife to William Shute aged 51 years died Janry ye 8th 1721–22

991. No 13 the Tomb of Samuel Winslow.

992. Here lyes the mortal part of William Clark Esqr An Eminent Merchant of this Town and An Honorable Counsellor for the Province Who Distinguished Himself as a Faithful and Affectionate Friend a Fair and generous Trader· Loyal to his Prince Yet always Zealous for the Freedom of his Country A Despiser of Sorry Persons and little Actions, An Enemy to Priestcraft and Enthusiasm, Ready to relieve and help the Wretched, A Lover of good Men of Various Denominations, and a Reverent Worshipper of the Deity

993. Elizth Daur to Mr James & Mrs Anna Clemens died Septr 6·h 1749 Aged 11 Months & 14 days

994. Sarah ye daur of Capt James and Mrs. Anna Clemans Aged 14 days decd Augst 14 1737

995. Here lyes buried ye body of Capt Robert Miers aged 57 years decd December ye 20th 1733

996. Here lies the body of Mrs Elizabeth Miers aged 62 years decd June 23d 1739

997. Relique Johannis Clarke Armig laudatissimi Senatoris et Medicinae Doctoris Probitate Modestia et Mansuetudine praeclari Terram reliquit Decem 5 1728 aetat 62 Nomen et Pietas manent post Funera

998. Sacred to the memory of Miss Mercy Jones who died April 7 1805 Aged 20 years & 6 months
(poetry 12 lines)

999. Here lies buried ly Body of Mrs Sarah Goold wife to Capt James Goold died Oct 1th e1764 aged 73 years

1000. Here lyes ye body of Mr Job Coit aged 49 years who died Janry ye 12th 1741

1001. Here lyes buried the Body of Mr Nathl Coit died May ye 22d 1747 aged 31 years

1002. Joseph Coit son of Mr Joseph & Mrs Dorothy Coit Died July 17th 1748 Aged 8 weeks

1003. Here lyes the Body of Mr Job Coit Junr who died Feby ye 22^d 1744 in ye 28th year of his age

1004. Here lies ye body of Mr^s Lydia Coit wife of Mr Job Coit aged 56 years Died July 9th 1751

1005. Prudence Porter wife to Thomas Porter first dau^r of Samuel & Hannah White aged 27 years & 9 mo died July ye 3^d 1709

1006. Here lies buried the Body of Mr Richard Sherrin aged 53 years died Dec ye 25th 1746

1007. In Memory of Mary Armstrong dau^r of Mary Huntley who departed this Life Sept 28th A D 1798 in the 36th Year of her Age

1008. In Memory of Mary Huntley who departed this life Sept 28th 1798 in the 64th Year of her age

(poetry 4 lines)

1009. Mary Perkins dau^r of Isaac & Mary Perkins aged 11 years 3 mo & 28 dayes deceased July ye 13th 1718

1010. In memory of John Ripley Junr Son of John & Jane Ripley who died March 19th 1809 in the 10th year of his age

1011. In memory of David Ripley who died May 28 1802 aged 9 months Also in memory of Rachel Ripley who died Octr 13th 1804 Aged 2 years children John & Jane Ripley.

1012. Here lyeth buried ye Body of John White aged about 50 years dec^d ye 6 of August 1690   [Said to be properly 1695. Ed.]

1013. In Memory of Mr Isaac White deceased Decr 10th 1795 Aged 62 years

1014. Here lyeth buried ye body of Capt William Greenough aged about 52 years dec^d August ye 6th 1693

1015. Here lies Ye Body of Mrs Elizabeth Stone wife of Mr William Stone who departed this life March ye 15th 1763 in the 57th year of her age

1016. Joseph son to Joseph & Hannah Calley aged about 7 years dec^d Novr ye 28 1678

1017. Hannah Ca.. Relict of Jose.. Cally Aged .. years deceas. August y^e .. 1693

1018. Here lyes ye body of Mrs Elizabeth Forsyth wife to Capt Alexander Forsyth died July ye 28th 1726 in ye 30th year of her age

1019. Nathaniel Marston died April 28th 1764 Aged 4 years and 7 months.   Hannah Marston died April 28th 1764 Aged 11 months and 10 days

1020. Here lieth ye body of Kezia Needham wife to John Needham aged 37 years & 3 Mo Died Janu^r ye 17th 1704–5

1021. To the memory of Martha daughter W^m & Nancy Grubb who departed this life Sept 21st 1805 aged 1 year & 16 days

(poetry 4 lines)

1022. In memory of Mrs Sarah Hunt wife of Jacob Hunt who departed this life May 18th 1805 aged 65 years.

1023. In Memory of Mr Joab Hunt who departed this life March 14th 1800 aged 62 years

1024. Joab Hunt's Tomb 1811. No 15

1025. .... Ward OBiit June 22^d 1790 Ætat 56 Also Catharine his wife OBiit Jany 3^d 1801 Ætat 64 Also James Seward grandson of James & Catharine Seward OBiit Sept 22^d 1792 Ætat 6 months

(poetry 2 lines)

1026. In Memory of Mr Daniel Manwaring Shipwright who died April ye 6th 1773 Aged 64 years

1027. Here lies Buried the Body of Mrs Mercy Sumner Wife to Mr Benj Sumner Died Feb^{ry} 22^d 1768 Aged 55 years

1028. Here lies buried the Body of Mrs Sarah Manwaring wife of Mr. Daniel Manwaring who Died of the small pox Jan^{ry} the 23^d 1764 Aged 48 years

1029. Here lyes buried ye Body of Anna Henchman wife to Nathaniel Henchman aged 37 years & 9 mo died Jany ye 7th 1706

1030. A Family Tomb
Elizabeth Grant died May 25, 1769 Æt 20
Moses Grant died August 18 1777   15 mos
Elizabeth Grant died Jan 28 1778 Æt 70
Samuel Grant died Nov 14 1784 Æt 79
Sarah Grant died March 14 1792 Æt 39
Mary Grant died Dec 3 1808 Æt 27
Moses Grant died Dec 22 1817 Æt 73
John Grant died Sept 19 1820 Æt 33
Ann Grant died April 17 183? Æt 77
Susan W. Grant died July 26 1818 Æt 31
Samuel Grant died Oct 2 1778 Æt 5

1031. Joanna daughter to James & Joanna Grant aged 1 year 10 Mo died May ye 20 1696

1032. James & Joanna Grant Aged 14 Mo ½ died September ye 1 1688

1033. Here lies the body of Joseph Grant the fourth died June 25th 1752 aged 5 years. Here lies the Body of Edward Grant died July 19, 1752 aged 3 years & 6 Mo
both sons of Mr John & Mrs Rebecca Grant

1034. Here lyes ye Body of Mary ye wife of Ceasor Augustus Servant of Mr Robert Ball Aged 25 Years Died May 28th 1759

1035. In Memory of James G., Son of John & Emely Sullivan died Feb'y 10th, 1807 Æ. 4 years 6 mo

1036. In memory of Elizabeth A Daughter of John and Mrs Emily A Sullivan who died June 24th 1812 aged 7 years

1037. In Memory of Charles G. Son of John and Emily Sullivan, died Aug' 15th 1815, aged 5 years

(poetry 1 line)

1038. In Memory of Thomas Valentine Sullivan son of Thomas and Rebecca Sullivan who died Oct' 29th 1795 aged 10 months & 9 days

1039. Here lie the remains of Mr. Timothy Gay Merchant who July 28 1799 in the 36th year of his age. He was diligent in business, faithful to his friends and affectionate to his family

1040. Here sweetly rests the ashes of Rebecca Porter Gay Second daughter of Mr Timothy & Mrs Jane Gay died Dec' 8th 1797 ; aged 4 years 2 months & 29 days

1041. Sacred to the Memory of Mrs Ann McMillian wife of Mr James McMillian who died Feb'y 28th 1805 aged 81

(poetry 4 lines)

Also In Memory of their son Mr Edward McMillian who died at the Island of St Thomas W. I. Dec' 22d 1804 aged 40.

(Poetry 1 line)

1042. Here lyes Buried the Body of Mrs Ann Mc Clarry yc wife of Mr John Mc Clarry who died May ye 1st 1748 aged 37 years 1 mo & 10 D'

1043. In Memory of Mrs Sarah McClary Widow of the late Mr John Mc Clary who departed this Life Oct' 8th 1797 aged 72

1044. In Memory of John Son of David & Rebcca Adlington who died Jany 17th 1816 in his 3 year also Rebecca aged 1 year died July 1st 1816

1045. Here lies buried the Body of Mrs Elizabeth Turrell the wife of Mr Joseph Turrell who died April the 12th 1765 in ye 36th year of her age also four of her offspring

1046 Here lyes buried the Body of Mr. Thomas Lawlor aged 61 years died Feb'y ye 26th 1743–4

1047. Here lyes ye Body of William Gooding aged 17 years died Jan'y 22d 1738–9.

1048. Here lies Buried the Body of Mrs Sarah Gooding the wife of Mr. Samuel Gooding aged 33 years & 4 mo who Died August the 21st 1749

1049. In Memory of Mrs. Seeth Rumney who died suddenly Jany 13th 1804 Æt 56 The late amiable consort of Capt Edward Rumney

1050. In Memory of Mrs Jane Henry Widow of the late M^r. Robert Henry died Oct 22d 1803 Æ 78 Also two Grandchildren Daughters of Col James & Mrs Jane Robinson, Jane Henry Robinson 1st died July 21 1804 Æ 16 months, Jane Henry Robinson 2^d died Oct 13 1807 Æ 16 months

1051. Roger Hacker son of Mr. Caleb and Mrs Elizth Hacker aged 9 months Died May 3^d 1750

1052. Here lies the Body of Mr Joseph Beath died Jan^{ry} 24th 1771 aged 57 years also Mrs Seeth Beath widow of Mr Joseph Beath died June 20th 1779 aged 66 years

1053. Here lyes ye Body of Isaac Aves son of Mr. Samuel & Mrs Mary Aves aged 27 years & 13 d^s dec^d Sept 24th 1739

1054. Here lies the Body of Mr John Richards who died Jan^{ry} 5th 1732 aged 29 years

1055. Here lyes buried ye Body of Mr. Edward Richards died February ye 11th 1747–8 aged 70 years

1056. In Memory of Mr. Joseph Richards Son to Mr. Edward & Mrs Mary Richards who died at Port Mahone January ye 18th 1742 aged 24 years

1057. Here lyes the body of Ales Richards wife to Philip Richards aged 47 years & 3 mo dec^d Feb^{ry} ye 26 1717–18

1058. No 19. 1811. J. Percival N. Parker

1059. No 20. Blank (Soldier's Home)

1060. Here lyes the Body of Elizabeth Avis dec^d May ye 6, 1730 in ye 48 year of her age

1061. No 17. Stephen Rhoades Jr died Sept 21 1835 aged 14 mos.

1062. Mrs Mary Ward died April 1 1853 aged 80

1063 Mrs Hannah Lock died April 16 1854 aged 80 years 7 mos.

1064. Here lyes the body of Elizth Harris daug^{hr} to Mr Samuel & Mrs Hannah Harris who dec^d Octr ye 10th 1744 aged 18 years

1065. Thomas Harris Aged one year died Feb^{ry} 28th 1742

1066. Mary Harris Aged Ten months died Novr 12th 1743 the children of Mr. Lach & Mrs Hannah Harris

1067. Elizth Harris aged 4 years 9 Mo & 18 D^s dec^d Octr ye 1st 1735

1068. Here lyes buried the Body of Mrs Mary Jarvis wife to Mr Elias Jarvis Junr aged 21 years died Septr 20th 1748

1069. Here lyes the body of Capt Nathaniel Jarvis aged 70 years who died Decr 13th 1738.

1070. Here lyes ye body of Elizabeth Jarvis wife to Nathaniel Jarvis died ye 15th of August 1709 in ye 38th year of her age.

8

1071. John H. Pitman's Tomb 1848. No. 48.

1072. Here lies buried the Body of Mr Peleg Wiswall late Master of the North Grammar School died Sept 2ᵈ 1767 in the 84ᵗʰ year of his age.

1073. Mary ye dauʳ of Mr James & Mrs Anne Jeffs aged 4 years 4 mo 12 ds decᵈ August yᵉ 1ˢᵗ 1734

1074. In Memory of Mrs Deborah Gardner wife of Capt Lemuel Gardner who departed this life 28ᵗʰ September 1792 aged 39 years. (1 line poetry)

1075. Here lyes buried the Body of Mr Michael Dennis who departed this life July the 11ᵗʰ 1763 in the 48 year of his age

1076. In Memory of Mrs Mary Adams widow of Capt John Adams who departed this life May 16ᵗʰ 1791 aged 38 years

1077. Here lyeth ye body of Abraham Adams Aged 60 years died April ye 6 1700

1078. Margaret Dauʳ to Mr John and Mrs Mary Adams Aged 8 Months Died Decʳ ye 2ᵈ 1733

1079. In Memory of Mr Thomas Christy who died Oct 21ˢᵗ 1798 aged 62 years

1080. In Memory of Mrs Hannah Christy wife of Mr Thomas Christy who died Octʳ 16ᵗʰ 1798 Aged 59 years

1081. In Memory of Thomas Christy died July 22ᵈ 1762 aged 12 months

1082. John Christy died Octʳ 5ᵗʰ 1784 aged 2 years & 9 months the children of Mr Thomas & Mrs Hannah Christy

1083. Here lies yᵉ Body of Sarah Christy Dauʳ of Mr Thomas & Mrs Hannah Christy died Oct 16ᵗʰ 1770 Aged 15 Months

1084. No 21.   Ezra Dyer's Tomb 1811

1085. Sacred to the Memory of Mr John Lambord, Cooper, who departed this life Nov 17ᵗʰ 1805 Æt 60

(poetry 5 lines)

1086. Here lies interred the mortal part of Simeon Skillin who departed this life February 27ᵗʰ 1778 Æ. 62 years

1087. Here lies buried the Body of Mrs Mary Skillin wife of Mr John Skillin Junʳ died Janʳʸ 28ᵗʰ 1763 aged 27 years.

1088. Here lies interred the mortal part of Ruth Skillin Relict of Simeon Skillin who departed this life May 29ᵗʰ 1786 Æ. 64 years

1089. Simeon Skilling Son to Mr Simeon & Mrs Ruth Skilling Aged 8 years he died Janʳʸ ye 23ᵈ 1748-9

1090. Here lyes ye Body of Mrs Elizabeth Lash wife to Mr Nicholas Lash who died Augˢᵗ 14 A.D. 1750 in yᵉ 44ᵗʰ year of her age

1091. Here lyeth buried y^c body of Nicolas Lash aged 10 years & 8 mo Dyed April ye 30th 1683

1092. Here lyes ye Body of Mrs Elizth Lash Wife to Mr Robert Lash who Dec^d Octr ye 12th 1727 Aged 58 years

1093. Elizabeth Lash Dau^r of Nickolas & Elizabeth Lash Died Sept y^c 6 1731 Aged 3 years & 6 Mo.

1094. Here lyes the Body of Mrs Abigail Richards dau to Mr Edward & Mrs Mary Richards died Nov ye 4th in ye 36th year of her age

1095. No 52. Benj Varney & Elizabeth Rogers 1805

1096. John Shel . . Thomas Foster Junr Tomb 1805

1097. No 54. Charles Holmes Henry Lane Daniel Johnson Tomb 1807

1098. No 58. Aaron Bancroft and Galen Holmes Tomb 1814.

1099. Sacred to the Memory of Susanna Johnson who departed this Life Augst 20th 1804 Aged 60 years John Johnson who departed this Life June 5th 1804 Aged 57 years

1100. Susanna Johnson Dau^r of John & Susanna Johnson Aged 7 months Dec^d Novem^{br} 2^d 1721 John Johnson son of John & Susanna Johnson Aged 9 years & 7 Months, Dec^d Oct^{br} 28th 1721

1101. Here lyes ye Body of Mrs Susanna Johnson wife of Mr John Johnson aged 63 years 9 Mo & 9 D^s Died Novr 23^d 1713

1102 Here lyes ye Body of Mrs Rebecca Mitchell wife of Capt Thomas Mitchell who departed this life Sept 3 1784 aged 59 years

1103. In Memory of Anna Miller dau^r of Mr William & Mrs Anna Miller who died May 7th 1782 aged 12 months

1104. In Memory of William N. Son of Ephraim and Nancy Steel who died Decr 21st, 1815 aged 3 mo & 6 days

(poetry 4 lines)

1105. Here lyes ye body of Mr Zachariah Johnson dec^d Decr ye 25th 1727 in ye 83^d year of his age

1106. Here lies ye body of Elizabeth Johnson aged 68 years dyed May ye 7 1701

1107. Here lyes ye body of Elizabeth Johnson wife of Zechariah Johnson who died April ye 8th 1717 in ye 63 year of her age.

1108. Here lyes ye Body of Mrs Anna Jeffs wife to Mr James Jeffs who dec^d July ye 22^d 1738 in ye 32^d years of her age

1109. No 59. Joshua Foster & Baker McNear Tomb 1815

1110. No 59. Samuel and Edmund Chessman's

1111. In Memory of Sewall, Son of Mr Sewall & Mrs Sally Fisk^e who died April 3^d 1817 aged 1 year

1112. Here lyes the body of Jonathan Kent, A.M. who deceased Decemb^r 30th 1760 Aged 43 Years. His education & temper of mind were liberal. He was no Sectary in Religion To Life or Death he was so indifferent that confiding in the Divine Providence He was satisfied with that lot & Portion by God for him Ordained in this Life and the future. Of himself he might truly say Et mea virtute me Involvo probamque pauperiem sine Dote quaero

1113. Here lyes ye Body of Mrs Mary Gardner widow to Capt Habakkuk Gardner who departed this life Decemb^r the 17th 1762 aged 56 years

1114. Here lyes ye Body of Mrs Johanna Lash wife to Mr Robert Lash who departed this life May the 39th 1771 aged 27 years

1115. Here lies buried the Body of Mr Thomas Adams who departed this life December 31st 1781 aged 68 years

1116. Here lies Buried the Body of Mrs Mary Adams Widow of Mr Thomas Adams Died Octr 15th 1795 aged 78 years

1117. Here lies buried the Body of Mr Richard Gooding who died suddenly May 16th 1756 aged 53 years, and 4 months

1118. Here lyes ye Body of Thomas Gooding Son of Mr Thomas & Mrs Mary his wife Died Feb^{ry} ye 21st 1742 aged 20 years & 8 Mo

1119. Here lies ye Body of Mrs Elizabeth Goodwing who Departed this Life April 8th 1762 aged 57 years.

1120. Here lyes ye Body of Mrs Elizabeth Tufton wife to Capt Thomas Tufton who died Augst ye 18th 1760 aged 35 years

1121. Robert Tufton Son of Capt John and Mrs Susanna Tufton Born June ye 10th 1716 and died April ye 28th 1717 Aged 11 Months and 17 days

1122. Here lyes buried the Body of Capt Benjamin Seward who departed this life February 10 1766 in the 29th year of his age.

1123. In Memory of Capt Edward Rumney who died April 6, 1808 Æt 63

1124. Miss Mary Richardson eldest Daughter of Mr Richd Richardson who died July 10th 1805 Aged 20 years

1125. In Memory of Mr Richard Richardson who died Jany 17th 1805 Aged 48 years

1126. In Memory of Mr Mary Richardson wife of Richard Richardson Deceased Sept 22^d 1789 in the 30th year of her age

1127. Here lyes ye Body of Moses Paul Payson son of Mr Jonathan & Mrs Mary Payson aged 12 years & 8 mo dyed Jan^{ry} 20th 1742

1128. Here lyes buried the Body of Mrs Mary Paul wife of Mr Moses Paul who died May 7 1742 In the 61st year of her age

1129. Here lyes buried the Body of Mr Moses Paul aged 53 years 3 months who dec^d Jan^{ry} ye 5 1730

1130. Aquila Paull ye son to Aquila & Sarah Paull aged 1 year & 9 Mo Died July ye 30 1714

1131. Here lyes ye Body of Samuel Mower son of Mr Ephraim & Elizth Mower died May ye 6th 1747 Aetatis 28 years

. 1132. Ephraim son to Ephraim & Elizabeth Mower aged 9 years & 10 months died Octob^r ye 2^d 1721

1133. Here lies buried the Body of Mr Nathaniel Brown who departed this life Novr ye 30th 1761 in the 48th year of his age

1134. In Memory of Mr John Hoson who died March 7th 1791 in the 69th year of his age

1135. Here lies ye Body of Samuel Gyles son of Mr Edward & Mrs Abigail Gyles died Octr 25th 1773 aged 4 years & 6 months

1136. Here lies the body of Mrs Elizabeth Gyles wife of Mr Edward Gyles who dec^d September the 10th 17.. in the 38th ..

1137. In Memory of Mrs Elizabeth Lane wife of Mr Levi Lane who died April 15th 1795 aged 40 years Also Ammi Lane died 1780 aged 19 years

1138. In Memory of Mrs Joanna Williston wife of Mr Joseph Williston Junr who departed this life Feb^{ry} 23^d, 1803 aged 28 years

1139. Here lies buried the Body of Mr Thomas Williston who died Dec 14th 1783 Aged 59 years

1140. Here lies ye Body of Mrs Jane Williston wife of Mr Thomas Williston who Died March 12th 1759 Aged 53 years

1141. Here lies Buried the Body of Mr Thomas Williston who exchanged this life for a better August 31st 1775 Aged 75 years

1142. Here lyes buried the Body of Mrs Sarah Townsend wife to Mr Thomas Townsend aged 86 years died Decr 1st 1750

1143. John Doncan son to Mr John & Mrs Keziah Doncan aged 13 months & 11 d^s dec^d May ye 29th 1736

1144. Here lies the Body of Mr. John Roberts son of Mr Benjamin & Mrs Priscilla Roberts aged 36 years & 3 mo died Jan^{ry} 9th 1765.

1145. Sacred to the Memory of Eliza Roberts dau^r of Rich^d & Mercy Roberts, obt Sept 12th 1803 Æt 13, 5 m

(poetry 4 lines)

1146. Here lies buried the Body of Mis Abagail Breading the Dau^r of Capt Philip & Mrs Abigail Breading who departed this life the 17th day December 1762 aged 13 years & 6 mo

1147. In Memory of Mrs Elizabeth Brown wife to Mr. Thomas Brown who died July ye 19th 1756 aged 37 years

1148. Mr. Thomas Brown who died March ye 11th 1760 aged 43 years and Elizabeth Brown dau^r to Thomas & Elizabeth Brown who died January ye 9th 1765 in ye 20th year of her age

1149. Thomas Brown son to Mr. Thomas & Mrs Jean ...

1150. Elizabeth Brown Dau^r of Thomas & Elizabeth Brown aged 16 months & 5 D^s dyed Octr ye 11th 1742

1151. Elizabeth Brown Daug^{tr} of Mr. John & Mrs Susanna Brown Died Oct^{vr} 31st 1739 aged 1 year 10 mo & 6 D^s

1152. In Memory of Mrs Elizabeth Brown who departed this Life the 22^d of May 1773 aged 58 years.

1153. William son to William & Abigail Merchant aged 3 years died Octr ye 16th 1721.   Martha dau^r to William and Abigail Merchant aged 10 mo & 9 days died Octr ye 16th 1721

1154. In Memory of Thomas L. Son of John & Jane Fiske died Sept 24 1815 aged 4 years

1155. Hannah Soames aged 7 months 22 days died ye 30 of ye 2^d moth 1674

1156. Hannah Daughter of John & Hannah Soames Aged 11 days dec^d June ye 19 1682

1157. Here lies ye body of Mrs Margary Sharp wife of Capt Jonathan Sharp died Decem^b 2^d 1763 aged 78 years

1158 .... es ye Body of ..... eth Kemble Ag. 4 years died December ye 19th 1712

1159. Here lyes ye Body of Katherine Kimble aged 53 & 9 mo wife to Timothy Kimble Died March ye 24th 1722

1160. Mary Parkman Died Novr 16th 1763 aged 18 years 3 months & 8 days, Sarah Parkman died June 10th 1765 aged 14 years 1 mo & 5 days the children of Mr Nath^{el} & Mrs Mary Parkman

1161. Nathaniel son of Nathaniel & Hannah Parkman aged 5 years ½ died April ye 27 1694

1162. Here lyes ye body of Capt Samuel Mole Aged 35 years dec^d August ye 21st 1727

1163. In Memory of Mrs. Hannah Brigham wife of Mr. John W. Brigham who died May 7th 1801 aged 27 years

1164. In Memory of Rachel C. Cole who died Jan 23 1800 aged 3 mos, In Memory of Isaac Cole who died Oct. 20 1801 aged 9 mos children of Charles Cole Junr & Rachel his wife

1165. In Memory of Edward Cole son of Capt Jacob & Mrs Hannah Cole died Novr 20th 1787 in the 10th year of his age

1166. Here lies the Body of William Cole Son of Mr Jacob & Mrs Hannah Cole Aged 11 months Dyed July 6th 1767

1167. .. re lyes ye Body of Prissella Woodward wife to Mr Nathl Woddard dec^d Decr ye 29th 1722 in ye 35th year of her age

1168. Here lyes buried ye Body of Mr John Foster who departed this life the 12th of Octr Anno D 1746 aged 57 years 8 months and 3 days

1169. In Memory of Miss Hannah Tilton wife of Mr. William Tilton who died Nov 11 1808 Æt 38

1170. Here lies interred the body of Mr Nathaniel Lewis Merchant of Great Yarmouth in the county of Norfolk old England who departed this Life May 12th 1778 Aetatis Suae 42

1171. Here lyes ye Body of John Mackenzie son to John and Sarah Mackenzie Aged 16 years and 9 mo died Nov. ye 13th 1721

1172. Here lyes ye Body of Mrs Mary Newhall Wife of Mr Eleazer Newhall Aged 41 years Dec^d Feb^ry 9 1739

1173. In Memory of Hannah Newhall wife to Mr Henry Newhall departed this life April 29th 1785 aged 71 years.
(poetry 4 lines)

1174. Here lies the Body of Mr Henry Newhall died March 30th 1753 in ye 58th year of his age

1175. John Nicoll son of Mr James & Mrs Eunice Nicoll aged 20 months died Sept ye 11th 1747.

1176. Here lyes ye Body of Mrs Mary Bennet wife to Mr John Bennet aged about 29 years dec^d March ye 28th 1728

1177. In Memory of Mr Alexander Baker who died May 22^d 1801 aged 72 years, In Memory of Mrs Mary Baker who died Decr 29th 1801 aged 59 years

1178. Here lyes ye Body of Samuel Baker aged 5 weeks died September ye 27 1689

1179. Here lyeth ye body of Joseph Baker son to Thomas & Sarah Baker Aged 11 years & neire 3 months Died April ye 23 1702

1180. Mary . . to John . . Baker . . Dec^d . . ye 2^d . .

1181. Nathaniel Baker son to Thomas & Sarah Baker aged about 5 years deceased May the 30, 1702

1182. Here lyeth buried ye body of Sarah Baker wife to Thomas Baker aged about 45 years died August ye 14 1700

1183. Elizabeth Baker ye daughter of Thomas & Sarah Baker aged 6 weeks died ye 14 of July 1688

1184. Here lyes buried ye body of Mrs Rebecca Baker wife to Mr Thomas Baker aged near 60 years died July ye 29 1708

1185. Here lyes buried the Body of Mr Josiah Baker who departed this life April ye 12th 1760 in ye 70th year of his age

1186. Here lyes ye Body of Mrs Elizabeth Baker wife to Mr Josiah who died June 10th 1753 aged 65 years

1187. Erected in Memory of Mr Philip Rose who departed this life March 20th 1800 aged 27 years

1188. Here Lies Buried the Body of Mrs Dorcas Tyler wife of Mr Elisha Tyler who Departed this life Decemr the 28th 1770 Ætat 29

1189. Here lyes ye body of Mrs Margaret Tyler wife to Mr Moses Tyler aged 21 years 8 Mo decd Novr ye 25th 1724

1190. Here lyes buried the Body of Mrs Mary Page wife to Mr John Page aged 29 years died April 6th 1750

1191. In Memory of Mr John Crease who died Decr 8th 1800 in the 33d Year of his age
(poetry 4 lines)

1192. Sacred to the Memory of Mr Samuel Lord Who died July 29, 1808 Æ 56

1193. Died Nov 5th 1804 Mrs Eliza Maria Revere Æt 28 a native of the city of New York wife of Mr Edward Revere of Boston, Silversmith
(poetry 4 lines)

1194. Isabella Richardson died July 20th 1730 aged 1 year & 2 mo

Anne Richardson died July 22d 1730 aged 2 years & 2 mo
Ye children of Mr Richard & Mrs Anne Richardson

1195. In Memory of Mrs Catherine Richardson Wife of John Richardson who died Octr 7th 1792 Aged 71 years

1196. In Memory of Mr John Richardson who died Novr 14th 1793 Aged 77 years

1197. In Memory of Mr Thomas Richardson who died Novr 7th 1796 Aged 42 years

1198. Thomas Richardson Son of Mr John & Mrs Katherine Richardson Died Febry 13th 1752 Aged 1 year & 8 months

1199. Here lies Interred the Body of the Revd Andrew Eliot D.D. Pastor of the New North church who Died Sept 13th 1778 Ætat 60

1200. John Son of John & Lydia Gunderson, died Nov 12 1817 Æt 7 years

1201. Here lyes buried the body of Mrs Elizth Millburn wife to Mr William Millburn Aged 23 years Died April ye 8 1747 Also the Body of Francis Gouge Aged 12 years died April 8 1747

1202. Martyn.

1203. Here lies ye Body of Edward Page son of Mr Edward & Mrs Rebeckah Page Aged 5 Years Died Septr ye 8th 1760

1204. Mrs Abiel Salter

1205. Here lyes yᵉ Body of Mrs Elizabeth Stephens wife to Mr John Stephens aged 38 years decᵈ Novʳ 19ᵗʰ 1723

1206. Here lies the Body of Mrs Elizabeth Whitman widdow of Mr Francis Whitman who Departed this Life May the 25ᵗʰ 1768 Aged 74 years

1207. Francis son of Francis & Elizabeth Whitman Aged 10 Days Died August yᵉ 15 1715

1208. Elizᵗʰ dauʳ to Francis & Elizᵗʰ Whitman Aged 21 Mo & 8 dˢ Decᵈ Octʳ ye 5 1721

1209. Abigail Whitman Dauʳ to Mr Francis & Mrs Sarah Whitman Aged 19 Months Died Novʳ 8ᵗʰ 1756

1210. Here lies yᵉ Body of Alexander Seares Lord, son of Jonathan & Sarah Lord Who Died March the 26ᵗʰ 1762 Aged 7 months. Here lies ye Body of Hannah Lord Dauʳ of Jonathan & Sarah Lord who Died Novʳ the 2ᵈ 1759 Aged 4 Months

1211. Around this monumental stone lies intered the remains of eight children of Samˡ & Mary Lord. Samuel Lord Junʳ aged 8 months. Polly Lord aged 1 month Polly Lord aged 10 years. Sam Lord the second aged 4 years. Harriet Lord aged 1 year Thomas Lord aged 5 years, Thos Lord the second Aged 1 year. Maria Lord ...

1212. Here lyes yᵉ Body of Mr Thomas Scoot who died Sept yᵉ 3ᵈ 1733 Aged about 50 Years Also Here lyes yᵉ Body of Mrs Anna Scoot wife to Mr Thomas Scoot who died May yᵉ 6ᵗʰ 1734 Aged 59 Years & 6 Mo

1213. Here lyes the body of Mrs Sarah Scott Wife of Mr Thomas Scott Aged 32 years Dyed Sept 20ᵗʰ 1742

1214. In Memory of Thomas Barry who was drowned in Boston Harbour Aug 30, 1807 aged 21 years & 10 months

1215. In Memory of Mrs Patience S. Stevens who died Dec 23 1814 Æt 37

1216. Susannah Dauʳ to John & Grace Stevens aged nere 9 months died October yᵉ 4 1704

1217. Here lyes Buried the Body of Mrs Abigail Stevens wife of Mr Gammon Stevens who died September the 12ᵗʰ 1747 in the 26ᵗʰ year of age

1218. Mary Lemmex died Janʳʸ 18ᵗʰ 1809, aged 11 years and 6 months.

1219. In memory of Mr David Pulsifer who died Sept. 26ᵗʰ 1797 in the 56ᵗʰ year of his. In memory of Mrs Elizabeth Pulsifer Wife of David Pulsifer who died Decᵈ 2ᵈ 1807 in the 61ˢᵗ year of her age.

1220. This Stone is erected in Memory of Mrs Deborah Blake Wife of William Blake obt the 3ᵈ of Augst 1791 Aged 21 Years & 7 Months

1221. Here lyes y⁰ Body of Mr Thomas Bommor aged 74 years dec⁴ June 1ˢᵗ 1741. Here lyes .. body of Mrs Margaret Bommor wife of Mr Thomas Bemmor aged 72 years dec⁴ Feb'ʸ 22ᵈ 1741

1222. Here lies ye Body of Mrs Mary Bomor wife of Mr George Bomor Died Sept ye 15ᵗʰ 1767 in the 34ᵗʰ year of age

1223. In Memory of Miss Rebecca Perkins dagh' of Mr James and Mrs Sally Perkins who died March 16ᵗʰ 1802 Aged 19 Years 7 Months & 13 days

(poetry 4 lines)

1224. Isaac son to Isaac & Mary Perkins aged 14 Months & 12 days died May 13 1705

1225. Here Lies Buried the Body of Capt William Werling who Dep·rted this Life Feb'ʸ 17ᵗʰ 1749–50 In ye 32ᵈ year of his age also

1226. William Werling son of Capt William & Eliz'ʰ Werling. who died Jan'ʸ ye 20ᵗʰ 1748 Aged 12 months

1227. Mariners Tomb 1851, This Tomb is Dedicated to Seamen Of all Nations By Phineas Stow Pastor of the First Baptist Bethel Church, Boston 1851.

1228 Here ... y⁰ son of John & Elizabeth Blewstill Born 1710

1229. In Memory of Henry Rich who died Sept' 29ᵗʰ 1791 Ætat 2 Also Joanna Rich died Oct' 7ᵗʰ 1802 Aged 8 months; children of Capt Obadiah & Mrs Salome Rich

1230. Memento Mori Here lyes ye Body of Mr John Parmetar aged 75 years who departed this Life The 12ᵗʰ Day of February 1711–12 Fugit Hora Also here lyes y⁰ Body of Mrs Hannah Parmeter wife to Mr John Parmeter Aged 42 years Who deceased August ye 12ᵗʰ 1693

1231 Here lyes y⁰ Body of Mr Joseph Parmater Aged 40 Years & 3 Mo dec⁴ June yᵉ 26ᵗʰ 1726

1232. Deposited in the Mariners' Receiving Tomb Emily Wife of Rev. Phineas Stow of Boston who suddenly departed this life May 18, 1851 aged 42 years. The tribute of respect paid to the departed by seamen and friends is very ·consoling to the bereaved husband and his motherless daughter. Her devotion to the welfare of mariners gave her the appropriate appellation of The Sailor's Friend. Her excellent judgment made her a safe adviser in temporal and spiritual things. Cheerfulness and frankness were prominent features in her character. Monuments more durable than marble or brass are erected to her memory in loving hearts

(poetry 7 lines)

1233. Here lies the Bodies of Joseph & Polly Kettell children of Mr Joseph & Mrs Rebecca Kettell. Joseph died July 12 1783 Aged 2 years & 4 Months. Polly died Nov' 15 1783 Aged 14 months

1234. Here lies ye Body of Joseph Kettell son of Mr Joseph & Mrs Rebecca Kettell who died August 30ᵗʰ 1777 Aged 1 year

1235. ... eph .. o died Octⁿ .. Aged 2 years Rebecca Austin Kettell died Octʰʳ 14ᵗʰ 1773 Aged 1 year children of Mr Joseph & Mrs Rebecca Kettell

1236. Sigourney Tomb. No. 25

1237. Here lyes yᵉ body of Mrs Sarah Johnson wife of Mr Joseph Johnson aged 28 years died Janʳy yᵉ 24ᵗʰ 1744–5

1238. Sarah Johnson Dauʳ to Mr Jeffs & Mrs Sarah Johnson Aged 13 mouths decᵈ Sep yᵉ 12ᵗʰ 1740

1239. A tribute To the memory of Mr Hotton Porter Johnson died Jan 16, 1814 aged 20 years Erected by his Sisters

1240. Here lyes yᵉ Body of Mrs Sarah Johnson Wife of Mr Jeffs Johnson Aged 29 years & 18 Dˢ Died Octʳ 11ᵗʰ 1743

1241. No 46 Francis & Enoch James Tomb Built 1805

1242. No 108 Elijah Adams Tomb 1800.

1243. Sacred to the memory of Mr Elijah Adams who departed this Life Augˢᵗ 25ᵗʰ 1798 in the 61ˢᵗ Year of his age

(poetry 4 lines)"

1244. No. 103. Henry Hutchinson and James Penniman Tomb. 1808

1245. Here lyes yᵉ Body of Mr. Thomas Delaplace, Died Decʳ yᵉ 25th 1733, in yᵉ 60ᵗʰ yearof his age.

1246. Sacred to the memory Miss Polley Townsend who died March 9ᵗʰ 1787 aged 9 years & 3 months.

1247. also Judith, Ebenʳ, John, James R. & Benjⁿ B. Townsend children of Mr Nathan & Mrs Judith Townsend

1248 Here lyes yᵉ Body of Isaac Townsend Died Janʳy the 12ᵗʰ 1717–18 in the 34ᵗʰ year of his age

1249. Here lyes yᵉ body of Mrs Abigail Townsend widow to Mr Samuel Townsend aged 87 years & 8 mo decᵈ January yᵉ 2ᵈ 1728–9

1250. In memory of Mr Benjamin Pool who died Octʳ 5ᵗʰ 1795 aged 65 years Also In memory of Mrs Ann Pool wife of Mr Benjamin Pool Died May 13ᵗʰ 1803 Aged 83 years

1251. Here lyes Buried the Body of Mrs Mary White wife of Mr. Benjamin White died Feby 23ᵈ 1759 Aged 35 years

1252. Joseph White, Son of Mr. Samuel & Mrs Anne White Decᵈ Septʰʳ 21ˢᵗ 1721 in yᵉ 18ᵗʰ year of his age

1253. Mary White daughʳ of Samuel & Anne White aged 11 mo & 13 days Died Septᵐʰʳ the 3ʳᵈ 1714

1254. Here lyes yᵉ Body of Mrs Hannah Windsor wife to Mr Thomas Windsor who Died Novʰʳᵉ 25ᵗʰ 1745 aged 57 years

1255. Here lyeth ye Body of Abigail Hanyford wife of John Hanyford aged 75 years dec^d February ye 28th 1695–6

1256. Here lyes the body of Mr. John Adams who died Decem^r ye 18th 1747 in ye 58th year of his age

1257. Zechariah ... son of Abraham & Mary .. Adames aged 23 years died May 16 1703.

1258. No 23 Capt Richard Whellen Died Novr 25th 1803 Æ 64

1259. John, son of Capt. Alexander and Mrs Elizth Forsyth, aged 14 months, dec^d Sept. ye 18, 1727.

1260. Here lyes ye Body of Mr Benjamin Tomson aged 27 years Dec^d June ye 18th 1730

1261. Here lies intered the mortal part of Mrs Abigail James Consort to Mr Enoch James who departed this life April ye 3rd 1783 Æ 28 years

1262. Joseph Bennet son to Mr. George & Mrs Elizth Bennet Dec^d March ye 1st 1734–5 in ye 5th year of his age

1263. No 4 Daniel E Powars Tomb 1811

1264. No 5 Othniel French & John Lemans Tomb 1811

1265. No 37 W. Folsom & Joseph Bennett Tomb

1266. Andrew Crocker & Vollintine Tomb

1267. Here lies the Body of Mrs. Meriam James who departed this Life July 15th 1765 aged 73 years

1268. In memory of Mr Prince Chew who departed this life Oct 21st 1803 aged 38 years

1269. Capt Jonathan Snellings Tomb

1270. Joshua Snelling son of Capt Jonathan & Mrs Mary Snelling Died Jan^{ry} 26th 1748 aged 2 years & 2 mo Also Sarah Snelling Died Jan^{ry} 13th 1749 aged 7 years

1271. James Phillips son of Philip & Nancy Taylor died May 5 1818 aged 6 years

(poetry 5 lines)

1272. Here lies buried the Body of Mrs Dorothy Gafford Wife of Mr. Richard Gafford Died Feb^{ry} 26th 1764 in ye 38th year of her age

1273. Here lies buried three children of Capt Edward & Mrs Mary Taylor, Mary the eldest died June 9th 1803 Aged 11 Months & 14 days.

1274. Here lyes buried the Body of Mr James Bound aged 23 years dec^d Nov ye 6th 1738

1275. Here lies Buried the Body of Mr James Orr who died Sept ye 3, 1750 in the 36 year of his age

1276. Here lies the body of Mrs Margaret Orr dau^r of Mr Daniel & Mrs Jane Orr died May 7th 1753 in y^r 25th year of her age

1277. In memory of Henrieta Dau^r of Sarah & Henry Iwalt died June 3^d 1809 Æ 4 ys 4 mos & 3 D^s

1278. Jeremiah Merells aged about 70 years Dec^d August ye 25th 1679

1279. Here lies the Body of Mrs Elizabeth Ruby wife to Captⁿ John Ruby aged 65 years died Jany 19th 1754

1280. Here lies buried the Body of Mrs Elizabeth Wotton died March 21st 1769 ... d 50 years

1281. John A Graham child of Edw Anderson died Augst 11, 1818 Aged 27 mos

1282. Memento Mori Fugit Hora. Here lyes ye Body of John Ayres aged 62 years & A 11 months who departed this life ye 12th of August 1711

1283. No 9 Edward Cruft's Tomb 1805 Deposited Foster Cruft who died Nov. 16. 1800 Ætat 68

1284. No 42 S. Brintnall Tomb Built 1802

1285. No 42½ Hannah Barker and Mary F. Bartlett

1286. No 43 William McKean and Henry Swifts Tomb Built 1804

1287. No 44 Dephania Sampson & John Snelling Tomb 1805

1288. Doct^r Thomas Tait 1796

1289. Sacred to the memory of Mrs Elizabeth Distoff wife of Mr Jacob Distoff who departed this life April 7, 1806 Aged 31 years

1290. Mrs Mary Harvey 1782

1291. In Memory of Mrs Mary Harvey Widow of Capt Jonathan Harvey who died May 2^d 1782 in the 63^d Year of her age (poetry 4 lines)

1292. .. rah dau^r of Mr Abia & Mrs Mary Hollbrook Aged 10 Months Dec^d Sept 20th 1738

1293. No 45 Jona Wild & Asa Holbrook Tomb 1805

1294. Samuel the Son of Mr Samuel & Mrs Elizth Holbrook Aged 3 days died June ye 11th 1756

1295. Here lyes ye body of Grace Sterling wife to William Sterling aged 27 years Dec^d Feb^{ry} ye 1st 1721–22

1296. In Memory of Miss Eliza Long, 2^d Dau^r of Mr Abraham & Mrs Hannah Long who departed this life the 13 of April 1808 aged 5 years & 3 months

1297. Here lies interred ye body of Capt Peter Mortimer Brother to Mr James Mortimer who departed this life Augt 22 1773 aged 59 years. He was born in the city of Waterford in the Kingdom of Ireland

1298. No 8 Ann Curtis, Joseph Willcut Jr. Tomb 1811

1299. No 22 Joseph Willcut 1831, James W. Fenno's Tomb.

1300. ..vid Martin 1757

1301. Here lies buried the Body of Capt Roger Lucas Born in Oakford Died March 16ᵗʰ 1772 aged 58 years

1302. Here lies buried the Body of Mrs Sarah Lucas wife of Capt Roger Lucas Died March 26 1772 aged 48 years

1303. No 27 Peter Thomas' Tomb.   Sacred to the memories of Ann Thomas. Obt. Dec. 27, 1796. Æ 12 days.
    Ann R. Thomas, Obt. May 24 1804 Æ. 6 years.
    Samⁱ P. Thomas Obt Dec 14 1805 Æ. 14 months
    Son, still born Aug 11, 1806
    Elizⁱⁱ R. Thomas Obt May 4, 1821 Æ. 21 years
    Mary Thomes Obt July 8, 1821 Æ 48 years
    Children & wife of Thomas Kemble Thomas

1304. In Memory of Mr. Alexander Little who departed this life Sepᵗ yᵉ 25ᵗʰ 1785 aged 55 years

1305. Octʳ 11, 1806 No 86 Capᵗ Seth Webber's & Joseph Grammer's Tomb.

1306. Here lyes yᵉ body of Mrs Susannah Littleton wife to Mr Lewis Littleton Decᵈ Jaⁿʸ yᵉ 16 ... ¾ in ye 26 ... of her age

1307. Here lyes the Body of Mrs Hannah Tapper aged 85 years Died July yᵉ 14ᵗʰ 1742

1308 Sarah Dauʳ to Benjamin & Rebecca Stookas aged about 11 mo Decᵈ Augᵗ yᵉ 23ᵈ 1723

1309. John Son of Mr John & Mrs Dorcas Adams aged 10 weeks & 6 Dˢ Decᵈ April yᵉ 2ᵈ 1737

1310. Here lyes yᵉ body of Hannah Adams wife to John Adams aged about 50 years died Decʳ yᵉ 5ᵗʰ 1723

1311. Here lyes buried the body of Mrs Mary Adams wife to Mr John Adams died Augᵗ yᵉ 16ᵗʰ 1745 in yᵉ 69th year of her age

1312. In Memory of Almeda Daughter of Mr. Edward & Mrs Eunice Cutter died Sept 30ᵗʰ 1806 aged 19 months & 22 days

1313. Sigourney No 25 This stone replaced by D. A. & H. H. W. S. 1852.

1314. Here lies buried the Body of Mrs Jemimia Adams wife to Mr. William Adams who Departed this Life April 29ᵗʰ 1765 in the 39 year of her age Also Jemima Adams Daur of Mr. William & Mrs Jemima Adams Died March 14 1773 in yᵉ 5ᵗʰ year of her age.

1315. In Memory of Mr. John James who died Decʳ 22ᵈ Aged 47 in the year 1803

(poetry 8 lines)

1316. Martha Hillard Daughter to Edward and Lidia Hillard aged 2 years & a quarter Died yᵉ August 21 1687.

1317. Here lies ye Body of Sarah Ritchery wife of Prince Hall died Feb the 26th 1769 aged 24 years

1318. Here lyeth ye body of Elizabeth Lawson ye wife of John Lawson Aged 50 years Dec^d May ye 1st 1699

1319. This Stone is sacred to the memory of Capt William Burke who died May 24th 1787 Ætat 40, And of Mrs Mary Burke Wife of Capt William Burke who died Ja^ny 15th 1787 Ætat 38

1320. Here lyes ye Body of Mr Benjamin Snelling who died Novr 6 Anno Dom 1739 in ye 40th year of his age

1321. Here lyeth Bur... ye Body of John Snelling Aged about 38 years Dec^d February ye 17, 1699–700

1322. In Memory of Mr. Benj^a Doubleday who departed this life Sept 2^d 1784 aged 50 years

1323. Hannah Spencer J. S.

1324. In Memory of Mercy Wife of Wm Collins Hookaway died Octr 29th 1807 Ae 42

1325. Here lyes ye Body of Mrs Elizabeth Webber wife to Mr. Nath Webber dec^d March ye 11th 1731–2 in ye 60 year of her age

1326. In Memory of Mrs. Susanna Hemmenway Wife of Mr. Eben^r Hemmenway and youngest dau^r of Capt Christopher Hoskins. She departed this Life April 17th 1796 in the 34th year of her age.

(poetry 4 lines)

1327. Here lyes buried ye Body of Mr. Joseph Snelling who departed this life July ye 1st A. D. 1748 aged 53 years 2 months & 10 days.

1328. Here lyes buried ye Body of Anna Snelling Daut^r of Mr Joseph & Mrs Prissila Snelling who departed this life Jany the 30th 1766 aged 20 years.

1329. Here Lyes Buried ye Body of Mr. Joseph Snelling Who Dec^d Augu^t ye 15th 1726 Aged about 59 years.

1330. Samuel Snelling son to Joseph & Mary Snelling aged 4 mo Dec^d Sept ye 20th 1723.

1331. Rebecca Snelling Died June 21st 1730 Aged 1 year & 7 mo. Hannah Snelling Died June 22^d 1730 Aged 1 year & 7 mo. ye children of Joseph & Elizabeth Snelling.

1332. In Memory of Anna Snelling Daughter of Jonah & Mary Snelling died April 8th 1790 Aged 12 months.

1333. No. 3 The Armes & Tomb Belonging to the Family of Gee.

1334. In Memory of Ebenezer Wild who departed this life Decr 4th 1794 in the 37th year of his age He was a kind husband a tender parent and sincere friend

1335. In Memory ... Mr. Samuel Wild who died Octr 27 1784 aged 63 years

1336. Cushing .... 48 years and 4 mo died Novr ye 14th 1715

1337. Elizabeth Fowle Daughter of John & Katherine Fowle Aged 13 mo died December 2 1694

1338. ...yes Buried the Body of Mrs. Mary Wilson widow of Capt. Andrew Wilson Died Augst 17th 1753 Aged 89

1339. The Family Tomb of Nath^e Barber Esq., who lies here deposited, died Oct. 14, 1787 Æ^t 59. Also Mrs Elizabeth wife of Mr John F. Barber died April 24 1832 Æt 52 No. 28

1340. In Memory of Mr. William Barber who died August 20th 1801 Aged 52 years

1341. In Memory of Mrs. Mary Farmer who died Nov. 4th 1798 Ætat 68

(poetry 4 lines)

1342. In Memory of Mr. Abraham Hayward Son to Mr. Abraham & Mrs Abigail Hayward who died Novr 7 1781 aged 22 years. He was a dutiful son, a kind Brother & sincere friend. Also Thomas Haward died Feby 12th 1771 aged 2 years & 5 mos.

1343. In Memory of Mr. Abraham Hayward who died March 5th 1796, Aged 62 years

1344. Sacred to the memory of Mrs. Hephsibah Hayward who departed this Life Decr 23^d 1802 aged 68

1345. In Memory of Abigail Brewer Farmer who died Decr 10th 1804 aged 20 years.

1346. Here lyes ye body of Mr. Samuel Barber died Octr ye 21st 1746 in ye 51st year of his age

1347. Sarah Barber aged 13 days died October ye 26, 1693

1348. Polly Bentley Barber Daug^r of John & Hepzibah Barber who died Sep 12th 1800 Aged 1 year

1349. Here lyes the body of Mrs. Elizabeth Langdon widdow to Mr. Edward Langdon Aged about 96 years Dec^d Dec y 28th 1737

1350. Here lyes intered the Body of Mr William Pitman aged 45 years dec^d Decr ye 17^{t}h 1732.

1351. Here lies intered the Body of Deacon Josiah Langdon who died Novr the 5th 1742 in the 55th year of his age
Edwd Langdon Junr Ob^t 30th April 1755 Æt 31
Nathl Langdon Obt 27th Dec 1757 Æt 63
Susanna Langdon Obt 3^d Septr 1760 Æt 65.
Eph^m Langdon A.M. Obt 21st Novr 1765 Æt 33
Dea Edward Langdon Obt 25th May 1766 Æt 69
Mary Langdon only child of Edward Langdon Junr dec^d
Obt 8th Sept 1771 Æt 18.

1352 Skillin

1353. Here lies buried y⁻ Body of Mr. James Varney who died Jan'ʸ yᶜ 24ᵗ⁻ 1752 Aged 74 Also the Body of Mrs Jean Varney wife of Mr James Varney who died April 8ᵗʰ 1752 aged 80

1354. In Memory of Mr William Speed a native of Scotland died Augˢᵗ 21ˢᵗ 1808 Æ 53

1355. Mary Tolman died May 30ᵗʰ 1752 aged 5 years & 6 mo. Desire Tolman Died April 29ᵗᵸ 1755 aged 5 weeks & 22 Dˢ children of Samˡ & Mary Tolman

1356. Josiah Smith Aged 1 year and about 1 mo Decˡ Novbʳ 13ᵗʰ 1721, Nathaniel Smith Aged 3 years & about 7 mo Decˡ Novbʳ 15, 1721, children of John & Ruth Smith.

1357. In Memory of Ann Wilbur Smith, only child of Capt John & Ann Smith who died July 6 1815 Aged 3 ye 9 mo & 12 days.

1358. In Memory of 4 children of Capt John & Mrs Jane Guliker who are here intered viz John Guliker Junʳ who died 23ᵈ Augˢᵗ 1770 aged 13 days, John Guliker Junʳ who died 7ᵗʰ Augˢᵗ 1781 Aged 14 months, Thomas Guliker died 29ᵗʰ June 1783 aged 10 days. Mary Guliker died 23ˡ Decʳ 1784 aged 6 years

1359. John Smith's Tomb, 1812 No. 33.

1360. Here Lyes the Body of Mr. John Holland aged 63 years died Sept 9ᵗʰ 1736. Also Mrs Susannah ye wife of Mr John Holland aged 69 years died July 13ᵗʰ 1741

1361. Sacred to the memory of Mrs Elizabeth Kenny who departed this Life Sept 10ᵗʰ 1807 in the 42ᵈ year of her age

(poetry 4 lines)

1362. Loyd son of Sarah and Hannah Ball aged 15 dayes deceased ye 7ᵗʰ of Novʳ 1716.

1363. Here lies buried the Body of Mr Robert Balls who departed this Life Octʳ 10ᵗʰ 1774 in the 75ᵗʰ Year of his age

1364. Here lies buried Ye Body of Mrs Martha Balls the wife of Mr Robert Balls who departed this Life May 30, 1765 aged 82 years

1365. No. 16 Col Edward Proctor

1366. Thomas ye son of Edward & Elizabeth Proctor aged 4 mo decᵈ April yᶜ 12 1697

1367. No 15 Hooton & Watts Family Tomb

1368. Here lies buried the Body of Mr Aaron Boardman aged 43 years died June yᶜ 9ᵗʰ 1754

1369. Mrs Bethesda Bordman

1370. Sacred to the Memory of Mr. John Green of this town who died May 28ᵗʰ 1806 in the 72ᵈ Year of his age

1371. Capt Joseph Ingraham died Juhe 1811 Æ 48

1372. Here lyes yᵉ body of Elizabeth wife of Henry Ingraham died Janʳʸ yᵉ 17ᵗʰ 1717–8 in yᵉ 62ᵈ year of her age

1373. Here lyes the body of Mr John Welch aged 55 years decᵈ Novʳ ye 23 1713

1374. Mary daur to Mr William & Mrs Deborah Welch aged 6 months decᵈ July yᵉ 11ᵗʰ 1729

1375. Mary daur to Mr William & Mrs Deborah Welch aged 1 mo & 3 dˢ decᵈ Decʳ yᵉ 22ᵈ 1732

1376. Here lies the Body of Mrs. Phebe Richardson wife of Mr Benjamin Richardson who departed this Life May yᵉ 3ᵈ 1768, In the 37ᵗʰ Year of her age

1377. Here lyes yᵉ Body of Mrs Mary Bassett Widow of Mr Francis Bassett who Died Octʳ 12ᵗʰ 1743 in yᵉ 66ᵗʰ year of her age

1378. Andrew Sigourney Tomb No 6

1379. Here lyes yᵉ Body of Samuel Aves Son to Mr Samuel Aves aged 20 years decᵈ Otʳ yᵉ 3ᵈ 1727

1380. Here lies the Body of Mrs Rebeckah Aves wife of Mr Samuel Aves and Dauʳ of Mr Robert & Mrs Sibella Breck Died July 29ᵗʰ 1772 in yᵉ 34ᵗʰ year of her age

1381. Capt John Harvey died Febʸ 16ᵗʰ 1814 aged 54

1382. In Memory of Capt Nathaniel Doak who died Febʸ 23 1819 Æt 35 years

1383 No 22 Family Tomb of W. Monroe. J. Mead. J. D. Ingersoll

1384. Here lyes buried the body of Mary Langley wife to Mr William Langley Aged 43 years & 6 Mo Died Sept yᵉ 23 1743

1385. Erected in Memory of Mr Samuel Hill who died April 27 1804 Ætat 38

1386. In Memory of Mrs Prudence Hill Widow of Mr Abraham Hill of Cambridge died Janʳʸ the 26ᵗʰ 1775 Aged 78 years.

1387. Samuel Hill & Edmund Parsons   Tomb   1820
poetry 2 lines

1387a. 1722 Greenwood. No. 57.

1387b. Here lyeth interred yᵉ Body of Nathaniel Greenwood, aged 53 years, Departed this life July the 31, 1684.

1387c. Here lyes buried yᵉ Body of Mr. William Burrough, aged about 70 years, decᵈ April yᵉ 21ˢᵗ 1717.

1387d. Sacred to the Memory of three children of Elisha and Mary Norcross : William died Octʳ 23ᵈ 1802, aged 5 years and 2 mᵒ ; Mary died Septᵗ 25ᵗʰ 1802, aged 2 years : and an Infant Daughter.

1387e. Edward Peirse, son to Mr Moses and Mrs Eliz^th Peirse, aged 1 year & 8 m^o dec^d June ye 18th 1730.

1387f. Thomas Stoddard, son of Mr Thomas & Mrs Abigail Stoddard, aged 1 year & 2 m^o Died Sept ye 3^d 1743.

1387g. Rebecca Edes, Dau^r to Mr Will... & Mrs Rebecca Edes, died Sept. 20, 1758. Aged 1 year & 4 months

1388. In Memory of Miss Mary Fitzgearld Daug^r of Mr Michael & Mrs Honnor Fitzgearld who died Sep^t 30th 1787 aged 19 Years

1389. No 9 Ichabod Macomber Charles Howard and Ezekiel Sawin's Tomb

1390. Major Nathaniel Heath died May 5th 1812 Ætat 80 His wife Mrs Mary Heath died Octr 12th 1809 Ætat 72

(poetry 4 lines)

1391. Sacred to the memory Lt. Robert Clarke a native of New Boston N. H. who died May 19, A. D. 1813. Ætat 34

1392. Mary dau^r of Josiah & Pressellah Clark aged 4 years & 9 Mos Died Novr ye 4th 1719

1393. Here lies buried the Body of .. Mrs Priscilla Ola.... who departed this . March 12, 1756 Aged 76

1394. Mrs Sarah Storer.

1395. Here lyes ye Body of Mrs Mary Treat Wife to Mr Joseph Treat Aged 49 years Dec^d May ye 6, 1742

1396. Capt Elijah Nickerson & Thomas Hopkins 1804

1397. Sacred to the memory of Capt Nathaniel Glasier who departed this life May 27th in the year of our Lord 1812 aged 30 years

(poetry 2 lines)

1398. In Memory of Mrs Susanna Dunn wife of Capt James Dunn who died March 1 1815 Æt 25

1399. Sacred to the memory of Mr Thomas Fisher a native of Manchester Old England who departed this life June 27th 1805 aged 30

1400. Capt Michael Randols died Aug 11, 1812 Æt 45

(poetry 4 lines)

1401. Here lyes ye body of John Underwood aged 57 years died Jan^ry ye 11th 1706

1402. In Memory of Joseph Warren Underwood Son of Mr John and Mrs Eliz^th Underwood Died June 5th 1783 aged 7 years & 6 mo

1403. Here lies ye Body of Mary Underwood Dau^r of Mr John & Mrs Eliz^th Underwood Died Sept 30th 1769 aged 14 months

1404. In Memory of Mrs. Hipsabah Underwood Widow of John Underwood died 27ᵗʰ July 1785 aged 72 years

1405. Thomas Sulliv.. John Barber & John Sullivan Tomb 1802

1406. Here lies the Body of Mr. John Barber who Died Decʳ yᵉ 2ᵈ 1758 in yᵉ 35ᵗʰ year of his age

1407. .ere lyes the Body of Mr John Barber Aged 47 years Died April 25ᵗ 1748

1408. In memory of Mr Joseph Blake who died Dec 2, 1805 Æt 26

1409. In memory of Henry Blake Senʳ died Oct 25ᵗʰ 18 Æ 56

1410. Here lyes yᵉ Body of Mrs Marcy Willson wife to Mr William Willson decᵈ Decʳ yᵉ 15ᵗʰ 1719 Ætatis sua 21 years & 7 months

1411. Ingersoll

1412. Here lies the Body of Mrs Ann Thomas wife of Capt William Thomas who departed this Life Novemʳ 27 1767 aged 89 years

1413. Here lies Buried the Body of Capt William Thomas Aged 76 years

1414. Capt Thomas Lambert Died May 12ᵗʰ 1813 Ætat 32

1415. In Memory of Theodore James Obt Sepʳ 25 1813 aged 28 months Also Francis Edward Obt Feb 17 1815 Aged 20 months two children of Samuel & Sally Brewer

1416. Here Lyeth Buried Yᵉ Body of Ann Yᵉ Wife Of Joseph Penwell Aged about 60 Years Deceased December Yᵉ 3 1688

1417. Nathaniel Bremer, Elsie Cook & George Darracott's Tomb

1418. ... lyes yᵉ Body .. Mr. Christopher Capron aged 53 years decᵈ Novʳ yᵉ 14ᵗʰ 1721

1419. Here lyes yᵉ Body of Mr Josiah Stone aged 62 years & about 5 mo decᵈ July yᵉ 26ᵗʰ 1717.

1420. In Memory of Mrs Rebecca Car wife of Mr John H. Car died May 17ᵗʰ 1805 Æ 26

1421. Thomas son to John & Susanna Wilkins aged 18 months decᵈ July yᵉ 19, 1679

1422. Here lyes yᵉ body of Mrs Susanna Wilkins wife to Mr John Wilkins aged 76 years decᵈ Octʳ ye 24ᵗʰ 1724

1423. Here lyes the body of Mrs Sarah Willson wife to Mr George Willson Aged 32 years Died May 21ˢᵗ 1749

1424. Here lyeth yᵉ Body of Abigail Everden ye wife of William Everden Aged 38 years decᵈ August yᵉ 15 1696

1425. Ann Brown Elizabeth Hudson & Joseph Callender's Tomb 1823 No 24

1426. Here lyes buried yᵉ Body of Miss Grace Ierland Relict of Capt John Ierland who died Octᵇʳ 2ᵈ 1730 aged 77 years 5 mo & 1 day

1427. Here lyes yᵉ Body of Mary Ireland Daughter of Mr John & Mrs Grace Ireland Aged 24 years Decᵈ Novᵐᵉʳ 10ᵗʰ 172..

1428. Here lyes yᵉ Body of Mr George Worthylake died Novʳ yᵉ 3ᵈ 1718 in yᵉ 45 year of his age. Ruth Dauʳ of Mr George & Mrs Ann Worthylake died Novʳ yᵉ 3ᵈ 1718 in yᵉ 15ᵗʰ year of her age. Here lyes ye Body of Miss Ann Worthylake died Novʳ yᵉ 3ᵈ 1718 in yᵉ 40 year of her age

1429. Susanna Whittreadg aged 7 years died May yᵉ — 1694

1430. Here lies the Body of Mrs Abigail Whiteridge wife to Mr Richard Whiteridge Aged 52 years Decᵈ Janʳʸ ye 30 1724–5

1431. Here lyes yᵉ Body of Sarah Whitridge Wife to Richard Whitridge who died January 31ˢᵗ 1733–4 Aged 68 years

1432. John Cookson Tomb.

1433. Here lies intombed the body of Mrs Margaret Webb who died Decʳ 11ᵗʰ 1813 aged 74 years

1434. Joseph son of Joseph and Deborah Webb aged 9 months died June the 30 1708

1435. Joseph son to Joseph & ... Webb ... days .. Augᵗ 1714

1436. Erected In memory of Mr Thomas S.·Webb son of Mr Nehemiah & Mrs Sarah Webb of Falmouth County of Barnstable He died Sept 17ᵗʰ 1798 Aged 18 years & 9 months

1437. Jabez & Nathaniel Fishers Tomb

1438. Sacred to the Memory of Mr Richard Roberts son of Mr Richard and Mrs Mercy Roberts who departed the life June 16ᵗʰ 1812 aged 26

(poetry 4 lines)

1439. No 19. In memory of Dorothy Roberts wife of Robert Roberts died Decʳ 31 1812 Aged 28

1440. Sarah Stone Dauʳ of Mr William & Mrs Elizabeth Stone aged 20 years Died May 15ᵗʰ 1752. Anna Stone Dauʳ of Mr William & Mrs Elizabeth Stone aged 13 years Died May 28ᵗʰ 1752

1441. Here lyes yᵉ Body of Mr. Benjamin Stone aged about 42 years died December yᵉ 15 1706

1442. Here lyes buried the Body of Mrs Mercy Stoddard wife to Mr Arthur Stoddard aged 26 years Decᵈ Febʳʸ ye 14ᵗʰ 1738–9

1443. Here Lyes Ye Body of Mrs Judet Colesworthy Wife of Mr Gorge Colesworthey Aged Twenty-One Years And Three Months And 25 Days Old Died The 23 Day of April 1729

1444. In Memory of Mr Nathaniel Colesworthy Sen' who died Sept 20 1802 : Æ 53. Also Mr. Nathaniel Colesworthy Jun' who died April 22 1808 Æ 27 Nath¹ Colesworthy died Oct 20, 1779 Æ 2, Sally Colesworthy died May 9, 1780 Æ 6 mo Charles Colesworthy died Aug 9 1793 Æ 5.

1445. Here lyes the mortal part of Nath¹ Colesworthy who died Oct' 21ˢᵗ 1802 Aged 32 and also of Polly his wife who after his death was the wife of William Green, She died Feb'ʸ 11ᵗʰ 1805 June ye 18ᵗʰ 1745

1446. Mr George Colesworthy Aged 40 years & 2 mo Dyed Aged 29

1447. Erected in Memory of Mr Thomas Webb Son of Mr Nehemiah & Mrs Sarah Webb...

1448. Samuel son of Joseph & Deborah Webb aged 14 days died ye Oct' 31ˢᵗ 1717

1449. Ann daughter to Christopher & Ann Webb Aged 1 year 5 Dˢ decᵈ Oct' yᵉ 30 1774

1450. Here lies buried the Body of Major John Ruddock Esq Died 2ᵈ Sept 1772 aged 59 years & 2 months. He was in commission for the Peace & Justice of the Quonun for the County of Suffolk for 13 years. He commanded his Majesty's North Battery in Boston 13 yʳˢ & was a selectman for the same Town 9 yʳˢ. Could a heart that felt, and a hand that relieved the Miseries Attendant upon humanity — Could the truest patriotism Equally superior To the frowns of power and the rage of party,Which with invisible constancy Asserted and defended universally, (For he was a citizen of the world) The rights of mankind Could undeviating integrity In every office which he dignified by holding, Joined to the most impartial Dispensation of justice — In fine, could extensive virtue worth Rescue from the tomb, Reader, thou hadst not been told Here lies Ruddock. Depart! Imitate his virtues And with him Merit the eulogium of thy country

1451. John son of Fortune & Abel Reddock Aged 9 months died October ye 12ᵗʰ 1709

1452. Abiell dau' to Fortune & Abiell Reddock aged 6 weeks died July yᵉ 22 1707

1453. .. memory of William Meacham who died Sep 3 1805 Aet 43 William P. Meacham, son of William & Ruth Meacham died July 30 1804 aged 6 mos

1454. A Tribute To the memory of Mrs Ruth consort of Mr William Meacham died August 13 1811 Aged 33 years. Erected by her son George L. Meacham

1455. In Memory of Capt Caleb Hayden died on the 2ᵈ day of July Anno Domini 1795 in the 57ᵗʰ Year of his Age

(poetry 6 lines)

1456. Here lies Buried the Body of Capt Richard Watts aged 30 Years Died March y⸱ 8ᵗʰ 1749–50

1457. Joseph son to John & Elizabeth Wilkins agod 14 Mo died Dec yᵉ 9 1702

1458. Susannah Dauʳ of Stephen & Mary Paine died Novʳ ye 26 1719 in the 9ᵗʰ year of her age

1459. Daniel Ware son to Daniel & Hannah Ware Aged 13 Mo & 12 days dyed January y⸱ 8ᵗʰ 1693–4

1460 In memory of Mrs Hariot wife of Mr Henry Jacobus Revinason who died May 27ᵗʰ 1812 in her 20ᵗʰ year

1461. James Bartlett, John Thayer, Joseph Uranns Tomb 1813 No. 25

1462. In Memory of Ebenezer Frost Bartlett son of Mr Roger & Mrs Anna Bartlott Aged 9 weeks died June 27ᵗʰ 1765

1463. In Memory of Mr John Nelson who departed this. Life May 5ᵗʰ 1806 aged 46 years

1464. Here lyes y⸱ Body of Mrs Joanna Hunt wife to Mr Ephraim Hunt aged about 52 years decᵈ August y⸱ 20ᵗʰ 1731

1465. Edward Bells Tomb 1828 No. 47.

1466. Memento Mori Fugit Hora, Here lyes ye body of Mary Bell wife to Thomas Bell Aged 30 years 7 Mo & 20 days who deceased y⸱ 15ᵗʰ of September 1710

1467. In memory of James B. Smith died June 17ᵗʰ 1805 Æ 48. Also his Wife Susannah Smith died March 25ᵗʰ 1809 Æ 57

1468. In Memory of Thomas R. Snow Son of Martin & Eleanor Snow; who died Sept 25ᵗʰ 1813 Aged 1 year

1469. No 88. Oct 11. 1806. John Loring's Tomb.

1470. No 93 Elijah Loring

1471. Here lyes Buried y⸱ Body of Deacon John Barret Aged 47 Years, who Decᵈ Octᵇʳ the 1ˢᵗ 1721

1472. Here lies y⸱ Body of Samuel Barrett & Son of Mr William & Mrs Abigail Barrett died Octʳ 30ᵗʰ 1767 Aged 12 Months & 25 days

1473. Here y⸱ body of Rebeccah Barrett wife to Deacon John Barrett decᵈ May y⸱ 16ᵗʰ 1731 in ye 59ᵗʰ year of her age

1474. No 45 Joshua Loring, John F. Newton 1819

1475. In memory of Jacob H. Son of Nathaniel & Rebecca Emmes who was drowned July 23 1807 Ae 10 Joshua H. Mann who was killed by the falling of the wall of the Columbian Museum Janry 15ᵗʰ 1807 Ae 16.

1476. In memory of Philander Wayne who died Augˢᵗ 28ᵗʰ 1817, aged 3 months & 16 days, & Lydia Ellen Sanger, who died May 21ˢᵗ 1819 aged 6 months & 26 days children of Nathan & Lydia L. Barrett

1477. Asahel Stockwell & Daniel Wise No. 1.

1478. In Memory of John Capen the second son of Mr Hopestill and Mrs Patience Capen who died Feb 19th 1770 Aged 7 years.

1479. In Memory of Isaac Howard Davis only child of John & Eliz⁺ Davis died May 8th 1807 Æ 20 mos & 8 days
(poetry 2 lines)

1480. No. 46 Michael Dalton and William F. Clark Tomb

1481. Nathaniel & Edward Clark sons of Nathnie & Elizabeth Clark; Nathanᵢ Aged 15 days Edwaᵈ 20 days; both died in September 1712

1482. In Memory of Mr Eunice Clark wife of Mr Samuel Clark died 19 Jany 1794 63 years & 8 months.

1483. Here lies buried the Body of Mrs Ann Coping aged 62 years Decᵈ Augᵗ yᵉ 26ᵗʰ 1731

1484. Simeon Boydens Tomb 1825 No. 26.

1485. Charles Gyles son to Mr. Edward & Mrs Elizᵗʰ Gyles died May the 16th 1754 aged 5 years

1486. Charles Gyles son to Mr Edward and Mrs Elizᵗʰ Gyles aged 1 month Died March yᵉ 9th 1745–6

1487. Here lyes intered ye Body of Mr John Pullen Decᵈ Jan'y yᵉ 9th 1717–8 in ye 61ˢᵗ year of his age

1488. Here lyes the Body of Mary Pullen wife to Captⁿ John Pullen aged 56 years died March yᵉ 4th 1712–13

1489. Here lies buried the Body of Mrs Annis Pulling Wife to Mr John Pulling Obt 11th Augˢᵗ 1771 aged 27 year & 10 mo

1490. Here lyes yᵉ body of Mary Maccollo wife to Thomas Maccollo aged 34 years decᵈ July yᵉ 15th 1739

1491. James son to Thomas and Mary Maccolloy aged one year decᵈ Octʳ yᵉ 26 1736

1492. No. 48 Nathaniel Nottage & Jonathan Loring Junʳ Tomb 1828

1493. Here lyes yᵉ Body of Samuel Babcock died Octʳ yᵉ 24th 1721 in yᵉ 31ˢᵗ year of his age.

1494. Erected to the Memory of five children of Mrs Hopestill & Mrs Patience Capen, namely William died Jan 14 1770 Aged 1 day, John the second died Sept 3, 1771, Aged 5 months, and 14 days; John the third died Apr 10, 1773, Aged 5 months and 20 days; Elizabeth the first died Oct 13 1772 Aged 4 years 6 months & 27 days ; Elizabeth the second died Oct 7 1775 Aged 1 year.

1495. No. 7 David Mardens Tomb 1828

1496. John Pritchard son to William and Mrs Atterlanter Pritchard died March 17th 1757 Aged 14 years 3 months & 13 days

1497. Here lyes ye body of Peter Prichet aged about 31 years dec^d Novr ye 26th 1721 Sarah dau^r to Peter & Sarah Prichet aged 16 mo dec^d Oct ye 6 t 1721.

1498. Thomas son to Nathaniel and Su... Loring, A.. weeks 2 D... Dec¹ Novr ye 21st 1715

1499. No 24. Thomas Green & John Lewis's Tomb 1812.

1500. No. 19. Benja Lewis, Jane Bayley & Elizabeth Thomas Tomb 1820

1501. In Memory of Abigail Allcock dau^r of Mr Robert & Mr; Abigail Allcock died Octr 26th 1784 Aged 19 months.

1502. Here lyes ye Body of Mr Joseph Pratt deceas^d August y^r 27t^h 1719 & buried Septr ye 11 in ye 30th year of his age

1503. Here lies ye body of Deborah wife to Timothy Prat Aged 45 years dec^d September ye 26, 1679 as also 3 children lies by her left hand

1504. Here Lies buried ye Body of Mary Pratt Wife to Caleb Pratt : who Dec^d Octo^r y 26 1721

1505. Turell Tuttle's Tomb 1801

1506. Here lies buried the Body of Mary Boucher dau^r to Deacon Thomas & Mrs Ann Boucher Died Sept 2^d 1767

(poetry 4 lines)

1507. Elizabeth Turner

1508. Here lyeth buried ye body of Mary Warram daughter to William & Mary Warram aged about 2 months dec^d ye 13 of July 1681

1509. William McClennen & Joseph Jones Tomb 1812

1510. Here lyes buried the body of Mrs Elizabeth Jones wife to Mr John Jones Aged 25 years died July the 9th 1744

1511. No 30. Josiah Marshall's Tomb 1812

1512. In Memory of George Wardell youngest son of Capt John Wardell who died Decr 5th 1802 aged 2 years and 7 months (poetry 2 lines)

1513. Jane McTaggett .. Dau^r of Mr Peter .. & Mrs Margaret McTaggett Aged 2 years & 3 Mo died Decr 31st 1751

1514. Sacred to the Memory of Capt. James Smith who departed this Life July 1st 1803 aged 43 years

1515. Here lyes ye Body of Mrs Elizabeth Smith Widow to Mr Thomas Smith Who Died Jan^{ry} 23¹ 1753 Aged 75 Years

1516. Elizabeth daughter to John & Jane Smith aged 1 year & 10 days died Sept ye 12 1702

1517. Sacred to the memory of Mrs Elizabeth Smith Wife of Capt James Smith who departed this life July 1st 1803 Aged 43 years

1518. Mary McClarry Dauʳ of Mr John & Mrs Anna McClarry aged 5 weeks died Augˢᵗ 15 1744 Ann McClarry Aged 16 months & 4 da died Augˢᵗ 10ᵗʰ 1747

1519. Here lieth ye Body of Tickleemanbeck Aged about 22 years died 28 April 1702

1520. In Memory of Abel Barbadoes who died March 22 1817 aged 66

1521. Hannah Robie Dauʳ to Joseph and Prissella Robie aged 11 weeks & 3 Dˢ decᵈ March yᵉ 28 1726

1522. Here lies yᵉ body of Margaret Colley a free negro died May 4ᵗʰ 1761 aged 75 years

1523. William, son to Bartholomew & Mary Gedney, aged 6 weeks Died Decʳ yᵉ 7ᵗʰ 1725 ; William son to Bartholomew & Mary Gedney Aged 14 days Died Decʳ yᵉ 14ᵗʰ 1726.

1524. This Stone perpetuates the Memory of Mrˢ Elizabeth Herman wife of Mr Leopold F. Herman who departed this life June 5ᵗʰ 1797 aged 20. Also their daughter Eliza aged 5 mo and 13 days died July 24ᵗʰ 1796

1525. Here lyes yᵉ Body of George Hiller aged about 32 years died August yᵉ 22ᵈ 1721

1526. Here lies buried the body of Mr Henry Roby who departed this life Nov 9ᵗʰ 1807 Aged 85 years

1527. Henry Roby son to Mr Henry & Mrs Elizabeth Roby aged 5 years & 2 months Died June yᵉ 13ᵗʰ 1752

1528. Here lyes yᵉ body of Henry Robie son to William & Elizᵗʰ Robie aged 18 years decᵈ July yᵉ 20ᵗʰ 1721

1529. In Memory of · Mrs Sarah Roby wife of Mr Henry Roby who departed this Life May 19ᵗʰ 1805 Aged 78

1530. Mary Robey dauʳ to Mr Joseph and Mrs Mary Robey Aged about 1 year..

1531. Robert King son of Mr Henry & Mrs Sarah King aged 13 months & 9 days dyed Sept 19ᵗʰ 1742

1532. No 49 Jacob Hilers Tomb Built 1805

1533. Sarah Daughter of John & Jane Snelling aged 12 years 10 mo & 17 Dˢ died december yᵉ 17 1702

1534. No 16. Adams Bailey Jr, Samuel Noyse, Marcy Blanchard Tomb 1821

1535. Here lyes yᵉ body of Israel Bailey decᵈ Augᵗ yᵉ 6ᵗʰ 1721 in yᵉ 32ᵈ year of age

1536. To the Memory of Mrs Elizabeth Hayden consort of Capt Caleb Hayden who departed this Life September 23ᵈ 1790 Aged 55 years.

(poetry 4 lines)

1537. Thomas Wells book publisher died Dec 31 1829 aged 49 year T. Gilman Wells son of Thomas & Eliza Wells died Jan 24 1848 aged 25 years 5 months

1538. Sarah Wells Dau^r to Mr Johu & Mrs Hannah Wells died Aug^st ye 7th 1733 Aged 11 years

1539. Here lyes the body of Mrs Joanna Mills widow of Mr John Mills who died March ye 26th 1733 in the 83^d year of her age

1540. Davis Whitman 1804

1541. In Memory of William son of Mr William Mills & Mrs Betsey his wife he was drowned August the 25th 1792 in the 6th year of his age

1542. Benj^a Amos. Joshua & John Binuey's Family Tomb 1801.

1543. No —, 1807 Thomas Page's Family Tomb.

1544. Here lies Intend the Mortal part of Mr Edward Page who Departed this Life November the 10th 1784 aged 68 Years

1545. Here lyes ye Body of Mrs Rachel Young Wife to Mr An..ony Young who Died Nov^br 1st 1732 in ye 49th year of her age

1546. Here lies the body of Mr William Yonge who died June the 5 1750 in the 48 year of his age.

1547. Abraham Millet Tomb 1821   No. 12.

1548. Mc Leod.

1549. Thomas y^r son of Thomas & Rebecca Wels aged 9 months and 4 days died October ye 7 1702

1550. In Memory of Charlotte Gould daughter of James & Sally Gould who died Aug 26, 1805 aged 19 months & 10 days

(poetry 2 lines)

1551. Sarah Goldthwait, Sarah daughter to John & Sarah Goldthwait aged 9 Mo & 19 days died Oct. ye 7, 1702

1552. No 28. Noah Lincoln & Jonathan Thaxter's Tomb 1812

1553. This Stone is erected in Memory of Miss Polly Tidmarsh Barker who died Sept 24th 1798 Aged 17 Years.

(poetry 2 lines)

1554. In Memory of Miss Eliza eldest daughter of Mr William Mills & Mrs Betsey his wife died August 20th 1809 Æ. 17 years & 6 mo

1555. No 14 Rufus Baxter, Eliza Stephens 1821

1556. In Memory of Capt John Crozer * who died April 27th 1801 aged 42 years

1557. .. ere lies Buried the Body of Patrick Sinnett . who died Aug^st 4 1767 .. 35 years

---

* Or Grozer.— Ed.

1558. In Memory of two children of Christopher & Eliza Lincoln both named Christopher Lincoln first died March 18ᵗʰ 1810 Æ 4 years & 4 Month second died April 19ᵗʰ 1813 Ae 11 months

1559. Here lyes yᵉ body of Thomas Barker Aged 38 years decᵈ April yᵉ 5ᵗʰ 1723

1560. In Memory of Thompson Ingerfield Son of Mr Paul and Mrs. Silence Ingerfield died July 28ᵗʰ 1788 Ae 15 years

1561. Here lyes buried ye body of Mary Shortriggs Wife to William Shortriggs aged 39 years died ye 9ᵗʰ 1703

1562. Samuel Hichborn Jr. & Gedney Kings' Tomb 1812 No 29

1563. Here lies the Body of Phebe Lane consort to Capt Ebene zer Lane who departed this Life 12ᵗʰ Novʳ 1781 in the 33ᵈ year of her age

1564. In Memory of Levi Lane died June 23ᵈ 1806 Æ 52

1565. Here lyes buried the body of Mrs Susannah Tomson the wife of Capt Thomas Tomson who departed this life October yʳ 10ᵗʰ 1747 In the 27ᵗʰ year of her age

1566. Here lyes yᵉ Body of Mrs Mary Tompson wife to Mr Thos Tomson Aged 25 years Decᵈ Sept ye 8ᵗʰ 1723

1567. Thomas Capen Tomb 1811

1568. In Memory of Daniel Sharp son of Samuel R. & Mrs Ruth Greene who died Octʳ 2ᵈ 1814 aged 7 monˢ and 14 days

1569. In Memory of Miss Nancy Green youngest daughter of Thomas & Mrs Mary Green who died Dec 18, 1800, aged 11 years
(poetry 2 lines)

1570. No 30. Henry Clap & Jonathan Forbs Tomb 1819

1571. Sacred to the Memory of Mrs. Elizabeth Fernald amiable wife of Capᵗ Abraham Fernald (Also in Memory of her Husband and children), who died Febʳʸ 27ᵗʰ 1804 in the 34ᵗʰ year of her age

1572. Sacred to the Memory of Mr John Learned who died Decʳ 14, 1800 Ætat 31

1573. Mary dauʳ to Mr. James and Mrs Deborah Robins aged 1 year & 8 mo died Novʳ yᵉ 18ᵗʰ 1747

1574. Here lyes the Body of Mr Peter Harratt aged 42 years Decᵈ Febʸ 20ᵗʰ 1739–40

1575. Katharine Harratt Dauʳ to Mr Peter & Mrs Katharine Harratt aged 4 months Decᵈ Novʳ yᵉ 6ᵗʰ 1733

1576. Here lies an infant son of Mr Ebenʳ & Mrs Phebe Lane Born and died Decʳ 8 h 1780

1577. In Memory of Levi, Infant son of Levi & Elizabeth Lane died July 23ᵈ 1790

1578. Elijah L. Green No. 77

1579. No. 74. Ezra Hawkes & Thomas Gould Tomb 1812

1580. He.. ... Bur... the body of Mr Jonathan Brown who died June yᵉ 14ᵗʰ 1746 in yᵉ 63ᵈ year of his age

1581. T. Oliver

1582. Mr. John Cooper

1583. Mrs Mary Johnson

1584. Here lies Buried the Body of Polly Robins Dauʳ of Mr James & Mrs. Susannah Robins Died March 28 1778 aged 6 Years

1585. In Memory of Mrs Susanna Robins wife of Mr James Robins, who died March 26ᵗʰ 1796 aged 49 Years Also two of their children, Deborah Robins died Janʳʸ 20ᵗʰ 1783, Aged 11 months

1586. William Warner Robins died March 25ᵗʰ 1784 Aged 4 months

1587. In Memory of Mrs Abigail Robins Wife of Mr James Robins they were married the 4ᵗʰ and she died the 17ᵗʰ of Dec 1796. Aged 55 years

1588. Sacred to the Memory of Captain Jonathan Cary who departed this Life Decʳ 29ᵗʰ Anno Domini 1801 Aged 85 Years A full believer in the Universal Religion (poetry 4 lines)

1589. Thomas Lark son to Thomas & Rachel Lark Aged 2 years 11 months died Novʳ yᵉ 30ᵗʰ 1723

1590. In Memory of Deaⁿ Jonathan Brown who departed this Life on the 12ᵗʰ day of August 1785 Aged 78 years.

1591. Elizabeth dauʳ to William & Elizabeth Nickholson aged About 2 years decᵈ Janʸ ye 24 1713

1592. No 31 George Low & Abiah P. Low Tomb 1836 Abiah P. Low died May 28 1846 aged 51 years 7 months

1593. This Stone is erected in Memory of Capt Caleb Hopkins Junʳ who died Octʳ 19ᵗʰ 1791 in the 39ᵗʰ year of his age

1594. Here lies buried the body of Mrs Susannah Somes the wife of Capt Nehemiah Somes died Sept 3ᵈ 1770 aged 23 years

1595. Clark.

1596. Here lies buried the body of Mrs Susannah White wife of Mr John White died June 4ᵗʰ 1769 aged 48 years.

1597. Here lyes yᵉ body of Mr Samuel White decᵈ January the 16ᵗʰ 1727–8 in ye 59ᵗʰ year of his age

1598. Edward Pitts yᵉ son of James & Elizabeth Pitts died Decᵉʳ ye 28 1709 aged 3 months

1599. Here lyes yᵉ Body of Mrs Christian Pits widow of Capt John Pits aged 69 years Decᵈ Febʳʸ yᵉ 8ᵗʰ 1736–7

1600. Here lyes ye body of Elizabeth Pitts daughter to James & Elizabeth Pitts aged 15 years & 4 mo died May ye 6ᵗʰ 1709

1601. No 36. Ross Family Tomb. And^w Ross died Novr 1st 1814 Æ 37. William Ross died April 1st 1816 Æ 42. John Ross died April 5th 1841 Æ 64 Mary & Rose died June 20 1846 Æ 72

1602. Here lies the Body of Betsey Hopkins Daur^r of Michael & Joanna Hopkins died Aug^{-t} 29th 1783 aged 15 months & 17 days

1604. Sarah Dodge Dau, to Mr James & Mrs Mary Dodge aged 13 months died May 14th 1748

1605. W. Sherburne

1606. Here lies the Body of Mrs Elizabeth Ballord the wife of Mr Samuel Ballord who departed this life March the 16th 1763 in the 45 year of her age

1607. Samuel Ballord died Sept 4th 1744 aged 8 months & 2^{ds}, Timothy Ballord died Nov. 30 1747 aged 9 months & 11 ds... of Mr S...

1608. Sarah ye daughter of John & Sarah Dolbeare aged 10 months Died July ye 17, 1701

1609. In Memory of Capt Joseph Dolbeare who died Decr 7 1794 Aged 30 years

1610. Phebe Ballord

1611. No 31 Isaac S. Tompkins and Josiah Brown 1845

1612. In Memory of Mrs Nabby Dodge wife of Capt James Dodge who departed this life March 28th 1796 aged 25 years

1613. Here was buried Mrs Fanny Dissmore wife of Capt Thomas Dissmore who lived 35 years and died the 29th of December 1788 it being the anniversary of her Bi ...

1614. B. Henderson

1615. Here lies buried the Body of Capt Thomas Eeles aged 55 years died Novr ye 16th 1748

1616. Here lies ye Body of Mrs Elizabeth Hubbard who died Feb^{ry} ye 5th 1758 Aged 19 years

1617. Here lyes ye body of Mr Obadiah Read, Dec^d Feb^{ry} ye 19th 1721–2 in the 82^d year of age

1618. Here lies ye body of Mrs Esther Reed wife to Mr. Richard Reed Aged 73 years Died April ye 3 1725

1619. Here lies buried the Bo.. of Mrs Elizabeth Read wife of Mr Edward Read who departed this Life Feb^{ry} 1st 1783 in the 24th year of her age

1620. Mary Tree Dau^r of Mr Francis and Mrs Bridget Tree Born Jan^{ry} ye 7th 1773 and Died Feb^{ry} ye 5th 1773

1621. No. 32 Mr John Fenno & Capt John Howes Tomb 1819

1622. In Memory of Mrs Abigail How wife of Capt John How Obt Augt 15th 1805 Æt 29

1623. In Memory of Mrs Margaret How wife of Mr. Edward How died July 23ᵈ 1776 aged 29 years

1624. Here lies Buried the Body of Capt William Trefry Aged 56 years Died May yᵉ 6ᵗʰ 1761
(poetry 2 lines)

1625. Here lies Buried the Remains of John Scollay son of James Scollay & Susanna his wife who died Nov yᵉ 17ᵗʰ 1763 Aged 10 years

1626 N. S. Prentiss

1627. Sacred to the Memory of Mrs Marcy Hammatt wife of Capt Benjamin Hammatt who died Janʳʸ 6ᵗʰ 1796 aged 69 years

1628. Here lies the body of Elizᵃ Starr dauʳ of Joseph & Hannah Starr who deceased June 8ᵗʰ 1800 Aged 6 years & 3 months

1629. Here lies buried yᵉ body of Mrs Mary Hammatt wife of Capt Benjʳ Hammatt who departed this life Janʳʸ 25ᵗʰ 1762 Aged 45 years

1630. A.D 1811. J. Piercival. N. Parker.
(poetry 2 lines)

1631. Joseph Young son of William & Hannah Young Died Octbʳ 5ᵗʰ 1731 Aged 1 Month & 9 days

1632. Mrs Elizabeth Hammond wife of Capt. Gardner Hammond, died April 15 1810 aged 45 years
poetry 4 lines

1633. Ward Jackson & Heman Lincoln's Tomb 1819   No. 33.

1634. In Memory of Mrs Susannah Foster wife of Mr. Jonathan Foster who died Octʳ 15 1794 Aged 39 years

1635. Here lies buried the body of Capt Philip Viscount aged 62 years who departed this life Sepʳ yᵉ 22ᵈ 1751

1636. John son to Mr. Philip & Mrs Dorcas Viscount aged 20 months Decᵈ Octʳ ye 14ᵗʰ 1734

1637. Here lies the Body of Mrs Dorcas Viscount widow of Capt Philip Viscount who departed this life May yᵉ 30ᵗʰ 1769 aged 75 years

1638. In Memory of Daniel Heard, Son of John & Susan Heard 3ᵈ who died March 11, 1811, aged 1 month Also Mary Ann Heard who died May 1ˢᵗ 1814 aged 17 months & 8 days

1639. J. & N. Hall

1640. Sacred to the memory of Joseph Howard Esq Who died July 20 1808 Æ 54
(poetry 6 lines)

1641. T. & J. Lewis

1642. Sacred to the Memory of Miss Rosetta Jane Lewis Dauʳ of John & Jane Lewis who died Augᵗ 11ᵗʰ 1812 aged 12 years.

1643. .... .ies the body of .illiam Mellens ..parted this life ... ye 10th 1755 ....e 40th year .. his age

1644. Here lies the Body of Mrs Katharine Mellens wife to Capt William Mellens who died Oct 11th 1767 Æ 55

1645. Here lies the Body of Mrs Katherine Hoskins wife of Capt Christopher Hoskins died Jan^{ry} 5th 1769 aged 34 Years

1646. Bassett

1647. Here lyes the body of Mr John Vaughan of Braunton in Deavon Mariner who departed this life the 12th of July aged 26 years 1746.

1648. Here lyes buried ye body of Mr William Blackwell aged ye 14th of July 1...

1649. No 5 William & John Howe's Tomb 1820

1650. Thomas K ... and Ezra Haw .. 1814

1651. In Memory of Mrs Rebecca Howe Wife of Mr Nath' Howe died Feby 1st 1806 Æ 37

1652. Jacob Rhodes Howe son of John Howe Junr died Feby 11th 1807 Æ 3 years.

1653. Here lyes the Body of Mrs Mary Poole aged 50 years Dec^d July 28th 1737

1654. Here lies buried the Body of Mrs Lydia Parsons Widow of the late Revd Jonathan Parsons of Newbury Port Departed this life April 17th 1778 aged 47 years.

1655. No. 5. Francis Masse. Leonard Spaulding, John Gale's Tomb

1656. In Memory of Mrs Hannah Young widow of Mr William Young died Octr 13th 1790 aged 87 years

1657. In Memory of Miss Hannah Young who died Sept 24th 1796 in the 64th year of her age

1658. Here lyes the body of Mr William Sanders aged 63 ycars Died Octr ye 31st 1745

1659. No 23 Alex^r Vannevar & Jacob Barstow's Tomb 1819

1660. Here lies buried the Body of Mr James Dodge who Died Nov^{br} ye 24th 1759 Aged 46 Years

1661. Here lyes Buried the Body of Mr Samuel Spring died April 6th 1752 in the 22^d year of his age

1662. No 7 John Wyers Tomb 1820

1663. Ephraim son to Zechariah & Mary Wier aged 1 year & 6 Mo Died Feb^{ry} ye 3 1714–15

1664. Here lyes ye body of Zachariah Wyer Nov 23^d 1717 in ye 42 year of his age.

1665. Here lies buried ye Body of Mr Richard Bradburn Son of Mr Joseph Bradburn of London who departed this life Jan^{ry} 2^d 1739 in ye 21st year of his age

1666. No 26 Edmund Winchester Tomb 1819

1667. In memory of Mrs Sarah Skirrow who died March 10th 1805 Æt 62

1668. Daniel son to Mr James & Mary Dodge Died Sept 28th 1752 Aged 1 year

1669. Mrs Susanna Willard.

1670. In Memory of Mr John Milk who died July 11th 1808 Aged 43 years. Also James died July 16th 1792 Æ 14d^s. Eleanor died Nov 7th 1794 Æ 14 mo & 17 d^s. Susanna died Augst 4th 1802 Æ 7 years. Children of Mr John & Mrs Eleanor Milk.

1671. No 29 James Sherman's Family Tomb 1801

1672. In Memory of Mary Ann only Daug^h of Mr William & Mrs Mary Ann Homer died April 1 1816 Æ 4 years & 4 months (poetry 2 lines)

1673. Here lyes ye Body of Anna Burrill Daughter of Mr Samuel & Mrs Mary Burrill died Octr 7th 1773 aged 10 months

1674. Here lyes ye body of Jonathan Frost son to Samuel & Elizabeth Frost aged 21 years died Jany ye 23 1706

1675. Eben^r Frost died Novr 1773 Æ 54

1676. John Frost 1776.

1677. Here lies the Body of Mr. Roger Lobb who departed this Life May ye 4th 1760 Aged 51 years

1678. Here lyes buried the Body of Mrs Jane Pimm wife to Mr John Pimm Aged 49 years died May 26th 1748

1679. Here lyes ye body of Mary Burrill Dau^r of Mr Saml Burrill & Mary his wife died April 5th 1777 aged 9 years & 6 months

1680. Here lyes Y^e body of Mrs Jane Burril wife to Mr Joseph Burril Who Died Jan^{ry} 20th 1740 aged 46 years

1681. No 31 Josiah Snelling's Tomb 1803

1682. In Memory of Joseph Snelling son of Josiah & Mary Snelling dec^d April 27th 1799 Aged 24 years

1683. In Memory of Josiah Snelling son of Mr Josiah & Mary Snelling Died Feby 11th 1783 Aged 5 years 10 months & 10 Days

1684. Her. ....d th. .... of Mr John Langdon aged 82 years dec^d Decr y^e 6th 1732

1685. Here lies intered the Body of Mrs Joanna Feveryear wife to Mr Grafton Feveryear aged 33 years decd April ye 10th 1727

1686. Here lyes y^e Body of Silvanus Vickers aged 38 years Dec_p June ye 29th 1721 Mary dau^r to Silvanus & Ann Vickers Aged 5 Mo Dec^d. Augt ye 17th 1721

1687. Here lies Buried the Body of Deacon Grafton Feveryear who departed this life March the 30th 1755 Aged 66 years

12

1688. Here lyes y^e Body of Sarah Norton wife to David Norton Aged 49 years Dec^d October 30th 1721

1689. Here lyes ye Body of Mr Joseph Crawley who died March 6th Anno Dom 1738–9 aged 69 years

1690. No 32 Daniel and Samuel Adams Tomb 1813. Mrs Susan wife of Samuel Adams died Jan^ry 25th 1813 aged 27

1691. Here lyes ye body of David Adams aged 65 years Died July ye 3^d 1705

1692. In Memory of Mrs Rebecca Young who died March 29 1808 Aged 79 years

1693. Capt William Ward's Tomb.

1694. Here lyes ye Body of Mrs Margaret Fletcher wife of Mr William Fletcher aged 55 years died Feb^ry ye 9th 1747–8.

1695. Here lyes ye body of Mrs Sarah Fletcher widow of Capt Robert Fletcher Aged 62 years & 9 Mo Dec^d Decr ye 20th 1736

1696. Adam Knox son of Mr Adam & Mrs Martha Knox Aged 22 months dyed Octr ye 17th 1745

1697. In Memory of Susan Wilbur only child of James & Dorcas Trask who died Aug 7, 1814 Aet 10 Months

1698. No 11 Robert Barber's Tomb 1811

1699. ...uel Heath Aged 7 years and 3 mo died May 23^d 1752 Deborah Heath Æ 12 years died Jany 7th 1753 The children of Mr Saml & Mrs Eliz^th Heath

1700. No 16 Joseph Austin Tomb.

1701. In Memory of Wm Bowles Austin, son to Mr Joseph & Mrs Lydia Austin who died Septr 15 1792 Aet 4 years

1702. No 9. Jacob Rhoades Tomb 1811

1703. Here lyes the Body of Mr Caleb Norwood Aged 51 years Dec^d December ye 27th 1735

1704. Martha Dau to Mr John & Mrs Hannah Ludgate Aged 10 days dec^d Jan^ry ye 3^d 1734

1705. Here lyes the Body of Mr John White aged 63 years died Dec. ye 1st 1746. Also the body of Mrs Katharine White wife to Mr John White aged 6 years Died Feb^ry ye 3^d 1746–7

1706. Here lyes buried the body of Capt Richard White Aged 40 years who died Jan^ry ye 4th 1748

1707. No. 34 William Hall & Cornelius B. Simmons Tomb 1819

1708. Here lies buried ye Body of Mr Alexander Scammell who departed this life December 27th 1766 In the 64 year of his Age

1709. Here lies the body of Mrs Mary Scammell wife of Mr Alexander Scammell who died Aug^ust the 15th 1760 aged 57 Years

1710. No 2 William Badger & Thomas Richardson's Tomb 1842

1711. Here lies buried the Body of Mr Nathaniel Brown son of Mr Nathaniel & Mrs Mary Brown died Dec^emr 8th 1759 in the 23^d year of his age

1712. Here Lyes Buried the Body of Mr Nathaniel Emmes who Departed this Life April y^r 7th 1750 Aged 59 years and 8 Months

1713. Nathl son to Mr Joshua & Mrs Margaret Emmes Aged 3 Months Died Jan^ry ye 5th 1748-9

1714. Mary Dau^r to Nathaniel & Mrs Hannah Emmes Aged 6 months Dec^d July ye 17th 1729

1715. In memory of Mary daughter of Nathaniel & Mary Emmes who died Octr 11 1812 aged 14 months

1716. Nathaniel son to Nathaniel & Hannah Emmes aged about 9 mo dec^sd Novr y^c 23^d 1718

1717. Here lies Buried the Body of Mrs Hannah Emmes wife to Mr Nathaniel Emmes who Departed this Life June 1st Aged 67 years

1718. John Emmes son of Nathl & Rebecca Emmes died Jan^ry 1st 1806 Ae 17

1719. No 21 Francis Holmes & Benj^a Cushing's Tomb 1819

1720. In Memory of Mrs Mary Cushing Wife of Benjamin Cushing who died March 14th 1800 aged 38 years

1721. Here lyes the body of Mr John Cushing died Feb^ry ye 10th 1743 in ye 10th year of his age

1722. Here lyes buried the Body of Mrs Mary Brown widow of Mr Nathl Brown died March 5th 1780 Aged 78 years.

1723. Here lies buri.. the body of Mrs Ann Brown widow of Mr William Brown died Sept 1st 1751 aged 74.

1724. Here lyes buried the Body of Mr William Brown died June the 4th 1745 in the 74th year of his age

1725. No 4 Utley, Heath, Rayner, Reed, & Baker's Tomb 1819

1726. No 8 Joseph Wheeler's Tomb 1820

1727. Here lyes ye Bod. of Mr John Brown Who Died Novem^br 29th Anno Dom 1742 Aged 47 years

1728. In Memory of Mr John Brown son of Mr Eben^r & Mrs Mary Brown died March 6th 1782 in the 27th year of his age

1729. Here lyes ye Body of Mrs Mary Brown Wife of Mr Ebenezer Brown Who died January ye 10th 1766 Aged 48 years

1730. Here lies ye Body of John Brown son to Capt John & Mrs Eliz^th Brown who died March the 27th 1764 Aged 26 months

1731. Here lyes buried the Body of Mrs Ann Brown wife to Mr Willm Brown aged about 57 years dec^d March ye 31st 1731

1732. Here lyes ye Body of John Brown son of William and Anne Brown aged 21 years & 3 m^o dec^d Octo^br 14 1721

1733. No 21 Eben Gay & Eli Veazie's Tomb 1819

1734. No 29 Bradley Cumings & Simon W. Robinson's Tomb

1735. Here lyes y⁰ Body of Mary Moore daughᵗʳ of Capt Richard & Mrs Mary Moore of Oxford who dec⁰ˡ May y⁰ 27ᵗʰ aged 19 years

1736. John y⁰ Son of John & Mary Robinson Aged 17 months Died August y⁰ 2, 1690

1737. No 18 Nathaniel Parker's Tomb 1828

1738. No 27 Thomas Frothingham & Others Tomb 1819

1739. No 28 James Davis Tomb 1821

1740. No 47 James Davis, Warren Jacobs & Seth Lothrops Tomb 1805

1741. In Memory of Mrs Eliza Davis wife of John E. Davis who died Feb. 14, 1806 Aged 24

1742. Here lies y⁰ Body of Capt James Dennen aged 40 years 4 months & 3 days died August 11ᵗʰ 1757

1743. Here lyes y⁰ body of Mr John Cadwell aged 66 years Dec⁰ Janʳʸ y⁰ 2ᵈ 1732–3

1744. Dorothy Greenough Aged 4 Years & 8 Months Dyed Ye 2 October 1667

1745. Mr Caleb Parker Tomb 1745

1746. William Rayner son of Willᵐ & Charlotte Rayner died Sept 14ᵗʰ 1803 Aged 9 years

1747. In memory of Mrs Elizabeth Wife of Mr Jonathan Wright Daughter of Mr John Howe Senʳ died Octʳ 7ᵗʰ 1806 Ae 44

1748. In Memory of Mrs Rebecca Mayo who died Aged 56 years

1749. No 2 Ebenezer Shute and Jonathan Turner Family Tomb 1806

1750. [Eben Shute, born in Malden, Jan 5 1775 died in Boston May 23 1850, Susannah Shute his wife, born in Kingham, Nov. 22, 1773 died in Boston Feb 1 1847. And their children and grand children, Caleb B. Shute born July 7, 1806 died April 4 1840, Joseph B. Shute born April 28, 1808 died June 15, 1840, Susan G. Stetson (wife of Joshua Stetson) born June 9, 1815, died August 9, 1844. Frances child of Ebenʳ Shute Jr born May 27. 1838 died August 31, 1838 Frances (child of Ebenʳ Shute) born Jan 17, 1832 died Oct 7 1836, Susan (child of Caleb B. Shute) born April 5 1836 died August 26, 1839, Sarah Stetson (child of James M. Shute) born May 14 1844 died the same day, Susan Stetson (child of James M. Shute) born Oct 5, 1845 died May 8, 1846. *The above are not inscribed on the stone, but are copied from Bridgman.*]

1751. Elinour Dau' to Samuel & Ann Moor aged 2 years and 4 Mo dec^d June ye 27, 1730.

1752. Here lyes buried the body of Mr Samuel Moor who dec^d Jan^{ry} ye 28th 1739 in ye 45th year of his age

1753. Mrs Rachel Young

1754. Nicholas Upsall Aged About 70 Years Dyed Y^e .... Of August 1666.

1755. No 17 Robert Ripley's Tomb 1843

1756. Joseph Cocke Aged 46 Years Dec^d January Ye 15 1678–9

1757. No 11 George Vannevar Tomb 1845

1758. Samuel Rhodes son to Capt William Rhodes & Mary his wife who died Oct 9th 1759 aged 12 years & 4 months

1759. Here lyes buried the Body of Mr Thomas Verien Died Novr ye 22^d 1747 In the 86th year of his age

1760. Here lyes Buried the Body of Mrs Hannah Verien wife to Mr. Thomas Verien who died March ye 7th 1736–7 Aged 73 years, & 4 months

1761. Here lies buried ye body of Elizabeth Venteman wife to John Venteman aged about 32 years Deceased February ye 14th 1709–10

1762. Here lyes ye body of Mrs Mary Venteman wife to Mr John Venteman Aged 39 years dec^d March ye 16th 1723

1763. No 10. Eliza Wakefield & Henry Goodrich Tomb 1811

1764. John son to Obadiah & Rebecca Wakefield aged above 6 mo died April ye 25th 1712.

1765. Here lyes buried ye Body of Ann Wakefield wife of John Wakefield aged 32 years & 9 mo Dec^d January ye 1st 1712.

1766. Here lyes buried ye Body of Mr. Robert Duncan Merch^t who departed this life January ye 24th 1752, in the 50 year of his age

1767. Here lies buried the body of Mrs Isabella Duncan wife to Mr. Robert Duncan who departed this life Feby 2^d 1749–50 in ye 38th year of her age.

1768. J. Greenogh.

1769. Capt. Saml Nichols & Mr. Jesse Kingsbury Tomb 1825 No 12

1770. Here lies the body of Mrs Elizabeth wife of Mr Oliver Luckis Junr who Departed this life July the 22^d 1766 aged 40 years & 7 mo

1771. Here lyes ye Body of Mrs Elizabeth wife to Mr Oliver Luckis, who departed this life Nov^{br} 8th 1767 aged 23 years & 7 months

1772. Here lyes Buried ye Body of Mr. Oliver Luckis Junr who died May 12th 1749 in ye 33d year of his age.

1773. Here lyes Buried ye Body of Mrs Rebekah Luckis wife of Mr Oliver Luckis who died June the 18 1764 aged 68 years

1774. Here lyes buried yᵉ Body of Mr. Oliver Luckis . Departed this .. .. ᵇʳ yᵉ 18 1755

1775. Robert Thompson & John Wade. No. 14. 1811

1776. Here lyes yᵉ Body .. Mrs Patience Starling wife to Mr William Starllng Junʳ who died June 2ᵈ 1760 aged 40 years also John Starling their son died Sept. 1ˢᵗ 1760, aged 14 years

1777. Nathˡ.. John & Charles Wells Tomb 1811

1778. No 96 John Wells & Samuel Tuttle's Family Tomb 1807.

1779. Mary Wells Aged 9 months decᵈ Decʳ yᵉ 1, 1678

1780. Here lyes buried the body of Mrs Bridget Lad departed this life Novʳ yᵉ 2ᵈ 1743 in the 79 year of her age

1781. No 39 Amasa Winchester Tomb 1815

1782. No 6 Edward & John Sargent & Ann Burchsted's Tomb 1820

1783. Here lies ye Body of Mrs Hannah Pierce wife of Mr Samuel Pierce who departed this life May 7 1784 aged 46 years

1784. Here lyes ye Body of Mrs Mary Pierce wife to Mr. Jonathan Pierce of Charlestown aged 81 years Died Decʳ yᵉ 18ᵗʰ 1744

1785. Here lyes ye Body of Elizabeth Peirce wife to Mr. John Peirce Aged 63 years decᵈ April yᵉ 7ᵗʰ 1723

1786. John .. to .. Isaac .. Agness Pier ... aged 1 year Dec... 1721

1787. Mary Daughtʳ to Isaac and Grace Pierce aged 18 months Died June ye 7ᵗʰ 1715

1788. Here lyes the body of Tamazen Peirce Dauʳ of Mr. Isaac and Mrs Agnis Peirce aged 19 years died March ye 21ˢᵗ 1749–50

1789. Here lyes yᵉ body .. Mrs Elizabeth Pie.. Wife of Mr Jos.. Pierce.. Died .. yᵉ 6 17.. in yᵉ ..

1790 No 20. Elliott, Kimball & Pratt's Tomb 1819

1791. Here lyes yᵉ Body of Mrs Grace Palmer Wife to Mr George Palmer who departed this life June yᵉ 5ᵗʰ 1750 Aged 45 years

1792. No 13 Isaac Jenkins. Luther Felton, Earl Goddard & Solon Jenkins Tomb 1821.

1793. Thomas son to Samuel & Elizabeth Jenkins Aged 9 Mo & 18 dˢ decᵈ May yᵉ 28 1730

1794. In memory of Miss Martha Jenkins Dauʳ of Capt Peter & Mrs Mary Jenkins died July 16ᵗʰ 1797 Aged 13 years

1795. Thomas Jenkins son of Mr Peter & Mrs Martha Jenkins Died August yᵉ 27ᵗʰ 1748 Aged 3 years & 8 Mo.

1796. John son of Daniel & Sarah Jenkins Aged 17 months. dec^d
Sept ye 16th 1717

1797. Sacred to the memory of Thomas Waterman son of Thomas
& Mary Waterman who died June 17, 1808 aged 1 year & 5 months

1798. In Memory of Joseph Hammatt obt Feb^{ry} 19th 1798 Æ 48

1799. In Memory of Mr John Polley son of Mr Simeon & Mrs
Mary Polley who died Octr 3^d 1787 in the 23^d year of his age
(poetry 2 lines)

1800. No 13 William Hartt's Tomb and Samuel Hartt's Tomb
1841

1801. In Memory of Mrs Sarah Champney wife of Capt Caleb
Champney died Octr 13th 1800 Aged 60 years
(poetry 2 lines)

1802. No 40. Andrew J. Allen and Thomas Mickell's Tomb

1803. Here lies buried the body of Mr Nathaniel Hodsdon who
died April 5th 1757 Aged 76 years

1804. Ann Hodgdon dau^r to Mr Nathaniel & Mrs Ann Hodgdon
Aged 20 months Dec^d May ye 18th 1733

1805. Here lyes the Body of Mrs Ann Hodgdon wife of Mr Nathl
Hodgdon who died June ye 9th 1748 Aged 51 years

1806. Here lyes buried the body of Mrs Susannah Hodgdon the
wife of Mr Nathl Hodgdon aged 56 years & 3 months Dec^d May y^e
23^d 1730

1807. In memory of Mrs Martha Cabot who departed this life ou
Saturday, March 11th 1809 aged 60 years
(poetry 4 lines)

Also In memory of Mr George Cabot son of Mrs Martha Cabot
who departed this life on Sunday, Feb^{ry} 5th 1804 aged 20
Years After a long and distressing sickness which he bore
with meekness and resignation in hope of a glorious immortality.

1808. Samuel Winslow's Tomb 1826

1809. No 110. Samuel Winslow & Joseph Barnes Family Tomb
1811

1810. In Memory of Deaⁿ Samuel Holland who died August 17th
1798 Æ. 98

1811. No 41. Nathaniel Hammond & O & S. Davis Tomb 1819

1812. Here lies ye body of Mr Jacob Davis who departed this
Life March the 10th 1762 Aged 75 years

1813. Here lyes ye body of Mrs Mary Davis Wife of Mr William
Davis aged 86 years Died Jan^{ry} ye 19th 1745

1814. William son to William & Mary Davies aged 12 years & 9
months Died Decr ye 9 1710

1815. In Memory of Mr William Polley son of Mr Simeon & Mrs Mary Polley Died Decʳ 20ᵗʰ 1782 in the 24ᵗʰ year of his age

1816. No 44 Parker Emerson Jun & Warner Claflin's Tomb 1815

1817. In Memory of Mrs Ann Beers widow of Mr William Beers who departed this life Decʳ 18ᵗʰ 1784 aged 79 years

1818. No 38 S. Yendells Tomb 1816 and Thomas Hudson's

1819. In memory of Eliza Yendell dau of Samuel & Sally Yendall who died Oct 30 1805 Aet 9

1820. No 57 Peter Bingham's and Andrew Harrington's Tomb 1814

1821. Sacred to the Memory of Caleb Dinsdal Champney Obt Oct 4ᵗʰ 1802 Æ. 26.

(7 lines)

1822. No 34 Nathˡ Faxon's Tomb 1814

1823. Here lyes buried the body of Mrs Thankfull Lutwyche who departed this life May yᵉ 6ᵗʰ 1734 in yᵉ 45ᵗʰ year of her age

1824. No 7 Capt Samuel Eames & George Redding's Tomb 1811

1825. In memory of a son of George T & Elizabeth M. Hope was born Augᵗ 29ᵗʰ A. D. 1811

1826. In Memory of Samuel Hope Son of Robert & Ann Hope who departed this Life Octʳ 19 1815 Aet 13 months

1827. Mr John Ure

1828. Mrs Abigail Vassell died May 2ⁿᵈ 1816 aged 25 years

1829. No 1. Benjamin Sweetser & Enoch H Snelling Tomb

1830. In Memory of Mr David L. Sweetser son of Joseph & Lydia Sweetser who died June 3ʳᵈ 1803 Agᵈ 17 years

1831. Hannah Sweetser Dauʳ of Mr John & Mrs Sarah Sweetser Aged 3 years & 10 mo Died Decʳ yᵉ 11ᵗʰ 1745

1832. Sacred To the Memory of Mrs Rebecca Vinton Wife of Mr John Vinton who died Oct 15, 1807 Ae 31

1833. Joanna the Dauʳ of Mr John and Mrs Sarah Sweetser Aged 2 years Died Sept yᵉ 12ᵗʰ 1746

1834. In Memory of Mrs Mary Sweetser only Daughter of Mr Joseph & Mrs Mary Sweetser who Died Octʳ 30ᵗʰ 1784 Aged 47 years

1835. Memento Mori Fugit Hora Here lyes buried the body of Mr John Wilkins aged 35 years 9 months & 2 dayes who departed this life June yᵉ 17ᵗʰ 1710

1836. Here lyes yᵉ body of Mr John Wilkins decᵈ August yᵉ 17ᵗᵇ 1724 in yᵉ 25ᵗʰ year of his age

1837. No 56 Eben Frothingham's Tomb 1814

1838. Here lyes ye Body of Sarah Bennit wife to Samuel Bennit aged 75 years dec^d January ye 18 1682–3

1839. No 2. John H. Pray and J. G. L. Libby's Tomb 1832

1840. No 35 Ransford & Farrington's Tomb 1814

1841. No 6 Capt John Suter & Francis Walker's Tomb 1811

1842. Here lies the Body of Capt Richard Walker who died 24th Feb^ry 1774 In the 47th year of his age

1843. Sacred to the memory of Mrs Susanna Walker Relict of Capt Richard Walker who departed this life Aug^st 26th 1799 Aged 65

1844. In .... Mr Jo... who depar... .... April 27th 18.. Also Miss Nancy ...... who departed .... August 10th 1800 aged ..
(poetry 4 lines)

1845. No 49 Family Tomb of Daniel Dickenson who died June 23 1845 Aet 72 y^s

1846. Mrs Sarah Potts

1847. In Memory of David Gardner son of David S & Ann Ranney Obt March 22, 1815 Ae 15 mo

1848. Hiram Smith Family Tomb.

1849. Sacred to the Memory of William Sullivan Smith Obt Feb 2 1816 aged 17 days

1850. Hiram Smith Obt Aug 28 1817 aged 6 months

1851. Hiram Shurtleff Smith Obt April 29, 1818 Aged 11 months

1852. Julia Ann Smith Obt June 4, 1821 Aged 8 Weeks

1853. Benjamin Shurtleff Smith Obt Aug 22 1834 Aged 12 months

1854. Ruth Smith

1855. In Memory of Mr Francis Smith son of Mr John and Mrs Mary Smith who died Aug^st the 6, 1798 aged 20 years and 6 months

1856. Here lies ye body of Mrs Mary Smith aged 52 years died Feb^ry ye 5th 1727.

1857. In Memory of Mrs. Rebecca Smith Wife of Dea^n Richard Smith who departed this Life June 28th 1799 Aged 43 years

1858. Benjamin Shurtleff Smith Obt May 4 1824 aged 5 months 14 Days

1859. John Williams, son of Mr Henry & Mrs Mary Williams aged 9 Months, dyed Decr 27th 1736.

1860a. Thomas, son to John & Elizabeth Gaud, aged 3 weeks & 5 ds. Died Novr ye 15th 1708.

1860b. In memory of Mrs Martha Brown who died Sept. 20th 1795 aged 78 years.

1861. In Memory of Levi son of Elisha & Mary Cutler Obt Jan 7, 1821 Aged 6 months & 6 da

1862. In memory of Nancy Southwick wife of Mr. Henry Southwick who died June 20th 1801 Aged 20 years Also their Daughter Eliza Southwick who died March 14th 1801 Aged 7 months

1863. In Memory of Henry Rust Son of Mr Joseph & Mrs Ruth Rust who died Augst 18th 1791 Aged 16 months

1864. Here lies ye Body of Sarah ye wife of Andrew Willett Aged 38 years Died October ye 21 1693

1865. No 37. P. Capen's Tomb. 1815.

1866. Mrs Mary Otheman died 12th April 1802 Æ 45
[A. Otheman Junr her son died 18th Feby 1805 Æ 21
Mrs Hannah Otheman died 4th Jan^{ry} .... Æ 31
Edward McRedding died 10th June 1808 Æ 10 months
Godfrey Malone died April 30th 1815 aged 39
Anthony Otheman died Feby 9 1835 aged 85 years
Henry Otheman died May 25 1838 aged 47 years
Not inscribed on stone, but copied from Bridgman.]

1867. . who departe... April 27th 18.. Also Miss Nancy .. who departed .. August 10th 1800 Aged 10 ..

1868. Co... 2^d 1722–3 in ye 48th year of her age

1869. ... Aged .. 5 died

1870. Da.. Mrs Mary y^e .... Died May ye 19 aged 9 months

1871. Mat... Elizabeth D... of the City of New .. born 16th June 1782 died Jan^{ry} 14th 1798

1872. of Su.. Aged 26.. Died Sept. ye 23^d 1726

1873. Jonathan Pierce. 1804.

1874. Here lye .... body of Samuel .... aged 73

1875. In Memory of 6 children of Robert & Ann Miller Eliza died Augst 12th 1803, Ae 4 Mo ; Ann L. died Jany 30th 1806 Ae 15 Mo; Joseph died Octr 7th 1809 Ae 11 days; Benjⁿ died Decr 25th 1809 Ae 3 mo.; Chas died Octr 3^d 1810 Ae 3 wks; Jno W. died Sept 30th 1813 Ae 2 y^s

1876. y^e ..es died the 30 day of January 1673

1877. Here .. the ... Mar .. Wife .. Ag ..

1878. .. D 20 dayes dec^d Sept ye 20th 1723

1879. Mrs Mary Died May 19 Aged .9 Months

1880. No 89, Benjamin Comey & Leach Harris Family Tomb 1807

1881. No 90 Jany 10th 1807 Joseph & Philip Adams Family Tomb.

1882. No 94 William & Isa c Harri Tomb 1808

1883 No 95 Jany 10th 1807 Edward Chamberlain & Frederick Gould's Family Tomb

1884. No 91 Jan^{ry} 10th 1807 Norton Newcomb & Willm Leamard's Family Tomb

1885. No 92 Jacob Kent.

1886. R. Sacred to the Memory of Mr John Richardson Obt July 6. 1810 Aet 31 Also Mr Tho Richardson Obt July 29, 1811 Aet 24

1887. In Memory of Mr James Turner A Native of .... Derbyshire England who died Feby 19. 1813 Aged 43 years

1888. Alexander Cuscadin a Native of Londonderry Ireland who died April 16. 1811. Aged 26 year

1889. In memory of William McKenney a ative of Limerick who died April 16 1811 Aged 43 years

1890. Mrs Elizabeth Colesworthy wife of Mr Nath Colesworthy died Novr 11th 1810 in her 20th year

1891. Mrs Sarah Milton Died March 29th 1817 Aet 58

1892. Wm Farmer Died May 1st 1811 Aet 36.

1893. Mrs Susanah Munroe wife of Caleb B. Munroe who died Decr 14 1810 Aged 35. Also their son David Webb Munroe died March 22^d 1813 Ae 2

1894. Elizabeth Steel died April 26th 1817 Ae 58

1895. In Memory of Anna Mackay wife of James Mackay who died April 5th 1811 Aged 39 years

1896. In memory of Mr Samuel Beal who died May 10 1812 Aged 25 years

1897. Miss Sally B. McClary died May 14, 1811 Aet 23

1898. Mr Samuel Roach died July 14th 1811 Ae 47 y^{rs} 6 Mos

1899. Mrs Sarah Hurd died Jan^{ry} 29th 1809 Ae 28.

1900. Mrs Abigail Matthews died June 4th 1811 Ae 72

1901. Miss Jane Stimpson died April 9th 1812 Aged 20

1902. Leonard W. Pearson son of Amos and Charlotte Pearson died Feb 6, 1813 Aged 16 Mos.

1903. Mrs Avis Rickard wife of Mr Lewis Rickard died April 1 1813 Ae 31

1904. Sacred to the Memory of Mrs Abigail Barker wife of Mr William Barker Obt Decr 19 1812 Aged 37 years

1905. In memory of Mrs Sally Smith wife of Mr Edward Smith who died Octr 26th 1811 Aged 24. Miss Rebecca Smith 2^d Daughter of late Deaⁿ Richd Smith who died Novr 14th 1811 Aged 19. Also Rebecca Smith dau^r of Edwd & Sally Smith who died Jan^{ry} 24th 1812 Aged 19, Months Mr John Smith died Octr 15 1820 Aet 32

1906. Mrs Sarah Badger wife of John Badger died Sept 4 1811 Aet 46

1907. John L. Badger Died Octr 24th 1811 Aet 19 years

1908. James son of Zenus & Mary Nickerson died Sep 7 1821 Aet 11 months

1909. Mrs Elizabeth wife of Joseph Pallies who died Nov 4 1811 Aet 30

1910. William son of Joseph & Elizabeth Pallies died March 29 1812 in his 5th year

1911. In memory of William son of William & Abigail S. Mills who died Aug 21 1821 Aged 3 years 10 mo

1912. Joseph Burbeck son of Joseph & Elizabeth Burbeck died Novr 13th 1811 Æt 27 years

1913. Elizabeth Burbeck wife of Joseph Burbeck died Dec 10th 1815 Æt 53 years

1914. Mr. Joseph Burbeck died March 26 1820 Æt 62

1915. Henry Burbeck died May 27 1820 Æt 26.

1916. Mrs Mary Alley wife of Mr Richard Alley & Daur of Mr Timothy Winn late of Portsmouth who died Jan^{ry} 5 1812 aged 26

1917. Mr Eliphalet Jones died Decr 4th 1811 Æt 54

1918. ... died Sept 9 1821 Aged 13 mo

1919. Mrs Mary Black died March 27th 1812 Aged 56

1920. Rachael Coffin, Died Dec 17th 1813 aged 87 years

1921. John Peterson died Augst 11 1812 Æt 45.

1922. Mr Abigail Martain wife of Mr. Newhall Martain died Augst 22 1812 Aged 51 years

1923. Sacred to the momory of Sarah Cecilia Horace wife of Peter Horace who died ... . 1812 Æ ..

1924. Anne Pender Obt Oct 27 1815 Æ 8.

1925. Richard Pierce Obt Nov. 12 181 Æ 8 y & 7 mo.

1926. Miss Abigail Galloway died Feb^{ry} 25th 1813 aged 47

1927. James S. Coleman died April 25th 1813 aged 49 years

1928. In Memory of Mr. Siles Dudley who died Nov 26 1812 Æt 33

1929. Thomas T. Nudd died May 20th 1813 Æt 52

1930. .. Memory of . George Connell Native of ... Scotland

1931. Charlotte Hutchins dau^r of the late Capt Benjamin Hutchins died July 25th 1815 Aged 18 years

1932. Mary Randall wife of Wm. Randall died Sep 13th 1813 Aged 61

1933. In memory of Rebecca H. Pye who died Sept 19th 1822 Aged 7 years

1934. Mr Michael Williams of Charleston South Carolina who died Aug. 19, 1815 Aged 30

1935. Erected by George & Mary Dick to the memory of their Sister Emmy Dillaway who died Oct 11 1813 Æt 34

1936. In Memory of Mrs Elizabeth Flinn dau of John & Catherine McHeran who died Octr 15, 1813 Æt 21

1937 Miss Priscilla Daughter of Joseph & Mary Hayden died Oct 28th 1813 in her 16th year

1938. Prudence Clever died Novr 26 1813 Ætat 57.

1939. Capt John Harvey

1940. In Memory of Mr William Brazer who died Dec. 17 1815 Æt 39

1941. Sacred to the Memory of Mrs Hannah Smith Wife of Mr Levi Smith who died March 2 1811 Aged 32 years

1942. Holland Smith who died May 6 1811 Aged 21 years

1943. Frances Clark Bryant Daughter of Perez Bryant died April 14 1814 Aged 18 years

1944. Mary Ann Jones dau of Henry and Sally Jones died April 24th 1814 Aged 10 years

1945. In Memory of Mr Edmund Vaughan who died April 22 1814 Æt 33 years

1946. Revd Charles Warburton A native of England departed this life July 1st 1814 Aet 30

1947. Mr Elisha Wilton who died July 5 1814 aged 27 years and of Elisha Wilton Jun who died Oct 10 1814 Aged 3 Months Also Nathaniel Wilton died March 23 1819 aged 69

1948. Rachel Newcomb wife of Thomas Newcomb who died Augt 3d 1814 Aged 48

1949. Mary Simonds died Augt 4th 1814 aged 65

1950. In Memory of Mrs Rachel Bennett Wife of Mr Bezaleel Bennett who died Oct 9th 1814 Aet 60

1951. Lydia Nichols died Sepr 26 1814 aged 56

1952. In memory of Saml Foster Doggett died April 6, 1824 Aged 10 Mo only child of Saml & Laura Doggett

1953. Samuel H. Cary son of Jonathan & Mary Harris Cary Died Decr 1814 Aged 14 years & 5 mos

1954. Sacred .. the Memory of Mrs Josiah Hicks who departed this life January 27 1815 Aged 23

1955. In Memory of Mr William Gir... who died Oct 29th 181. Aged 29 years

1956. Abigail Goff died March 4. 1813 aged 75

1957. Sacred to the memory of Mrs Mary Fanning who departed this life April 9th 1815 Aet 82

1958. In Memory of Mrs Mary Beal Stevenson Wife of Mr Nathl H. Stevenson who died June 17, 1815 Aet 19

1959. Mrs Jane Wait wife to Dean John Wait who died July 4th 1815 Aged 57

1960. Sacred to the Memory of William Brown a native of London G. Britain who died May 27 1815 in the 44th year of his age

1961. In memory of Mrs Lettice White wife of Mr James White who died July 20 1815 Aged 64 Also of Mr James White who died April 12 1827 Aged 78

1962. In Memory of Mrs Harriot B. Hall, wife of Thomas Hall died Aug 21st 1815 Aged 24 years

1963. In Memory of Mr Isaac Richardson Obt Aug 22 1815 Ae 29 Also Mr Nathaniel Richardson Obt Sept 10 1815 Ae 34

1964. In Memory of Doct Anson Smith Late an inhabitant of Kingston upper Canada who Died Sept 25 1815 Aged 4 years

1965. Mrs Mary Williams wife of Mr Robert M. Williams died Oct 7, 1815 Aet 55

1966. Here lies departed the body of Samuel Richardson who was born in Dumfries Scotland 1764 & departed this life Oct 7 1815 Aet 51

1967. In Memory of Mrs Susanna Nazro Wife of Mr Matthew Nazro who died October 30th 1815 Aged 83

1968. Matthew Nazro died Nov 1 1816 Aged 82

1969. In memory of Thomas B. Sawyer who died October 23d 1815 aged 26 years

1970. In memory of Nancy wife of Alexr McGilvery died Decr 1st 1815 Aet 40

1971. Simeon C. Swan son of Daniel Swan died Oct. 27 1816 Aet 77

1972. In Memory of Widow Mary Drummond Who died Dec 15 1815 Aet 79 Also Miss Elizabeth Hudson Whe died Sept 27, 1816 Aet 69

1973. In memory of Miss Abigail Eaton who died Feby 5th 1816 Aged 24 years

1974. Elizabeth, daughter of Mr Samuel Andrews died March 12, 1816 Aet 17

1975. In Memory of Mr John P Thompson who died April 1 1816 Aet 52

1976. Elijah Tolman died June 22ᵈ 1816 Aged 67

1977. Mrs Hannah Stone Wife of Mr William Stone who died May 30 Aged 24 years 1816

1978. widow Elizabeth Williams died May 6, 1816 Aet 86

1979. Lucretia daugʳ of John & Hannah Venever died Augᵗ 31 1819 Aet 15 mo

1980. Mary Ann daugʳ of John & Hannah Venever died June 22, 1820 Aet 4 years

1981. Hannah F Venever wife of John Venever died Augᵗ 8, 1820 Aet 28

1982. Elizabeth Lash wife of John Lash died Sep 4 1819 Ae 64

1983. Sarah Pond wife of Moses Pond Died July 10 1816 aged 58 years

1984. Hannah Hill Sept 6 1816 Ae 88

1985. Hannah Hohn who died Sept 20, 1816 Aet 76

1986. Miss Lucy Macrith Died Janʸ 6, 1817 Aet 37

1987. Miss Ann F. Milne died Augᵗ 24 1820 Aet 17

1988. In memory of John S. son of Thomas & Maria Johnson who died Sept 9, 1829 aged 6 years

1989. In memory of Miss Ann G. Allquope who died Sept 19 1818 Aet 61

1990. Catharine Restieaux Daughter of Robert & Catharine Restieaux died Nov 17 1816 Aet 13

1991. In memory of Mary Morgan dauʳ of John & Hannah Morgan died Janʸ 16, 1815 in her 3ᵈ year

1992. In memory of Mrs Anna Kingman who died April 14, 1817 Aet 57 Also Mr John Kingman died June 18, 1814 Aet 57.

1993. Mrs Mary Gould Aged 37 years wife of Mr George Gould from the city of Bath England, Her death was occasioned By her clothes taking fire on the 7ᵗʰ day of April 1817 and survived 12 hours

1994. In Memory of Thomas P. Lane who died June 20 1817 Æt 28 years Also Mary Augusta Braynard died Oct 13, 1817 Æt 5 months

1995. In Memory of Capt William Cooke died June 23 1817 Æt 42 years

1996. Sarah Rogers wife of Moses Rogers died May 11 1817 Æt 26, Also in Fitz William N. H. their daur Sarah Blanding died Apl 22, 1817 aged 15 months

1997. Widow Christiana Vinall died June 25 1817 Æt 65 years

1998. Sarah Stevens wife of John Stevens died Nov. 6 1817 Æt

48

1999. Achsah Stevens dau' of John Stevens died May 24 1818 Æt 20

2000. In Memory of Mrs Elizabeth Foster wife of Mr James Foster who died Dec' 4ᵗʰ 1817 aged 63 and Mr James Foster who died August 31, 1818 Aged 69

2001. In Memory of Mr. Enoch Huse who died July 19, 1817 Æt 64

2002. Sacred to the memory of Mr. Patrick McKenna who departed this Life December 16, 1817 aged 40 a native of the co Monaghan Ireland Also

2003. James son of James Kelly died May 24ᵗʰ 1818 aged 2 yrs & 9 months.

2004. Here lies the remains of James Cavanough a native of Ireland who departed this life the year of our Lord 1818, March 16ᵗʰ Aged about 45 years

2005. Erected by James Hennesy in Memory of his Sister Elener Fitzgerald Wife of Martin Fitzgerald a native of the Co Kilkenny Ireland who died Feb'y 11, 1817 Æt 25.

2006. Widow Sarah Williams died April 25ᵗʰ 1818 aged 92.

2007 In memory of Mrs Bethiah Stevens who died June 13 1818 aged 54 years

2008. Sa... to the me.. Andrew G.. Son of William & Rebecca .. who died March .. 1832 aged 1 year & 11 months

2009. In memory of Clarissa Kingsbury wife of Fisher Kingsbury who died Oct 13 1818 aged 46

2010. In memory of Capt Simeon Kinsman who departed this life Jan 6, 1819 Æt 66 years

2011. Joseph Watts died Oct 29, 1816 Æt 49

2012. In memory of Miss Caroline Wyer who died March 4 1829 Æ 24

2013. In memory of Mrs Marcella Holmes died April 28, 1815 Æt 55 also Mrs Mary Kneeland died Jan 10 1819 Æt 33

2014. Sarah Roberts died Feb'y 15 1819 Æt 25 wife of Mr Daniel Roberts

2015. In Memory of Mr. Daniel Bemis who died Sept 30 1818 aged 59

2016. No 42 H. Merrill and L. L. Tarbell

2017. Isaac F. Rowe Tomb

2018. No 5 John Wilson & Richard Hosea's Tomb 1828

2019. Ephraim Milton, Henry Gurney & John B. Tremeres Tomb 1828   No 3

2020. Family Tomb of Lorenzo Alden who died July 2, 1857 aged 36 years   No 49

2021. Lydia Baker & Joel Richardson's Tomb 1828   No 50

2022. Lebbeus Stetson's Family Tomb 1828   No 52

2023. Abiel Buttrick. Abijah Patch, Artemas Tirrell & Thomas French's Tomb 1828.   No 53

2024. Benjamin Lawson & Joseph Lewis   Tomb. 1828.   No 54.

2025. William Dyke & Smith W. Nichols Tomb 1844   No 1

2026. Susan More . daughter to Ro.. Ann Moore . 1 yeare

2027. Here lyeth buried y⁰ body of Peter Ruck, y⁰ son of Samuell & Margaret Ruck, aged 24 years dyed December y⁰ 10ᵗʰ 1690

2028. William Hall. son of Andrew & Dorcas Hall aged 6 months died Janʳʸ 9ᵗʰ 1742–3.

2029. Thomas son of Robert & Elizabeth Rand aged 15 weeks died Sepᵗ y⁰ 18, 1711.

2030. Margret Clark Dauʳ to Joseph & Margret Clark Aged 1 year & 10 days, decᵈ Augᵗ y⁰ 15 1720

2031. Elizabeth Clark, Dauʳ to Joseph & Margret Clark aged 11 month & 25 days Decᵈ Augᵗ y⁰ 12, 1723

2032. Sarah y⁰ Daughter of Benjamin & Susana Worthylake, Aged 3 weeks died Janʸ 9, 1697.

2033. Here lyes y⁰ body of Ann y⁰ wife of William Edmans aged 80 years died October y⁰ 13. 168[6]

ERRATA.

In epitaph No. 1542, for Binuey read Binney.

"   "   "   1820, " Bingham read Brigham.

"   "   "   1884, " Leamard " Learned.

"   "   "   1, " Croer's " Crocker's.

To   "   "   131, add Tomb No. 112.

"   "   "   133, "   "   " 111.

"   "   "   135, "   "   " 113.

"   "   "   149, "   "   " 54.

ADDENDA

The following inscriptions are not found in Whitmore's "Copp's Hill Epitaphs. "Six were omitted in copying, and Edward MacDonald, superintendent, unearthed the others or found them around the neighborhood.

1. "David, son to David Copp and Obedience his wife, aged 2 weeks Dyed Dec. 22 1661."
2. "Thomas son to David Copp and Obedience his wife aged 2 years and 3 quarters."
3. Foot-stone." ' M. L."
4. "Jonathan Copp son of David Copp aged 12 years and 2 mo. Decd. Oct. ye 22d 1121."
5. "Isac son of Joseph and Elizabeth White aged 3 yrs & 6 mo Died Sept 3, 1732."
6. "Mary Glidden chd to Joshua and Elizabeth died March ye 8th 1709 in ye 16 year of her age"
7. In memory of John William son of John W and Elizabeth J. Ziegel who died Oct. 15 1814 aged 18 mos.'
8. "Frederick Christopher Ziegel who died Aug 3d,1815, aet 5 mos & 10 days."
9. "John Carthew age years and 7 mouths & days departed this life Nov ye 13 1696."
10. Recompense Wadsworth A. M. First Master of ye Grammar Free School of ye North End of Boston, aged about 24 years. Died June ye 9th 1713."
11. "Here Lyes ye Body of Mrs. Mary Welch wife to Mr. Eben'r Welch aged 21 Years. Died Septr ye' 5th 1730."
12. Ebenezer Welch son to Ebenezer and Mary Welch, aged 3 weeks and 2 days. Deceased Septr __ ye 6 1730."
13. Here Lyes ye Body of Sarah Goldthwait, wife to John Goldthwait, aged 35 years & 2 mo. dec'd Octr ye 31st, 1715."
14. "John the son of John & Hannah luck aged 18 days, Died the 4th day of Sept 1701."
15. "Here lyes the body of Mr. Thomas Millen, aged 58 years Deed Jan. 24, 1727-8."
16. "James Hill son of Mr. James and Esther Hill, aged 16 months, died July 24th 1744."
17. "Here lyes buried the body of Mr. James Hill, aged 36 years, died April ye 29, 1746."
18. "Here lyes buried the body of Mr. Daniel Collins, who died Aug. 29th 1758, in the 41st year of his age."
19. "Here lyes Buried the Rudy of Mrs. Easter Henchman, late widow of Mr. Richard Henchman aged 75 years. Dec'd May ye 5th 1731."
20. "Elizabeth Boone aged 2 years Dyed ye 13 October 1667."
21. "Miss Sarah Leate died Jan 19. I805. AE 80."
22. "Here lyes ye Body of Mary Roberts daur of Mr. John & Marcy Roberts died Sept 11th 1772 aged 1 year & 9 months."
23. "Here Lyes ye Body of Hannah Souther, wife to Joseph Souther, aged 53 Years, who departed this life August y' 20th 1711."
24. "Jeremiah Son to Mr. Jeremiah & Mrs. Hannah Bill aged 3 Years 6 mo Dec'd March ye l0th 1735-6."
25. "Ann Hett aged 38 Years Dec 4 June Y' 20th 1678."
26. "In Memory of Mrs. Abigail Breading died March ye 30th 1774 in the 60th Year of her age."
27. "Here Lyes ye body of Joseph Soames aged 24 Years & 6 mo died August Ye 2nd 1705."
28. Foot Stone. "Elizabeth Brame."
29. "Here Lyes ye body of Mrs. Sarah Storer Wife to mr Nathaniel Storer Dec 5 Sept Ye 22" 1745 in ye 52nd year of her age."
30. "In memory of Mary Sweetser Wife of Mr Joseph Sweetser wbo died April 9th 1784, in the 79 Year of her age."
31. "Edward Page Ye son of Mr Wm. & Mrs. Dorcas Page aged 6 Years died March ye 12th 1748-9."
32. Here lyes Buried Body of Mr. Edward Page Dec'd Jan ye 15 1736-7 aged 49 Years."
33. "Mary Page aged 5 Years Dec'd Aug'st 1730."
34. Elizabeth Barker Ye Daughter of Thomas & Sarah Barker aged 6 weeks died ye 4th July 1688."
35. "Elizabeth Coit Daughter of Sir Joseph & Mrs. Dorathy Coit aged 1 month died Aug. Ye 24th 1749."
36. "In Memory of Nathaniel Lamson of Mr Nathaniel Lamson & Elizabeth Lawson who died august Ye __ 1761 age 1 Year & 7 Mo Days."
37. Foot Stone. "Mrs. Elizabeth Lash."
38. "John Ruck Son to Thomas & Mary Ruck aged 20 months dec'd Sept ye 2nd 1715."

Section C

All About Section C

Section C indexes Copp's Hill markers that existed during a Historic Burying Grounds Initiative inventory taken in 1986. **Column 1** lists last names alphabetically. Here you also will find the type of stone, i.e. monument, footstone, etc. and that code is listed to the right under "Type." **Column 2** lists any dates that appear. **Column 3** indicates the condition and you will have to refer to the key at right, "Conditions," to understand the meaning of the abbreviations. Finally, **Column 4** tells the location. Using this, you can find from the three detailed maps in the Section D envelope the exact location of the marker or tombstone you want to find. Example: J-118 means Section J, tombstone 118. Take your time and enjoy looking up these long departed brethren who are a part of Boston of long ago.

Index Abbreviations

TYPE[1]

fs	footstone
m	monument
mk	marker
p	plaque
t	tomb
tm	tomb marker

CONDITION

ba	biological activity
bl	blistering
bs	bullet scars
chp	chipping
crk	cracking
del	delamination
eff	efflorescence
ers	erosion
fal	fallen
fla	flaking
frg	fragmented
grf	graffiti
ls	loss
ms	mower scars
oj	open joints
pa	painted surface
pt	pitted
rep	repaired
sc	scaling
soi	soiling
st	stains
sun	sunken
til	tilted

* Information from field observations
** Information from research
[1] Headstones are accompanied by a footstone where "fs" is noted. All markers are headstones unless noted otherwise.

Name	Date	Conditions	Location
Abrahams, Benjamin	1817/9/5	St,bl,fk,til,ms,chp	D-6
Abrams, William (tm)	1811	soi,grf,crk,ls,ba	C-416
Ad--, Elijah (tm)	--	grf, ls	A-349
Adams, Abigail	1764/1/17	til, eff,ls,ms,soi	F-178
Adams, Abraham	1700/4/6**	soi,fk,sc,til,chp	C-237
Adams, Alexander	1677/1/16**	soi, bl, til, ls	C-212
Adams, Elijah	1798/8/25	st. til, is, ms,chp	C-6
Adams, Elijah (fs)	1798/8/25*	st. fk, til,ls, chp	C-7
Adams, Elizabeth	1725/11/2	sun, chp, pt	F-241
Adams, Hannah	1723/12/5	del, til, ms	A-253
Adams, Isaac	1732/12/30	fk,sc,crk,eff,ms	F-256
Adams, James	1718/6/17	pa, sc, til, ls, ms	F-293
Adams, John	1737/4/2	fk, sc, sun, soi,ms	F-58
Adams, John	1783/3/1	fk, sc, soi, ls, ms	F-61
Adams, John	1747/12/18	ers,bl,fk,ba,soi,ms	F-63
Adams, John (fs)	1783	bl, fk, til, ins	F-62
Adams, Jonathan	1707/4/7	sc, sun, soi,ms,chp	F-141
Adams, Joseph	1745/8/13**	sc, crk, til,sun,ls	F-108
Adams, Joseph (bin)	1807/1/10	sun, ms, ba, soi	W-64
Adams, Judith	1798/8/22	st,eff,del,ls,ms	C-4
Adams, Judith (fs)	1798/8/22*	til, chp	C-5
Adams, Margaret	1733/12/2	fk, sun, ms, chp	F-92
Adams, Mary	1745/8/16	til, bs, ins, chp	A-250

Name	Date	Codes	Ref
Adams, Mary	1707/6/11	soi, del, til, ls	C-213
Adams, Mary	1791/5/16	til, sun, ls,chp,pa	G-4.
Adams, Mary	1795/10/15	pa,crk,til,sun,ls	G-12
Adams, Nathaniel	1690/3/29	soi, ba	C-169
Adams, Nathaniel	1745/5/26	bl, fk, pa, chp	F-290
Adams, Phillip (tm)	1807/1/10	sun, ms, ba, soi	W-64
Adams, Rebeckah	1731/12/22	soi, ers, sun, ls	C-166
Adams, Thomas	1781/12/31	pa,crk,til,sun,ls	G-12
Adams, Thomas	1781	til, chp, ms	G-13
Addams, Daveid	1705/7/3	soi, fk, bl, til,pt	C-228
Albry, Christon	1802/9/1	soi,ba,fk,sc,chp	A-121
Aibry, Christon (fs)	1802	soi,til,sun,ms,chp	A-53
Alexander, William (tm)	--	ls, soi, ba	W-56
Allcock, Abigail	1784/10/26	soi, ms, chp	A-267
Alley, Mary	1812/1/5	ba,bl,fk,crk,til	J-59
Allin, Ebenezer	1712/8/31	til, sun, ms	A-353
Allin, Edward (deacon)	1739/9/29	soi,ba,crk,fk,ls,ms	A-58
Amie, Lydia	1749/7/-**	sot, sun, ls	A-244
Anderson, John A.G.**	1818/8/11**	til, ls, sc	D-171
Anderson, Robert	--	del,til,sun,ls,ms	A-36
Andrews (tm)	--	sr, crk, chp	W-33
Andrews, Elizabeth	1816/3/12	soi, crk, ls,chp,ms	J-117
Archer, Ann	1738/9/20	sun, soi, ms, ba	H-75
Armstrong, Mary (fs)	1798	soi,bl,fk,til,chp	C-258
Armstrong, Matthew	1709/9/21	grf,sc,til,ls,ms	B-46

Name	Date	Codes	Ref
At–, – -cc	--	soi,fal,sun,ls ms	A-115
Atkins, Henry	1750/12/31	fk, til, sun, chp	F-201
Atkins, Henry** (tm)	1807**	ls, ba, sun, soi	W-58
Atkins, Isaiah	1767/5/13	fk, sun, ms	F-194
Atkins, John	1765/5/7	ba, til, ls, soi	F-202
Atkins, Silas (tm)	--	soi, st, ls, chp	W-11
Attwood, Alice (fs)	1770	fk,crk,til,ms,sr	A-43
Attwood, Mary	1729/3/18**	soi,fk,sun,crk,ls	C-273
Atwood, Elizabeth	--	soi,fk,til,sun,ls	C-275
Atwood, John (Deacon)	1714/8/26	soi, st. ba, til,ms	C-269
Atwood, Martha	1809/11/9	crk, pa, til, chp	G-213
Aubins, Thomas	1750/9/14	soi,crk,til,ls,ms	A-19
Augustus, Mary	1759/5/28	crk, ba, soi, chp	A-7
Austill, Elizabeth	1767/1/18	soi, til, ls, ms,pt	C-468
Austin, Joseph (tm)	--	soi, crk	J-7
Austin, William Bowles	1792/9/15	soi,st,fk,sc,chp,ms	A-131
Aves, Isaac	1739/9/24	soi, til, pa, chp	G-36
Aves, Rebeckah	1772/7/29**	ba, til, sun, ms	A-362
Aves, Samuel	1723/10/3	ls, crk, ba, ms	D-165
Ayer, Antoinette D. (m)	1839/8/28**	soi,ers,ba,crk,chp	I-24
Ayer, Emeline A. (m)	1842/1/21**	soi,ers,ba,crk,chp	I-24
Ayer, J. Cullen, **M.D.(rm)	1846/1/22**	soi,ers,ba,crk,chp	I-24
Ayers, John	1711/8/12	til, ba, st, soi	D-172
Ayers. Nathaniel	1731/12/4	pa, ls, til, sun,pt	F-275
Ayres, Abigail	1677/1/2	ba, ms, chp	F-213

Name	Date	Codes	Ref
B--, Sarah	1747/9/11	ls, ins, st. chp	G-202
B., A. (fs)	--	soi, ba, ms	A-343
B., E. (fs)	1809	del, rep, crk, frg	G-243
B., M. (fs)	--	fk, til, ba	F-82
B., T. (fs)	--	soi,grf,fk,sc,ms	B-52
Badcock, Rebeckah	1719/11/12	sun, ls, chp, ms	F-142
Badcock, Samuel	1721/10/24	crk, soi, ba, ms	D-141
Bailey, Israel	1721/8/6	soi, del, ms	C-115
Baker (tm)	1819	ba, chp, ms	H-76
Baker, Alexander	1801/5/22	sc, ls, ms, chp, pt	F-70
Baker, Elizabeth	1688/7/14	soi, crk, chp	A-245
Baker, ElizabeLh	1753/6/10	eff, crk, til, ms	F-94
Baker, Joseph	1702/4/28	soi, grf, ms	A-359
Baker, Joseph (fs)	--	soi, til, sun, ls	A-407
Baker, Josiah	1729/6/19	soi, bl, fk, sun	A-420
Baker, Josiah	1760/4/19	bl,fk,sc,til,eff,ms	F-71
Baker, Josiah (fs)	1729/6/19*	soi, til, sun, ls	A-421
Baker, Lydia (tin)	1828	soi,grf,bl,fk,crk	J-37
Baker, Mary	1801/12/27	sc, ls, ms, chp, pt	F-70
Baker, Nathaniel	1702/5/30	soi, bl, fk, til	A-392
Baker, Rebecca	1708/7/29	til, st, ms	A-405
Baker, Sarah	1700/8/14	crk, til, ls, ms	A-404
Baich, Elizabeth	1728/6/27	til, sun, ls, ms	D-134
Balford, Elizabeth	1763/3/16	fk, sun, eff,ms,soi	F-84
Ballard, Benjamin	1718/11/15	til, sun, chp	A-322

Name	Date	Abbreviations	Code
Ballard, Benjamin (fs)	1718/11/15*	til, sun, chp	A-323
Ballard, Dorcas	1737/1/25	soi, til, ms	A-315
Ballard, Dorcas	1719/6/22	eff,ba,crk,sun,chp	B-7
Ballard, Elizabeth	1769/12/20	soi, st, sc, ls	A-203
Ballard, Martha	1767/5/3	soi, sc, til, ms	A-204
Ballard, Mary	1769/12/18	soi, st, sc, ls	A-203
Ballard, Samuel	1744/9/4	ls, sc, ms, pt	D-62
Ballard, Sarah	1704/12/15	soi, til, ls, chp	A-423
Ballard, Timothy	1747/11/30	ls, sc, ms, pt	D-62
Balls, Martha	1765/5/30	til, sc, grf, ms	D-151
Balls, Robert	1774/10/10	til, crk, grf, ms	D-153
Balls, Robert (fs)	1774	sun, soi, ms, chp	D-154
Bankcamp, John	1805/3/21	sc, ba, soi, ms, sr	F-159
Bankcamp, John (fs)	1805/3/21*	fk, sc, soi, ms,chp	F-160
Barbadoes, Abel	1817/3/22	til, sc, ba, soi	A-2
Barber, Elizabeth (tm)	1832/4/24	crk, til, soi, chp	W-23
Barber, John	1726/12/4	soi, bli, crk, chp	C-207
Barber, John	1758/12/2	ers, ba, chp	D-71
Barber, Mary	1718/3/5	til, ls, soi, chp	C-352
Barber, Nathaniel (tm)	1787/10/14	cr1, til, soi, chp	W-23
Barber, Polley Bentley	1800/9/12	st, fk, til, ms,chp	C-415
Barber, Samuel	1746/10/21	til, sr, ms, chp	D-72
Barber, Sarah	1693/10/26	soi,ba,sc,til,chp	A-140
Barber, William	1801/8/20	ba,fk,crk,til,sun	C-428
Barker, Abigail	1812/12/12	soi, til, ls,chp,pt	J-52

Name	Date	Codes	Ref
Barker, Polly T. (fs)	1798	til, ms, ba, chp	D-115
Barker, Poily Tidmarsh	1798/9/24	til, ba, sot, ms	D-111
Barnard, Alce	1663	fk, pt, ms	H-11
Barnard, Elizabeth	1716/9/14	del, sc, ba, ms	H-81
Barnard, ElizabeLh	1683/9/4	ers, fk, chp, soi	H-88
Barnard, John**	1719/9/5	ls, ms, chp, soi	H-82
Barnard, Mary	1663	fk, pt, ms	H-11
Barnard, Mathew	1679/5/9	fk, pt, ms	H-11
Barnard, Richard	1745/5/31	sc, sr, ms	C-131
Barnard, Sarah	1685/10/5	ba, til, ls, ms	F-121
Barnard, Thomas	1730/5/16	eff, sc, crk,til,ls	H-86
Barnard, Thomas (Capt.)	1716/3/14	eff, ls, chp, soi	H-85
Barnicoat, John	1809/2/23	fk, crk, sun, sr	F-133
Barnicoat, John*(fs)	1809/2/23*	sr, til, chp	F-134
Barons, Leonard	1765/10/25	soi,fk,sc,til,ms	A-74
Barr, Susanna	1701/3/16	soi,ba,sc,del,tii	C-134
Barret, John (Dea.) (fs)	1721*	sc, til, ms	A-237
Barret, John (Deacon)	1721/10/1	soi, fk, Sc, del,ls	A-236
Barrett, John	--	soi, sun	A-229
Barrett, Lydia Ellen S.	1819/5/21	st,ba,til,ms,chp	D-3
Barrett, Philander Wayne	1817/8/28	st,ba,til,ms,chp	D-3
Barrett, Rebeccah	1731/5/16	fk, sc, ls, chp	A-238
Barrett, Rebeccah* (fs)	1731/5/16*	ers, del, frg, ls	A-239
Barrett, Samuel	1767/10/30	soi, til, ms	A-228
Barston, Jacob (tm)	1819	sot, st. bli, fk	I-10

Name	Date	Codes	Ref
Barter, James	1757/5/16**	fk, sc, til,sun, ls	A-70
Bartlett, Ebenezer Frost	1765/6/27	soi,ms,chp	A-76
Bartlett, James (tm)	1813	soi, st, chp	J-15
Bass, Moses (tm)	1819**	del, sun, St. ms	W-49
Bass, Phillip	1720/8/9	til, ba, ms, chp	H-79
Bass, Phillip (Capt.)	1761/6/10	eff, fk, ms, chp	H-77
Bass, Sarah	1692/7/7	fk, sc, til, ls, ba	H-31
Bass, Sarah	1746/4/26	bl,fk,sc,ls,ms,soi	H-71
Bassett, -- (tm)	--	sot, grf	J-9a
Bassett, Mary	1743/10/12	crk, til, ba, ms	D-164
Battens, John jr.	1762/4/1	fk, sc, eff, ls, ms	H-28
Baxter, Rufus (tm)	1821	soi, grf, ers, crk	I-20
Bayley, Jane (tm)	1820	soi, bl, fk	I-18
Beal, Abigail	1719/11/16	sun, ba, chp, ms	H-94
Beal, Caleb (fs)	1801	soi, bi, fk, chp	A-429
Beath, Joseph	1771/1/24	ba,pa,bl,til,pt,chp	G-38
Beath, Joseph	1780/7/28	soi, chp, pt, pa	G-104
Beath, Seeth	1779/6/20	ba,pa,bl,til,pt,chp	G-38
Beatley, Ralph (Capt.)	1804/10/16	grf,ba,til,ls,soi	C-426
Beeck, Tileman	1702/4/8	til, fk, ls, st	D-99
Beer, William	1759/12/11	soi, sun, chp, pa	G-57
Beer, William (fs)	1759/12/11*	til, sun, ls,ms,chp	G-58
Beers, Ann	1784/12/18	pa, st. chp	G-120
Beers, Ann (fs)	1784	st, sc, til, ms,chp	G-121
Beeth, Joseph (fs)	1784	fal, frg, ls,ms,chp	G-40

Name	Date	Codes	Ref
Beeth, Seeth (fs)	---/9/--	fal, frg, ls,ms,chp	G-40
Belcher, Elizabeth**	1828	soi,fk,del,til,sun	A-99
Bell, Edward (tm)	1710/9/15	soi, grf, bl, fk	J-32
Bell, Mary	1818/9/30	soi,fk,sc,crk,ls	A-54
Bemis, Daniel**	1733/7/23	st,grf,bl,fk,sc,soi	J-149
Bennet, Elis	1735/3/1	ba, fk, crk, til	C-126
Bennet, Joseph	--	ls, til, sr, chp,pt	F-182
Bennet, Joseph (tm)	1728/3/28	bl, fk, grf, soi	W-29
Bennet, Mary	--	sc,sun,eff,ms,chp	F-68
Bennett, Ellis (fs)	1814/10/9	soi, til, chp, pt	C-184
Bennett, Rachael	1765/7/31**	grf,del,fk,crk,ls	J-96
Bennett, Sarah	1765/7/31**	ba, sc, del, ms	C-144
Bennett, Sarah (fs)	1803	ba, chp, ms	C-145
Bennett, Sarah (fs)	1683/1/18	soi,grf,fal,ms	C-343
Bennit, Sarah	1748/9/9	soi,ba,fk,til,sun	C-92
Bentley, Susannah	1738/6/18	soi, til, sun, chp	A-422
Berry, Daniel	--	soi, crk, til, chp	A-416
Berry, Daniel (fs)	1695/5/17**	fk, til, sun, chp	F-3
Berry, Grace	1692/7/27**	st,eff,ers,del,sr	C-30
Berry, Margarett	1729/1/21	soi, ba,sc,sun,ms	C-174
Bickford, Abigail	1710/6/4	ba, crk, chp	C-403
Bickford, Edward	1696/11/7	soi, til, ms, chp	A-341
Bill, Abigail	1760/11/20	soi, ba, fk,til,chp	C-235
Bill. Hannah	1688/2/1	bl, crk, ls, soi	G-283
Bill, James		crk, til, st, soi	C-451

Name	Date		Code
Bill, Jeremiah	1736/3/10	crk, til, st. soi	C-451
Bill, Joseph	1748/2/3	soi, sc, til, ls,ms	C-266
Bill, Mabel	1766/8/7	soi, sc, til, ls,ms	C-266
Bill, Polly	1782/8/30	sol, bl, fk, til	A-388
Bistoff, Elizabeth	1806/4/7	st,crk,pt,ms,chp	D-5
Black, Mary	1812/3/27	soi,bl,fk,crk,til	J-60
Blackador, Mary	1751/10/23	pa, sc, til, chp	F-161
Blackman, Rebeca	1715/3/29	eff, sc, ms, chp	H-101
Blake, Deborah	1791/8/3	soi,grf,ba,fk,til	B-18
Blake, Deborah* (fs)	1791/8/3*	soi,til,sun,ms,chp	B-19
Blake, Henry	1805/10/25	fk, til, grf, ms	F-99
Blake, Joseph	1802/12/2	soi, crk,ms	C-56
Blanding, Sarah	1817/4/22	st, grf, bl, fk,chp	J-130
Boardman, Aaron	1754/6/9	til, grf, ba, ms	D-157
Bodge, Hannah	1745/11/10	sc, til, ls, chp	E-70
Boies, Margaret	1779/10/21	sc, sun, ms, sr, ba	F-117
Bommor, Margret	1741/2/22	ba,del,crk,ls,ms	B-16
Bommor, Thomas	1741/6/1	ba,del,crk,ls,ms	B-16
Bomor, Mary	1767/9/15	del, crk, sun, ms	A-361
Booden, Agnis	1684/3/8	soi, fk, til, ls	A-350
Bostan, James*	1818/3/--	ba, ers, crk, chp	J-136
Boucher, Mary	1767/9/2	st, grf, til, ms	D-9
Bound, James	1758/11/6	til, crk, grf, ins	D-167
Bound, James *(fs)	1758/11/6*	til, ms, chp	D-169
Bowles, Joshua (fs)	--	fk,del,crk,sun,chp	A-186

Name	Date	Codes	Ref
Bowles, Joshua jr.	1772/6/3	soi,ba,sc,crk,ms	A-132
Bowles, Joshua*	1794/8/31**	soi,fk,crk,til,ls	A-136
Bowles, Mary (fs)	--	fk,del,crk,sun,chp	A-186
Bowman, John	1730/7/4.	soi, del, til, sun	A-275
Boyden, Simeon (tm)	1825	soi, grf, bl, fk,sr	J-16
Boynton, William (tm)	1809**	sun, bl, fk, chp	W-53
Bradburn, Richard	1739/1/2	sun, sc, eff,ls,ms	F-7
Braine, Elizabeth (fs)	--	sun, del, chp	H-93
Bray, Marion L.	1968	soi, ba	I-la
Braynard, Mary Augusta	1817/10/13	soi,grf,ba,bl,fk,sc	J-131
Brazier, William	1813/12/17	grf,ba,bl,chp,pt	J-85
Breading, Abigail	1774./3/30	bl, fk, del, eff,ms	F-251
Breading, Abigail*(fs)	1774/3/30*	bl, fk, eff, clip	F-252
Breading, Phillip (Capt.)	1764/11/22	bl, fk, del, eff,ms	F-251
Breading, Phillip (fs)	1764	bl, fk, eff, chp	F-252
Breck, Hannah	1741/9/29	til, ms, chp	A-376
Breck, Samuel	1809/3/20	grf, st, til, frg	A-386
Breed, Nathaniel	1765/1/27	soi, del, ls, dr,ba	C-60
Breed, Sarah (Fs)	1740	crk, bl,fk,frg,ms	F-97
Brewer, Francis Edward	1815/2/17	bl,fk,sun,til,pa	G-235
Brewer, Nathaniel (tm)	--	ba, soi, til, chp	W-16
Brewer, Theodore James	1813/9/25	bl,fk,sun,til,pa	G-235
Brick, John	1713/2/16	soi, til, ls, chp	A-389
Brick, John (fs)	1713/2/16*	Bl, fk, til, chp	A-390
Briggs, John	1721/11/--**	st, ers, sun, ms,pa	C-57

Name	Date	Codes	Ref
Briggs, John	1717/9/14	flk, Sc, sun, ls, ms	F-104
Brigham, Hannah	1801/5/7	eff, sc, crk, til	H-35
Brigham, Hannah (fs)	1801/5/7*	flk, til, chp	H-41
Britnall (tm)	--	bl,flk,sc,del,til	W-34
Bronsdon (tm)	--	soi	W-1
Broun, Lydia ,	1680/7/30	soi,flk,fal,ls	A-42
Brown, Ann (tm)	1823	soi,bl,flk,sc,crk,sr	W-18
Brown, Ann**	1731/3/31	ls, pa, chp, soi	G-117
Brown, Charity	1754/4/13	st, til, pa, chp	G-173
Brown, Elizabeth	1773/5/22	soi,ba,crk,til,ms	C-293
Brown, Elizabeth	1803/12/11	sc,til, pa, ba	F-173
Brown, Elizabeth	1756/7/12	crk, soi, frg, ls	F-247
Brown, Elizabeth	--	crk, soi, frg, is	F-247
Brown, Elizabeth	1742/10/11	soi,crk,til,ls,ms	G-46
Brown, Elizabeth	1803/12/11	rep, til, sun, soi	G-275
Brown, Elizabeth (fs)	1773	soi, grf, flk,til,ins	C-291
Brown, Elizabeth (fs)	1803	til, soi, ls, chp	F-258
Brown, Hannah	1810/3/29	flk, frg, rep, chp	H-83
Brown, Hannah (fs)	1810	crk, sun, chp	H-84
Brown, Job	1742/11/29	frg, ls, soi, til	G-263
Brown, John	1782/3/6	soi, st. ba, ms,	D-68
Brown, John	1721/10/14	pa, til, soi, chp	C-118
Brown, John	1764/3/27	fal, soi, chp, ms	G-180
Brown, John (fs)	1782	til, soi, ms, clip	D-158
Brown, John (fs)	1748/3/11**	sun, soi, chp, pt	G-175

Name	Date	Codes	Ref
Brown, John*	1748/3/11**	sun, del, til, chp	G-174
Brown, Jonathan	1746/6/14	til, ls, fk, ms	D-70
Brown, Jonathan (Dea.)**	1785/8/12	ls, soi, ms, chp	D-66
Brown, Martha	1795/9/20	til, sun, soi, ba	G-253
Brown, Mary	1766/1/10	ers, crk, ba, soi	D-69
Brown, Mary	1780/3/5	soi,ba,pa,chp,pt	G-113
Brown, Mary	1728/11/25	pa, soi, sun, chp	G-127
Brown, Nathaniel	1761/11/30	soi,st,bl,chp,pt	G-112
Brown, Nathaniel	1759/12/8	soi, til, pa,pt,chp	G-114
Brown, Nicholas	1801/5/14	sc, til, pa, ba	F-173
Brown, Nicholas (fs)	1801	til, soi, ls, chp	F-258
Brown, Samuel	1768/8/7	crk, sc, sun, soi	G-166
Brown, Sarah	1754/2/17	til, sun, soi, chp	G-169
Brown, Sarah	1772/5/16	crk, til, bl,fk,st	G-244
Brown, Thomas	1760/3/11	crk, soi, frg, ls	F-247
Brown, William	1743/6/4	ba, til, pa,chp,soi	G-116
Brown, William	1751/9/6	soi, st. ms, chp	G-167
Brown, William*	1815/5/27	ba, crk, chp, ms	J-103
Brown,--	1761/7/14	bl, fk, soi, frg, ls	F-184
Bruce, Elizabeth Ann	1815/3/12	pa, fk, til, chp	G-149
Bryant, Frances Clark	1814/4/14	soi, ba, til, chp	J-88
Buckley, Joanna	1717/3/4	soi, is, ba, ms	C-425
Buckley, Joanna	1802	soi, bl,fk,crk,til	C-465
Buckley, John (Capt.)	1799/8/9	bl,fk,til,soi,ba,ms	C-442
Buckley, John jr.** (t)	1798/8/23	soi, del, is, chp	C-71

Name	Date	Notes	Ref
Buckley, Mary	1793/10/21	soi,bl,til,pt,st,ms	C-438
Buckley, Richard	1767/5/21	bl,fk,crk,ba,soi,ms	C-440
Buckley, Thomas	--	ers, til, sun	D-8
Buckly, Joanna**	1802/1/3**	fk, til, frg,ls,ms	C-423
Buckly, Joseph (Capt.)	1764/1/2	grf,fk,dei,crk,til	C-421
Buckly, Joseph (fs)	1764/1/2*	soi, crk, til, chp	C-422
Bucknuin, Marcy	1719/4/4	soi, til, ls,ms,chp	A-21
Buel, Hannah	1760	soi, fal,ls,chp,pa	G-93
Burbeck, Elizabeth	1815/12/10	soi, crk, til,pt,ms	J-57
Burbeck, Henry	1820/5/27	soi, crk, til,pt,ms	J-57
Burbeck, Jerusha	1777/7/27	st, sc, ms	C-350
Burbeck, Jerusha (fs)	1777	bl, fk, til, ls, ms	F-216
Burbeck, Joseph	1811/1/13	soi, crk, til,pt,ms	J-57
Burbeck, Joseph	1820/3/26	soi, crk, til,pt,ms	J-57
Burbeck, William (Col.)	1785/7/22	grf,fk,til,ms,chp	C-348
Burchsted, Ann	1820	soi, ba, bl, fk, sc	I-7
Burdsell, Jane	1721	soi, til, chp	A-438
Burke, Mary	1781/1/15	sc, del, ba, soi	E-5
Burke, Mary (fs)	1787/1/15*	ls, ms	E-6
Burke, William	1787/5/24	sc, del, ba, soi	E-5
Burke, William (fs)	1787/5/24*	ls, ms	E-6
Burr, Nancy	1804/10/3	soi, ba,fk, til,ms,	B-72
Burril, Jane	1741/1/20	soi,sc,til,sun,pa	G-54
Burrill, Anna	1773/10/7	soi, til, ls, chp	G-56
Burrill, Mary	1777 4/5	til, chp, ba, pa	G-55

Name	Date	Codes	Ref
Burrington, Elizabeth	1723/6/2	soi,grf,fk,sun,ms	B-54
Burrough, William	1717/4/21	eff,sc,til,chp,ba	B-41
Burt, family** (m)	--	ba,ers, frg	C-208
Bushnell, Custin	1718/7/13	ba,fk,sc, crk, is	A-67
Butler, Ann	1783/5/18	soi,bl, fk, pa	C-217
Butler, Ann (fs)	1783	pa, til, chp,St	G-216
Butler, John	1748/6/14.	pa, bl, til, soi	G-215
Butler, Mathew	1743/7/30	soi, til, sun, ms	G-210
Butler, Sarah	1751/10/9	bl, til, sun,chp	G-209
Butler, Susanna	1738/10/5	bl, til, soi,chp	G-212
Butler, Thankfull	1741/10/1**	sc, sun, soi,chp	G-211
C., -. (fs)	--	sc, til	A-242
C., E. (fs)	--	fk, til, sun,chp	B-2
C., N. (fs)	--	fk, til, sun,chp	B-2
C., R. (fs)	--	sc, til, ls	C-160
C., S. (fs)		sc, crk, til,ms,chp	C-306
Cabot, George	1804/2/5	bi, fk, til, ms,soi	E-10
Cabot, Martha	1809/3/14	bi, fk, til, ms,soi	E-10
Caddall, Jerusha	1771/11/14	fk, til, ba, chp	H-24.
Cades, Abigail	1777/9/3	bli, fk, chp	C-318
Cades, Joanah	1792/10/9	soi,ba,fk,bl,ms,chp	C-261
Cades, Mary	1783/8/18	bl, fk, til, chp,ms	C-320
Caldwell, John	1733/1/2	fk, sun, ms,chp,ba	F-23
Callender, Joseph (tm)	1823	soi,bl,fk,sc,crk,sr	W-18
Calley, Joseph**	1678/11/28	soi, sun, ls	C-155

Name	Date	Codes	Ref
Cambell, William	1773/1/18	til, ls, ms	A-402
Cambell, William (fs)	1773/1/18*	til, sun, ms	A-403
Campbell, Alexander	1770/8/4	sun, fk, grf,chp	D-145
Capen, Hopestill	1807/3/2	fk, ls, ms	A-291
Capen, Hopestill (fs)	1807	til, ms, chp	A-292
Capen, John	1770/2/19	til, ms, chp	A-297
Capen, John (fs)	1770	soi, til, ms,chp	A-298
Capen, Martha	1780/4/23	soi, grf, ms,chp	D-19
Capen, Martha (fs)	1780/4/23*	ba, ms, chp	D-20
Capen, P. (tm)	1815	soi, sc, pt	J-24
Capen, Patience	1791/1/19	soi, til, ms	A-294
Capen, Patience (fs)	1791*	til, is, ms, chp	A-293
Capen, Thomas (tm)	1811	soi, st. ls	J-11
Capen, Thos. Stoddard	1761/12/21	soi, til, ms	A-283
Capen, Wm. & 4 children	1770/1/14	soi, del, til, ms	A-288
Capron, Christoper**	1721/11/14	del,crk,til,sun,ls	C-28
Capron, Joanna	1721/11/30	soi,ba,del,til,ls	C-168
Carnes, Edward (tin)		grf, frg, pa	W-6
Carnes, Thomas	1818/12/22	soi,ba,fk,ms,chp	A-61
Carter, Jane	1772/7/28	soi, ba	D-139
Carter, John	1765/11/26	soi, ba	D-139
Carterit, Amos	1731/9/26	fk,sun,chp,ms	A-75
Carthew, Hannah	1714/1/20	soi,ers,sc,sun,ls	B-17
Cary, Jonathan	1801/12/29	til, ba, soi,shp	D-114
Cary, Samuel H.	1814/12	soi, crk, ba,chp	J-98

Name	Date	Codes	Ref
Chadwell, Moses(Capt)(fs)	--	ers, sun, soi,ms	F-230
Chadwick, Stephen Kent	1790/4/27	grf, crk, til	A-324
Chadwick,Stephen Kent(fs)	1790/4/27*	soi, fk, til	A-325
Chamberlain, Jane (fs)	--	soi, til,ls, chp	C-222
Chamberlin, Edward (tm)	1807/1/10	sun, soi, chp,ms	W-60
Champney, Caleb D. (fs)	1802	chp, til, crk, ins	G-126
Champney, Caleb Dinsdal	1802/10/4	st, pa, ls, til	G-125
Champney, Sarah	1800/10/13	st, chp, pa	G-122
Champney, Sarah (fs)	1800	soi, fk, chp	G-123
Chandler, Edward (fs)	--	soi, til, ls	A-417
Chandler, Joseph** (tin)	--	sun, ls, bl, fk	W-47
Chew, Prince (fs)	1803	soi, crk, til, ms	D-15
Christy, Hannah	1798/10/16	soi,st,ba,pa,chp,pt	C-85
Christy, Hannah (fs)	1798	frg, til, soi, ms	G-193
Christy, Sarah	1770/10/16	st, soi, pa, ls	G-146
Christy, Thomas	1798/10/21	soi,sc,crk,chp,pa	G-2
Christy, Thomas	1762/7/22	soi,til,sun,chp,pa	G-86
Christy, Thomas (fs)	1798	soi, til,ms,chp,pa	G-3
Chub, Benjamin	1722/12/4	ba, til, ms	A-371
Clap, Pliny (tm)	1819	grf,bl,fk,ls,ms,chp	I-1
Clark, -- (tm)	--	grf	J-8a
Clark, Benjamin (tm)	--	sun, bl, fk, sc	W-51
Clark, Buckland	1748/11/6	til, sun, ls, ms	A-13
Clark, Edward	1712/9	ba,fk,til,ls	B-26
Clark, Elizabeth	1751/10/20	til, sun, ls, ms	A-13

Name	Date	Attributes	Code
Clark, Elizabeth	1722/8/12	ba, til, sun,chp,ms	C-332
Clark, Hannah	1764/2/13	soi, til, ls,ms,chp	C-287
Clark, John (tm)	--	sun, bl, fk, sc	W-51
Clark, Jonas	1790/11/28	til, crk, fk, sc	C-359
Clark, Joseph (Capt.)	1760/3/7	til, crk, ms, soi	C-367
Clark, Josiah	1726/8/27	soi, til, ms, chp	A-299
Clark, Josiah (fs)	1726/8/27*	til, ls, soi	A-305
Clark, Margaret	1761/1/11	fk, til, soi, ms	C-362
Clark, Margret	1720/8/15	ba, til, sun,chp,ms	C-332
Clark, Martha	1769/3/20	soi, grf, fk,crk,ms	C-401
Clark, Mary	1719/11/4.	soi,ba,fk,til,sun	B-3
Clark, Nathaniel	1712/9	ba,fk,til,ls	B-26
Clark, Robert	1813/5/19	ba, pt, chp	J-62
Clark, Sarah	1799/8/9	soi, ba, til	C-288
Clark, William (tm)	1743**	bl,fk,sc,soi,chp	W-1O
Clark, William F. (tm)	--	soi, ers, pt	J-30
Clarke, Johannis (tm)	1728/12/5	pa, soi, sun	W-9
Clarke, Rebecca	1763/1/2**	del,soi,fal,frg,ls	C-444
Cleasby, Abigail	1718/8/20	ers, fk, til, chp	H-37
Cleasby, Sarah	1716/11/21	soi,crk,til,ls,ms	A-73
Cleasby, Sarah	1716/11/23	soi,crk,til,ls,ms	A-73
Clemens, Elizabeth	1749/9/6	st. sr. chp	C-147
Clesby, Ezeriel	1720/4/27	soi,ba,sc,sun,ls,ms	A-62
Clever, Prudanc	1813/11/26	soi, til, chp	J-82
Clough, Ann	1772/4/2	soi,fk,crk,til,ms	A-160

Name	Date	Codes	Ref
Clough, Ann (fs)	1772	til, sun, ms, soi	A-272
Clough, Elizabeth	1745/11/6	soi, grf, ms	A-216
Clough, Mehetabel	1717/10/5	soi, til, sun, ls	A-215
Clough, William (fs)	1798	til, chp. Ms	F-145
Cocke, Joseph	1679/1/15	st, til, ms sr	C-50
Codner, James	1784/8/5	eff, fk, sr, ms	F-41
Codner, Jaines	1715/7/2	ers, Sc, fal, ls	H-So
Codner, William	1769/9/12	fk, soi, ms, pt	H-52
Cogswell, Abiel	1782/1/19**	del, frg, sc, rep	G-230
Cogswcll, Abiel (fs)	1782/1/19**	rep, crk, til, chp	G-231
Cogswell, Abigail	1804/2/12**	del, frg, sc, rep	G-230
Cogswcll, Abigail (fs)	1804/2/12**	rep, crk, til, chp	G-231
Coat, Elizabeth	1749/8/24	fk, til, sun, ms	A-246
Coit, Job	1741/1/12	fk, del, crk, sun	A-336
Coit, Job jr,	1744/2/22	soi, grf, ls	A-241
Coit, Joseph	1748/7/17**	fk, fal, ls	A-251
Coit, Lydia	1751/7/9**	sun, ms, ba	A-337
Coit, Nathanial	1747/5/22	soi, sc, til, ls	A-240
Cole, Edward	1787/11/20	crk, til, soi, sr	A-15
Cole, Edward (fs)	1787	ba, til, ms, chp	A-97
Cole, Essac	1801/10/20	til, soi, ms, chp	H-38
Cole, Rachel C.	1800/1/23	til, soi, ins, chp	H-38
Cole. William	1767/7/6	soi,til,ls,ms	A-50
Coleman, Elizabeth	1798/9/5	soi, grf, crk	A-427
Coleman, Elizabeth* (fs)	1798	soi, del, ls	A-428

Coleman, Temperance	1798/9/13	soi, grf, crk	A-427
Colesworthey, Judet	1729/4/23	soi, til	C-111
Colesworthy, Charles	1793/8/9	soi, st, ms	A-210
Colesworthy, Elizabeth	1810/11/11	soi, grf, crk,pt, ms	J-45
Colesworthy, Nathaniel	1802/9/20	soi, st, ms	A-210
Colesworthy, Nathaniel	1779/10/20	soi,, st. ms	A-210
Colesworthy, Nathl. jr.	1808/4/22	soi, st, ms	A-210
Coleworthy, N. jr.*(fs)	1808/4/22*	til	A-211
Coleworthy, N.*(fs)	1802/10/10/21*	til	A-211
Coleworthy, Nathaniel	1802/10/21	soi, ls, ms, ba	A-212
Coleworthy, Sally	1780/5/9	soi, st, ms	A-210
Coleworthy,Nathaniel(fs)	1802*	st, chp	A-213
Collins, Daniel	1718/10/30	eff, ms, chp	H-96
Collacott, Richard	1686/7/7	soi,fk,sun,chp	B-51
Colle, Margaret	1761/5/4	soi,sc,til,ls,ms	A-49
Collins, Charity	1771/10/25	til, crk, sr, ba	D-106
Collins, Clement	1787/4/24	bl, fk, til, ms, ba	H-26
Collins, Daniel	1758/8/29	soi, ers, til, ls	C-96
Collins, Lydia	1789/6/10	soi, pa, til, chp	G-129
Collins, Lydia (fs)	1789	soi, fk, sc, ms,chp	G-130
Collins, Mary	1761/12/4	til, fk, ls, soi	D-107
Collins, Patience	1760/6/25	fk, ba, soi, ms,	D-108
Collins, Patience (fs)	1760/6/25*	til, ls, ms, soi	D-183
Collins, Sarah	1778/10/18	soi,til,sun,ms,chp	C-326
Collins, Sarah	1771/3/29	Sc, til, eff, ms	H-30

Name	Date	Codes	Ref
Collins, Sarah (fs)	1771	til, chp, ms	H-34
Colman, James S.	1813/4/25	grf, ba, chp, pt	J-68
Coiner, Benjamin (tm)	1807**	sun, ls, sr, soi	W-65
Coiner, Ellinor (fs)	--	soi, ls	A-320
Coiner, John (fs)	--	soi, ls	A-320
Coney, Mary	1750/1/30	pa, ls, til,soi,chp	F-286
Connel, Pattrick	1763/6/11	crk, sr. ms, soi	D-75
Connel, Pattrick (fs)	1763	crk, til, grf, chp	D-166
Connor, Johanna	1799/12/29	soi, ba, del,ls,ms	C-345
Cook, Ellis (tm)	--	ba, soi, til, chp	W-16
Cookson, J. (tm)	--	soi, grf	J-7a
Cooper, Abigail	1719/3/19	soi, til, ls, ms	A-345
Cooper, John (fs)	--	til, sun, soi, ms	E-57
Cooper, John Lambord	1805/11/17	st, chp, pa	G-88
Coping, Ann	1731/8/26	soi, til, chp	A-314
Copp, Amy	1718/11/28	til, del, ms	C-353
Copp, David	1712/2/24	soi,bl,til,sun,ls	C-218
Copp, David	1661/12/22	soi, crk, til, ms	C-264
Copp, David	1713/11/20	bl, fk, crk,til,ls	C-456
Copp, Goodeth	1670/3/25	soi, ba, sun, ms	C-280
Copp, Obedience	1678/5/30	til, ls, soi, ba	C-358
Copp, Obedience (fs?)	--	ms, sr, chp	C-39
Copp, Thomas	1678/7/25	soi, crk, til, ms	C-264
Corlew, Elijah	1804/5/25	til, sc, soi, rep	H-42
Coverly, Thomas (fs)	1778**	soi,fk,sc,til	A-133

Cox, Sarah	1733/11/17	crk, til, sun, soi	G-234
Crawford, David	1738/11/20	fk, crk, til, soi	F-166
Crawley, Joseph	1738/3/6	til, del, ba, ms	E-44
Crease, John	1800/12/8	til, crk, ba, ms	D-180
Crease, John (fs)	1800/12/8*	til, soi, ms	D-181
Creighton, Mary**	1801/4/5	fk, til, frg, ls	H-48
Crighton, Ann	1717/4/25	ba, sun, chp	C-74
Crocker (tm)	--	sr, crk, chp	W-33
Cullam, Lydia	1761/11/3	soi,grf,sun,chp,ms	C-256
Cumby, Rebecca	1731/4/26	sc, del, ls, soi	H-10
Cumby, Robert (fs)	1717	fk, sun, ms	H-2
Cummings, Bradley (tm)	--	soi,grf,fk,crk,ls	I-2
Cushing, Ann	1759/8/15	soi, til, chp	A-287
Cushing, Benjamin (tm)	1819	soi, st, bl, fk	I-8
Cushing, Jeremiah	1722/7/18	soi, fk, til, ls	A-205
Cushing, Jeremiah	1755/10/24	soi, til, chp	A-287
Cushing, John	1743/2/10	grf, sc, til, ls	A-230
Cushing, Mary	1800/3/14	soi. crk, til, sun	G-220
Cutler, Levi	1821/1/7	soi, sc, til, ms	G-184
Cutter, Almena	1806/9/30	fk, ba, ms, chp	F-S1
Cutter, Elizabeth	1801/6/13	fk, sc, crk, sun,ms	F-42
Cybuat, Mary	--	sc, til, sun, soi	G-214
D. I. H. (fs)	--	chp, ms	D-47
D. E. (fs)	--	sc, ba, frg, ms,chp	H-67
D. M. (fs)	1721	ba, til, ls	A-91

Name	Date	Codes	Ref
Dalton, Michael (tm)	--	soi, ers, pt	J-30
Darling, Betsy	1809/3/23	crk, bl, fk, sc	A-5
Darling, Betsy (fs)	1809	fk, sc, grf, ms	A-11
Darracott, George (tm)	--	ba, soi, til, chp	W-16
Davies, William	1710/11/9	soi,ba, til, ls	C-161
Davis, Isaac Howard	1807/5/8	st, til, sun, ms	D-42
Davis, Jacob ,	1762/3/10	soi, sun, chp	A-426
Davis, James (tm)	1821	grf, ba, til, ms	I-3
Davis, Martha	1686/8/7	soi,ba,til,ms,chp	C-262
Davis, O. (tm)	1819	soi, crk	J-26
Davis, S. (tm)	1819	soi, crk	J-26
Delaplace, Thomas	1733/12/25	pa, til, bl,chp,soi	F-284
Demeret, Mary	1737/3/20**	sun, til, chp	F-169
Demery, --	17--	til, sun, frg, ls	A-433
Demery, Charles	1717/11/22	ba, del, til, chp	C-76
Demery, John	1783/3/13	fk, til, sun, is	A-432
Deinount, Dorcas	1738/5/19	soi,, til,sun,ls,chp	C-214
Demount, Dorcas (fs)	--	soi, til, sun, ls	E-65
Dennen, James (Capt.)	1757/8/11**	fk, sc, sun, ls,chp	F-22
Dennis, Michael	1763/7/11	st, til, ls, chp,pa	G-5
Dennis, Michael (fs)	--	soi, pa, chp, pt,ba	G-87
Dethick, John	1738/7/2	ba,bl,fk,sc,sun,ls	C-324
Diamond, John	1763/3/B	soi,st,fk,del,crk	A-152
Diamond, John (fs)	1763	soi,ba,fk,ls,ms,chp	A-158
Diamond, Margaret	1769/5/9	soi,st,fk,del,crk	A-152

Name	Date	Codes	Ref
Diamond, Margaret (fs)	1769	soi,ba,flk,ls,ms,chp	A-158
Diamond, William	1711/9/20	flk, eff, del, ls	H-36
Dickenson, Daniel (tm)	1828	st,bl,flk,sun,ls,chp	J-141
Dickerson, Henry	1720/3/21	soi, ers, til	C-110
Dillaway, Eminy	1813/10/11	ba, bi, til, chp,pt	J-79
Dimond, Hannah	1743/5/4	soi,st,ba,crk,til	A-149
Dissinore, Fanny	1788/12/29	flk,sc,crk,til,sun	F-5
Dissinore, Fanny (fs)	1788/12/29*	Soi, til, chp	F-6
Dixwell, Martha	1722/10/3**	Soi,flk,crk,til,ls	A-94
Dixwell, Mary	1745/9/19	Soi,flk,til,sun,ms	A-92
Dixwell, Mary	1721/9/28	ba, is, ms	A-98
Dixwell, Mary* (fs)	1745/9/19*	crk,til,sun,ls	A-93
Dobel, Abiagil	1769/11/5	ers, flk, sun, soi	F-176
Dobel, John	1773/4/8	bl, crk, sun, ms	F-177
Dobel, John (Capt.) (fs)	1773	til, soi, ls, chp	F-262
Dobel, John jr (Capt) (fs)	1763	bl, flk, sc, ls, soi	F-260
Dobel, Joseph	1810/3/19	flk, sr, frg, ls, ms	F-175
Dobel, Mary	1790/12/3	flk, Sr, frg, ls, ms	F-175
Dodd, James (tm)	1821	soi, bl, flk	I-15
Dodd, John (tm)	1821	soi, bi, flk	I-15
Dodd, William (tm)	1807	sr, bl, flk, chp,soi	W-31
Dodge, James	1759/11/24	sun, ba,ms,chp,soi	E-39
Dodge, Nabby	1796/3/28	flk, til, eff, ms	F-18
Dodge, Nabby (fs)	1796	flk, chp, ins, soi	F-19
Dodge, Sarah	1748/5/14**	til, sun, ba, ms	F-83

Name	Date	Codes	Ref
Dolbeare, John (Capt.)	1794/12/7	soi,ba,til,ms,sr	A-196
Dolbeare, Sarah	1701/7/17	soi, eff, til, chp	C-102
Doncan, John	1736/5/29	pa, ls, sc, soi	F-279
Dorr, Dorothy	1765/4/16	soi,sc,del,crk,ls	A-120
Dorr, Harbottle	1746/6/19	soi,ba,fk,til,ls	A-117
Dorrington, John	1772/3/14	soi, ba, fk,sun,chp	C-236
Doubleday, Benjainin*	1784/9/2	soi, chp, pt, pa	G-72
Doubleday, Benjarnin* (fs)	1784/9/2*	sun, chp, ms	G-73
Doubleday, Susannah	1773/9/5	til, soi, ba, chp	D-123
Doublede, Dorcas	1740/3/3	pa, soi, crk, chp	G-76
Doublede, Dorcas (fs)	--	st, bi, chp, ms	G-77
Douglass, Susanna	1773/5/1	Bl, fk, crk, chp	W-20
Douglis, Elizabeth	1726/1/22	til, ms, soi	E-61
Dowrick, Martha	1757/10/16	soi,bl,fk,crk,til	C-436
Dowrick, William	1749/3/10	bl, fk, crk,til,ls	C-464
Draper, Moses	1693/8/14	soi,st,grf,fk,crk	A-147
Drowne, Elizabeth	1728/3/15	soi,del,til,crk,ls	A-170
Drowne, Elizabeth (fs)	1728/3/15*	til, chp, ms	A-171
Drowne, Joseph	1721/10/31	soi,del,crk,til,ms	A-167
Drowne, Katherine	1754/4/21	soi,grf,til,chp,ms	A-164
Drowne, Katherine (fs)	1754/4/21*	soi,ba,fk,til	A-166
Drowne, Leonard	1729/10/31	soi,fk,del,crk,til	A-163
Drowne, Mary	1726/2/11	soi,del,til,crk,ls	A-170
Drowne, Mary (fs)	1726/2/11*	til, chp, ms	A-171
Drowne, Sarah	1795/9/26	soi,grf,sc,til,ms	A-162

Name	Date	Codes	Ref
Drowne, Sarah (fs)	1795	chp	A-223
Drowne, Shem (Dea) (fs)	1774/1/13*	soi,ba,fk,til	A-166
Drowne, Shein (Deacon)	1774/1/13	soi,grf,til,chp,ms	A-164
Drowne, Shem (fs)	1770	soi,fk,crk,til,ls	C-159
Drowne, Shem jr.	1770/5/6	soi,grf,ms	A-161
Drowne, Simeon	1734	soi, fk, ms, chp	A-22
Drowne, Thomas	1795/2/20	soi,grf,sc,til,ms	A-162
Drowne, Thomas (fs)	1795	chp	A-223
Drummond, Mary	1815/12/15	ba, pt, chp	J-115
Dudley, Silas	1812/11/26	soi,ba,chp,pt	J-70
Dumblide, Sally	1796/2/26	fk, sc, sr, til	D-48
Dumblide, Sally (fs)	1796	til, chp, ms	D-49
Duncan, Issabella	1750/2/2	fk,sc,ers,eff,til	F-26
Duncan, Robert	1752/1/24	bl, fk, crk, til	F-25
Dunn, Susan	1815/3/17	soi,crk,til,chp	J-99
Dupee, I (tm)	--	soi. grf	J-4a
Dupee, Issac (m)	1846/8/31	ers, ba, grf, soi	G-297
Dutch, Harris	1712/9/10	fk, sc, til	A-327
Dyer, Ezra (tm)	--	soi, grf, crk,sc,ls	J-10
Dyer, Ezra (tm)	1811	soi, fk, chp	J-12
Dyke, William (tm)	1844	soi., grf, bl, fk	J-42
E., D. (fs)	--	fk, til, ba	C-424
Eames, Samuel	1811	ba, sc, til,sun,chp	J-53
Earle, Abigail	1729/7/27	--	F-95
Eaton, Abigail	1816/2/4	st, chp, pt, ms	J-116

Name	Date	Codes	Ref
Emmes, Henry	1725/2/12	soi,ba,crk,til,ms	C-289
Emmes, Jacob H.	1807/7/23	soi,grf,ba,ms,chp	C-304
Emmes, Jacob H.* (fs)	1807/7/23*	ba, til, ms, chp	C-305
Emmes, John	1806/1/1	grf, ba, crk,ms,chp	C-298
Emmes, Joshua	1772/8/6	ba, bi, fk, chp	C-300
Emmes, Joshua (fs)	1772/8/6*	ba, fk, sc, til, ms	C-299
Emmes, Margaret	1778/8/31	soi, ba, til,del,ms	C-302
Emmes, Martha	1747/1/27	soi,fal,ls,ms,chp	A-105
Emmes, Martha (fs)	1747/1/27*	ba,fk,chp	A-107
Ernines, Mary	1729/7/17**	soi, fk,sc, til,chp	C-231
Emmes, Mary	1812/10/11	soi, ba, til,ms,chp	C-295
Emmes, Nathanaell	1718/11/23	soi, ba, til, ms	C-285
Emmes, Nathaniel*	1749/1/5	soi,fk,sc,til,sc	C-294
English, William	1705/1/1	fk, sc, del, til	A-408
Eustis, Benjamin	1804/5/4	soi,grf,ms,pt,chp	D-40
Eustis, Flora	--/9/30**	sun	A-335
Eustis, George	1779/10/19	fk, til, ms, chp	H-99
F., S. (fs)	--	crk, til, ls, chp	F-170
Farington, Joseph	1721/11/5	ba,til,sun,ls,ms	A-63
Farmer, Abigail B. (fs)	1804/12/16*	til, sun, ls,ms,chp	F-45
Farmer, Abigail Brewer	1804/12/16	fk, sc, til, ms,chp	F-46
Farmer, John	--	frg, sun, crk, soi	D-146
Farmer, Mary	1798/11/4	soi, til, pt, chp	G-70
Farmer, Mary (fs)	--	soi,til, chp	G-71
Farmer, Paul	1701/12/26	soi, sun, ls,chp,pa	G-1

Name	Date	Codes	Ref
Farmer, Paul (fs)	1791	ba, til, chp, pa	G-9
Farnam, Elizabeth	1694/4/26	soi, til, ls, ms	A-415
Farnham, Elizabeth	1799/3/20	soi,ba,til,ms,sr	A-197
Farnham, Martha	1819/3/23	til, crk, ba, ms	D-64
Farnham, Ruth	1799/5/23	soi,grf,fk,ls,ms	C-418
Farnum, Charles	1678/1/21	soi, ms, ba	C-363
Farnum, John	1702/1/20	grf,crk,til,ls,ms	C-432
Farnum, Jonathan	1804/12/6	til, sun, crk, ls	C-371
Farnum, Jonathan	1768/10/13	grf,crk,til,sun,ls	C-439
Farnum, Joseph	1678/11/30	til, fk, sc, soi	C-370
Farnum, Susana	1700/9/23	soi,del,ls,sr,ms	C-35
Farnum,-- sr.	1686/12/6**	sc, til, sun, ls	C-372
Farrar, James (tm)	1806	bl, fk, ls, soi, ms	C-471
Fernald, Elizabeth	1804/2/27	fk, sun, eff, ba,ms	F-12
Fernald, Elizabeth (fs)	1804	fk, chp, ba	F-13
Feveryear, Grafton (Dea.)	1755/3/30**	del, bl,fk,til,sun	G-208
Fisher, Thomas	1805/6/27	crk, sun, ba, chp	F-209
Fisk, Sewall	1817/4/13**	soi,til,sun,pa,ms	G-23
Fisk, Thomas L.	1815/9/24	frg, ls, ms	H-6
Fitzgearld, Mary**	1787/9/3	pa, ls, bli, sun,soi	F-276
Fitzgerald, Elenor	1817/2/11	soi,bl,fk,sun,chp	J-139
Fletcher, Margaret	1747/2/9	sun, fk, ba, ms,chp	F-8
Fletcher, Sarah	1736/12/20	til, ls,ba,soi,chp	E-2
Flinn, Elizabeth	1813/10/15	ba, til, sun, chp	J-80
Folsom, J.W. (tm)	--	bl, fk, grf, soi	W-29

Name	Date	Codes	Ref
Forbs, Jonathan	1819	grf,bl,fk,ls,ms,chp	I-1
Forist, Mary	1728/9/2	soi.,fk,sc,sun	D-36
Foster, John (fs)	1746	fk, crk, ls, chp,ba	F-218
Foster, Susanah	1794/10-/15	sun, ms, ba, soi	E-37
Foster,--	1716/8/3	del, sun, ls, rep	F-214
Fowle, Elizabeth	1694/12/2	soi, del, til,ls,ms	C-282
Fowle, Robert (fs)	--	til, ba, soi, ms	A-12
Frackner, Thomas (tm)	1806**	sun, soi, ms, chp	W-69
Freeland, James	1802/7/20	crk, chp, ms, soi	G-277
Freeland, James (fs)	1802	soi, st, chp, ms	G-285
Freeman, Alice	1735/2/21	st,fk,til,crk,frg	C-412
French, Adarri (tm)	1806	bl, fk, ls, soi, ms	C-471
Frost, Ebenezer	1773/11	soi,fk,ba,ls,ms	A-77
Frost, John (fs)	1776	til, ls, ms, chp	D-53
Frost, Jonathan	1706/1/23**	ba,fk,sc,crk,til,ls	A-16
Frothingham, Thomas (tm)	1819	soi,bl,fk,crk,til,	I-4.
Fuller, Eliza	1806/9/16	til, soi, sr, chp	C-473
Fuller, Eliza* (fs)	1806/9/16*	bi, fk, til,soi,chp	C-472
Furber, Richard	1753/2/15	fk, sc, crk, sun,ms	F-245
Furbur, Elizabeth	1790/5/10	sc, pa, til, ms, ba	F-237
Furbur, Elizabeth*(fs)	1790/5/10*	til, chp, ms	F-238
Furbur, Richard	1749/3/8	sc, eff, ms, chp	F-243
G., A. (fs)	--	Ls, chp	H-21
G., J. (fs)	--	til, chp, ms	F-47
Galloway, Abigail	1813/2/25	soi,bl,fk,til,chp	J-66

Gamman, Grace	1702/7/27	soi,ba,fk,sun,ms	8-66
Gardner, Deborah	1792/9/28	soi, st, til, pa	G-6
Gardner, Elisy	1800/11/17	bi, fk, sc, crk,ms	F-103
Gardner, James	1802/3/22	eff, fk, sc, til,ms	F-101
Gardner, James (fs)	1802	crk, ms, chp	F-102
Gardner, Mary	1743/5/22	til, del, ba, ms	D-110
Garish, Lydia	1698/1/8**	ba, sc, til, ls	C-120
Gatte, Patrick	1746/11/19	til, chp, st. soi	G-232
Gatte, Thomas	1745/12/7	soi, til, chp, ms	C-168
Gaud, Thomas	1708/11/15	ba, sc, til	A-82
Gay, Ebin (tin)	1819	bl, fk, crk, pt	I-14
Gay, Rebecca P. (fs)	1797	fk,sc, til, ls	C-405
Gay, Rebecca Porter	1797/12/8	soi,st,fk,ba	C-107
Gay, Thomas	1799/7/28	soi,grf,fk,crk,til	C-4O4
Gay, Timothy (fs)	1799	ba, fk, sun, ms,chp	C-406
Gayetty, Joseph	1808/2/13	crk, fk, til, ms,ba	H-69
Gayetty, William	1802/7/15	crk, fk, til, ms,ba	H-69
Gedney, King (tm)	1812	grf, bl, fk, crk,sr	J-19
Gedney, William	1725/12/7	st,ba,bk,fk,sun,ls	C-176
Gedney, William	1726/12/14	st,ba,bk,fk,sun,ls	C-176
Gee (tm)	--	grf, til, chp, ba	W-2
Gendall, Lydia (fs)	--	del, soi, ba	H-98
George, Daniel	1684/7/18	st. ba, sc, ls	C-185
Gilburt, Mary	1733/12/30	soi, grf, crk,ms,pt	C-240
Gilburt, Mary (fs)	1733/12/30*	Soi, bl, fk, til,chp	C-239

Name	Date	Codes	Ref
Giles, Hannah	1805/8/12	soi,grf,fk,crk,chp	C-260
Giles, Hannah (fs)	1805/8/12*	soi, crk, ms, chp	C-260a
Gill, Elizabeth	1666/9/28	grf, fk, crk,til,ms	C-308
Gill, Elizabeth	1687/10/1	soi, fk, crk,ms,chp	C-321
Gill, John	1671/12/10	grf, fk, crk,til,ms	C-308
Gill, John (fs)	--	soi, til, ls, ms	C-344
Gill, Nathanaeli	1720/10/3	til, crk, del, ba	C-383
Gill, Obadiah (Deacon)	1700/1/6	soi, ba, ins, chp	C-314
Gill, Samuel	1683/5/29	soi,crk,del,til,ms	C-341
Gill, Sarah	1691/4/20	ba, til, ms, chp	C-310
Gill, Thomas	1666/12	grf, fk, crk,til,ms	C-308
Gillander, Joseph	1774/5/31	soi, sun, ms, chp	F-168
Gilma, Peter jr. (fs)	1804	til, ba, ms, chp	F-157
Gilman, Abigail	1802/7/3	bl, fk, ba, ms,chp	F-153
Gilman, Abigail (fs)	1802	bl, fk, ms, chp	F-155
Gilinan, Bethiah	1806/1/22	fk, sc, soi, ms	F-149
Gilman, Bethiah (fs)	1806	til, ba, chp	F-150
Gilinan, Lydia	1796/3/6	bl, fk, til, ba,chp	F-151
Gilman, Lydia (fs)	1796	fk, sc, til, sun	F-152
Gilinan, Peter	1807/4/12	fk, ba, pa, ms	F-147
Gilman, Peter (fs)	1807	crk, soi, ms, chp	F-148
Gilman, Peter jr.	1804/7/11	ba, ms, chp, soi	F-156
Gladding, Anna	1801/6/18	fk, ba, ms	F-105
Gladding, Anna (fs)	1801	Sun, ms, chp	F-106
Glasier, Nathaniel	1812/5/27	ba,bl,fk ,sc,til,chp	J-63

Name	Date	Codes	Ref
Glidden, Sarah	1739/10/16	bl,fk,til,sun,ms,ba	C-431
Goff, Abigail	1815/3/4	soi,til,sun,chp	J-100
Goff, John	1807/1/26	fk, crk, ms, pt	F-35
Goffe, Abigail	1744/8/21	soi, crk, sun, chp	G-291
Goffe, John	1716/7/2	ls, bl, sun, soi	G-186
Goffe, Samuel	1740/9/11	ba,fk,til,sun,ms	A-88
Goldthwait, Sarah	1713/10/31	ba,ers,crk,til,ls	C-99
Gooding, Richard	1756/5/16	ba, til, chp, pa	G-11
Gooding, Sarah	1749/8/21	crk, fk, st. chp	G-227
Gooding, Thomas	1742/2/21	crk, sun, chp, ms	G-221
Gooding, William	1739/1/22	soi,bl,til,chp,pa	G-39
Goodrich, Henry (tm)	1811	soi, crk, chp	J-2
Goodwill, T. (tm)	--	soi, grf, ba	J-lOa
Goodwin, Benjamin	1792/11/30	st,fk,crk,til,ms,sr	C-86
Goodwin, Hannah	1775/10/25	st,fk,crk,til,ms,sr	C-86
Goodwin, John	1712/6/21	soi, til, chp, ms	C-460
Goodwin, Mary	1759/7/6	bl, fk, crk,soi,pt	C-462
Goodwin, Sally	1781/8/23	fk, ba, soi, ms,chp	F-179
Goodwin, Sally	1781	bl, til, chp	G-42
Goodwin,Nancy	1775/10/21	st,fk,crk,til,ms,sr	C-86
Goodwing, Elizabeth	1762/4/8	ba, ms, chp	E-73
Goold, James	1764/10/11	soi, ls	C-153
Goold, Thomas	1707/2/27	til,sun,ls,ms,chp	D-34
Gooldttwait (fs)	--	ls, ba, ms, chp	E-43
Gording, Abraham	1706/9/27	ba.fk,sc,til,ls,ms	B-68

Name	Date	Codes	Number
Gording, Hannah	1725/3/3	ba,sc,crk,til,ls	B-53
Gore, Chris (tm)	1810**	sun, ls, bl, fk,soi	W-46
Gouge, Francis	1747/4/8	ls, ms	A-338
Gould, Charlotte	1805/8/26	til, crk, ba, ms	D-113
Gould, Charlotte* (fs)	1805/8/26*	til, ba, ms, chp	D-112
Gould, Mary	1817/4/17	grf, crk, sun, chp	J-129
Grammer, Joseph (tm)	1806/10/11	sun, soi, ms	W-68
Grant (t)	--	oj	C-58
Grant, Edward	1752/7/19	ba, del,crk,til,ms	C-335
Grant, Edward	1682/6/19	soi, fk, til, ls,ms	C-336
Grant, Edward	1797/6/28	soi,grf,fk,crk,ms	C-339
Grant, Edward (fs)	--	soi, til, ms	C-337
Grant, Edward (fs)	1797/6/28*	fk, del, til, ms	C-338
Grant, Joanna	1696/5/20	st. ba, sc, ls	C-128
Grant, Joseph	1752/7/25	ba, del,crk,til,ms	C-335
Grant, Sarah	1690/3/25	soi, ba, til, ms	C-334
Grater, Mary	1741/6/21	til, crk, ms, pt	E-69
Graves Eliphal (fs)	1717/4/15*	Soi, til, ls, chp	C-225
Graves, Daniel	1739/7/10	fk, sc, til, ms, pt	F-107
Graves, Elliphal*	1717/4/15	soi, fk, til,ls,chp	C-224
Gray, Susannah* (fs)	1798/7/9**	ba, sun, ms, chp	A-145
Gray, Susannah**	1798/7/9**	st,grf,fk,crk,ls,ba	A-144
Green, Anne	1730/6/23**	del,sc,crk,til,eff	F-127
Green, Elizabeth	1766/4/27	soi,ba,fk,til,ls	A-124
Green, Elizabeth (fs)	--	soi, ls, ms	A-178

Name	Date	Description	No.
Green, Hannah	1718/1/3	Bl, fk, sun, ls,soi	C-469
Green, John	1800/5/28	til, crk, fk, sr	D-159
Green, John *(fs)	1800/5/28*	soi, ba, ms, chp	D-160
Green, John Sr.	1702/2/25	bl, fk, crk, til	C-474
Green, Nancy	1800/12/18	pa, ba, chp	F-86
Green, Nancy (fs)	1800/12/18*	fk, ba, chp	F-87
Green, Polly Coleworthy	1805/2/11	soi, ls, ms, ba	A-212
Greenough, Dorothy	1667/10/20	soi, ba, til, sun	A-410
Greenough, Elizabeth	1688/5/23	ba, ms	A-366
Greenough, J. (tm)	--	soi, grf, ba	J-1a
Greenough, William (Capt)	1693/8/6	soi, fk, crk, til	A-400
Greenough, Sarah	1676/9	soi, til, chp, pt	C-245
Greenwood (t)	--	ls, pa, ba, soi	G-294
Greenwood, Mary	1774/9/21	soi,ba,fk,til,pit	B-27
Greenwood, Mary (fs)	1774/9/21	ba,fk,sc,til,ms	B-28
Greenwood, Nancy	1802/5/5	eff,fk,sun,ms	B-22
Greenwood, Nancy (fs)	1802/5/5*	ba,fk,til,sun,chp	B-23
Greenwood, Nathaniel	1684/7/31	fk,sc,til,sun,ms	B-20
Greenwood, Nathaniel*	1730/7/7	ba,sc,til	B-30
Greenwood, S. (tm)	--	soi, ba	J-2a
Greenwood, Samuel	1711/12/10	soi, ls, chp	A-280
Greenwood, Samuell	1711/8/9	ba,bl,fk,del,crk,	B-21
Griffen, Isaac	1693/7/29	soi, fk, til, ms	A-317
Grouard, Elizabeth	1730/5/21	soi, tili, chp, ms	G-269
Grouard, Elizabeth	1747/7/5	bl,til,ls,soi,st	G-272

Name	Date	Codes	Ref
Grouard, Joseph	1746/11/19	bl,fk,crk,til,ms	G-273
Grover, Dean	1734/8/15	soi, st, ba, chp	C-249
Grover, Dean (fs)	--	soi, til	C-100
Grozer, Anna	1722/4/8	ba,til,ls,ms	D-33
Grozer, John (Capt.)	1801/4/27	til, pa, ba, chp	F-75
Grubb, Martha	1805/9/21	soi sc,til,chp,pa	G-21
Guliker, John jr.	1770/8/23	crk, fk, sr, ins,p'c	D-143
Guliker, John jr.	1781/8/7	crk, fk, sr, ms,pt	D-143
Guliker, Mary	1784/12/23	crk, fk, sr, ms,pt	D-143
Guliker, Thomas	1783/6/29	crk, fk, sr, ms,pt	D-143
Gurney, Henry (tm)	1828	soi, grf, bl, fk	J-38
Gyles, Abigail**	1740/7/2**	fk, frg, ls	F-222
Gyles, Charles	1745/3/9	fk, sun, til, ms	F-196
Gyles, ElizabeLh	17--/9/10	fk, sun, ls, ms	F-200
Gyles, Mary	1795/4/13	bl, fk, sun,ms,soi	F-192
Gyles, Mary	1777/10/22	crk, chp, sr, soi	F-199
Gyles, Mary	1757/10/30	bl,fk,del,sun,eff	F-250
Gyles, Samuel	1777/10/25	pa, ls, soi,chp,ba	F-270
H., H, (fs)	--	ba, sc, til	C-137
H., I.(fs)	--	ers, sun, chp, soi	H-23
H.J. (fs)	--	sun, fk, chp	F-32
H.M.A. (fs)	1816	soi,til, chp, ms	G-60
Hall Harriot	1815/8/21	grf,crk,sun,chp,ms	J-107
Hall, J. (tm)	--	soi,grf	J-5a

Name	Date	Codes	Ref
Hall, Jacob (tm)	--	st.soi,ba,bl,fk,chp	W-15
Hall, N. (tm)	--	soi,grf	J-5a
Hall, Prince	1807/12/7	grf, til, ls, ms	D-16
Hall, Prince (m)	1895/6/24	soi, grf	D-17
Hall, William	1743/1/9**	crk, sun, chp	A-142
Haly, Sarah	1752/5/15	bl, sun, soi, ms,pt	G-284
Haly, William	1760/4/6	bl,sun, soi, ms,pt	C-284
Hammatt, Benjamin (Capt.)	1805/4/7	crk, til, ba, pa	E-30
Hammatt, Joseph .	1798/2/19	del, til, ms, soi	E-32
Haminatt, Joseph (fs)	1798	til, ms	E-33
Hammatt, Marcy	1796/1/6	fk,ba, ms	E-21
Hammatt, Marcy (fs)	1796	del, ba, ms	E-22
Hammatt, Mary	1762/1/25	til, fk, del, sr,ms	E-56
Harnmatt, Mary (fs)	1762/1/25*	fk, ms, chp	E-58
Hammond, Elizabeth	1810/4/15	til, ba, ms, chp	E-24
Hammond, Eiizabeth*(fs)	1810	soi, ms, ba	E-25
Hammond, Nathaniel (tm)	1819	soi, crk	J-26
Hancock, Ebenezer	1799/7/4	Soi, til, ms, ba	A-276
Hancock, Ebenezer (fs)	1799	soi, til, ls	A-277
Hannah, Elizabeth	1704/1/20	soi,ba,fk,ls,chp	C-163
Hannah, Mary	1701/7/31	soi,ba,fk,ls,chp	C-163
Hanyford, Abigail	1695/2/28	st,ls	C-24
Hardy, Francis	1807/10/26	sc,crk, til, chp	H-68
Hardy, Francis* (fs)	1807/10/26*	fk,sc, til, st,chp	H-87
Hardy, John	1808/8/28	sc,crk, til, chp	H-68

Name	Date		
Hardy, John* (fs)	1808/8/28*	flk,sc, til, st,chp	H-87
Hardy, Margaret	1809/9/16	sc,crk, til, chp	H-68
Hardy, Margaret* (fs)	1809/9/16*	flk, sc, til, st,chp	H-87
Hares, Hezekiah	1680/1/31	st,del, sr, chp	C-187
Hares, John	1674/10/23	st.del, sr, chp	C-187
Hares, William	1729/6/14	bl,flk, crk, ms, ba	F-235
Harper, Henretta	1795/5/23	st, til, chp, pa	G-52
Harper, Henretta (fs)	1795	til, sun, m, chp	G-53
Harratt, Katharine	1733/11/6	st. flk, til, ls, mns	C-177a
Harratt, Peter	1740/2/20	til, flk, ls, ms,soi	F-17
Harris, Ann	1778/6/28	st, ms	C-189
Harris, Ann (fs)	1778	st,ba, til, chp	C-250
Harris, Anna	1778/9/2**	til, sc, ms, soi	D-50
Harris, Anna (fs)	1778	til, ba, ms, chp	D-51
Harris, Catherine Butler	--	soi, bi, flk, ls	A-430
Harris, Elizabeth	1744/10/10	Soi, til, sr, pt	C-183
Harris, Hannah	1787/12/24	grf, ba, til chp	C-186
Harris, Hannah	1686/12/13	St,ba,sc,del,ls,ms	C-190
Harris, Hannah (fs)	1783	st,ba, del, chp	C-188
Harris, Hannah (fs)	-	soi, til, ls,ms,chp	C-243
Harris, Hannah* (fs)	1686/12/13	ba,til, sun	C-191
Harris, John	1770/12/8	ms,ba, chp, soi	D-52
Harris, Leach (tm)	1807**	sun, ls, sr, soi	W-65
Harris, Mary	1743/11/12	st,til, ms, chp	C-179
Harris, Nathaniel	1749/2/12	soi, grf, ls, ms	D-44

Name	Date	Codes	Ref
Harris, Nathaniel (fs)	1804	soi, til, ls	A-431
Harris, Nathaniel (fs)	1749/2/12*	til, sun, ls, ms	D-43
Harris, Nathl. Langdon	1804/1/14	soi, bl, fk, ls	A-430
Harris, Richard (Capt.)	1714/3/10	ba, ms, chp	A-367
Harris, Samuel	1741/3/20	soi,st,ba,sc,til,ms	C-177
Harris, Thomas	1742/2/28	st,til, ms, chp	C-179
Harris, Thomas (fs)	--	soi, ba, til, ms	C-263
Harris, William	1730/6/28	eff,ba,fk,sun,chp	B-5
Harris, William	1689/1/31	st,ba, sc, del,ls,ms	C-190
Harris, William* (fs)	1689/1/31*	ba,til, sun	C-191
Hartt, Lois	1751/11/5	soi,grf,fk,til, ms	A-191
Hartt, Lois (fs)	1751/11/5*	soi,ba,del,crk,til	A-192
Hartt, Mary	1733/8/2	soi,fk,sc,til,chp	A-193
Hartt, Ralph (Capt.)	1776/3/14	soi,fk,sc,del,crk,	A-195
Hartt, Samuel (tm)	1841	st, pt	J-4
Hartt, William (tm)	1841	st, pt	J-4
Harvey. John	1814/2/16	soi, til,sun,chp,pt	J-86
Harvey, Mary	1782/5/2	sun, crk, del, chp	E-7
Harvey, Mary (fs)	1782	til, del, ms, chp	D-173
Hasey, Martha	1676/5/4	soi, ba, til, chp	C-411
Hawkins, Jacob	1797/7/19	soi, til, chp,pa,pt	G-51
Hay, Theodocia	1757/5/31	til, sun, ls, ms	D-56
Hayden, Caleb (fs)	1795	til, grf, chp, soi	D-91
Hayden, Elizabeth	1790/9/23	til, ls, sc, ms	D-94
Hayden, Elizabeth (fs)	1790	til, ba, soi, ms	D-95

Name	Date	Codes	Ref
Hayden, Priscilla	1813/10/28	ba,bl,fk, crk,til,ls	J-81
Hayward, Abraham	1781/11/11	bl,fk,soi,pa,chp,ba	G-64
Hayward, Abraham	1796/3/5	pa, soi, st, chp	G-131
Hayward, Abraham (fs)	1781	soi,til,ls,chp,ms	G-65
Hayward, Abraham (fs)	1796	bl, fk, chp, ms,soi	G-132
Hayward, Hephzibah (fs)	1803	fk, ms, chp	A-34
Hayward, Hephzibah**	1803/12/23	soi,ba,fk,sc,ls	A-33
Hayward, Thomas	1771/2/19	bl,fk,soi,pa,chp,ba	G-64
Haywood, Anthony (Maj.)	1689/10/16	til, ba, ms, pt,chp	H-22
Haywood, Anthony (fs)	1689/10/16*	fk, til, ba, chp	H-27
Hazly, Richard (fs)	--	ers, eff, sun, ms	F-38
Hearst, Elizabeth (t)	1708/--/--	soi,ba,sc,fal,ls,ms	C-309
Heath (tin)	1819	ba, chp, ms	H-76
Heath, Deborah	1755/1/7	sc, ba, soi, chp	F-9
Heath, Mary	1809/10/12	ba, pt, chp	J-61
Heath, Nathaniel	1812/5/5	ba, pt, chp	J-61
Heath, Samuel	1752/5/23	sc, ba, soi, chp	F-9
Hemmenway, Joseph	1806/1/15	soi,grf,frg,ls,ms	C-254
Hemmenway, Joseph (fs)	--	soi, crk,til,ms, chp	C-251
Hemmenway, Susannah	1796/4/17	fk, sr, soi, chp	E-3
Hemmenway, Susannah (fs)	1796	til, ms, chp	E-4
Henchman, Anna	1706/1/7	soi,fk,sc,til,ms	B-33
Henchman, Easter	1731/5/s	soi, bi, crk,til,ls	C-211
Henchman, Richard	1725/2/15**	soi, grf, sun, ms	A-425
Henderson, B. (tm)		soi, grf	J-13b

Name	Date		Code
Henderson, Hemmen	1738/4/19	st,sc,dei,til,sun	C-130
Henry, Jane	1803/10/22	soi,ba,fk,crk, til	C-409
Henry, Jane (fs)	1803/10/22*	ba,fk,sc,til,ms	C-410
Herman, Elizabeth	1797/6/5	grf, til, chp, ms	A-265
Hett, Ann	1678/6/20	soi,fk,crk,frg,ls	C-312
Hewens, Jacob	1696/7/6	st, ba, del, sr	C-118
Hewens, Jacob jr.	1673/10/7	st, ba, del, sr	C-118
Hichborn, Samuel jr. (tm)	1812	grf, bl, fk, crk,sr	J-19
Hicks, Mary**	1747/12/30**	eff,ba,fk,ls,ms	B-24
Higgins, Patience	1760/2/4	til, sun, ba, soi	C-357
Hiler, Jacob (tm)	1805	bl, fk, sc, ls, soi	W-39
Hill, Mary	1714/10/20	soi,bl,ls,chp	C-203
Hill, Mary	1722/1/20	soi,ba,bl,crk,chp	C-257
Hill, Mary (fs)	--	soi, ers, chp	C-150
Hill, Prudence	1775/1/26	ba, ms, soi	C-366
Hill, Samuel	1804/4/27	del, crk, sr, chp	D-77
Hill, Samuel (fs)	1804/4/27*	del, fk, ms, soi	D-76
Hill, Samuel (tm)	1820	st,grf,ba,fk,crk,ls	I-6
Hiliard, Martha	1687/8/21	st, ls, ms, pt	D-12
Hilier, George	1721/8/22	ls, del, sc, ms, ba	D-103
Hillman, Peleg L.	1798/3/25	ba, ms	H-46
Hirsst, Mary	1717/11/23	soi, ba, ms	C-286
Hirsst, Hindreh	1717/1/30	sc, sun, chp, ba	H-90
Hoar, Wilimoth	1735/2/29	ers,fk,sc,crk,til	B-75
Hobby, Ann	1709/6/22	sc, til, chp, soi	H-13

Name	Date	Codes	Ref
Hobby, Ann	1711/4/3	fk, eff, chp	H-70
Hobby, Hannah	1690/6/26	fk, sc, soi, ms,chp	H-62
Hobby, John	1741/5/14	sun, soi, ms, chp	H-61
Hobby, John	1685/10/17	sc, ba, sun, ms,chp	H-63
Hobby, John (Capt.)	1711/9/7	Fk, Sc, til, ba, ms	H-72
Hobby, Richard	1711/4/13	fk, eff, chp	H-70
Hobby, William	1713/8/24	sc, til, chp, soi	H-13
Hodgdon, Susannah	1730/5/23	st, del,crk, ms,chp	C-43
Hodge, Sarah (fs)	--	fk, til, sun,ms,chp	F-242
Hodsdon, Nathaniel	1757/4/5	st,ers,til,sun,ms	C-47
Holbrook, Samuel	1756/6/11	soi,fk, til, ms,chp	A-130
Holbrook, Sarah**	1738/9/20	til, sun, ls,del,sc	E-8
Holden, (Infant)	--	bl,fk,crk,til,ls,ba	C-443
Holden, Nancy	1802/3/25**	bl,fk,crk,til,ls,ba	C-143
Holland, John	1736/9/9	fk, sc, soi, ms	D-148
Holland, Samuel (Deacon)	1798/8/17	til, soi, ms, chp	E-34
Holland, Samuel (fs)	1798	ms, chp	E-35
Holland, Susannah	1741/7/13	fk, sc, soi, ms	D-148
Holmes, Charles (tm)	1807	sc, crk, chp, soi	W-43
Holmes, Francis (tm)	1819	soi, st, bl, fk	I-8
Holmes, Henry P. (tm)	1839/1/4.	ba, grf, soi, sun	W-42
Holmes, Marcella	1815/4/28	soi,grf,crk,chp,ms	J-144
Holmes, Mary	1742/7/16	ba, bl, crk, chp	G-288
Holmes, Samuel (tm)	1821/7/3	ba, grf, soi, sun	W-42
Hood, Joseph	1729/12/14**	til, ba	C-373

Name	Date	Codes	Ref
Hood, Joseph	1713/9/4	ba, til, chp, ms	C-419
Hood, Lettuce	1747/7/10	crk,til,soi,ls,ms	C-430
Hood, Lettuce (fs)	--	fk, sun, ms, chp	C-374
Hooper, Rebekah	1675/10/15	soi, ba, til, ms	C-413
Hooton (tm)	--	ba, soi, bl, fk, til	W-12
Hope, (infant son)	1811/8/29	crk, til, sun, soi	G-228
Hope, Samuel	1815/10/19	crk, til, ms, soi	G-197
Hopkins, Betsy	1783/8/29	til,soi,ba,ms,chp	F-81
Hopkins, Betsy (fs)	1783/8/29*	soi, ls	F-74
Hopkins, Caleb jr.(Capt.)	1791/10/19	fk, sc, til, ba, pa	F-73
Hopkins, Enoch	177~/12/27	soi,st,grf,fk,ls,ms	C-202
Hopkins, Samuel	1767/9/23	soi, sun, ls, ms	C-255
Hopkins, Thomas (tm)	1804	fal	H-45
Hormbey, Mary	1755/6/11	st,ba,fk,crk,ls,ms	A-138
Horton, George	1710/5/9	soi, til, sun	A-397
Hosea, Richard (tm)	1828	grf,bl,fk,crk,ls,pt	J-35
Hoskins, Katherine	1769/1/5	til, soi, ba,ms,chp	E-15
Hoskins, Katherine (fs)	1769	til, ba, chp, soi	E-16
Hoson, John	1791/3/7	tili, soi, chp	F-264
Hough, Lydia	1683/2/26	soi,fk,sc,crk,til	B-34
Hough, Mary	1692/9/29	fk,sc,til,sun,ms	B-6
Hough, William	1714/11/8	ba,sc,crk,ls,chp	B-36
Hough. William (fs)	1714/11/8*	sc,til,ms,chp,ba	B-35
Hough, William jr.	1716/6/18	ba,sc,til,ms,chp	B-39
How, Margrett	1776/7/23	is, ms, chp	D-203

Name	Date	Codes	Ref
Inckenson, Daniel (tm)	1813/6/23	soi, ers, crk, pt	J-36
Ingerfield, Tompson**	1788/7/28**	soi, fk, sc, ls	A-269
Ingersol, D. (tm)	---	soi, grf	J-6a
Ingersoll, J. O. (tm)	--	ba, ers, crk	I-12
Ingersoll, Nehemiah	1782/8/25	til, sun, crk, ls	E-60
Ingersull*, Abraham	1752/6/15	ers, crk, til	H-108
Ingham, Abigail	1728/4/10	til, ls, soi, ba	C-368
Ingles, James	1703/2/6	soi,ba,fk,til,ms	C-132
Ingles, Joanna	1678/9/11	ba, fk, sc, ms, chp	C-87
Ingraham, Elizabeth**	1718/1/17	soi,ers,til	A-47
Ingraham, Joseph (Capt.)	1811/6	soi, grf, ba,pt,chp	J-49
Ingrsull, George	1721/8/19	crk, til, ls, ba	G-287
Ivory, Luce	1767/12/9	fk, sun, ms, chp	F-219
Jackson Eleazer (fs)	1809	bl, fk, crk,til	F-114
Jackson, Eleazer	1809/6/6	fk, ba, ms, chp	F-113
Jackson, Eleazer	1809/10/22	fk, ba, ms, chp	F-113
Jackson, Mary Ann	1809/7/24	fk, ba, ms, chp	F-113
Jackson, Walter	1809/6/21	fk, ba, ms, chp	F-113
James, --(fs)	--	sun, til, fk, sc	F-64
James, Abigail	1783/4/3	fk, ms, ba, soi	F-60
James, Enoch (tm)	1805	sr. soi, chp	W-36
James, Francis (tm)	1805	sr, soi, chp	W-36
James, John	1803/12/22	til, ls, fk,soi	A-3
James, John (fs)	1803	til, sc, chp, ms	A-4
James, Merriam	1765/7/15	soi,fk,sc,til,ms	A-46

Name	Date		ID
Jaruis, Eiizabeth*	1709/8/13	til, ls, ms,soi	A-260
Jarvis, --	1753/12/17	ls, ms	A-356
Jarvis, Charles (m)	1807/11/15	ba, ers, crk	A-385
Jarvis, Elizabeth	1760/5/9	soi, del, ls, ms	A-351
Jarvis, Elizabeth	1760/2/13	del, til, ls, ms	A-354
Jarvis, Elizabeth (fs)	1760	soi, til, ls, ms	A-381
Jarvis, Leonard (Col.)	1770/9/30	grf, fk, til, crk	A-352
Jarvis, Sarah	1747/12/15	soi,crk,til,ms	A-189
Jeffs, Anna	1738/7/22	soi, til, ls,chp,pa	G-20
Jeffs, Mary	1734/8/1	del,til,sun,ls,chp	G-24
Jenkin, John	1717/9/16	ba,soi,sc,til,ls	C-172
Jenkins, Martha	1797/7/16	pa, til, ba,soi	G-207
Jenkins, Martha (fs)	1797	fk, til, chp, ba	G-245
Jenkins, Thomas	1730/5/28	soi, st, crk, chp	G-268
Jognson, Sarah	1744/1/24	fk, sun, ms,chp	F-125
Johnson, Daniel (tm)	1807	sc, crk, chp, soi	W-43
Johnson, Elizabeth	1717/4/8	soi, chp	C-105
Johnson, Elizabeth	1701/5/7**	soi,crk,til,sun,frg	C-219
Johnson, John	1804/6/5	soi, sr, ba	D-119
Johnson, John	1721/10/28	eff, sun, ms, chp	F-129
Johnson, John (fs)	1721/10/28*	sun, ms, chp	F-130
Johnson, John S.	1829/9/9	soi,bl,fk,sun,chp	J-123
Johnson, Mary (fs)	--	del, chp	E-31
Johnson, Sarah	174.0/9/12	fk, til, ms,chp	F-50
Johnson, Sarah	1743/10/11	fk, ers, til,ms,chp	F-52

Name	Date	Notes	Ref
Johnson, Susanna	1745/11/23	fk, ba, ms, sr	F-128
Johnson, Susanna	1721/11/2	eff, sun, ms, chp	F-129
Johnson, Susanna (fs)	1721/11/2*	sun, ms, chp	F-130
Johnson, Susannah	1804/8/20	soi, sr, ba	D-119
Johnson, Zachariah	1727/12/25	soi,del,crk,til,ls	C-75
Jones, Benjamin B.	1813/10	st. fal	J-58
Jones, Betsy	1806/4/22	fk, crk, grf, ms	E-100
Jones, Betsy (fs)	--	fk, sc, crk,pa, ms	F-124
Jones, Eliphalet	1811/12/4	st, fal	J-58
Jones, Elizabc:th	1744/7/9	soi,grf,ba,fk,ls	A-146
Jor~es, Elizabeth**	--	soi, crk, ba	A-270
Jones, Joseph (tm)	1812	soi,grf,bli,fk,crk	J-17
Jones, Josiah	1744/1/17	til, ls, ba, soi	D-133
Jones, Mary (fs)	--	sc, til	A-208
Jones, Mary (fs)	--	til, soi	D-184
Jones, Mary **	1746/5/17	til, crk, frg, ls	D-135
Jones, Mercy	1805/4/7	st,crk,til,chp,pa	G-49
Jones, Mercy (fs)	1805/4/7*	soi, crk, ms, chp	G-48
Jones, Prudence	1828/11/19*	st, fal	J-58
Jones, Prudence Hall	1827/11/12	st. fal	J-58
Jones, Samuel	1731/26/8	ba, til, chp	C-194
Jones, Silas	1813/1	st. fal	J-58
Jonson, Thomas	1729/12/31	crk, ls, ba, soi	D-132
Josselyn, Emelinec D. (m)	1833/9/2	soi,ers,ba,crk,chp	I-24
Kaind, Artur	1687/3/24	soi, fk, ms, chp	C-247

Kellen, Elizabeth	1729/1/22**	soi,crk,til,sun,ms	A-81
Kellon, Thomas	1708/12/25	soi,grf,ms,chp,bs	D-41
Kemble, Elizabeth	1712/12/19**	sc, sun, ba	H-17
Kemble, Thomas	1689/1/29	fk, til, chp, soi	H-16
Kenney, Elizabeth	1753/5/6	til, ba, soi, ms	C-387
Kenney, Elizabeth	1807/9/10	til, crk, fk, ms	D-155
Kenney, Elizabeth (fs)	1807	til, sun, soi, ms	D-156
Kent, Jacob** (tm)	--	sun, ls, ms	W-62
Kent, John	1794/9/30	ls, sr, ba, ms	D-100
Kent, Jonathan	1700/12/30	crk, ba, ms, soi	D-162
Kent, William	1691/6/9	soi, grf, fk,til,ms	C-297
Kettell, Joseph	1783/7/12	ba,fk,sc,til,ms	B-58
Kettell, Joseph	1777/8/30	ba, fk, til, ms	B-60
Kettell, Joseph (fs)	1783/7/12*	fk,til,ms	B-59
Kettell, Joseph (fs)	--	fk,til,chp,eff	B-61
Kettell, Joseph (fs)	--	fk,til,chp	B-63
Kettell, Polley	1783/11/13	ba,fk,sc,til,ms	B-58
Kettell, Polley (fs)	1783/11/13*	fk,til,ms	B-59
Kettell, Rebecca A. (fs)	1773/10/14*	fk,til,chp	B-63
Kettell, Rebecca Austin	1773/10/14	fk,til,ls,chp,ms	B-62
Kimball, Elliot (tm)	1819	soi, bl, fk	I-16
Kimble, Katherine	1722/3/24**	chp, til, sun, ms	F-280
Kind, Jane	1710/4/3	soi,til,sun,ms,chp	C-248
Kind, John	1690/7/29	fk, sun, ms, chp	F-120
Kind, Mary	1662/8/15	fk, sc, sun, chp	H-9

Name	Date	Codes	Ref
Kind, Rachel	1690/7/6	soi, st. sun, ls	C-178
Kind, William	1666/2/14	fk, sc, sun, chp	H-9
King, Abigail	1770/11/13	til, ls, ba, soi	C-390
King, Elizabeth	1715/11/29	eff, ba, chp, ms	H-1
King, Josiah	1786/3/24.	soi, ba, crk,til,ms	C-346
King, Josiah (fs)	1786/3/24*	til, ins, chp	C-347
Kingman, Anna	1817/4/14	soi,grf,fk,sc,chp	J-128
Kingman, John	1817/6/18	soi,grf,fk,sc,chp	J-128
Kingsbury, Clarisa	1818/10/13	soi, ba, ers, chp	J-148
Kingsbury, Jesse (tm)	1825	soi,grf,crk,sc	J-3
Kingston, --	1721/9/9	sc, sun, is, ms,eff	F-118
Kingston, William	1720/2/8	soi,st,til,sun,chp	G-177
Kinsman, Pelatiah	1727/4/21	fk, crk, pa, chp	H-S
Kneeland, Mary	1819/1/10	soi,grf,crk,chp,ms	J-144
Kneeland, S. K. (tm)	1820	soi,ba,bl,fk,crk	I-11
Knight, Samuel	1721/10/25	del, soi, ls	G-176
Knox, Adam	1745/10/17	sun, ms, chp	D-61
Knox, Ann	1760/1/25	soi,ba,crk,til,sr	A-38
Knox, Ann (fs)	1760	soi,chp,ms	A-39
Knox, Martha	1748/5/15	til, is, del, ms	D-82
L., E. (fs)	--	fk, sun, chp, ms	F-180
L., E.(P) (fs)	--	fk, til	A-180
L., J. (fs)	--	soi, st. til, chp	G-89
L., M. (fs)	--	crk, til, chp, ba	H-40
Lack, Edward	1760/2/29	sun, soi, ms, chp	G-178

Name	Date	Codes	Ref
Lad, Briget	1743/11/2	fk, til, ba, ms	F-30
Laish, Nicolas	1685/4/30	soi,ba,fk,sc,sun	C-164
Lake, John	1690/6/27	soi,sc,del,til,sr	C-142
Lake, Thomas	1676/8/14	st. ba, crk,til,ms	C-143
Lambert, Thomas (Capt.)	1813/5/12	sc, grf, chp, pt	J-69
Lamson, Elizabeth	1766/8/10	bl, til, sun, soi	G-279
Lane, --	1780/12/8	fk, sun, pa, ms	F-88
Lane, Elizabeth	1795/4/13	Til, sun, soi, pa	F-271
Lane, Henry** (tm)	1807	Sc, crk, chp, soi	N-43
Lane, Levi	1806/6/23	Til, grf, soi, chp	F-193
Lane, Levi	1790/7/23	fk, Sc, til, soi	F-207
Lane, Levi (fs)	1790	chp, ba, sr, soi	F-190
Lane, Levi (fs)	--	soi, bl, fk, chp,ms	F-191
Lane, Phebe	1781/11/12	sun, fk,soi,ms,chp	F-14
Lane, Phebe (fs)	1781	ls, chp, ba, ins, pt	F-15
Lane, Thomas P.	1817/6/20	soi,grf,ba,bl,fk,sc	J-131
Langdon, Elizabeth	1713/12/18	ers, fk, del, chp	C-61
Langdon, Elizabeth	1713/9/14	sun, del, crk, ls	D-59
Langford, Hannah	1796/11/19	soi,ba,til,ls,ms	C-427
Langley, Mary	1743/9/23**	ba,til,sun,ms	B-43
Langley, Mary (fs)	1743/9/23**	soi,fk,sc,fal,ls	B-40
Lark, Thomas	1723/11/30	til, ls, ms	A-346
Larrabee, Abigail	1729/7/3	soi, ba, til,sun,ms	C-232
Larrabee, Benjamin	1730/5/9	soi, bl, fk, ls, pt	C-230
Larrabee, Benjamin (fs)	--	soi, ba, til, chp	C-226

Lasenby, Marcy	1732/8/31	soi, til,sun,ls,chp	G-31
Lash, Elizabeth	1727/10/12	soi, sun, chp	C-165
Lash, Elizabeth	1731/9/6	soi, crk, til, ls	C-167
Lash, Elizabeth	1750/8/14.	soi,st,til,sun,chp	G-94
Lash, Elizabeth	1819/9/4	grf, bl,fk, ls, chp	J-120
Lash, Elizabeth* (fs)	1750/8/14*	soi, til, chp, pt	G-99
Lash, Johanna	1771/5/29**	soi, til,sun,chp,ms	G-14
Lasinby,Thomas	1747/6/24.	s'c,ba,del,til,ms	D-2
Late, Edward	1734/5/13	bl, fk, ba, til,chp	F-189
Lawlor, Thomas	1744/2/26	soi, ba, til,chp,pa	G-41
Lawson, Elizabeth	1699/5/1	til, ba, ms, chp	A-363
Learnard, William	1807/1/10	fk, sun, del, ms	W-63
Learned, Elisha** (tm)	--	sun, ls, bl, fk	W-47
Learned, John	1800/12/14	st, crk, ms, chp	C-8
Leate, Sarah	1805/1/19	bi, fk, ba, ~il,chp	F-189
Lee, Deborah	1763/4/3**	soi,pa,bl,fk,sc,crk	W-4
Lee, Thomas (tm)	1766/7/6	soi,pa,bl,fk,sc,crk	W-4
Leland, Mary	--	soi,sun,chp	A-113
Leman, John	--	soi, til,sun,chp,pt	J-54
Lewis, Benjamin* (tm)	1820	soi, bi, fk	I-18
Lewis, J. (tm)	--	soi, ba	J-2b
Lewis, Joseph	1729/11/23	til, sun, ls, ms,ba	E-59
Lewis, Mary	1806/12/31	bl,fk,crk,til,grf	H-33
Lewis, Nathaniel	1778/5/12	del, crk, pa,ba,chp	F-163
Lewis, Nathaniel (fs)	1778	pa, ba, chp	F-164

Name	Date	Codes	Ref
Lewis, T. (tm)	1809/2/-	soi, ba	J-2b
Lewis, Thomas (t)	1824/8/8	soi, ers	G-295
Lewis, Thomas jr. Ct)	1832	soi, ers	G-295
Libby, J. G. L. (tm)	174-/4/4	soi, st. grf, fk, bl	J-40
Lidstone, Thomas	1810/3/18*	ls, del, soi, ms, ba	E-72
Lincoln, C. C.* (fs)	181-/4/12	fk, sun, til, chp	F-110
Lincoln, Christopher	1810/3/18	fk, sc, til, is, ms	F-109
Lincoln, Christopher C.	1812	fk, sc, til, ls, ms	F-109
Lincoln, Noah ('cm)	1752/3/6	grf, bl, sr, pt	J-18
Lioston, Elizabeth	1785/9/25	soi, bl, til, pa	G-278
Little, Alexander**	--	fk, ls, chp	F-56
Littlefield, Rebecca (fs)	1760/5/4	soi,ba,crk,ms	A-157
Lobb, Rodger	--	soi,fk,ba,ls,ms	A-77
Lobb, Rodger (fs)	1853/4/16**	soi,ba, ls, chp, ms	A-68
Lock, Hannah (tm)	1808/4/13	ers, crk	J-8
Long, Eliza	1808/4/13*	til, crk, sun, del	D-176
Long, Eliza (fs)	1762/3/26	til, sc, ba, ms	D-175
Lord, Alexander Seares	1739/11/2	soi,ba,bl,crk,til	C-322
Lord, Hannah	--	soi,ba,bl,crk,til	C-322
Loring, Elijah** (tm)	1806/10/11**	til, sl, sr, soi	W-61
Loring, John** (tm)	1828	fk, ls, soi, ms	W-66
Loring, Jonathan (tm)	1819	soi, fk, sc, crk,bl	J-34
Loring, Joshua (tm)	1689/11/25	soi st, grf, bl	J-29
Loud, Elizabeth	1836	til, soi, pa, ms	F-266
Low, Abiah P. (tm)		soi, grf, ers, pt	J-21

Name	Date	Codes	Ref
Macomber, Ichabod (tm)	--	soi, ba, bl, fk	I-13
Malcom, Ann	1770/4/4	Til, grf, ba, ms	D-85
Malcom, Ann (fs)	1770	til, grf, soi, ms	D-101
Malcom, Daniel	1769/10/23	til, del, ls, grf	D-86
Malcom, Daniel (fs)	1769	ls, ms, sc, ba	D-102
Malcom, Michael	1775/2/18	grf, ba, ms	D-84
Malcom, Sarah	1800/9/13	bl, fk, sc, ms, ba	F-33
Malcom, Sarah (dau.)	1800/9/13	bl, fk, sc, ms, ba	F-33
Malcom, Sarah (fs)	1800	ba, ms, chp	F-34
Malcomb, Sarah	1767/9/23	crk, sc, ls, ms	D-83
Manley, John	1767/9/7	soi, ba, ms, chp	A-66
Manwaring, Daniel	1773/4/6	soi, ls, ms, chp	A-257
Manwaring, Daniel (fs)	1773	soi, til, ms	A-258
Manwaring, Sarah	1764/1/23	crk, ms, chp	A-256
Marden, David (tm)	1828	soi, bl, fk	J-31
Marshal, Francis	1740/8/23	soi, til, sun, chp	G-261
Marshall, Francis	1767/7/24	bl, sun, soi, chp	G-225
Marshall, Josiah (tm)	1812	grf, fk, crk,sr,rep	J-20
Marshall, Marcy	1712/4/18	til, ba, ls, ms	C-355
Marston (tm)	--	soi, bl, til, ls	C-212
Marston, J.B. (tm)	1810**	sun, ls, bl, fk,soi	W-46
Martain, Abigail	1812/8/22	soi, ba, sc,sun,chp	J-64
Martyn, Michael	1680/3/26	soi,ba,til,ms	C-328
Martyn, Michael (Capt.)	1700/10/27	til, sr, ba,chp,soi	E-1
Marvin, Mary	1714/7/24	ba, til, ls, ms	C-395

Mason, Lydia	1803/12/30	soi,eff,til,sr,chp	C-94
Mason, Sampson	1807/8/28	soi,eff,ba,til	C-95
Mason, William	1732/9/23	crk, fk, sc, sun	H-32
Mason, William	172-/11/25	til, eff, ms, chp	H-43
Mather, Cotton** (t)	1727/2/13	soi,eff,crk,fk,ls	I-23
Mather, Increase (t)	1723/8/27	soi,eff,crk,fk,ls	I-23
Mather, Samuel (t)	1785/6/27	soi,eff,crk,fk,ls	I-23
Mather, Sarah	1737/2/21	til, crk, sc, soi	D-78
Mathews, Abigail	1811/6/4	soi,ba,fk,crk,chp	J-50
Maverick, John	1720/1/24	til, sun, ms, chp	F-221
Maverick, John	1734/7/17	fk, crk, til, ls	F-226
Maverick, John (fs)	1734/7/17*	bl, fk, crk, ms,chp	F-227
Mavericke, Mehitabel	1747/6/30	bl, fk, crk, til,ms	F-224
Mavericke, Mehitabel (fs)	--	bl, fk,til,soi,chp	F-195
May, Thomas	1710/11/10	til, ls, ms, chp	A-313
Mayo, Rebecca	--	pa, crk, sc, chp	G-201
McCiarry, Ann **	1747/8/10	ls, ms, bl, fk, soi	A-10
McClarry, Mary **	1744/8/15	ls, ms, bl, fk, soi	A-10
McClary, Sarah (Fs)	1797	sun,pt,ms	D-39
McClennen, William ('cm)	1812	soi,grf,bl,fk,crk	J-17
McClintock, Aaron	1800/5/5	bl, fk, chp, ms,soi	F-53
McClintock, Aaron*(fs)	1800/5/5*	bl, fk, crk, ms,chp	F-69
McClin'cock, Martha	1798/10/13	bl, fk, chp, ms,soi	F-53
McClintock, Martha*(fs)	1798/10/13*	bl, fk, crk, ms,chp	F-69
McGilvery, Nancy	1815/12/1	soi,fk,sc,crk,chp	J-114

Name	Codes	Ref
Milk, Eleanor	soi,st,del,pa,chp	G-68
Milk, James	soi,st,del,pa,chp	G-68
Milk, John	fk, chp, pt, pa	F-289
Milk, John	soi,st,del,pa,chp	G-68
Milk, Susanna	soi,st,del,pa,chp	G-68
Millar, Lydia	bl, fk, til, ls, ms	C-454
Miller, Ann L.	crk, til, chp, soi	H-80
Miller, Anna	sc, crk,til,chp,ms	G-105
Miller, Benjamin	crk, til, chp, soi	H-80
Miller, Charles	crk, til, chp, soi	H-80
Miller, Eliza	crk, til, chp, soi	H-80
Miller, Jno. W.	crk, til, chp, soi	H-80
Miller, Joseph	crk, til, chp, soi	H-80
Miller, Samuel	soi, til, ls	C-156
Miller, Sarah	soi,st,crk,til,ls	C-157
Millet, Abraham (tm)	ba, bl, fk	I-19
Millins, Thomas	st. til,sun, ls,sr	C-16
Mills, Eliza	soi, st. ba, chp,ms	G-280
Mills, Joanna	soi,ba,til,ls,ms	A-51
Mills, William	ba, sun, soi, chp	G-281
Milton, Ephraim (tm)	soi, grf, bl, fk	J-38
Milton, Sarah	soil grf, crk,pt,ms	J-45
Mole, Samuel (Capt.)	soi,ers,sun,ls,ms	B-70
Moor, Elinor	st, sun, ms, chp	A-40
Moor, Samuel	soi,fk,sc,crk,til	A-41

Milk, Eleanor 1794/11/7
Milk, James 1792/7/16
Milk, John 1756/5/19
Milk, John 1808/7/11
Milk, Susanna 1802/8/4
Millar, Lydia 1678/12/11
Miller, Ann L. 1806/1/30
Miller, Anna 1782/5/7
Miller, Benjamin 1809/12/25
Miller, Charles 1810/10/3
Miller, Eliza 1803/8/12
Miller, Jno. W. 1813/9/30
Miller, Joseph 1809/10/7
Miller, Samuel 1697/6/10
Miller, Sarah 1755/2/6
Millet, Abraham (tm) 1821
Millins, Thomas ---/1/24
Mills, Eliza 1809/8/20
Mills, Joanna 1733/3/26
Mills, William 1792/8/25**
Milton, Ephraim (tm) 1828
Milton, Sarah 1817/3/29
Mole, Samuel (Capt.) 1727/8/21
Moor, Elinor 1730/6/27
Moor, Samuel 1739/1/28

Name	Date	Codes	Ref
Moore, Mary	1730/5/27	til, sun, eff,sc,ms	F-24
Mortimer Hannah	1773/8/21	ls, crk, grf, sol	D-97
Mortimer, Hannah (fs)	1773/8/21*	til, ls, ms, ba	D-98
Mortimer, James	1773/8/18	ls, crk, grf, soi	D-97
Mortimner James (fs)	1773/8/18*	til, ls, ms, ba	D-98
Mortimer Peter (Capt.)	1773/8/22	til, sc, ba, grf	D-178
Mortimer, Peter (fs)	1773/8/22*	til, crk, ba, soi	D-177
Mounfort, John (tm)	1724/1/6	soi, st, ba, chp,pt	W-13
Mountford, J. (tm)	--	soi, grf, ba, pt	J-3a
Mountfort, Benjamin (tm)	1721/3/10	soi, st, ba, chp,pt	W-13
Mountfort, Jonathan (t)	1724	rep, crk, chp, soi	G-296
Mower, Ephraim	1721/10/2	chp, til, sun, ms	G-170
Mower, Samuel	1747/5/6	soi, til, pa,chp,pt	G-111
Mulvana, Sarah	1805/7/4	eff, crk, chp, ms	H-73
Mulvana, Sarah* (fs)	1805/7/4*	crk, ba, ms, chp	H-74
Mumford, Mary	1688/1/24.	soi, ls	C-151
Mumford, William	1704/12/18	soi, ba, til, ms	C-283
Mumford, William	1718/11/21	frg, crk, soi, ba	C-356
Munroe, David Webb	1813/3/22	soi,fk,crk,til,sun	J-46
Munroe, Elizabeth Steel	1813/4/26	soi,fk,crk,til,sun	J-46
Munroe, Susanah	1810/12/14	soi,fk,crk,til,sun	J-46
Munroe, W. (tm)	--	ba, ers, crk	I-12
N., M. (fs)	--	fk, sc, til, chp	F-233
Nash, R-	1726/1/6	fk, sc, sun, ls, ms	F-119
Nazro, Susannah	1815/10/30	grf, crk,ba,chp,ms	J-113

Name	Date	Abbreviations	Code
Norton, Sarah	1721/10/30	til, soi. bl, pt	C-449
Norton, Thomas	1714/9/21	ls, ms, chp	C-393
Norwood, Caleb	1735/12/27	sc, soi, st, chp	G-218
Nottage, Nathaniel ('cm)	1828	soi., fk, sc, crk,bl	J-34
Nowel, Mary**	1739/5/29**	soi, til, sun,ls,ms	C-327a
Nowell, --		del, sun, ls, ms	A-372
Nowell, Deborah	1794/5/6	til, ba, ms	A-370
Nowell, George	1742/6/8	crk, til, frg, ls	F-183
Nowell, Lidia	1704/12/18	soi, grf, til	A-374
Nowell, Michael	1696/8/27	soi, til, ba, ms	A-369
Nudd, Thomas T.	1813/5/20	til, clip, pt, ms	J-71
Oliver, T. (tin)	--	soi, ba	J-12a
Orr, Margaret	1753/5/7	soi,sc,del,til,ls	A-48
Owen, Mary	1767/12/14	del, crk, til, soi	G-182
Owen, Mary (fs)	1767	st. til, soi, chp	G-183
P. T. (fs)		soi,ba,fk,til,chp	B-55
P., W. A. (fs)	--	sc, til, chp, ms	H-25
Page, Edward	1784/11/10	til, sc, soi, chp	D-142
Page, Edward	1737/1/15	til, del, crk, ls	D-188
Page, Edward	1785/7/27	til, fk, ba, soi	D-191
Page, Edward	1748/3/12	fal, ls, soi	D-192
Page, Mary	1750/4/6	til, sun, ls, ms	D-187
Page, Mary	--	til, del, crk, ls	D-188
Page, Thomas ('cm)	1807	til, sun, sc,ms,soi	W-67
Paine, Susanah	1719/1/26	soi, bi, til,ls,chp	C-223

Name	Date	Codes	Ref
Paker, Thomas	1723/4/5	st,sc,til,ms,sr,st	C-53
Pallies, Elizabeth	1811/11/4	soi,st,crk,til,ls	J-56
Pallies, William	1812/3/29**	soi,st,crk,til,ls	J-56
Palmer, Grace	1750/6/5	til, ls, ms, ba	E-9
Palmer, Grace (fs)	1750/6/5*	til, ms	E-11
Par--, Joseph	1726/6/26	del, ls	A-209
Parham, Rebecca	1753/4/28	til, ls, del, sc	D-120
Parham, Rebecca (fs)	1753/4/28*	Til, sun, ba, soi	D-121
Parham, Sarah	1752/5/27	til, ls, del, sc	D-120
Parham, Sarah (fs)	1752/5/27*	til, sun, ba, soi	D-121
Parker Ct)	--	soi,ers, crk,rep	C-400
Parker, John	1744/9/27	st,fk,crk,til,sun	C-244
Parker, John Jenkins	1758/5/17	frg, til, soi	G-237
Parker, N. (tm)	--	soi, grf, crk,sc,ls	J-1O
Parker, Sarah	1750/9/5	st,fk,crk,til,sun	C-244
Parkman, --nah	--	frg, ls, ms, chp	C-259
Parkman, Alexander	1748/3/6	soi, til, ls, ms	A-102
Parkman, Alexander (fs)	1748/3/6*	soi, til, ls, chp	A-103
Parkman, Benjamin (fs)	--	soi, bl, til,pa,ls	G-63
Parkman, Dorothy**	1741/4/9	soi,fk,del,ls	A-118
Parkman, Elias	1741/5/24	soi, fk, crk, ms	A-122
Parkman, Elias	--	fk, til, chp	A-185
Parkman, Elias (doctor)	1751/3/6	soi,fk,crk,til,ls	A-125
Parkman, Elizabeth	1746/4/13	soi,grf,ba,crk,til	A-109
Parkman, Elizabeth (fs)	--	soi,til,sun,ls,chp	A-184

Name	Date	Codes	Ref
Parkman, Elizabeth**	1746/11/1/1**	soi,fk,crk,frg,ls	A-123
Parkman, Esther	1746/1/12	soi,grf,crk,fk,til	A-111
Parkman, Esther (fs)	1746/1/12*	fk,sc,ls	A-112
Parkman, Nathanael	1694/4/27	ba, fk, sun, ms,chp	C-315
Parkman, Samuel	1767/8/10	soi,sc,crk,ls,ms	A-174
Parkman, Samuel (fs)	1767	soi,fk,del,crk,ls	A-172
Parkman, Sarah	1765/6/10	del,sc,til,sun,ls	F-292
Parkman, Susanah.	1743/11/6	fk,sc,crk,sun,ers	F-255
Parkman, William	1730/11/28	soi,grf,fk,del,til	A-175
Parkman, William	1730/5/4	pa, sc, sun, chp	F-291
Parmetar, Hannah	1693/8/12	fk, sc, del, sun	A-207
Parmetar, John	1712/2/12	fk, sc, del, sun	A-207
Parsons, Ebenezer	1805/8/31	ba, grf, soi, ms	D-127
Parsons, Ebenezer *(fs)	1805/8/31*	til, sc, soi, ms	D-128
Parsons, Edmund (tm)	1820	st,grf,ba,fk,crk,ls	I-6
Parsons, Lydia	1778/4/17	fk, ba, soi, ms,chp	E-18
Parsons, Lydia (fs)	1778	til, ba, ms, chp	E-38
Patridge, Robert	1802/11/10	st, til, ls, ms	C-17
Patridge, Robert (fs)	1802/11/10*	ms, chp	C-18
Patten, Barbra (fs)	--	sun, ba, chp	H-78
Paul, Mary	1742/5/7	soi,ba,til,sun,chp	G-107
Paul, Moses	1730/1/3	soi,ba,pa,crk,chp	G-110
Paull, Aquila	1714/7/30	ba, til	A-311
Paull, Moses	1730/3/25	crk, til, chp, soi	G-164
Paull, Sarah	1730/3/25	soi, crk, 'cii, chp	G-164

Payson, Ann (fs)	1774	bl, fk, sc, chp,soi	G-223
Payson, Mary	1743/6/3	fk, crk, til, soi	G-162
Payson, Mary (fs)	--	soi, til, chp, ms	G-224
Payson, Moses Paul	1742/1/20	del,fal,frg,ls,pa	G-106
Payson, Moses Paul (fs)	--	bl, til, sun, sr	G-163
Payson, Samuel	1741/10/11	til, grf, soi, chp	G-229
Pearson, John	1729/10/7	fk,crk,tii,sun,ls	A-181
Pearson, Leonard W.	1813/2/6	soi,ba,fk,crk,chp	J-50
Pearson, Martha	1728/9/26	crk, ba, soi, chp	C-458
Peggy, Dorcas	1720/10/24	fk,til,sun,eff,ms	F-239
Peirce, Elizabeth	1723/4/7	crk,til,ls,chp	A-116
Peirce, Jonathan (fs)	1804	fal, soi, ms	H-100
Peirse, Edward	1730/6/18	ba,sun,ms,chp	A-155
Peirse, Elizabeth	1721/11/1	sc, til, sun, ls	A-206
Pellens, Katherine	1767/10/11	crk, til, ls, ms	E-17
Penniman, James (tm)	1808**	sun, sr, soi, ms	W-52
Penwell, Ann	1688/12/3	soi, til, chp	C-109
Percival, I. (tm)	--	soi, grf, crk.sc,ls	J-10
Perkins, Mary	1756/7/8	eff,ba,til,sun,ls	C-138
Perkins, Mary	1718/7/13	soi, ba, til,chp,ms	C-182
Perkins, Rebecca	1802/3/16	til, sun, ls, fk	D-194
Perkins, Rebecca (fs)	1802/3/16*	til, sun, soi, ms	D-197
Person, George	1727/9/17	sc, til, sun, soi	G-249
Phillipes, Johanna	1675/10/22	ls, sun, ba, soi	C-452
Phillipes, John	1682/12/16	til, ba, ms, soi	C-369

Name	Date	Codes	Ref
Phillips, Abigail	1763/1/3	sc, til, soi, ms	H-54
Phillips, Dorcas	1763/1/9	sc, til, soi, ms	H-54
Phillips, James **	1818/5/5	til, ls, sc, ms	D-170
Pickerin, Elizabeth	1690/8/27**	Sc, til, ls, ms	A-310
Pierce, Hannah	1784/5/7	til, fk, ba	E-13
Pierce, Mary	1744/12/18	til, fk, ms, chp,ba	E-12
Pierce, Tamazen	1750/3/21	soi,fk,til,ms,chp	A-44
Pike, William	1721/9/23	soi, sc, chp	C-152
Pimm, Jane	1748/5/26	soi,sc,del,til,ms	C-139
Pitman, Betsy	1784/3/8	bl,fk,crk,til,ls	G-266
Pitman, Betsy (fs)	1784	soi, til, ms, chp	G-267
Pitman, Sally (fs)	1801	soi, til, ms, chp	G-267
Pitman, Sally*	1801/4/2	bl,fk,crk,til,ls	G-266
Pits, Christan	1786/2/8	pa, crk, til, sun	G-194
Pittom, John	1699/2/30	soi,ba,fk,sun,ls	A-156
Pittom, Mary	1713/3/17	soi,ba,fk,sun,ls	A-156
Pittomn, Matthew	1694/1/26	soi,ba,fk,sun,ls	A-156
Pitts, Edward	1709/12/28	ba, sc, til, ls, ms	B-1
Pitts, Elizabeth	1709/5/6	soi,ba,sc,til,ls,	B-37
Polley, John	1787/10/3	pa, soi,st. chp	G-119
Polley, John (fs)	1787	soi, til, ms, chp	G-171
Polley, William	1782/12/20	pa, chp, pt, st	G-124
Pompoy, Mary	1790/5/8	bl, st, soi, chp	G-260
Pond, Moses** (tm)	1852**	sun, sot st, chp	W-55
Pond, Sarah	1816/7/10	grf, crk, chp,ms,pt	J-122

Name	Date	Symbols	Ref
Pool, Ann	1803/5/13	crk, ls, ms	C-13
Pool, Benjamin	1795/10/5	crk, ls, ms	C-13
Poole, Mary	1737/7/28	crk, sun, fk, ms	E-36
Porter, Prudence	1709/7/3	til, sun, ba, ms	C-381
Poter, Thomas (Capt.)	1738/4/11	til, ls, eff, ms	C-389
Powell, Michael	1672/12/28	til, soi, ls, chp	C-467
Pratt, -- (tm)	1819	soi, bl, fk	I-16
Pratt, Deborah	1679/9/20	soi,fk,crk,ms,chp	B-50
Pratt, Joseph	1719/8/27	st, ls, ms, chp	D-11
Pratt, Mary	1721/10/26	soi, til, chp	C-159
Pratt, Mehetabel	1750/8/8	ba, sc, crk, ms,chp	C-316
Pray, John H. (tm)	1832	soi, st. grf, fk, bl	J-40
Prentiss, N. 5. (tm)	--	soi, grf	J-lla
Prichet, Peter	1721/11/26	soi, sun	A-395
Prichet, Sarah	1721/10/6	soi, sun	A-395
Pritchard, John	1757/3/17	crk, til, frg, ls	A-268
Proctor, Eliza Lane	1802/10/15	fk, sc, sun, frg,ms	F-205
Proctor, Harris C.	1818/3/9	til, ms, chp, soi	D-73
Prout, Elizabeth	1694/1/19	st, ba, sc	C-36
Pullin, John	1718/1/9	soi, ba, fk, ls	C-69
Pullin, Mary	1713/3/4	soi., ers, chp	C-70
Pulling, John	1771/1/18	frg, is, ms	F-139
Pulling, John (Capt.)	1787/1/25	til, ls, fk, soi	C-361
Pulling, John (Capt.)(fs)	1787	til, crk, ba, soi	C-360
Pulling, Martha	1753/1/31	til, fk, del, soi	C-364

Name	Date	Codes	Ref
Pullington, Benjamin	1735/6/11	sc, ls, ba, soi, ms	C-382
Pulsifer, David	1797/9/26**	soi,ba,sc,til,ls,ms	B-13
Pulsifer, David (fs)	1797/9/26**	fk,del,frg,ls,ms	B-14
Pulsifer, Elizabeth	1807/12/2**	soi,ba,sc,til,ls,ms	B-13
Puisifer, Elizabeth (fs)	1807/12/2**	soi,fk,crk,ms	B-15
R., H. (fs)	--	crk, til, chp, sr	A-14
R., R. (fs)	--	soi, ls, chp	C-216
Rand, Thomas	1711/9/18	til, ls, ba	A-414
Randall, Abigail	--	sun, soi, ms, chp	G-17B
Randall, Mary.	1772/6/26	soi, fk, sc, ms	A-224
Randall, Mary	1813/9/13	st,bl,fk,til,chp,pt	J-76
Randall, Sarah	--	sun, soi, ms, chp	G-178
Randalls, Richard	1730/10/10	st, soi, til, ls	G-179
Ransford, Edward	1717/12/27	ba,fk,sc,crk,chp,ms	B-32
Ransford, Susannah	--	del, til, sun	A-334
Rawlings, Caleb	1682/1/12	soi, til, ms	A-285
Rawlings, Caleb	1678/8/16	soi, til, ms	A-285
Rawlings, Elizabeth	1683/8/12	soi, til, ms	A-285
Rawlins, Love	1743/12/10	soi,del,crk,ms,ba	A-101
Rawlins, Love* (fs)	1743/12/10*	crk, ls	A-100
Rayner (tm)	1819	ba, chp, ms	H-76
Rayner, William	1805/9/14	til, sot, st. chp	G-262
Read, Eleanor (fs)	1798	ba,fk,chp,ms	B-45
Read, Elizabeth	1783/2/1	st, ls, ms, chp	C-42
Reade, Annah	1680/9/13	bl,fk,crk,ls,soi,pt	F-265

Name	Date		Code
Reade, Elizabeth	1713/2/16	bl,fk,crk,ls,soi,pt	F-265
Reade, Esdras	1680/7/27	soi, til,ls, ms	A-406
Reade, Sarah	16--/-/-	soi, til, ls, mns	A-406
Redding, George	1811	ba, sc, til, sun,chp	J-53
Reed (tm)	1819	ba, chp, ms	H-76
Restieaux, Catherine M.	1816/11/17**	ba, ers, chp, pt	J-127
Revere, Eliza, Meria	1804/11/5	til, sr, ms, pt	F-212
Rhoades, Jacob (tm)	1811	soi,sc,crk,frg,ls	J-1
Rhoades, Stephen (tm)	1835/9/21	ers, crk	J-8
Rhodes, Samuel	1759/10/9	ba, crk, til, chp	G-115
Rich, Henry	1791/9/29	soi,ba,crk,ms	D-30
Rich, Henry* (fs)	1791/9/29*	til,ms,chp,pt	D-31
Rich, Joanna	1802/10/7	soi,ba,crk,ms	D-30
Rich, Joanna* (fs)	1802/10/7*	til,ms,chp,pt	D-31
Rich, Salome** (tm)	1807**	ls, ba, sun, soi	W-58
Richard, Ales	1718/2/26	soi,fk,crk,ls,sr	A-29
Richards, Edward	1748/2/11	st, fk, sc, chp,pt	G-29
Richards, Edward (fs)	--	sc, ls, chp, ms	G-30
Richards, John	1732/1/5	st,til,sun,ls,chp	G-33
Richards, John (fs)	--	ls, til, crk, soi	G-16C
Richards, Joseph	1742/1/18	st, fk, sc, chp,pt	G-29
Richards, Mary	1713/10/22	ba, crk, sun, ms	A-364
Richards, Mary	1760/1/20	pa,sc,til,frg, ls	G-26
Richardson, Anne	1730/7/22	sc, til, sun, eff	F-236
Richardson, Catherine	1792/10/7	ba, st, ms	C-392

Name	Date	Codes	Ref
Richardson, Isaac	1815/8/22	soi,bl,fk,crk,chp	J-108
Richardson, Isabella	1730/7/20	sc, til, sun, eff	F-236
Richardson, Joel (tm)	1828	soi,grf,bl,fk,crk	J-37
Richardson, John	1793/11/14	sc, soi, ms, chp	C-391
Richardson, John	1810/7/6	soi, st. grf, ls	J-44
Richardson, Mary	1805/7/15	st,grf,fk,til,sun	C-397
Richardson, Mary	1789/9/27	soi,grf,fk,st,pt,ms	C-399
Richardson, Nathaniel	1815/9/10	soi,bi,fk,crk,chp	J-108
Richardson, Phebe	1768/5/3	grf, ba, ms, chp	D-161
Richardson, Phebe (fs)	1768	sc, ls, ms	D-163
Richardson, Richard	1805/1/17	st,grf,fk,til,sun	C-397
Richardson, Richard* (fs)	1805/1/17*	soi, ms, chp	C-398
Richardson, Samuel	1815/10/7	soi,fk,crk,til,sun	J-111
Richardson, Thomas	1752/2/13	til, soi, ls, ms	C-394
Richardson, Thomas*	1811/7/29	soi, st, grf, ls	J-44
Richardson,Catharine (fs)	1792	bl,fk,til,chp,soi	C-446
Rickard, Avis	1813/4/4	soi,ba,fk,crk,chp	J-50
Ridgway, L. (tm)	1819	crk, sr, chp, soi	W-30
Ripley, -- (fs?)	1804	del, ls	C-66a
Ripley, David	1802/5/28	soi, ba, ls	C-98
Ripley, David**	1802/5/28**	soi, ls	C-66
Ripley, John jr.	1809/3/19	soi, sun, chp	C-67
Ripley, John jr. (fs)	1809/3/19*	del, chp	C-68
Ripley, Rachel	1804/10/13	soi, ba, ls	C-98
Ripley, Rachel**	1804/10/13**	soi, ls	C-66

Name	Date	Codes	Ref
Robins, William Warner	1784/3/25	til, fk, ba,ms,chp	E-53
Robinson, Elizabeth	1697/7/7	bl, fk, til, ls, pt	C-450
Robinson, Jane Henry 1st	1804/7/21	soi,ba.fk,crk,til	C-409
Robinson, Jane Henry 2nd	1807/10/13	soi,ba,fk,crk,til	C-409
Robinson, S. W. (tm)	--	soi,grf,fk,crk,ls	I-2
Robinson,Jane H. 1st (fs)	1804/7/21*	ba,fk,sc,til,ms	C-410
Robinson,Jane H. 2nd (fs)	1807/10/13*	ba,fk,sc,til,ms	C-410
Roby, Henry	1807/11/9	grf,fk,crk,chp,ms	C-84
Roby, Henry* (fs)	1807/11/9*	grf, ms, chp	C-85
Roby, Sarah	1803/5/19	st, fk, crk, ms, ba	C-81
Roby, Sarah (fs)	1803/5/19*	soi, til	C-82
Rogers, Elizabeth (tm)	--	bl,fk,chp,sun,ba,sr	W-41
Rogers, Sarah	1817/5/11	st, grf, bl, fk,chp	J-130
Rose, Phillip	1800/3/20	sc, til, ba, ms,chp	F-93
Ross, Andrew* (tm)	1814	soi,grf,bl,crk,pt	J-23
Ross, John (tm)	1841	soi,grf,bl,crk,pt	J-23
Ross, Margaret* (tm)	1846	soi,grf,bl,crk,pt	J-23
Ross, William* (tm)	1816	soi,grf,bi,crk,pt	J-23
Rous, Sarah**	1705/8/29	soi, sc, til, ls,ms	C-181
Rouse, Rebeckah	1742/8/15	soi, crk, til, frg	A-312
Rouse, William	1705/1/20	soi,ba,fk,sc,til,ls	C-175
Rowe, Isaac F (tm)	--	soi, st	J-27
Ruby, Ann	1741/9/19	til, fk, ms, ba,	D-104
Ruck, John	1715/9/2	soi, ba, chp	C-20
Ruck, Peter	1690/12/1	ls, bl, fk, soi	A-6

Rumney, Edward (Capt.)	1808/4/6	st, ba,pa,til,chp	G-102
Rumney, Edward* (fs)	1808/4/6*	st, til, chp, ms	G-103
Rumney, Seeth	1804/1/13	soi, til, chp	G-37
Russel, Susannah	1721/10/17	til, sun, chp	A-271
Russell, Hannah	1737/3/21	sc, til, sun, soi	G-222
Russell, John.	1709/9/28	soi,sc,crk, ls,chp	B-38
Russell, Mary	1750/9/29	til, sun, pt, soi	G-165
Rust, Henry	1791/8/18	til, sun, sr, chp	C-197
Rust, Henry (fs)	1791/8/18*	til, ms, chp	C-198
Ruck, Margrett	1687/7/8	til, sun, ms, ba	C-354
S., E. (fs)	--	soi, til, chp	C-274
S., E. A. (fs)	--	ba, ls, ms	D-37
S., G. (fs)	--	ba, sc, til	C-137
S., J. G. (fs)	--	ba, ls, ms	D-37
S. , S. (fs)	--	grf, ls	A-231
Sa., Martha	1748/2/3	pa, ls, bl, fk, chp	F-287
Salisbury, Elizabeth	1688/2/17	ba, til	A-311
Salisbury, John	1704/12/15	fk, dci, crk, til	A-319
Sanders, William	1745/10/31	til, sun, ms, chp	E-67
Sargent, Edward (tm)	1820	soi, ba, bl, fk, sc	I-7
Sargent, Elizabeth	1770/5/19	soi, fk, sc, ls	A-442
Sargent, Elizabeth (fs)	1770	soi, st, fk, til	A-443
Sargent, John (tm)	1820	soi, ba, bl, fk, sc	I-7
Sargent, Thaddeus	1773/1/26	fk,til,sun,ms	B-25
Sarvise, Sarah	1739/8/4	st, ba, fk, ls	C-125

Name	Date	Abbreviations	Code
Sawin, Ezekil (tm)	--	soi, ba, bl, fk	I-13
Sawyer, Thomas B.	1815/10/23	soi, crk, til, chp	J-112
Saxton, John	1786/7/31	bl, fk, crk, til, ls	C-453
Saxton, Nathanel	1677/9/15	soi, ba	C-270
Saxton, Samuel	1693/7/21	fk, sc, til, eff	H-39
Saxton, Thomas	1680/11/6	fk, til, sun, chp	H-15
Saxton, Thomas (fs)	--	st, ba, ls, ms	C-402
Scammell, Alexander	1766/12/27	del, soi, ba, ms	D-116
Scammell, Mary	1760/8/15	crk, grf, ba, ms	D-117
Scarlet, Humnphry	1740/1/4	fk,til,ms,chp,soi	C-145
Scarlet, Mehetable	1733/6/26	sr, ls, soi, chp,ms	C-476
Scollay, John	1763/11/17	til, ms, del, ba	E-26
Scoot, Anna	1733/9/3	sc,crk,til,sun,is	B-9
Scoot, Anna (fs)	1733/9/3*	fk,sc,del,crk,til	B-10
Scoot, Thomas	1733/9/3	sc,crk,til,sun,ls	B-9
Scoot, Thomas (fs)	1733/9/3*	fk,sc,del,crk,til	B-1O
Scott, Mary **	1754/11/23**	is, sc, crk, ms	C-386
Scott, Sarah	1742/9/30	soi,ba,fk,del,ms	A-177
Seamen's Monument (m)	1851	grf, ls	D-1
Seares, Alexander (Capt.)	1758/3/17	soi,fk,sc,crk,ms,ba	C-327
Scares, Hannah	1769/6/25	ba, fk, crk, sr,ms	C-317
Scares, Hannah (fs)	1769	bl,fk,sc,til,ms,chp	C-319
Seares, Robert	1732/12/29	ba,sc,crk,til,ms,pt	C-325
Seccombe, John	1721/9/25	sc,crk,til,ls,chp	A-126
Seccombe, John (fs)	--	sun, ms, chp	F-2

Selley, Abigail	1721/9/25	Ls, chp	A-119
Servise, Maria	1742	Til, sun	C-133
Session, Ebenezer	1813/10/13	pa, bl, fk, til, chp	G-200
Seward, (?) (fs)	--	til, sun, chp, ms	G-100
Seward, Benjamin	1766/2/10	st, chp, pa	G-7
Seward, C. (fs)	--	til, sun, chp, ms	G-100
Seward, Catherine	1801/1/31	st, sun, ls, chp,pa	G-10
Seward, James	1790/6/22	st. sun, ls, chp,pa	G-10
Seward, James	1792/9/22	st, sun, ls, chp,pa	G-10
Seward, James (fs)	--	til, sun, chp, ms	G-100
Seward, Sarah	1800/3/14**	ba,pa,til,sun,ms,pt	C-35
Seward, Sarah (fs)	1800/3/14**	st, ls, ms, chp	G-34
Seward, Thomas	1800/11/27	ba,pa,til,sun,ms,pt	G-35
Seward, Thomas (fs)	1800/11/27*	st, ls, ms, chp	G-34
Shapp, Daniel	1814/10/2	frg, ls, til, soi	G-1O1
Sharin, Richard	1710/10/29	grf,del, til,sr,chp	C-200
Sharp, Gibbins	1770/10/24	soi, til, ls, ms	A-347
Sharp, Gibbins (fs)	1770	sc, til, ms	A-348
Sharp, Margery	1763/12/2	til, ms, chp	H-12
Sharp, Sarah	1756/6/9	soi, til, ls, ms	A-342
Sharrow, George	1743/10/6	st, sc, del, til,sun	C-130
Shaw, Francis (Esq.) (fs)	1784	soi, ls, chp	A-437
Shaw, Joseph sr.	1701/7/5	til, ba, ms, soi	C-380
Shaw, Sarah (fs)	1799	soi,ba,til,ms,chp	C-278
Shaw, Susannah	1737/5/12	til,sun,ls,ms,chp	D-25

Name	Date		Ref
Sheaffe, Elizabeth	1732/3/17**	soi, ba, fk,sun,chp	C-238
Sherburne, Abigail	1778/4/8	grf,fk,crk,til,chp	C-420
Sherburne, W. (tm)	--	soi, ba	J-13a
Sherman, James (tm)	1801	ba, sun, soi, chp	W-24
Sherran, Richard	1746/12/25	grf,ba,til	C-192
Sherrin, Sarah	1715/8/26	grf,ba,fk,sc,til,ms	C-199
Shirley, James**	1749/8/2	soi,sun,ls,ms,chp	A-56
Shut, Richard	1703/10/2	sc, til,sun,ls,soi	C-437
Shute, Elizabeth	1665/2/2	ba, soi, til, pt	C-461
Shute, Elizabeth	1691/9/8	bl,fk,sc,crk, ls,pa	C-466
Shute, Lydia	1721/10/3	ls, fk, crk, del	C-378
Shutt, Hannah	1709/4/29	bl, fk, soi, crk	C-463
Shutt, Mary	1709/9/16	bl, fk, soi, crk	C-463
Sigourney (tm)	1852	soi, chp	W-19
Sigourney, Andrew (tm)	--	soi, ba, ers	J-33
Simonds, Mary	1814/8/4	soi,bi,fk,til,sun	J-93
Singleton, Ann	1805/9/3	til, grf, ba, soi	D-140
Singleton, George	1805/1/24	ba, ms, soi	D-138
Singleton, James Carter	1800/11/26	til, ms, soi, sr	D-136
Singleton, Samuel H.	--	ba, ms, soi	D-138
Sinnitt, Patrick	1767/8/4	soi,st,fk,sc,ls,ms	A-143
Skillin (tm)	--	soi, pa, st,bl,fk	W-14
Skillin, Mary	1763/1/28	soi, til, chp, pt	G-92
Skillin, Ruth	1786/5/29	soi,st,chp,pt,pa	G-96
Skillin, Ruth (fs)	1786	soi,st, pa, chp, ms	G-97

Skillin, Simeon	1778/2/27	soi, ba,til,pt,chp	G-90
Skillin, Simeon (fs)	1778	soi, sun, chp, ms	G-91
Skilling, Simeon	1748/1/23	soi,bl, til, sun,ls	G-32
Smallpeace, Furnell	1712/8/28	soi, st, fk, sun	A-440
Smith, Arthur**	1708/5/17**	soi,ba,del ,is	C-173
Smith, Benjamin (tm)	1805	bl,fk,del,crk,st,ba	W-32
Smith, Elizabeth	1803/7/1	crk, ba, ms, chp	D-54
Smith, Elizabeth	1753/1/23	til, crk, grf, soi	D-87
Smith, Elizabeth (fs)	1803/7/1*	sun, ms, chp	D-55
Smith, Francis	1798/8/6	pa, st, soi, chp	G-264
Smith, Francis (fs)	1798	soi, fk, crk, til	G-265
Smith, Hannah	1811/3/2	ba, til, chp	J-87
Smith, Holland	1811/5/6	ba, til, chp	J-87
Smith, James B.	1805/6/17	til, crk, bl, fk	D-88
Smith, James B. *(fs)	1805/6/17*	til, soi, ms	D-89
Smith, John (tm)	1812	soi, grf, bl, fk, sr	J-22
Smith, Josiah	1721/11/13	ls, ba, ms	D-179
Smith, Mary	1727/2/5	soi, fal, frg, ms	A-382
Smith, Nathaniel	1721/11/13	ls, ba, ms	D-179
Smith, Rebecca	1799/6/28	st,del,til,sun,ms	C-40
Smith, Rebecca	1811/11/14	bl,fk,crk,til,sun	J-55
Smith, Rebecca	1812/1/24	bl,fk,crk,til,sun	J-55
Smith, Rebecca (fs)	--	sun, ls, ms, grf	C-5S
Smith, Sally	1811/10/26	bl,fk,crk,til,sun	J-55
Smith, Susanna	1809/3/25	til, crk, bl, fk	D-88

Name	Date	Codes	Ref
Smith, Susanna *(fs)	1809/3/5*	til, soi, ms	D-89
Smith, Wilbur	1815/7/6	sun, fk, soi, chp	G-161
Snelling (tm)	180-	ers, soi	W-26
Snelling, Anna	1766/1/30	soi,crk,til,chp,pa	G-74
Snelling, Anna	1720/4/8	st, sun, chp, ms	G-75
Snelling, Anna	1766	soi, crk, chp, ms	G-79
Snelling, Anna (fs)	1790	pa, til, st,chp	G-137
Snelling, Benjamin	1739/11/6	soi, chp, pt	G-78
Snelling, Benjamin (fs)	1739/11/6*	st, til,sun,ls, chp	G-80
Snelling, Elizabeth	1737/4/1	crk, sun, st, soi	G-185
Snelling, Hannah	1730/6/22	pa, chp, crk, til	G-136
Snelling, John	1699/2/17	bl,fk,til, ls, sun, ms	G-276
Snelling, Joseph	1748/7/1	soi, til, ls,pa,chp	G-83
Snelling, Joseph	1726/8/13	pa, sun, chp, soi	G-134
Snelling, Joseph	1799/4/27	st, ba, chp, pa	G-138
Snelling, Joseph (fs)	1799	ls, chp, ms, til	G-142
Snelling, Joseph (fs)	--	ers, chp, soi	G-144
Snelling, Joshua (tm)	1748/1/26	sr, ba, crk, til	W-27
Snelling, Josiah	1783/2/11	pa, chp, til, sun	G-135
Snelling, Mary	1719/8/29	sun, soi, ls, chp	G-289
Snelling, Mary	1724/1/28	eff, del, soi, ms	H-55
Snelling, Nathaniel	1745/5/26	pa, til, st, ba	G-141
Snelling,Nathaniel (fs)	1745/5/26*	til, sun, st, soi	G-145
Sneiling,Nathaniel (fs)	--	bl, soi, ls, ms,chp	G-188
Snelling, Priscilla	1791/8/2	fk, eff, sun, ms	H-57

Name	Date		Code
Snelling, Priscilla (fs)	1791	fk, fal, ms	H-58
Snelling, Rebecah	1777/4/20	pa, crk, chp, soi	G-143
Snelling, Rebecah (fs)	1777/4/20*	chp, til, ms, st	G-139
Snelling, Rebecca	1802/5/20	fk, crk, ms,chp	H-59
Snelling, Rebecca (Es)	1802	fk, ba, til	H-60
Snelling, Rebeckah	1730/11/7	del, sun, pa, st	G-133
Snelling, Rebeckah	1730/6/21	pa, chp, crk, til	G-136
Snelling, Rebeckah (fs)	--	til, eff, chp	H-56
Snelling, Samuel	1723/9/20	soi,st,crk,sun,ls	G-84
Snelling, Sarah (tm)	1742/1/13	sr, ba, crk, til	W-27
Snow, Ephraim (tm)	1808**	sun, bl, fk,soi	W-54
Snow, Larkin (tm)	1808**	sun, bl, fk,soi	W-54
Soames, Hannah	1674/2/30**	ers, pt, chp	H-8
Soames, Hannah	1682/7/19	soi, til, ba, ms	H-89
Soames, John Sr.	1700/11/16	sc, crk, ba, ls, ms	H-91
Soames, Joseph	1705/8/2	til, sun, chp	H-92
Somes, Elizabeth	1685/9/16	til, ba, ms,chp	H-J9
Somes, Susannah	1770/9/3	fk, sc, ba, ms,soi	F-77
Somes, Susannah (Es)	1770	til,fk,ls,chp,soi	F-72
Souter, Hannah	1711/8/20	st, del, ls, ms, ba	C-19
Speed, William	1808/8/21	soi, ba, crk, til	C-268
Spence, John (fs)	1852**	sun, soi, st. chp	W-55
Spring, Robert (fs)	--	bl, til, ba, chp	F-78
Spring, Samuel	1752/4/6	sc, ba, ms	E-42
Starling, John	1760/9/1	til, sc, eff, ls	F-28

Name	Date	Codes	Ref
Starling, Patience	1760/6/2	til, sc, eff, ls	F-28
Starr, Eliza	1800/6/8	til, ls, grf, soi	D-122
Starr, Elizabeth	1802/7/2	ba,crk,til,ls,ms	C-342
Stephens, Elizabeth	1723/11/19	til, sun, crk, soi	D-193
Sterling, Grace	1722/2/1	til, crk, ls, sr	D-174
Stetson, Lebbeus (tm)	1828	soi, grf, bl, fk	J-41
Stevens, Abigail	1747/9/12	soi,ba,fk,sc,crk,ms	B-67
Stevens, Abigail (fs)	1747	ba, bl, fk, crk	B-73
Stevens, Edward**	1712/8/31**	ba,sc,ls,ms	A-64
Stevens, Eiiza (tm)	1821	soi, grf, ers, crk	I-20
Stevens, Elizabeth (t)	--	grf, ba	D-124
Stevens, Erasmus	1750/6/22	fk, sc, pt, soi	D-124a
Stevens, Erasmus (t)	--	grf, ba	D-124
Stevens, Erasmus (t)	1750/6/22	grf, ba	D-124
Stevens, John	1721/4/2	eff,ba,sc,del,sun	B-65
Stevens, John	1747/11/11	sun, sc, ls, ms, ba	F-1
Stevens, John	1739/9/29	sun, soi, ls, ms	F-96
Stevens, John	174.8/9/26	ba,sc,crk,sun,ms	B-56
Stevens, John (fs)	1748/9/26*	eff,fk,sun,chp	B-57
Stevens, John (t)	--	grf, ba	D-124
Stevens, Mary	1785/5/9	soi,st,fk,ls,chp,ms	A-85
Stevens, Mary (t)	--	grf, ba	D-124
Stevens, Mary*	1785/5/9*	soi,fk,ms,chp	A-86
Stevens, Patience S.	1814/12/23	soi,eff,fk,til,ms	B-12
Stevens, Sarah	1723/11/30	crk,til,chp	A-165

Name	Date	Codes	Ref
Stevens, Thomas	1761/5/6	soi,sc,crk,til,ls	A-84
Steves, Erasmus	1721/11/1	til, ls, crk, ms	D-80
Stimpson, Jane	1812/4/9	soi,ba,fk,crk,chp	J-50
Stoddard, Abigail	1761/7/23	crk, til, soi	A-302
Stoddard, Elizabeth	1732/2/20	soi, til, ba	A-284
Stoddard, Elizabeth (fs)	--	soi, ms, chp	A-296
Stoddard, Hannah	1755/12/29	til	A-306
Stoddard, Hannah (fs)	--	soi, ms	C-162
Stoddard, Mercy	1739/2/14	crk, ms, chp	A-295
Stoddard, Tabitha	1734/6/3	fk, til, ms, chp	A-290
Stoddard, Thomas	1743/9/3	til, soi, chp, ms	A-281
Stoddard, Thomas (Capt.)	1763/4/12	til, ms	A-300
Stoddard, Thos. (fs)	1763*	til, ms, chp	A-301
Stone, Ann	1752/5/28	sun, frg, ls, chp	C-25
Stone, Benjamin	1706/12/15	ba, til, ls, ms	C-119
Stone, Elizabeth	1763/3/15	soi, til, ls, chp	C-97
Stone, Josiah	1717/7/26	soi, ers, ms, chp	C-29
Stone, Margaret	--	sun, ls, ms	F-29
Stone, Nicolas	1689/12/9	soi, eff, ls	C-104
Stone, Sarah	1752/5/25	sun, frg, ls, chp	C-26
Stookas, Sarah	1723/8/--	fal, ls, soi, ms	D-186
Storer, --	--	pa, frg, sc	G-153
Stowe, Elizabeth S. (tm)	1845/1A	soi, ba, bl, fk, sc	I-7
Stretton, Bartholomew	1686/1/9	ms, chp, ba	E-66
Stretton, Eliphai	1725/1/19	ms, chp, ba	E-66

Stretton, Elizabeth	1727/5/4	ba, chp, ms	E-64
Stride, John	1724/12/5	crk, ls, ms	A-69
Strong*, —	1798/9/28	soi, ba, ls	C-195
Stuart, Adam (fs)	--	crk, ls, rep, soi	F-261
Sullivan, Charles, G	1815/8/15	soi,bl, til,sun,pa	G-45
Sullivan, Elizabeth A.	1812/6/24	soi,pa,st,crk,til	G-47
Sullivan, James G.	1807/2/10	soi,pa,st,crk,til	G-47
Sullivan, Thomas U.	1795/10/29	pa, til, soi,chp,pt	G-203
Sullivan, Thomas U.(fs)	1795	pa, til, st, soi	G-190
Sumers, Charles**	1682/1/25	ba,bl,fk,sc,ls,chp	C-313
Sunderland, John (Capt.)	1724/9/11	fk,sc,crk,sun,eff	F-39
Sunderland, Nathaniel	1699/6/22**	fk,del,til,ls,ms	B-49
Sutherland, George (tm)	1809	bi, fk, til, sun,sr	W-50
Swaen, Sarah	1711/2/10	soi,del,crk,til,ms	A-104
Sweester, Joanna	1746/9/12	chp, sun, soi, ba	G-198
Sweet, Ebenezer	1802/4/14	bl,fk,sc,crk,sr,ms	F-211
Sweet, Ebenezer*	1802/4/14*	bl,fk,sun,til,pa	G-235
Sweet, Ebenezer*(fs)	1802	til, chp, sr, sun	F-229
Sweet, Henry	1800/1/13	bl,fk,sc,crk,sr,ms	F-211
Sweet, Henry*	1800/1/13*	bl,fk,sun,til,pa	G-235
Sweet, Henry*(fs)	1800	til, chp, sr, sun	F-229
Sweet, Jabez	1805/9/6	bl,fk,sc,crk,sr,ms	F-211
Sweet, Jabez Henry	1807/5/20	bl,fk,sc,crk,sr,ms	F-211
Sweet, Jabez Henry*	1807/5/20*	bl,fk,sun, til,pa	G-235
Sweet, Jabez*	1805/9/6*	bi,fk,sun,til,pa	G-235

Name	Date		Ref
Sweet, Jabez*(fs)	1805	til, chp, sr, sun	F-229
Sweet, John	1685/4/25	bl, fk, ba, chp	H-44
Sweet, Susanna	1666/7/16	bl, fk, ba, chp	H-44
Sweetser, David	1803/6/3	st, sc, til, ms	A-218
Sweetser, David L.* (fs)	1803/6/3*	soi, grf, til, ls	A-217
Sweetser, Hannah	1743/12/11	til, chp, ms, soi	G-199
Sweetser, Mary	1784/4/9	st, sc, til, ms	A-218
Sweetser, Mary	1784/10/30	soi, st, ls	A-219
Sweetser, Mary* (fs)	1784/4/9*	soi, grf, til, ls	A-217
Sweetser, Mary* (fs)	1784/10/30*	fk, ms, chp, pt	A-220
Swier, Lucy	1795/10/14	sc, fal, ls, ms,soi	H-97
Swift, Edee	1795/10/12	soi, st, ms, chp	C-123
Swift, Elijah	1803/5/9	ba, sun, frg, ls	C-124
Swift, Elijah* (fs)	1803/5/9*	soi, til, chp	C-122
Swift, Mary**	1764/4/9**	til, is, ms	C-31
Swift, William	1765/4/1	st,til,sr,ms,chp	C-33
T., T. (fs)	--	ba, sc, del, til	C-83
Tapper, Hannah	1742/7/14	soi, del, til, ms	A-248
Tarbell, L. L. (tm)	--	soi, ls	J-28
Tarbox, Jonathan	1769/5/3	soi,fk,crk,til,ls	A-55
Tarbox, Jonathan	1760/7/7	til, ms, chp	A-190
Tarbox, Mary	1763/1/19	soi,st,grf,fk,chp	A-187
Taylor Mary	1803/6/9	bi, til, soi,ms,chp	C-435
Taylor, (Child)	--	bi, til, soi,ms,chp	C-435
Taylor, (Child)	--	bi, til, soi,ms,chp	C-435

Name	Date		Ref
Taylor, Abigail	1774/10/26	crk, til, ba, ms, sr	F-144
Taylor, Jane	1807/4419	ba,crk,til,ls,ms	C-342
Templer, Thomas	1745/8/3	soi, fk, sr, ba,ms	F-171
Thacher, Margaret	1719/9/14	eff, ba, ls, ms	H-20
Thatcher, Mary	1708/11/30	soi, del, ls, chp	C-59
Thaxter, Jonathan (tm)	1812	grf, bl, sr. pt	J-1B
Thayer, John (tm)	1813	soi, st, chp	J-15
Thayers, Cotton** (tm)	1806**	sun, soi, ms, chp	W-69
Thicker, Ebenezer	--	chp, til, sun, st	G-155
Thomas, (son)	1806/8/11	soi, sun, chp	W-21
Thomas, Abigail	1717/5/4	til, ms, ba, soi	C-365
Thomas, Abigail (fs)	1717	til, crk, fk, ms	C- 376
Thomas, Ann	1767/11/27	sc, crk, sun, ls	A-393
Thomas, Ann (tm)	1796/12/27	soi, sun, chp	W-21
Thomas, Ann R. (tm)	1804/5/24	soi, sun, chp	W-21
Thomas, Elizabeth (tm)	1820	soi, bl, fk	I-18
Thomas, Elizabeth K. (tm)	1821/5/4	soi, sun, chp	W-21
Thomas, Harvey	1750/9/12	crk, soi, pa, ls	F-274
Thomas, Martha	1756/6/4	ba, til, sun	A-202
Thomas, Mary	1821/7/7	soi, sun, chp	W-21
Thomas, Peter (tm)	--	soi, sun, chp	W-21
Thomas, Samuel R. (tm)	1805/12/14	soi, sun, chp	W-21
Thomas, William	174-/3/-	til, sun, ls, ms	E-71
Thomas, William (Capt.)		til, sun, chp, ms	A-308
Thompson, John P.	1816/4/1	soi,bl,fk,crk,til	J-119

Name	Date	Notes	Ref
Townsend, James	1738/4/18	pa, crk, sun, chp	F-269
Townsend, James P.	--	del, ls, ms, chp	C-3
Townsend, Jeremiah	1690/9/6	st,fk, til,chp,soi	C-434
Townsend, John	1783/6/27	st, ers, sun,ms,chp	C-1
Townsend, John	--	del, ls, ms, chp	C-3
Townsend, John (fs)	1783/6/27*	fk, chp	C-2
Townsend, Judith	1771/19/16	st, ers, sun,ms,chp	C-1
Townsend, Judith	--	del, ls, ms, chp	C-3
Townsend, Judith (fs)	1771/10/16*	fk, chp	C-2
Townsend, Nathan	1772/10/17	st, ers, sun,ms,chp	C-1
Townsend, Nathan	1777/4/16	st, ers, sun,ms,chp	C-1
Townsend, Nathan	1786/10/12	st,eff,del,ls,ms	C-4
Townsend, Nathan (fs)	1772/10/17*	fk, chp	C-2
Townsend, Nathan (fs)	1777/4/16*	fk, chp	C-2
Townsend, Policy	1787/3/9	del, ls, ms, chp	C-3
Townsend, Ruth**	1713/10/23	fal, ls	A-94a
Townsend, Sarah	1750/12/1	pa, bl, fk, til,sun	F-282
Travis, Daniel	1720/5/9	fk, sc,til,sun,chp	C-311
Travis, Daniel Sr.	1689/1/19	grf,fk,del,til,is	C-93
Treat, Mary	1742/5/6	bl, til, soi, chp	G-240
Treat, Robert	1749/8/5	eff, sun, ms, chp	F-167
Trefry, William (Capt.)	1761/5/61	crk, sun, ms, chp	E-27
Tremere, John B. (tm)	1828	soi, grf, bl, fk	J-38
Trench, Othniel	--	soi, til,sun,chp,pt	J-54
Trew, Richard	1756/10/8	bl, fk, sun, chp	G-187

Name	Date	Codes	Ref
Troth, John (Capt.)	1781/9/9	soi, til, ls, ms	A-263
Troth, John (Capt.) (fs)	1781	til, ms, bs	A-264
Troth, Judith	1786/5/17	del, crk, til, sun	A-261
Troth, Judith* (fs)	1786*	sc, del, til, ls	A-262
Trout, Sarah	1753/8/25	bl, fk, sun, ls,soi	F-198
Troutt, William	1749/3/31	soi,grf,dei,crk,st	A-141
True, Richard	1744/8/29	grf, sc, soi, ms,st	G-292
Tucker, Daniel	1739/7/17	del, til, soi, chp	H-103
Tucks, Martha	1729/11/4	ba,del, sun, ls	C-136
Tufton, Elizabeth	1760/8/18	soi,, til, chp,pa	G-8
Tufton, Robert	1717/4/28	til,sun,chp,ms,soi	C-448
Tufton, Robert	--	pa, til,sun, ls,chp	G-25
Turell, (four offspring)	--	soi, pa, til, chp	G-43
Turell, Elizabeth	1765/4/12	soi, pa, til, chp	G-43
Tureil, Elizabeth (fs)	1765/4/12*	soi, bl, crk,til, ls	G-14
Turner, Elizabeth (fs)	--	sc, sun, ls, ms	F-223
Tutile, Hannah	1736/5/15	sc, ba, soi, ms	F-158
Tuttle, Joses	1712/7/17	soi, til, ls, chp	F-263
Tuttle, Samuel (tm)	1807	ls, soi, chp	W-59
Twing, Rebecca	1717/1/5	soi, fk, crk	A-441
Tyer, Wiiliam**	1666/1/14	soi, sc, til, ls,ms	C-181
Tyler, Dorcas	1770/12/28	fk, til, sr, pt	D-189
Tyley, Elizabeth	1727/911	soi,chp	A-108
Underwood, Hipsabah	1785/7/27	soi,fk,sc,ms,chp	A-30
Underwood, Hipsabah	1785	ba,fk,chp,ms	A-31

Name	Date	Notes	Ref
Vickers, Silvanus	1721/6/29	ba, til, ms, chp	C-349
Vinall, Christiana	1817/6/25	st. crk, sun, chp	J-133
Vinton, Rebecca	1807/10/15	pa, til, sun, chp	G-195
Vinton, Rebecca* (fs)	1807/10/15*	til, sun, ms, chp	G-196
Viscount, Dorcas	1769/5/30	st. fk, sc, ls	A-222
Viscount, John	1734/10/14	soi, sc, til, sun	A-227
Viscount, Phillip	1751/9/22	st. grf, til, chp	A-225
Vollintine (tm)	--	sr. crk, chp	W-33
W--, Samuel	1784/10/27	soi, st, til, ls	D-7
W., E. (fs)	--	til, ls, ms, soi	D-204
W., R. (fs)	--	ba, til, ms	A-303
Wade John (tm)	1811	soi, ers, crk	J-5
Wadsworth, Susanna	1704/4/3**	crk, til, sun, frg	A-401
Wair, Lydia	1705/1/2	soi, til, ls, ba	A-274
Wakefield, Ann	1712/1/1	sc, til, ms	A-357
Wakefield, Ann (fs)	1712/1/1*	sc, til, ls, ms	A-365
Wakefield, Eliza (tm)	1811	soi, crk, chp	J-2
Wakefield, John	1712/4/27	soi, til, sun	A-339
Wakefield, Rebacca	1715/5/28	til, ls, bs	A-333
Wakefield, Samuel	1809/11/12	Bl, crk, til, chp	G-271
Walker, Richard (Capt.)	1774/2/24	bl,fk,crk,pa,rep,st	G-191
Walker, Richard (fs)	1774	pa, til, chp, soi	G-204
Walker, Susanna	1799/8/26	pa, soi, pt, chp,ba	G-192
Walker, Susanna (fs)	1799	crk, til, ms, soi	G-206
Walters, Joseph	1709/5/24	soi, sun, ls	A-396

Warburton, Charles (Rev.)	1814/7/1	soi,st,crk,chp,pt	J-90
Ward, Fransis	1690/6/10	soi,eff,ba,fk,sc	B-74
Ward, Mary (tm)	1853/4/1	ers, crk	J-8
Wardell, George	1802/12/5	til, ms, chp, ba	D-92
Wardell, George (fs)	1802	til, del, soi, ms	D-93
Ware, Daniel	1694/1/8	ba, fk,crk,til,chp	C-323
Warran, Mary	1681/7/13**	soi, ba, til,ms,chp	C-301
Water, John	1799/10/24	soi,fk,sc,til,ms	A-139
Waterhous, Rachel	1727/1/23	til, ba, ms, chp	D-182
Waterhous, Rachel	1727/1/3	til, ba, ms, chp	D-182
Waterhouse, John	1746/7/1	soi, til, ls, ms	A-200
Waterman, Thomas	1808/6/7	fk, sc, crk, ms,soi	H-104
Waterman, Thomas (fs)	1808	ls, ms, ba	H-29
Waters, Mary	1802/6/7	crk, sr. soa, ms	D-96
Waters, Sampson (Capt.)	1693/8/13	fk, sc, til, pa	F-4
Waters, William	1691/6/15	soi, ba, bl,fk,ls ,ms	B-64
Waters, William	1757/8/10	bl,fk, crk,sun, eff	F-253
Watson, James	1738/7/22	soi, grf, crk, til	A-326
Watson, Mary**	1743/10/1	soi, til, ls	A-331
Watters, Rebeckah	1745/4/9	fk, sc, srk, ls	A-221
Watts (tm)	--	ba, soi, bl, fk, til	W-12
Watts, Lydia	1700/9/29	sc, del, til, ls, ms	C-117
Watts, Richard (Capt.)	1750/3/8	soi, del, crk, til	A-316
Way, Kathron	1689/4/28	bl, fk, sc, til, ms	F-232
Webb, Ann	1714./10/30	soi, til, ls	A-358

Webb, Davied**	1722/10/9**	crk,til,sun,ls,pa	G-66
Webb, Joseph	1714/8/--**	st. sc, til, ls	A-211.
Webb, Joseph*M	1708/6/30	soi, til, ls	A-234
Webb, Margarot (tm)	1813	grf, pt, soi	G-298
Webb, Samuel	1717/10/31	soi, til, sun, ls	A-235
Webber, Ehzabeth*	1732/3/11	bl,del,til,ls,chp	G-81
Webber, Seth (Capt.) (tm)	1806/10/11	sun, soi, ms	W-6B
Welch, John	1713/11/23	soi, til, sun, ls	A-413
Welch, Rebekah	1767/10/23	bl, fk, sc, til,ms	F-215
Wells, Charles (tm)	1811	soi, sc, ls	J-9
Wells, Mary	1678/12/1	soi, ba, del,sun,ms	C-281
Wells, Richard	1680/9/8	sc, del, sun	A-249
Wells, Samuel	1804/11/13	til, sun, fk, crk	D-198
Wells, William	1808/8/8	crk, soi, chp, ms	D-199
Wells, Williain (fs)	1808	til, crk, sc, ms	D-200
Weiis,Nathaniel John (tm)	1811	soi, sc, lis	J-9
Wels, Thomas	1702/10/7	eff,sc,del,ls	C-88
Whelien, Richard** (tm)	1803/11/25	bl,fk,crk,ls,chp	W-17
White, -- (fs?)	--	fal, ls	C-79
White, Elizabeth	1748/4/15	bl, fk, sc, ls, ms	F-31
White, Hannah	1736/12/9	til, ls, fk, ba	C-384
White, Hannah	1718/4/8	til, ba, soi, ms	C-388
White, Hannah (fs)	--	til, sun, del, soi	C-377
White, Issac	1732/9/3	ers, bl, fk, crk,ls	F-48
White, James	1827/4/12**	ba, ers, ms, pt,chp	J-106

Name	Date	Notes	Code
White, John	1690/8/6	st. sc, til, chp	C-54
White, John	1746/12/1	sun, fk, ms, ba	F-10
White, Joseph	1721/9/21	til, sun, ls, ms	A-378
White, Joseph* (fs)	1721/9/21*	sc, til, ms, soi	A-379
White, Katherine	1747/2/3	sun, fk, ms, ba	F-10
White, Lettice**	1815/7/20**	ba, ers, ms, pt,chp	J-106
White, Marcy	1778/4/13	til, sc, st. soi	D-131
White, Mary	1702/10/10**	soi, til, sun, ls	A-377
White, Mary	1714/9/3	soi, til, chp, ms	A-380
White, Mary	1759/2/23	st, fk, crk, ls, pt	C-10
White, Mary	1727/10/--	til, ba, soi, chp	C-455
White, Mary (fs)	1759/2/23*	til, sun, ls, chp	C-11
White, Richard	1748/1/4	del, grf, ms, chp	D-60
White, Samuel	1727/1/16	del, til, sun, ms	A-375
White, Susannah	1769/6/4	fk, sc, til, ba,chp	F-79
White, Susannah (fs)	1769	sc, til, ls	F-80
Whitehead, Samuel	1719/8/26	til, sun, chp, ms	G-172
Whitemore, John	1748/4/21	crk, til, sc, chp	G-248
Whiteridge, Abigail	1724/1/30	soi, til, ls	A-282
Whitman, Abigail	1756/11/8	soi,sc,sun,ms	A-182
Whitman, Elizabeth	1768/5/25	soi,grf,fk,crk,ls	A-179
Whitman, Francis	1715/8/15	soi, grf, fal, ls	A-384
Whitman, Samuel	1715/517	ers,ls,ms	A-188
Whitridge, Sarah	1734/1/31	sc, til, sun,ls,pa	F-295
Whittemore, Elizabeth(fs)	--	sc, til, sun, chp	G-251

Name	Date	Codes	Ref
Whittemore, Gershom	1795/11/1*	soi,til,ms	A-199
Whittemore, Gershom**	1795/11/1	soi,st,ba,ls,ms	A-198
Whi'ctemor'e, Hannah	1694/1/15	bl, crk, til, ls	A-436
Whittemore, Lydia	1750/1/15	crk, ls, fk, til	G-247
Wilbur, Susan	1815/7/18	bi, fk, crk, til	G-219
Wild, Ebenezer	1794/12/4	soi, til, chp, pa	G-62
Wild, Jonathan (tm)	--	ls, ms, chp	A-18
Wild, Samuel (fs)	1784	st,ba,til,ms	D-35
Wiliston, Joanna (fs)	--	sun, soi, ms	E-40
Wilkins, John	1710/6/17	soi,ba,fk,sun,ls,mns	B-69
Wilkins, John (fs)	1674/8/17*	soi, til	C-107
Wilkins, John	1674/8/17	del,crk,tii,sun,ls	C-108
Wilkins, Susannah	1724/10/24	soi, til, chp	C-109
Wilkins, Thomas	1679/7/19	soi, ers, til, ba	C-106
Willard, Josiah (Deacon)	1807/8/20	soi, fk, sc, til	A-278
Willard, Josiah* (fs)	1807/8/20*	soi, del, til	A-279
Willard, Susanna (fs)	--	soi, ba, fk, sc	A-173
Wilicut, Joseph ('cm)	1831	soi, chp	J-13
Willet, Sarah	1693/10/21	pa, ls, crk, sun,ba	F-268
Williams, Elizabeth	1759/3/1	sc, ba, ls, soi, ms	H-4
Williams, Elizabeth	1690/8/12	til, sun, soi, ls	H-7
Williams, ElizabeTh	1816/5/6	grf, bl,fk, ls, chp	J-120
Williams, Jeremiah	1721/10/30	ba, til, chp	C-408
Williams, John	1736/12/27	soi, til, sun, chp	C-229
Williams, Mary	1815/10/7	soi, crk, chp, ms	J-110

Name	Date	Codes	Ref
Williams, Rachel	1708/3/25	til, ms, chp, soi	A-255
Williams, Sarah	1618/4/25	soi,st,bl,fk,chp,ba	J-140
Williston, Ann	1775/9/28	grf, ba, ms, pt,chp	F-90
Williston, Ann (fs)	1775	sun, ms, chp, pt	F-91
Williston, Jane	1759/3/12	soi, til, chp	G-255
Williston, Joanna	1803/2/23	pa, til, chp, ms	F-277
Williston, John	1776/4/7	grf, ba, ms, pt,chp	F-90
Williston, John	1809/10/8	fk, til, eff, ms,ba	F-111
Williston, John (fs)	1776	sun, ms, chp, pt	F-91
Williston, John*(fs)	1809/10/8*	fk, til, ba, ms	F-112
Williston, Thomas	1783/12/14	crk, fk, sun, st	G-257
Williston, Thomas	1775/8/31	ba, fk, chp, soi	G-259
Williston, Thomas (fs)	1775	til, sun, chp, soi	G-256
Williston, Thomas (fs)	1783	bl, fk, sun, chp	G-258
Willson, Marcy	1719/12/15	sc,sun,chp,eff	B-42
Willson, Mary	1753/8/17**	st, crk, ls, ms, sr	C-51
Willson, Sarah*	1749/5/21	soi,fk,crk,ls	A-183
Wilson, John (tm)	1828	grf,bl,fk,crk,ls,pt	J-35
Winchester, Edmund (tm)	1819	grf,ba,bl,fk,crk,pt	I-5
Winslow, Mary	1681/6/12	grf, ba, til, chp	C-242
Winslow, Samuel	1680/10/14	soi,sc,crk,til,ls	C-241
Winslow, Samuel (tm)	--	bl,fk,sc,soi,chp	W-10
Winslow, Sarah	1667/4/4	ba, ls, ms, chp	C-327b
Wiring, William (Capt.)	1749	til, ms, chp	D-29
Wirling, William	1748/1/20	soi,grf,ba,ms,chp	D-28

Name	Date	Codes	ID
Wirling, William (Capt.)	1750/2/17	soi,grf,ba,ms,chp	D-2B
Wiswall, Elizabeth	1747/12/1	st, til, sun, bl	G-159
Woodbury, Andrew	1721/10/21	til, ls, ms, ba	A-360
Woodbury, Hannah	1733/7/28	fk, sc, crk, til	A-332
Wooddard, Prissilla	1722/12/29	fk, sc, til, eff,ms	F-220
Woodward, Elizabeth	--	til,sun,ms,chp	D-32
Woodward, Elizabeth (fs)	--	soi, bl, til, ls	C-220
Worthylake, Ruth (Fs)	1718	fk, sc, til, pa, ls	F-294
Worthylake, Ann	1718/11/3	bl,fk,sc,til,pt,ms	F-257
Worthylake, Ann (fs)	1718	fk, sc, til, pa, ls	F-294
Worthylake, George	1718/11/3	bl,fk,sc,til,pt,ms	F-257
Worthylake, Ruth	1718/11/3	bl,fk,sc,til,pt,ms	F-257
Worthylake, Susanna	1703/11/10	soi, del, til, ls	A-412
Wright, Jonathan	1806/10/7	til, fal, fk, sr	D-201
Wyer, Zachariah	1717/11/23	soi,ers, del, ls	C-103
Wyers, John (tm)	1820	soi,grf, bl, fk	I-9
Wyman, Hezekiah	1808/10/24	soi,pa, sr, ba, ms	F-115
Wyman, Hezekiah (fs)	1808/10/24*	ms, chp	F-116
Y., R. (fs)	--	til, soi, ba, grf	D-195
Yendell, S (tm)*~	1816**	soi, ers,crk, ls,pt	J-25
Yendell, Eliza	1805/10/30	crk, til, bl, fk	A-8
Yendell, Eliza *(fs)	1805/10/30*	til, del, bl, fk	A-9
Young, Hannah	1790/10/5	sc, ba, soi, ms,chp	E-47
Young, Hannah	1796/9/24	del, ba, soi, ms	E-49
Young, Hannah (Fs)	1790	ls, crk, ms, ba	E-48

Name	Date		Code
Young, Hannah (fs)	1796	til, sun, ms, soi	E-50
Young, Joseph	1731/10/5	ls, sun, ms, chp	E-2B
Young, Rachel	1752/11/1	til, ls, crk, ms	D-129
Young, Rachel (fs)	--	--	E-41
Young, Rebecca	1808/3/29	sr, soi, ba, ms,chp	E-45
Younge, William	1750/6/5	til, sun, grf, ms	D-185
Ziegel, Frederick C.	1815/8/3	crk, til, soi, ms	G-293
Ziegel, John William	1814/10/14	crk, til, soi, ms	G-293
Ziegel, John William*(fs)	1814	crk, til, chp, st	G-140

NOTES

NOTES

ACKNOWLEDGEMENTS

We wish to thank the following for their help and support in writing and publishing Boston's Copp's Hill Burying Ground Guide.

Kathryn Coggeshall, project manager Historic Burying Ground Initiative, Parks & Recreation Department, City of Boston, and her associate Sherry A. Frear, masters candidate, class of 1999, Historic Preservation Planning, Cornell University, Ithaca, NY, for their help on current grave status used in Section C. Also for the excellent maps we used at the back of this work and to Douglas Southard of The Bostonian Society for research answers.

Posthumously to Wm. Whitmore and Thomas Bellows Wyman for their labors 120 years ago in publishing their first work *Copp's Hill Epitaphs*, which was so well researched and indexed, and which we publish entirely in Section B. Thanks also to Eric E. Grundset, library director, National Society Daughters of the American Revolution, Washington, for copying the rare original text.

Laurel K. Gabel, trustee and research coordinator for the Association for Gravestone Studies of Pittsford, NY, edited and helped us better understand burying grounds and the stone maker's work. Thanks to Patrick Leehey, research director, Paul Revere Memorial Assn., Boston. Prince Hall material came from Earnest L. Carthan, past master and editor of Illinois Prince Hall Freemasons Journal.

Thanks to Robert A. Pinsky and Christian Nathan Wells, both of Oak Park, IL, computer and technical support; and Leigh Dezelan, also of Oak Park for her cover and inside layout and design. Dr. Robert Louis Welsch, adjunct curator of anthropology at The Field Museum of Chicago and visiting professor of anthropology at Dartmouth College, Hanover, NH, deserves thanks for editing and research advice and Alfred F. Young of Oak Park, IL, senior research fellow at The Newberry Library, Chicago, and author of *The Shoemaker and the Tea Party* and *Masquerade: The Adventures of Deborah Sampson Gannett in the American Revolution,* for his research and editiorial assistance and advice. Also to Sarah Leslie Welsch, director of marketing and sales for University Press of New England for copyright and marketing assistance.

Thanks also to Thomas R. Crowdis Jr. of Acton, MA, and Richard A. Purdy, executive director, Massachusetts Charitable Mechanic Assn. of Quincy, for their Boston Tea Party and Charitable Mechanic information. Thanks also to the *Boston Globe* and Mrs. Raymond (Ann) Fleck, honorary president general, National Society, Daughters of the American Revolution, Walpole, MA, for supplying lists of Tea Party members from the Boston Tea Party DAR Chapter.

Finally, to Suzanne Austin Wells, my wife, for her support and encouragement, for taking the current photographs of Copp's Hill Burying Ground, and her editorial and design assistance, especially on Sec C. ⚓

Remembrance

FOR THOSE WHOSE REMAINS
ARE BURIED HERE,

"LIFE IS CHANGED NOT ENDED."

FOR THOSE OF US WHO HONOR THEM,
MAY IT BE SAID AT OUR DEPARTING:

"WELL DONE, THOU GOOD AND
FAITHFUL SERVANT,

ENTER INTO THE JOY OF THY LORD."

Festival of All Souls, 2 Nov. 1998

Selected Bibliography

Adams, Thomas, *Historical Sketch of Boston, Settlement, Rise and Progress*, Boston, Alfred Mudge & Son, 1879.

American Puritans, Issue 41, 1994, *Christian History Magazine*, published by Christianity Today, Carol Stream, Illinois.

Bahne, Charles, *Complete Guide to the Freedom Trail*, Cambridge, MA, Newtowne Publishing, 1985, updated 1998.

Bridgman, Thomas, *Epitaphs from Copp's Hill Burying Ground*, Boston, Thomas Bridgman, 1851.

Crawford, Mary Caroline, *Old Boston Days & Ways*, Boston, Crawford, Little, Brown, & Co., 1909.

Drake, Samuel Adams, *Old Boston Taverns & Clubs*, Boston, W. A. Butterfield, 1917.

Dunwell , Stephen and Linden, Blanche M., *Boston Freedom Trail*, Boston, Back Bay Press, 1996.

Eastburn, J. B., *Charter and Ordinances*, City of Boston, Boston, City Printers, 1834.

Evacuation Day Memorial, 150th Anniversary of Evacuation of the British, March 17, 1901, Boston, Municipal Printing Office, 1901.

MacDonald, Edward, *Old Copp's Hill & Burial Ground with Historical Sketches*, Boston Edward MacDonald, superintendent, printed by Benjamin Parks, 1882; Revised 1900.

Norton, John, *Historical Sketch of Copp's Hill Burying Ground with Inscriptions and Ancient Epitaphs*, Boston, John Norton, 1907, Revised 1913.

Roberts, Oliver Ayer, *Ancient & Honorable Artillery Company of Massachusetts History, Vol. II & III*, Boston, Alfred Mudge & Son, printers, 1897.

Shurtleff, Nathaniel B., *A Topographical & Historical Description of Boston*, Boston, 2nd Edition, 1872.

State Street Trust Company Series Booklets, by Walton Advertising & Printing, Boston:
"Some Interesting Boston Events," 1916.
"Mayors of Boston," 1914.
"40 of Boston's Immortals," 1910

Thwing, Annie Haven, *Crooked & Narrow Streets of Boston*, Boston, Marshall Jones Co., 1920.

Winsor, Justin, *Memorial History of Boston 1630 -1880, Vols. 1 - 4*, Boston, James R. Osgood & Co., 1881. ☙

How to use this index

The original index to the Whitmore book has been updated and includes entries for Sections A and C. The entries listed below are for Section B unless a prefix is used, i.e., "A-8," for Section A, page 8.

Numbers for Section B are usually listed by entry not by page. When you find a name to look up from the index, leaf through the Section B pages looking for the entry numbers. Example: "Abrams 9" means entry 9 in Section B, which happens to be found on page 1 of Section B.

Roman numerals indicate a page at the beginning of Section B. For example, for entry "xvi," look in the front of Section B for page xvi, then run down that page for the name you are looking for.

Completely read the letter category of the name desired; read all the "E's" for a name like Eckles; it may be listed as Eecles. Other examples: Larned may be Learned; or Patridge for Partridge; or Twing for Thwing. Early-day people often spelled their names like they sounded. Those early-day names were spelled, when pronounced in a New England accent of that time, much differently than we would spell them today.

Also check alphabetical lists on A-26, A-36, A-38. Most of these names are not indexed.

Even if the name you are looking for is not in this particular index, that person may well be buried in Copp's Hill. See Page 58 on "Where Else to Look."

Manley, 441.
Mann, 1475.
Manwaring, 1026-8.
Marden, 1495, xviii.
Mariners Tomb, 1227,
A-23.
Marshall, 298, 906-7,
1511, xvii.
Marsters,(Masters) 663.
Marston, 131 (pg. B-105),
1019, xvi, A-31.
Martain, 1922.
Martin (Martyn), 193-4,
1202-30,1300, viii, x,
xiii, xxiii A-23.
Marvin, 939.
Mary (a slave), 1034.
Mason, 652-4, 73-74.
Massachusetts, History of,
A-15.
Mass. Mutual, A-19.
Masse, 1655, xviii.
Mather, 1, 2, xv, A-9, A-10,
A-14, A-24, A-40.
Mather Church, A-10.
Mathews, 1900.
Maverick, 84-5,94,492-3.
Maxwell, 787.
May, 281.
Mayo, 1748.
McClennan, 1509, xvii.
McClarry, 1042-3,1518,
1897.
McClintock, 416-7.
McDonald, Supt. Edwd.,
A-35, A-44.
McGilvery, 1970.
McKean, 648, 1286, xiv.
McKenney (McKenna),
1889, 2002.
McKenzie, 1171.
McMillian, 1041.
McNear, 1109.
McLeod, 1548.
McQuedy, 409.
McTaggart, 1513.
Meacham, 1453-4.
Mead, 1383, xix, A-31.
Mechanics, MA Charitable
Mechanic Assn., pgs. A-
38, 39 alphabetically
Mellens, 1643-4.
Mellendy, 405.
Merchant, 374, 1153.
Merells, 1278.
Merrill, 2016, xvii.
Merritt, 675-6.
Merry, vii, xii.

Michell (Mitchell),llO2.
Mickell, 1802, xvii.
Middlecott, xvi.
Miers, 995-6.
Miles, 52.
Milk, 328, 1670 A-23.
Millburn, 1201.
Milne, 1987.
Milton, 1891,2019,xviii.
Mills, 1539-41,1554, 1911,
xvi.
Miller,717-8-9, 1103,
1875.
Millet, 1547, xviii.
Millen, page 106.
Minot, xiii.
Mole, 1162.
Moore, 1735-51-52, 2026.
Morgan, 1991.
Morrison, 601-3.
Mortimer (Mortamore,
Mortmer), 767-79-94-95,
1297.
Mountfort,792-3, viii, xi,
xiii, xiv, xxii, A-24, A-32.
Mt. Auburn, A-19; A-52.
Mower, 1132-3.
Mulvana, 680.
Mumford, 190-1-2, A-41.
Munroe, 1383, 1893, xix.

N
Nazro, 1967-8.
Neat, xv.
Neck, 509.
Needham, 1020.
Nelson, 1463.
Neville, 20.
Newcomb, 1884, 1948, xv.
New Brick Church, A-10,
A-24.
New Guinea, African
American area, A-6.
Newell 341, 916 960.
Newhall, ll72-3-4.
Newman. 378-9-8, xvii,
A-7.
Newton, 1474, xvii.
Nickels, 530.
Nicoll, 1175.
Nichols, 325,650,922,
1769, 1951, 2025, xvi.
Nicholson, 1591. Samuel,
A-11.
Nickerson, 1396,1908, xv.
Norcross, 1387 d, xiv.
Norton,945-6-7, 1688.
Norwood, 1703.

Nottage, 1492, xvii.
Nowell, 180-1,605-6-7-9-
11-14,814.
Noyse (Noyes), 1534, xvii,
xviii.
Nudd, 1929.

O
Oakes, 900.
Ola(--), 1393.
Old North Church (2nd)
A-9, 10.
Oliver, 911, 1581, xv.
Onesimus, 418-9.
Orange, viii, x, xiii.
Orr, 1275-6.
Osborn, xiv.
Otheman, 1866.
Owen, 898.

P
Page,797,879,1190,1203,
1543-4,xv, page 106.
Paine, 1458.
Palfrey, xiii.
Pallies, 1909-10.
Palmer, 680-1, 1791.
Parham, 684.
Parker, 952-3-4-61,1058,
1630,1737-45, ix, xii, xiv,
xv, xvi, xvii, A-24.
Parkman, 261-2-3-4-5,
347-8-9, 356, 365, 366-
7-8-9, 943,1160-1.
Parmater, 1230-1.
Parry, 463.
Parsons, 395, 796, 1387,
1654, xviii, xix.
Partridge (Patridge), 735.
Patch, 2023, xviii.
Pattern, 784.
Paul, 903-4,1128-9-30.
Payson, 8@6, 1127.
Peak, xviii.
Pearson, 163-5, 1902, xvi.
Pecker, viii, ix.
Peggy, 655.
Pell, ix, xi, xv.
Pellinton, 246.
Pender, 1924.
Penniman, 395,1244, xvi,
xviii.
Penwell, 1416.
Percival (Piercival),
1058,1630, xvii.
Perkins, 589,1009,1223-4.
Person, 164.
Peterson, 1921.

C-105

A note from the editor...

We appreciate you as a reader. If there is additional information we have overlooked or if you have ideas on how we might make this book more useful, let us know. Write us at Chauncey Park Press, 735 N. Grove Ave., Oak Park, IL 60302-1551, or email at chauncey@wells1.com

How to order this book

You may order additional copies of Boston's Copp's Hill Burying Ground Guide by sending a check or money order for $24.00 to Chauncey Park Press, 735 N. Grove Ave., Oak Park, IL 60302-1551.

Section D

The Section D envelope contains complete maps of Copp's Hill Burying Ground. Some tombs on these maps will have two numbers. One designates the original number and the other is the renumbered designation given in the 1880s.